Youth Development in India

I0894609

This book provides a comprehensive understanding of youth development and protection in the Indian context. It reviews the demographic and socio-economic background and future prospects of Indian youth. It discusses the role of family and culture in the upbringing and development of youth, changing political and socio-economic situations, and the influence of parents and teachers in shaping the future of the youth. The book highlights the nature of adversities faced by children and youth and the subsequent impact on their mental health and well-being. It also examines the efficacy of various skill development programmes and national and international policies designed for the youth.

The book will be of interest to students, teachers, and researchers of population sciences, population studies, psychology, childhood studies, development studies, sociology, and youth studies. It will also be of interest to policymakers and NGOs working with children and youth.

Sibnath Deb is Professor and Director at the Rajiv Gandhi National Institute of Youth Development (RGNIYD), under the Ministry of Youth Affairs and Sports, Government of India. Before joining RGNIYD, he taught at Pondicherry University and University of Calcutta. He is also Adjunct Professor at School of Justice, Faculty of Law, Queensland University of Technology, Australia. He has 30 years of teaching, research, and administrative experience. He has supervised 21 PhDs and published 15 books. He has been a recipient of Visitor's Award, 2019 for his academic and research contributions.

Bishakha Majumdar is a faculty member of Organizational Behaviour and Human Resource Management at the Indian Institute of Management Visakhapatnam, India. With a PhD from IIM Indore, she has been engaged in teaching, corporate training, research, and consultancy in Human Resource Management and Psychology for more than ten years. She has authored several research papers, case studies, and book chapters in the areas of people management and public policy, besides co-authoring the book *Disadvantaged Children in India: Empirical Evidence, Policies and Actions* (2021) with Sibnath Deb, and has received multiple awards for her research contributions.

Aleena Maria Sunny is a faculty member at the Department of Applied Psychology, Rajiv Gandhi National Institute of Youth Development (RGNIYD), India. She is also a PhD Scholar at the Department of Applied Psychology, Pondicherry University. Her three co-authored publications with Sibnath Deb include *Community Psychology: Theories and Application* (2021); *Disadvantaged Children in India: Empirical Evidence, Policies and Actions* (2021); and *Childhood to Adolescence: Issues and Concerns* (2021).

"*Youth Development in India* is the most comprehensive book available describing the strengths, challenges, and opportunities of youth in India. This book is destined to become a classic in the youth development literature. It contains practical, strength-based suggestions for promoting youth development that will be of interest to administrators, government officials, educators, and mental health practitioners who are interested in thinking deeply about ways to empower youth in any country".

Brian A. Gerrard, *Chief Academic Officer, Western Institute for Social Research, Berkeley, California & Emeritus Faculty, Counseling Psychology Department, University of San Francisco, USA*

"Professor Deb is the leading thinker on young people in India today. He and his co-authors are to be congratulated on this milestone book. This text is important for several reasons. Firstly, it provides the most comprehensive overview of young people in India to date, and it does so in a way that will be accessible to undergraduate and international audiences, who might be new to the themes here. Secondly, the opportunities and challenges faced by India's and the world's young people have been highlighted by the growth of information technologies and the onset of a global pandemic. There is much the world can learn from the recent Indian experience, especially when it comes to the experiences of young people. Finally, the text is to be applauded for taking an optimistic view of young people, focussing on themes of empowerment and building capacity for leadership".

John Scott, *Professor and Head, School of Justice, Queensland University of Technology, Australia*

"This book will be invaluable for those who work with children, whatever their professional background. It is up to date, relevant to a modern society and written by experienced scholars who know what they are talking about".

Kim Oates, *Emeritus Professor, Child and Adolescent Health, The University of Sydney, Australia*

Youth Development in India

Future Generations in a Changing World

Sibnath Deb, Bishakha Majumdar, and Aleena Maria Sunny

Routledge
Taylor & Francis Group
LONDON AND NEW YORK

First published 2022
by Routledge
4 Park Square, Milton Park, Abingdon, Oxon OX14 4RN

and by Routledge
605 Third Avenue, New York, NY 10158

Routledge is an imprint of the Taylor & Francis Group, an informa business

British Library Cataloguing-in-Publication Data
A catalogue record for this book is available from the British Library

Library of Congress Cataloging-in-Publication Data
A catalog record has been requested for this book

ISBN: 978-0-367-71561-8 (hbk)
ISBN: 978-0-367-77275-8 (pbk)
ISBN: 978-1-003-17058-7 (ebk)

DOI: 10.4324/9781003170587

Typeset in Sabon
by SPi Technologies India Pvt Ltd (Straive)

The book is dedicated to the youth

Contents

Figures

Tables

Foreword

This book provides a comprehensive overview of the challenges facing youth in India. The authors have captured the wide scope of youth development, and identify pressures and barriers that can limit the horizons and wellbeing of young people. Importantly, this book is constructive. It is positive. Unlike some texts in this field internationally, the narrative does not problematize adolescence and early adulthood. The authors have an optimistic approach and describe educational, health, social and political systems and robust programmes that aim to support and empower youth to achieve their potential.

Professor Sibnath Deb, Dr. Bishakha Majumdar, and Aleena Maria Sunny should be congratulated for taking on the massive task of drawing together complex ideas into a coherent story about youth development. The context is in India but the themes are universal. There is so much information available now in many different forms and media that it is difficult for students and professionals to find a clear path forward for their thinking, planning, and action. The authors have done a great service. They synthesize diverse evidence and clarify what is most important across the vast landscapes in which young people live. This book has a wonderfully collaborative spirit. Young people are not seen as "the other", they are partners with whom problems are solved together. Strategies to engage with youth are woven through the fabric. The authors champion youth social and political leadership and active collaboration with teachers and mental health professionals. Solutions to heavily difficult problems, such as child abuse, online safety, digital identity formation, and strained relationships with parents and peers, require strong policy, strategic support, and technical skill, but most of all, an egalitarian ethos and mutual respect.

Our future is being shaped by the complex social forces described here. This book is relevant for early-, middle-, and late-career professionals and students; it gives us pause to reflect on what is known and what needs to be achieved in the future.

Michael Dunne
Adjunct Professor, Australian Centre for Health Law Research, Queensland University of Technology, Australia; and
Co-Director, Institute for Community Health Research, Hue University, Vietnam

Preface

The society is changing fast with increasing industrial and economic growth, increased level of income of middle- and upper middle-class families, change in lifestyles and human values, outlook about life, mobility of people for better career growth and overall quality of life, which impact the younger generations to a great extent, both positively and negatively. At the same time, existing disparity with respect to quality of life of rural and urban populations and in terms of industrial and economic growth, educational and health care facilities, and opportunity for employment have also impacted the life and career development of the rural youth. Youth from rural belts are in a disadvantageous position as compared to youth from urban areas, in terms of facilities. Quality parental care and guidance, child safety, equal opportunity, and quality education are essential for getting potentially skilled youth. India is very rich in terms of demographic dividends and it is expected that skills of youths will transform India as atmanirbhar (self-reliant) in the days to come.

Nevertheless, Indian youths of present generations experience tough competitions for admission in good educational institutions and job opportunities. On the other hand, technological advancements in terms of information technology have revolutionized human civilization by creating more job opportunities. Improved communication facilities are connecting people through mobile phones and computers, by using social networking sites. The availability of information through the Internet makes children and youth well informed about various issues. Today's children and youth are in an advantageous position in terms of having information fast through mobile phones and its various applications. As the technological advancements create opportunities for the children and youth, it also poses some challenges too, which are distracting the attention of the youth from studies towards mobiles and make them vulnerable to risk behaviour.

Youths are potent in bringing changes in the society and they need guidance and support. They should also be empowered to think independently for their welfare and take personal decisions. Increasing youth participation in civic activities, political, and decision-making processes is clearly evident in various spheres of life, which give a platform to youth to share their voices. The youth must also be introduced to the vital essence of one's personality and their outlook must not be limited to mere materialist pursuits. However, more initiatives need to be taken to make the youth politically conscious both in rural and urban areas so that at the time of casting their votes they are able to examine the background of the candidates judiciously and accordingly they decide to vote for a competent candidate who will in turn address their issues. In addition, emphasizing quality education and creating equal opportunity for the youths will make a big difference in terms of their socio-political consciousness in the changing situation and also make them more responsible.

The Ministry of Youth Affairs and Sports, Government of India (GoI) have come out with various schemes for the holistic development of youths. For the better physical and mental health of youth, FIT INDIA programme is worth mentioning. The Ministry of Youth Affairs and Sports, GoI annually confers awards to national young leaders for their outstanding contributions in various sectors to encourage them to excel further and serve as role models. Besides, the Ministry also provides national youth awards to youth and NGOs in recognition of their contribution for nation-building activities apart from bestowing awards to outperforming NSS and NYKS volunteers. Another such initiative is the V-Awards instituted by United Nations Volunteers in collaboration with the Ministry of Youth Affairs and Sports for volunteering activities which carries worldwide recognition. The New Education Policy 2020 of the Ministry of Education, GoI will have positive impacts on children and youth for their career growth because of its unique features viz., emphasis on aptitude and interest-oriented education, vocational education, multiples exit options, multidisciplinary and collaborative approach in higher education and so on.

However, COVID-19 has brought major challenges for children and youth. It has not only affected them psychologically but also disrupted the normal functioning of educational institutions and put them in uncertainty about their future education and career. A large number of youth working in private sectors lost their jobs, while a bulk number of youths could not go abroad for higher studies. Despite all the challenges posed by COVID-19, a large number of youths are actively engaged in creating awareness about safety measures and providing support to needy people in different parts of the country.

Various online intervention programmes conducted by different educational institutions including the Rajiv Gandhi National Institute of Youth Development have helped a large number of youths to remain engaged in academic activities and gain knowledge. In addition, an online programme on mental health had helped youths to deal judiciously with stressful situations.

Youth needs professional guidance and/or sensitization for enhancing their functional capacities, which will in turn help them to remain focused in life and make sincere efforts to achieve their vision of life. Basic functional capacities include recognizing the purpose of life, having personal vision, setting clearly defined goals, prioritizing tasks, achievement orientation, self-awareness, enhancing self-esteem and self-efficacy, promoting self-adaptive behaviours, enhancing critical thinking and responsible decision-making, solving problems effectively, building positive relationships, demonstrating leadership and initiative and effective communication, handling challenges without stress (recognizing and regulating emotions), observance of values and ethics, adherence to rules and norms, working effectively in teams, re-evaluating personal accomplishments, setting long-term goals, to name a few. Every educational institute should engage professional psychologists for assessing students' aptitude and interest and addressing their issues and challenges and providing them professional support to enhance their self-confidence. If necessary, parents should be involved in intervention programmes for students' welfare.

The broad aim of this volume is to provide a comprehensive picture of Indian youths, their status, and their role as well as responsibilities in nation building. The issues, challenges, and concerns of the youth in the changing socio-political situation across the society are discussed at length in this volume, and culture-specific viable remediable measures are suggested.

The book comprises 10 chapters. Chapter I discusses the need for early childhood quality care, including safety, and its important role in the holistic growth of a child and child development. It further highlights upon orientation needs on the socialization processes during the formative years, in addition to discussing the need for basic facilities like nutrition, medical care, safety and education, as well as love and affection of parents for overall development of children. The necessity of child protection is elaborated in this chapter. Chapter II highlights the background characteristics of the Indian population in general and youth in particular, in addition to examining the status of the youth with special reference to their educational background, health, employment, civic engagement, and migration, as well as social inclusion. The chapter also presents a comparative picture of the status of youth in different states as per the data of Youth Development Index 2017. Chapter III focuses upon the role of the family and the home environment on the development of a child and the various predictors for healthy child and youth development. Based on the changing dynamics of the family environment in the present times, the chapter proposes need-based measures for ensuring a healthy home environment.

Chapter IV begins with an overview of the role of teachers in shaping the behaviour of the students in the educational institutions. Thereafter, the chapter highlights the influence of community leaders in community development with support from local youth, especially taking care of the safety and education of the underprivileged children. The role of young community leaders, spiritual leaders, political leaders, film personalities, sport personalities, and significant others are elaborated in this chapter with live examples in motivating and inspiring thousands of youths in civic engagements during any crisis phase. Chapter V explores youth development in the context of the changing political and socio-economic conditions today, with a specific focus on the subcontinent, possessing one of the largest youth populations in the world. Chapter VI highlights the nature and extent of adversities experienced by the youth, the causes, and consequences behind the same. Further, the chapter discusses the causes and consequences of youth's involvement in socially deviant activities and risk behaviour. Chapter VII explores the impact of virtual access on the development of youth today, the positive and negative effects of the Internet, and the policy interventions that are needed to make the Internet a youth-friendly space. Chapter VIII provides an introduction to the definition and characteristic features of mental health and mental fitness to further elaborate on the mental health of Indian youths. Chapter IX discusses the contribution of youths in two interrelated areas of nation building, namely, social development and policy formulation, in addition to discussing youth engagement at times of any crisis, for community mobilization or to come out of the crisis. The last chapter (Chapter X) focuses on various skill development training programmes that have been adopted and implemented by various government and non-government organizations. Further, the chapter discusses various national and international policies and programmes for youth development and recommends measures for the effective growth and development of the youth.

It is believed that this volume will be beneficial for young researchers working with children and youth, academicians, community leaders, youth organizations, national and international funding agencies working with children and the youth, NGO personnel working in the field, child protection officers, NSS and NKYS volunteers, local administrations looking after youth welfare-related schemes and projects and also for policy makers.

Acknowledgements

Writing a book requires reading of a lot of study material and journal articles, in addition to discussions with professionals working in the same field. We express our gratitude to all the authors and editors of different books and journal articles, individuals and reports, for enlightening us with a lot of innovative ideas in writing this volume.

We express our sincere gratitude to Hon'ble Prime Minister of India, Shri Narendra Modi for his vision about India, i.e. making India a self-reliant country or Atmanirbhar Bharat, and his confidence on youths, as well as his encouraging messages towards the youth of the country, to become a part of the process of new India. The vision of the Prime Minister and his dynamic leadership has inspired the authors to take up this project. The role of former Hon'ble Minister of Youth Affairs and Sports, Government of India (GoI), Shri Kiren Rijiju for his dynamic role in implementing various youth development policies and programmes in India was highly motivating for the authors to add additional knowledge to the existing knowledge concerning youth development, from academic and social perspectives. I am sure we will be able to take many more youth development activities under the able leadership of present Hon'ble Ministers, Ministry of Youth Affairs and Sports, GoI viz., Shri Anurag Singh Thakur, and Shri Nisith Pramanik. Continuous encouragement from Mrs. Usha Sharma, IAS, Secretary, Ministry of Youth Affairs and Sports, Government of India and her concerns about various youth development policies and programmes, particularly, capturing the perspectives of various stakeholders about draft National Youth Policy 2021 and bringing out the Youth Development Index 2021 and running online skill-based professional courses for youth during COVID-19 pandemic, were highly motivating for the authors to work for in this volume. The role of Shri Asit Singh, IRS, Joint Secretary, Ministry of Youth Affairs and Sports, GoI was instrumental in implementing different programmes for youth development in Rajiv Gandhi National Institute of Youth Development (RGNIYD) and in writing of this book.

Our personal discussions with some of our friends and colleagues were very beneficial in putting issues related to youth development from right perspectives. In particular, we thank Dr. K. S. Ravichandran, Registrar, Dr. P. Muralidassan, Admin (Consultant), Prof. Vasanthi Rajendran, Head of

CTOCB, RGNIYD, David Paul, Training Officer, Ram Kumar, Technical Officer of -RGNIYD, Ministry of Youth Affairs and Sports, Government of India and Kaustuv Chakraborty, a scholar from Pondicherry University, for providing inputs and support during the preparation of the volume. Authors also extend special thanks to Shayana Deb – a Post Graduate Student of Behavioural Science of CHRIST (Deemed to be University), Bengaluru for her assistance in carrying out literature reivew for four chatpers.

1 Child protection and youth development

The world is rapidly changing in terms of social dynamics, international relationships, lifestyles of common people, and technological advancements. Undoubtedly, technological advancements benefit the global population. People are now able to connect with each other globally and have easy access to all information through the internet and social media. Children and youth are immensely benefited by technological advancements in gathering knowledge related to their studies and scientific advancements. At the same time, easy internet facilities consume valuable time and sometimes people compulsively use the internet and/or stay engaged in social media for long periods, thus creating emotional and social distance among people psychologically. Further, circulation of wrong information on social networking sites causes a great deal of confusion. Children and youth also become dependent on the internet, which often diverts their mind in negative directions and affects their studies.

In this changing scenario, human rights-related issues are getting special attention of policymakers at the international and national levels because of the active role of both print and electronic media and the ever-growing research-based evidence related to violence against vulnerable populations, including children and youth. In the given situation, responsible journalism is important so that only relevant, authentic, and educative information is circulated through the media. Child rights and protection of children from adversities have also drawn the attention of the policymakers. The word 'child protection' sounds great. It manifests upon the notion of a healthy, prosperous, and peaceful society. Child protection and youth development have a close connection and there is a vertical relationship. Early childhood quality care during the formative stages (i.e., conception of birth to six years) is very crucial since it is the stage of a child's rapid growth. Early childhood is a critical stage in the development of the human brain, which greatly influences the pathways of both physical and mental health as well as the behaviour of a child in later life. Any deficiency during this formative stage has an adverse effect on overall human development. Care during early childhood broadly includes safety, nutrition, medical care, play, etc. Orientation on the socialization process and congenial and happy family environments are crucial for healthy emotional development of children

DOI: 10.4324/9781003170587-1

and in turn, they feel emotionally secure. Quality parental care ensures healthy emotional bonds between the parent and the child, which has a lifelong impact on a child's emotional security.

If a child gets proper care, guidance, a happy family environment and safety during childhood, they will grow healthy, both in terms of mental and physical health and social relationships. A child will also have a positive outlook towards life. They will study sincerely and will become potential human resources and responsible citizens contributing towards social growth and development. The concept of child development has also gathered special attention from international policymakers of human resource development and management. It has been realized that without ensuring basic care and support facilities to every child, it would be very difficult to harvest the optimal potential of a child and make them professionally well equipped for taking an active role in the society.

Let us discuss the contributing factors for healthy child growth and development. It will not be an exaggeration to state that child protection issues should be taken care of by the parents prior to birth. Mother's health status, lifestyle, food habits, and medical care have very important roles in delivering a healthy child. For example, before conceiving, potential parents should have a discussion, in order to remain mentally prepared to take the additional responsibility of a child and provide utmost care for their proper development. Proper upbringing of a child requires care from both the parents. In a number of cases, it has been observed that a child experiences neglect where parents beget a child without planning. Parents should also be prepared to accept the reality if they get a child with some disability.

During pregnancy, a mother should have a healthy diet, periodic health check-ups, avoiding drugs or alcohol and taking other remedial measures for delivering a healthy baby. Evidence demonstrates that drinking and/or smoking during pregnancy has adverse impacts on the health of a newborn (Olegård et al., 1979a; Olegård et al., 1979b; Powers, McDermott, Loxton, & Chojenta, 2013). For example, smoking during pregnancy may cause low birth weight of a newborn and altered cardiorespiratory responses, in addition to various cognitive and behavioural outcomes in children, including attention deficit hyperactivity disorder (ADHD), conduct disorder, impaired learning and memory, and cognitive dysfunction (Knopik, 2009).

In India, there are numerous social myths and misconceptions about child-rearing practices, like colostrum should not be given to a child immediately after birth, a child should not be fed when the mother suffers from stomach upset, and so on. Parents should be very careful about misconceptions which harm the proper upbringing of a child.

In urban India, most of the deliveries take place in hospitals in the hands of a doctor or a trained health care provider. However, in the rural areas, it happens mostly at home and in a large number of cases, deliveries are done by untrained individuals or elderly women, which may cause negligence and risk. Delivery of a child at home by a trained medical or paramedical professional is important so that all appropriate measures are taken in delivering a healthy child. In this regard, an Indian study conducted in rural Karnataka tried to understand the factors influencing the place of delivery and reasons for preferring home deliveries in rural areas (Mutharayappa & Prabhuswamy, 2003). The study reported that trained *dai* is limited in the primary health care centres and sub-centres in rural areas. As a result, over half of the deliveries are unsafe. The factors which are playing important roles for home deliveries include time of delivery, illiteracy, economic conditions of women, customs of the natal home, transportation, and place of stay of the health workers. Moreover, most health centres do not have female medical officers in position, and the lack of staff and inadequate facilities at sub-centres and hospitals aggravate the issue. Nearly half the infants die due to maternal causes among women who arrange deliveries at home. The causes of infant deaths were premature delivery, infection in the umbilical cord, being accidentally hit on the head while delivery, breech presentation, severe anaemia of mother, etc. Based on the findings, the authors suggested that good antenatal services need to be provided to potential parents and women should take adequate rest and proper nutrition during pregnancy. Women should also be sensitized to prefer hospital delivery in the hand of a medical doctor or a trained *dai*.

Child mortality and morbidity could be reduced substantially by regular breastfeeding. At the same time, providing colostrum immediately after birth enhances the immune capacity of a child. However, misconceptions prevail in the rural belts of India and other developing countries about colostrum. Because of various social myths and misconceptions, colostrum is not given to a large number of newborn children in India and thus deprives the child of better immune capacity. In rural areas, myths and misconceptions about colostrum include affecting the stomach of the newborn, it is dirty as it was stored in the mother's breast for a long period, it should be poured down the river with a belief that it would ensure sufficient milk in the mother's breast, etc. Given these misconceptions, a large number of women in rural areas do not feed colostrum to their newborns (Madhu, Chowdary, & Masthi, 2009). One intervention study in Bangladesh observed that peer counselling significantly improved breastfeeding practices (Haider, Ashworth, Kabir, & Huttly, 2000). The authors recommend the introduction of peer counselling among mothers and child health care programmes in developing countries.

Mothers' educational background, occupation, income, lifestyle, and mental health as well as outlook have a very significant role in quality upbringing of a child, which largely decides the mother's child care behaviour (McLoyd, 1989; McLoyd, 1990). Support from extended family members in the upbringing of a child is essential when a mother is working and they require some care and guidance.

Providing timely immunization and periodic health check-ups for minor health problems of a child is very important in addition to a balanced diet as well as love and affection. One African study reported that "timely initiation of vaccination could contribute to higher rates of immunization schedule completion and improving the reach and impact of vaccination programmes on child health outcomes in Sub-Saharan Africa" (Janusz et al., 2021). During childhood, children are vulnerable to fever, diarrhoea, and other health problems for which home-based remedial measures need to be followed, especially oral rehydration solution in case of diarrhoea. Diarrhoea is the third leading cause of childhood mortality in India and is responsible for 13% of all deaths every year among children under five years of age (Lakshminarayanan & Jayalakshmy, 2015). Every year, about 30,000 children die in India because of diarrhoea. Regarding persistent diarrhoea among children aged 0–71 months in northern rural India, Bhan et al. (1989) conducted a prospective follow-up study of 963 children for 12 months through weekly household visits. The incidence rate of persistent diarrhoea was found to be 6.3 per 100 children, irrespective of gender and seasonal variations. There were no significant sex-related differences in the incidence of the disease and the overall seasonal distribution of acute and persistent diarrhoea was similar.

So far as intervention for diarrhoea is concerned, homemade oral rehydration therapy (ORS) is found to be highly beneficial in keeping a child healthy and avoiding dehydration. A number of international studies carried out in countries like Nepal, Iran, Ethiopia, and Nigeria reported that the caregivers lacked knowledge about home management of diarrhoea (Abdinia, 2014; Ghasemi, Talebian, Masoudi Alavi, & Moosavi, 2013; Olakunle, Valentine, Kamaldeen, & Buhari, 2012). Similarly, the practice of providing home-based ORS was also poor in Nepal, Iran, Pakistan, and Kenya (Abdinia, 2014; Berisha, Hoxha-Gashi, Gashi, & Ramadani, 2009; Osonwa Kalu, Eko Jimmy, & Ema, 2016; Shah et al., 2012). Evidence demonstrates that lack of knowledge and understanding about remedial home-based measures for addressing diarrhoea of small children is the cause of deaths of thousands of children every year in developing countries like India (Million Death Study Collaborators, 2010). In this regard, health workers have a very significant role to sensitize parents with low levels of education about basic health care-related issues and minor health problems in the areas where medical facilities are not available.

Given this background, the role of the mother in early childhood care and child protection has got the special attention of national and international child care policymakers and almost every country has come out with a child care policy, in line with the United Nations policy related to child care.

Defining child protection

There are different definitions of child protection used by different national and international organizations. They are almost similar with little variations in terms of arrangement of words and terminologies. In simple words, child protection means safeguarding children from all adversities which cause harm to them and affect their normal growth and development. In other words, child protection means protecting the rights of the children as outlined by the UN Convention on the Rights of the Child (1989). Article 19 of the UN Convention on the Rights of the Child provides for the protection of children in and out of their homes while the sustainable development goals emphasize on quality education. Child protection is also empowering children with education and engaging them in various decision-making processes related to their welfare and interests. The terms 'Child Protection' and 'Safeguarding of Children Interests' are used synonymously in different literatures.

A number of international organizations are working around the world for child protection and they have their own definitions. For example, according to the Save the Children (a UK-based international welfare organization),

> Child Protection is any measure or initiative that addresses or prevents children from situations of violence, abuse, neglect and exploitation. It refers to protecting children from or against any perceived or real danger/risk. It helps to reduce their vulnerability in harmful situations. It also means protecting children against social, psychological and emotional insecurity and distress. Child Protection must ensure that no child falls out of the social security and safety net and those who do, receive necessary care and protection to be brought back into the safety net. While protection is a right of every child, some children like street children, children with disabilities, children of commercial sex workers, child labourers etc. are more vulnerable than others and need special attention. Child Protection is relevant for all settings-home, school, neighbourhood, community, and institutional/residential care.
>
> (www.savethechildren.in)

UNICEF has come out with another definition of child protection. It refers to

> preventing and responding to violence, exploitation and abuse against children – including commercial sexual exploitation, trafficking, child labour and harmful traditional practices, such as female genital mutilation/cutting and child marriage.
>
> (www.unicef.org)

Necessity for child protection and its implication

Child protection is necessary for ensuring the fundamental rights of every child and for the optimal utilization of their potentials for national growth and prosperity. Every child should receive adequate nutrition, medical care, and a healthy and safe environment, in addition to unconditional love and affection from the parents, which are prerequisites for the healthy growth and development of a child. Like other countries, the Indian Constitution also guarantees equity and equality to every citizen in addition to other fundamental rights.

A large number of children experience academic pressure from parents for better performance. Sometimes, it is so intense that some children cannot withstand the pressure and suffer from anxiety, depression, and suicidal ideation (Deb, Strodl, & Sun, 2015). Every year, about 28 students commit suicide because of academic failure (National Crime Records Bureau, 2018). This issue requires the attention of academic administrators for the sensitization of parents.

Ensuring a protective environment for children means preventing and responding to neglect, violence, abuse, maltreatment, and exploitation of children. According to UNICEF,

> strategies to be adopted for protective environment include strengthening government commitment and capacity to fulfil children's right to protection; promoting the establishment and enforcement of adequate legislation; addressing harmful attitudes, customs and practices; encouraging open discussion of child protection issues that includes media and civil society partners; developing children's life skills, knowledge and participation; building capacity of families and communities; providing essential services for prevention, recovery and reintegration, including basic health, education and protection; and establishing and implementing on-going and effective monitoring, reporting and oversight.
>
> (www.unicef.org)

In order to achieve the above strategies, there is a need to have proper coordination among government, national and international organizations, working with children, to review and implement various intervention programmes, organizing sensitization programmes for parents, teachers, doctors and law enforcement agencies and personnel working in NGOS, sharing of experiences of best practices, empowering children with knowledge about their rights and giving them courage to report any incident of abuse and neglect, ensuring security to the victim and his/her family, providing safe shelter and vocational training to disadvantaged children, rescue of trafficked children and putting them in safe shelter, adopting child protection policy in every educational institution, periodic review of the implementation of legislations and policies in the truest sense and documentation, as well as research, on contemporary issues for generating more evidence.

First-hand work experience of the authors suggests the need to bring professionalism among the NGOs and empower them with knowledge regarding research and systematic documentation. Lack of quality research and poor documentation is a big challenge for most of the NGOs working with disadvantaged populations, to design systematic and need-based intervention programmes. Instead of rivalry relationships among the welfare organizations, there should be a supportive environment to provide maximum benefit to the disadvantaged children and/or to avoid duplication of

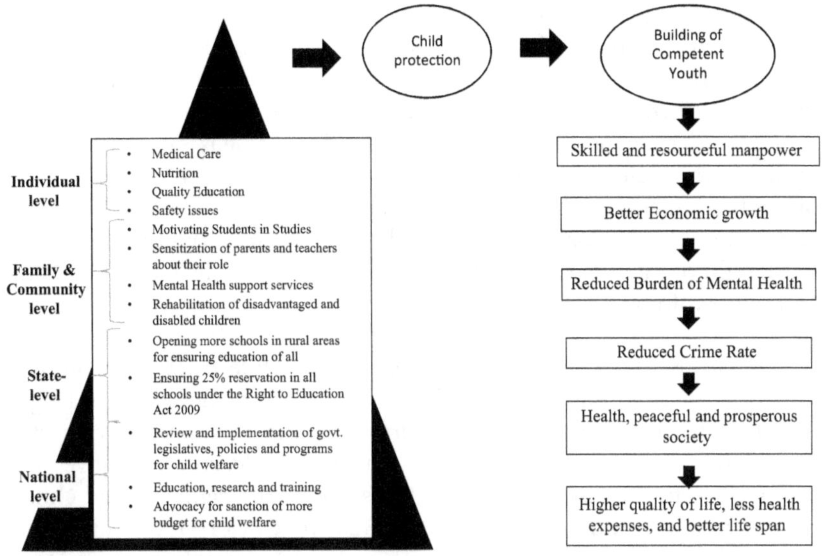

Figure 1.1 A conceptual model for faster economic growth and healthy society through child protection and youth development.

Source: Deb, S. (2017). Prof. Anima Sen Memorial Lecture titled 'Child Protection: The Key for Better Growth Statistics and Harmony in the Nation' delivered at the Indian Science Congress, Jan. 3–7, 2017, Sri Venkaterswara University, Tirupati.

services. Joint and well-coordinated programmes will be of great help to the children, who are in need of care and support services. From time to time, NGOs should get their activities evaluated by an outsider to understand the effectiveness of their services and shortcomings, if any, and accordingly, they should change their service delivery mechanism.

Child protection will not only bring out the full potential of every child but also make them responsible, skilled, and productive citizens. They will grow into a good human being and their presence will create a positive psychological ambience within the family, community, and work environment. In addition, child protection will ensure achieving the target of sustainable development goals and contribution of children and youth towards national growth and prosperity. The following conceptual model illustrates the overall benefit of child protection for potential youth development and for long-term positive impact on society (Figure 1.1).

Rights of the child

International measures for the protection of child rights

The increasing rate of child abuse, neglect, and exploitation has become a serious concern for international policymakers towards ensuring safety for every child, which translated into various policies and programmes across the society. For example, The United Nations Convention on the Rights of the Child (UNCRC, 1989) is one such international yardstick for protection of child rights. Most of the countries are signatory to the same convention, including India. The UNCRC (1989) motivated most of the nations across the world to come out with their own legislative measures and social policies considering the local situation. The UNCRC has 54 articles clearly outlining the different dimensions for the protection of child rights. Some of the fundamental rights of the children as outlined in the United Nations Convention on the Rights of the Child (1989) include right to life, right to food, right to medical care, right to nutrition, right to shelter, right to safety and non-exploitation, etc. For example,

> article 28 talks about the right to education while article 24 protects the rights of children in terms of health and medical care. Article 15 gives children freedom to express their views and opinions. During childhood, every child likes to play with other children and it gives them maximum pleasure. Article 31 talks about the rights of the child to leisure, play, and participate in cultural events. Corporal punishment is highly prevalent at home and in the schools across the society. Articles 19 and 37 take care of the protection of children from any form of abuse, exploitation, torture, or neglect. This issue is taken care of by the UNCRC under article 31. Likewise, article 32 protects children from economic exploitation and work that threatens his/her health, education and development. Finally, the UNCRC also obliges State parties to take all appropriate legislative, administrative, social and educational measures to protect children from all forms of abuse and exploitation (article 19).

National legislative measures for protection of child rights

Child protection is one of the areas of priority of the Government of India and it is clearly evident in the Indian Constitution (1949). The Indian Constitution highlights the importance of protection of various rights of the children and it guarantees four fundamental rights to all citizens viz., justice, liberty, equality, and fraternity. For example,

> Article 14 guarantees equality before the law while Article 15 prohibits discrimination based on gender, caste, race, and religion. Thereafter, Article 21A directs all States to provide free and compulsory education to all children between the ages of six and fourteen years. A large number of children across the society are involved in child labour in poor conditions and they are denied of education and proper nutrition. In some places, the working condition is extremely unhygienic and harmful. For prevention of child labour, Article 24 of the Indian Constitution prohibits children under 14 from being employed in factories and mines and from working in any hazardous employments. Child trafficking is rampant in developing countries like India. Article

> 23 prohibits the trafficking of human beings and forced labour. Freedom of religion is conferred by Article 25. Exploitation of children for commercial purposes is a common phenomenon. Article 39 directs policy to ensure that children are protected from inappropriate work and from all forms of exploitation. In addition, the Government of India has taken up various legislations for addressing the problems of children and for ensuring their rights.

In addition, there are specific laws for the protection of children from abuse, maltreatment, and exploitation. For prevention of children from abuse, there are a number of provisions in the Indian Penal Code (1860). These include, The Immoral Trafficking Act (1956), The Protection of Women from Domestic Violence Act (2005), The Prohibition of Child Marriage Act (2006), The Child Labour (Prohibition and Regulation) Act (1986), The Right of Children to Free and Compulsory Education Act (2009), The Protection of Children from Sexual Offences Act, 2012 (POCSO Act, 2012), The Commissions for Protection of Child Rights Act (2005), The Juvenile Justice (Care and Protection of Children) Act (2015), The Pre-Conception and Pre-natal Diagnostic Technique (Prohibition of Sex Selection) Act (1994), The Persons with Disabilities (Equal Opportunities, Protection of Rights and Full Participation) Act (1995), The Guardian and Wards Act (1890), The Young Persons (Harmful Publications) Act (1956) and so on.

The above legislative measures for protection of child rights in India are clear examples of the sincere efforts by the government of India to protect children from all forms of abuse and neglect. However, the main problem lies with the implementation of the laws in the legitimate sense. An Indian study revealed that parents, teachers as well as community members lack proper understanding about healthy child upbringing, child rights, and legislative measures for child protection (Deb & Mathews, 2012). The issue requires the attention of all respective state governments to take appropriate measures.

Critical comments about some of the child protection-related legislations

Any legislation passed by the government requires awareness and proper clarification about the particular legislation among the law enforcement agencies for which there should be orientation programmes on the newly enacted legislation for detailed discussion so that personnel of law enforcement agencies will have full clarity about their role, jurisdiction, various provisions of the law as well as good understanding about the coordination with other allied agencies. Second, there should be periodic review of a legislation to examine its implementation process and barriers in implementing the same, if any so that course corrective measures can be taken. After two to three years of implementation of a particular law, personnel of law enforcement agencies will be in a better position to figure out the challenges and obstacles to address the issues for effective implementation of the same.

In reality, none of the processes are followed in most of the legislations because of various reasons. Therefore, when a particular incident of child sexual abuse and/or maltreatment occurs and it comes to the knowledge of law enforcement agency, it does not get proper attention and they fail to book a case under appropriate section of a law resulting denial of justice. Lack of coordination between child welfare committees, police, doctors, rehabilitation homes, and mental health support facilities is another hindrance in delivering holistic care and protection to children. Undoubtedly, there is an impact of child protection-related legislations to improve the situation; it may not be fully successful in achieving its objective. For want of review and/or mid-term evaluation of any legislation, it is very difficult to make a comment on its achievement. Nevertheless, any legislation has certain limitations. For example, the Immoral Trafficking Act (1956) was implemented 65 years back. If we look at the number of cases booked under this law, the figure is very negligible as compared to the actual number of violations of the law. The main reasons for poor reporting of cases include ignorance about the law among the common people, even if there is a report by any victim, there was no action from the police, illiteracy among victims, lack of support facilities, no faith in the system, etc.

Domestic violence is a hidden problem in India. Most of the women who experience domestic violence do not report the incident to the police out of a feeling of embarrassment, fear of further victimization, and/or to protect the image of the family and bear the pain lifelong. In order to address the issue, the Protection of Women from Domestic Violence Act (2005) was passed by the Indian Parliament with an objective to protect women from harassment and all forms of domestic violence like physical, mental, economic, and sexual. According to the National Crime Records Bureau (NCRB), 2018 report, about 40% of total 4.05 lakh cases of crimes against women are registered under Section 498A of the Indian Penal Code (IPC). A large number of them are minors i.e., within 18 years of age. Although this law encouraged a good number of women to come forward to report the incident of domestic violence, awareness at the community level by the local administration and NGOs about the law might encourage others to report the incident for justice. But the hard reality is that the women from marginalized communities do not have the courage to report the incident since they are totally dependent on their husbands economically and because of lack of social support facilities.

The Prohibition of Child Marriage Act (2006) is another important law in India for the interest of healthy growth of girl child. Girl child marriage is rampant in India and it is linked to cultural practices and social reality. Early marriage is not only detrimental for the healthy physical growth of a girl child, it affects their education, career, and overall quality of life. Parents from poor families consider a girl child as a burden and therefore, they wish to arrange their marriage at an early age because of lack of safety, poverty, not giving importance in providing education since they will go to somebody's house after marriage, and finally preference for boy child. Limited cases are reported under this law. Any responsible citizen should report such cases to the appropriate authority (i.e., either child protection committee or local police) if it comes to their knowledge. Cultural acceptance and indifferent attitude of the larger society are responsible for poor implementation of the law. Determining the age of a minor child is challenging since most of the people in rural areas do not have a birth certificate. Social consciousness and awareness about the law are necessary to bring a change.

Although the Child Labour (Prohibition and Regulation) Act (1986) was implemented with good spirit, it could not achieve its objective satisfactorily because of various reasons like poverty, lack of social support during crisis in a family, lack of monitoring by labour inspectors in each state, etc. In India, about one-fifth of the families are still living in poor conditions and as a result they prefer to engage their small children in economic activities for survival instead of sending them to school. Some of the places where children work are hazardous, which includes fire cracker industries, garment factories, agriculture, mining, construction, hotels, bars, restaurants, and markets, etc. In a large number of such industries, working conditions are not hygienic and children hardly get any rest and are provided only minimum wages. This issue requires immediate attention of the Ministry of Labour and Employment.

As per The Juvenile Justice (Care and Protection of Children) Act (2020), every police station should have a female juvenile officer so that children and women victims of sexual abuse feel comfortable to report the cases. In reality, female juvenile officers are available in the police stations. Another limitation of the police station is the lack of privacy while taking the first investigation report (FIR) for confidentiality of information. Ensuring safety to the sexual abuse victims after reporting the incident to the police or child welfare committee is another big challenge as it discourages victims and their families from reporting the incident because of perceived threats. Victims of sexual abuse suffer from conditions like post-traumatic stress, fear, anxiety, and guilt which requires immediate mental health support to give them confidence and to make them realize that they are not responsible for the incident and encourage them to resume daily life activities and link them with other support facilities. In fact, post-incident mental health support facilities are not available across the society leaving the victim vulnerable to long-term mental health challenges and social stigma.

Like other legislative measures, the Protection of Children from Sexual Offences Act, 2012 (POCSO Act, 2012) is another law for safety of children from sexual abuse. This act lacks clarity regarding the involvement of two minors in sexual activity, i.e., how to deal with such a situation if parents of a particular child complaints about the issue. Delivering timely justice to the victim as mentioned in the law because of caseloads in the courts is one of the cornerstones of the POCSO Act, 2012. Timely registration of the FIR, followed by an immediate medical examination is essential. However, police face a lot of challenges for doing the same and often there exists communication gaps between police and medical professionals in addressing the issue. Insensitivity among some of the doctors while checking a sexually abused child causes trauma.

To ensure education for all children, The Right of Children to Free and Compulsory Education Act was passed by the Indian Parliament in, 2009. This act ensures compulsory primary education for all children without any capitation fees. For instance, Section 3 of this act stated that every child between the ages of six and fourteen shall have the right to free and compulsory education in a neighbourhood school until the completion of his/her elementary education. This law also reserves 25% seats for admission of children from disadvantaged communities in the schools. Section 17 of this act prohibits age-old cultural practices like physical punishment and mental harassment of the child. In reality, ignorance about this law and its various provisions among common people and school teachers was the barrier in achieving its objective.

> The main challenge lies with the implementation of this act in ensuring reservation of 25% seats for children of socially backward communities because of lack of awareness. In this case, also, it is the obligation of the Directorate of School Education of the respective state government to implement the law in the truest sense, ensuring 25% seats for children of socio-economically background families. However, monitoring mechanisms for checking the implementation of the law and taking corrective measures is a big challenge.

In another study Deb et al. (2016) reported that the factors which are responsible for violence against children include poor reporting, inadequate knowledge among law enforcement agencies, lack of training of concerned personnel, ineffective implementation of the law, and lack of provisions in the legislations for mandatory reporting by professionals and social agents close to children like teachers, doctors, nurses, public representatives, etc. Deb et al. (2016) further stated that there is a need to review the legislation periodically for taking corrective measures in addition to emphasizing on periodic monitoring and evaluation of legislations.

Ignorance among common people, irrespective of educational background, regarding child protection-related legislative measures is another big challenge to deliver justice and ensure protection of children across the society from all adversities. Therefore, awareness about law enforcement agencies and child protection-related legislations among general population is required and it should be done with the help of electronic and print media, non-governmental organizations, youth clubs, local administration, youth volunteers of Nehru Yuvak Kendra, community and spiritual leaders, anganwadi and health workers, and Gram Panchayat members at the community level. Last but not the least, the State Commission for protection of child rights has a very important role to monitor the child safety issue closely to avoid further victimization of an already exploited child.

Policies and programmes for welfare and well-being of children

Several policies and programmes have been undertaken by various Ministries of the Government of India for overall welfare of the children and for protection of their rights. Some of the policies include the National Policy for Education (1986), National Policy for Children (1994), the National Policy for Empowerment of Women (2001), the National Health Policy (2002), the National Charter for Children (2004), the National Plan of Action for Children (2005), the Integrated Child Protection Scheme (2009), the National Policy for Children (2013), New Education Policy, 2020, and many more.

Implementation of policies and programmes takes a lot of time for planning and execution, especially in a country like India, because of cultural and social diversity as well as political challenges.

> Overpopulation, lack of trained manpower, lack of priority of child protection issue in reality, lack of knowledge about the developmental characteristics of children, poor reporting of abuse to the police or appropriate authorities, lack of coordination among different agencies involved in child protection and lack of a voice of the innocent children about their rights and so on

as reported by Deb et al. (2020). Although all social policies benefited a large number of children across the country, the final outcome is not satisfactory. Close monitoring of implementation of social schemes and proper coordination among both governmental and non-governmental organizations are necessary. The broad objectives of some of the important child welfare schemes are discussed in the following sections:

The Integrated Child Protection Scheme (ICPS, 2009)

This is one of the most comprehensive social welfare schemes for protection of child rights. The broad objective of the scheme is to

> contribute to the improvement in the well-being of children in difficult circumstances, as well as to the reduction of vulnerabilities to situations and actions that lead to abuse, neglect, exploitation, abandonment and separation of children. These will be achieved by: (i) improved access to and quality of child protection services; (ii) raised public awareness about the reality of child rights, the situation and protection in India; (iii) clearly articulated responsibilities and enforced accountability for

child protection (iv) established and functioning structures at all government levels for the delivery of statutory and support services to children in difficult circumstances; (v) introduced and operational evidence based monitoring and evaluation.

Specific objectives of the scheme include

> (i) institutionalizing essential services and strengthening structures; (ii) enhancing capacities at all levels; (iii) creating database and knowledge base for child protection services; (iv) strengthening child protection at family and community level; (v) ensuring appropriate inter-sectoral response at all levels; and (vi) raising public awareness.

An NGO titled "Human Liberty Network" located at Alambagh, Lucknow, Uttar Pradesh carried out a study in 2019 to identify the gaps in implementing the ICPS following a qualitative study covering 52 children from 8 districts of Uttar Pradesh viz., Azamgarh, Prayagraj, Varanasi, Mirzapur, Chandauli, Sant Kabir Nagar, Kushinagar, and Gorakhpur. Findings revealed a number of gaps and barriers for effective implementation of ICPS. For example, first, the composition of the Child Welfare Committee (CWC) in half of the districts covered in the study was short of required members. Second, there are no institutional services for children in need of care and support services in half of the districts while in the remaining half of the districts, accommodation is inadequate. Third, lack of transportation and absence of escorts are hurdles for sending children in need to the government institutions for safe shelter. Fourth, as per the ICPS guidelines, the District Child Protection Committee (DCPC) does not meet periodically to discuss various issues. Fifth, individual care plans based on individual needs are totally missing. Sixth, follow-up with the family after reuniting the children is extremely difficult. Seventh, the quality of mental health support services provided for traumatized children is far below the minimum standard as most of the counsellors are not trained to deal with children who are emotionally sensitive. There are many more challenges observed by the study team. The findings of this study provide an overview of the reality and the situation is almost similar in every state as far as implementation of ICPS is concerned.

Nevertheless, based on the findings of the study, the organization suggested a number of measures for improving the situation and they include (i) periodic meetings of the child protection committees at district, block and village levels as specified in the ICPS, (ii) Formation of Annual District Child Protection Plan (DCPP) under ICPS, (iii) Monitoring of Individual Child-Care Plans (ICPs), (iv) Training and capacity building for scheme functionaries (v) Review of Child-care Institutions in Districts and setting a time-frame for regular monitoring of the rehabilitation homes and so on" (Source: Report of study on Integrated Child Protection Scheme (ICPS), conducted by Human Liberty Network, Lucknow, UP; https://www.humanlibertynetwork.org › 2019).

Integrated Child Development Services (ICDS, 1975)

This scheme was adopted by the government of India on October 2, 1975 with a view towards extending care and support services to children between the age of 0 and 6 years and their mothers. The main objectives of the scheme include

> (i) improving the nutritional and health status of children in the age group of 0–6 years; (ii) laying the foundation for proper psychological, physical and social development of the children; (iii) reducing the incidence of mortality, morbidity, malnutrition and school dropout; (iv) achieving effective coordination of policy and implementation amongst the various departments to promote child development, and (v) enhancing the capability of the mother to look after the normal health and nutritional needs of the child through proper nutrition and health education.

Supplementary nutrition, immunization, health check-ups, referral services, pre-school non-formal education, nutrition, and health education are the primary services provided by the ICDS at the community level.

Evaluation of any intervention programme is very important to gather understanding about efficacy of the programme and challenges in implementing the programme, if any. Findings of any evaluation are eye openers for the implementing agencies and it helps them to take course corrective measures to realize the maximum benefits of the project for the target groups.

The ICDS project was subject to evaluation by different agencies and findings of the evaluation study gave a proper understanding about its usefulness. For example, one study, covering 19 selected sample States and UTs, disclosed that

> 75.7% of AWCs maintained records properly. However, problems were noticed in records maintained by the remaining 24.3% of AWCs. Further, it was observed that 99% of AWCs were providing counselling to mothers on child health care and 68.6% of AWCs had intervened in improving the nutritional status of the children. So far as constraints of the AWCs are concerned, it was noticed that 22.5% of AWCs did not have the required medicines for the children. Scrutiny of health records maintained by AWCs for the month of December, 2013 revealed that 74.6%, 19.7% and 5.7% of children had Normal (N), Moderately Malnourished (MM) and Severely Malnourished (SM) health status respectively. Similarly, the health records of children enrolled in AWCs in January 2015 was 75.4% (N), 19.1% (MM) and 5.5% (SM). Space was a constraint for 41% of the AWCs. In the case of more than four-fifth of the AWCs (86.3%), drinking water was not a problem.
>
> (Report on Quick Evaluation of ICDS, June 2015)

CHILDLINE scheme:

The objective of the scheme is to encourage child victims or children in need of care for reporting of incidents of abuse and neglect and seeking support services. There is a 24-hour toll-free number (1098) through which a child can contact the concerned person for support and help.

First-hand field experience of the first author indicates that quality of online support and care services varies from centre to centre and it depends on sensitivity of the online counsellor, their educational background and training as well as passion for child welfare. However, there is a need to carry out a study to examine the effectiveness of online child care and support services.

Beti Bachao, Beti Padhao (BBBP):

This is another welcome initiative taken by the Government of India to protect the right to life of a girl child. There are two specific laws in India to prohibit the sex selection of a foetus and they include: (i) The Medical Termination of Pregnancy Act, 1971 (MTP), as amended in 2002, and (ii) the Pre-natal Diagnostic Techniques (Regulation and Prevention of Misuse) Act, 1994 (PNDT), as amended in 2002. Gender imbalance in some of the states of India viz. Punjab, Haryana, and Rajasthan are very alarming, which causes social challenges. The Kanyashree scheme of the Department of Women and Social Welfare, Government of West Bengal, is highly appreciable. The objective of this scheme is to ensure that girls pursue their academic endeavours and delay their marriage till they attain the age of 18 years.

Critical comments about some of the social policies related to welfare of the children

Like legislative measures, social policies and programmes require periodic review and necessary revisions based on interim assessment and/or evaluation as during the implementation process the personnel involved in the programme might encounter various challenges. Sometimes, evaluation of some of the social policies and programmes are carried out by an external agency and the agency submits the report highlighting the advantages and disadvantages of the programmes indicating the progressive measures, but no action is taken afterwards. If appropriate corrective measures are taken, any policy and/or programme will be able to achieve its long-term objectives to a great extent. There are several other factors which facilitate the smooth implementation of any programmes and broadly they include clear picture about the modalities for implementation of the programme, training of personnel involved in the programme and their involvement, community mobilization, participation of the community members and their cooperation, regular and timely release of fund and supply of necessary materials, cooperation and coordination among various allied agencies, periodic monitoring of the programmes, etc. If monitoring and evaluation of any programme is given importance and timely course corrective measures are taken, the fund sanctioned for a particular programme will give desired results.

International policies for welfare and well-being of global population including children

In addition to the Millennium Development Goals (MDGs, 2000), Sustainable Development Goals (SDGs) are also playing a very important role for the overall welfare and well-being of the human civilization. Out of the 17 goals, seven goals are directly related to child welfare and well-being and they include ending poverty and hunger, improving health and education, gender equality, ensuring availability and sustainable management of water and sanitation for all, and making cities more sustainable and safer. It is believed that by 2030, most of the nations would be able to achieve most of the goals of SDGs to improve the overall quality of life of common people, including children and youth.

Role of other international bodies and professional platforms for child protection

The umbrella organizations of the United Nations like the UNICEF, the International Labour Organization (ILO), and other professional bodies like the International Society for Prevention of Child Abuse and Neglect (ISPCAN) and Save the Children (SCF) are playing very important roles across the world to protect the children and youth from adversities and providing them a safe environment. They are organizing seminars, workshops, and conferences for sharing learning experiences of researchers and other professionals with each other and for the dissemination of knowledge about best practices.

Factors influencing early childhood care, safety and overall well-being of children and youth

Since the beginning of 2020, the COVID-19 pandemic has caused a lot of challenges for people from all sections of the society including children and youth. COVID-19 not only affected the school education and it confined children, adolescents, and youth at home resulting in psychological stress. The factors which contribute significantly towards child neglect and youth development are many. It varies from community to community. In the following section, the main contributing factors towards child neglect and abuse in India are discussed based on a first-hand experience:

(i) Pregnancy before marriage and its consequences

Pregnancy before marriage is a normal phenomenon in the developed countries and women do not experience any discrimination and/or social boycott for the same. Single parenting is socially accepted in developed countries while in developing countries like India, the larger society perceives and/or treats single parents differently. The following case study is a clear example of social discrimination experienced by a child for having a single parent.[1]

Case Study 1

A, aged 21, living in Hyderabad had a relationship with her classmate. They became close to each other and had physical intercourses, resulting in pregnancy. She was scared and reluctant to share the information with her family members, thus delaying her abortion. When she disclosed the information to family members, it was risky to go for abortion. Her family members wanted to arrange a formal marriage with the same boy. But the family members of the boy did not agree with the proposal causing a serious crisis. Finally, A's parents took her to her distant relative's place in a village and she delivered a boy child. Because of social stigma, she preferred to hand over the child to another family in this same locality. When the child grew up and was admitted in the school, the information about his parents' background was disclosed to the locality and the child continuously experienced humiliation and social boycott. As a result, the boy preferred to discontinue education and remain unskilled.

(ii) Unwanted pregnancy and its impact on children

Unwanted pregnancy after marriage is not common. However, it happens. A good number of couples have physical relationships without taking protective measures and sometimes it leads to pregnancy. In some cases, couples accept the reality and go ahead with the pregnancy and consider the child's upbringing seriously. On the other hand, in some cases, there is conflict among the couples about the issue i.e., whether to undergo the abortion or retain it. If either of the couples do not agree with the proposal to deliver the child and finally get a child because of the circumstances, the child might experience neglect while some women experience violence (Dixit, Ram, & Dwivedi, 2012; Hajizadeh & Nghiem, 2020; Stephenson, Koenig, Acharya, & Roy, 2008).

(iii) Preference for male child

India is a patriarchal society and there is a preference for male children although children, irrespective of gender, are equally potentially creative. Several Indian studies documented the same issue in different geographical locations covering different communities (Arnold, Choe, & Roy, 1998; Dudeja, Singh, Jindal, & Bhatnagar, 2013; Mitra, 2014; Mutharayappa, 1997).

Senior members of some families are very much obsessed with male children so that they can take the family tradition forward. Some couples, after getting two or three girl children, go for another child with the expectation to get a male child. In the process, the couples get three or four girl children. In some families, women are blamed for delivering a girl child without realizing that the father's gender is the determinant factor for the gender of a child. Nevertheless, preference for a male child causes neglect to the girl child.

(iv) Dependence of parents on substance and its impact on child upbringing

Taking alcohol or other substances by women of well-to-do families in the developed countries are regular affairs as they frequently attend parties and/or social gatherings. In developing countries like India, taking substances by pregnant women is a phenomenon in the urban belt, although it is not very common. However, if a mother takes alcohol or other substances, it might affect the health of the baby, as highlighted by several studies (Behnke et al., 2013; Law et al., 2003; Little, 1977; Olegård et al., 1979a; Olegård et al., 1979b; Ornoy & Ergaz, 2010).

(v) Parenting styles and its impact on children

Parenting styles have a significant role in quality upbringing of children and adolescents. Research evidence also indicates that besides parenting styles, parental behaviours have an important role in the upbringing of children and adolescents. Broadly, there are four types of parenting styles viz., authoritative, authoritarian, permissive (Baumrind, 1996), and uninvolved (Maccoby & Martin, 1983). Let us discuss in brief about each of these types of parenting styles for a better understanding of their advantages and disadvantages.

Authoritative parenting style

Parents of this category are highly responsive and they clearly tell their children about their expectations. They are also very supportive and extend it to their adolescents when needed. The following case study demonstrates parenting styles of authoritative parents:

Case Study 2

B a student of class VII, came back home after a tough day at her school. Her mother found her upset and inactive. The mother enquired about the matter and listened to B as she explained what had happened. It turned out that her teacher scolded her for misbehaving in the class. Her mother sat with her and discussed the incident in detail, reasoned out and negotiated the matter together with the involvement of B. Her mother clarified about the code of conduct and discipline to be maintained by B in the class. By the end of the discussion B herself identified where she went wrong and why her teacher scolded her.

(Deb et al., 2020).

Authoritarian parenting style

As compared to authoritative parenting, authoritarian parents lack responsiveness, rather they are very demanding. Parents of this category expect that their child will always be very obedient and strictly listen to the parents' instructions and/or rules of the family (Baumrind, Larzelere, & Owens, 2010). Further, they do not rely on their child and listen to their voices related to their career and family decision-making processes. They also discourage open discussions with their child about any issue (Gonzalez, Holbein, & Quilter, 2002). An example of the authoritative parenting style is provided below:

Case Study 3

C is a 7-year-old boy who, on an evening, was trying to fix one of his broken toy cars. His father was sitting next to him reading the newspaper and was not noticing what C was involved in. In the process of repairing, C accidently hit a glass of water which was kept on the table. It fell down and broke. His father became furious and harshly scolded him for being very untidy, careless, and undisciplined. He snatched away his toy car and told him that it would not be returned to him. C was hurt and locked himself in his room away from his father's sight.

(Deb et al., 2020)

Permissive parenting style

Parents of this category actively engage in child care and they do not have high expectations from their child. They discuss various issues with their child, even family-related decision-making processes. They give liberty to their child to think differently instead of setting rules for their child. However, they set a few behavioural expectations from the child (Baumrind et al., 2010). Once the child attains adolescence, they do not closely monitor the child's behaviour. These parenting styles cause externalizing behaviour of the children (Luyckx et al., 2011) and some of the children get involved in risk behaviour and pay less attention to studies (Querido, Warner, & Eyberg, 2002). A study disclosed that permissive parenting has been associated with low self-esteem of children and less engagement in studies, causing poor academic performance (Ginsburg & Bronstein, 1993). The following case study illustrates the styles of permissive parenting:

Case Study 4

D and her parents were attending a birthday party in their society. Soon D and her friends were having fun by running around and playing with balloons. Her mother was found to be watchful of D while she played; she had fallen down a couple of times and her mother picked her up and comforted her. As the game continued, D began to bother other children by fighting with them and by bursting their balloons. A few of them stopped playing with D and ran back to their mothers crying and complaining. But D's mother did not take any initiative in disciplining D or giving her appropriate guidelines.

(Deb et al., 2020)

Uninvolved parenting style

Parents of this category are indifferent about their child's welfare. They also do not extend support to their child at times of crisis (Baumrind et al., 2010). In other words, parents of this category are low in responsiveness and low on demands. This is the worst parenting style among the four broad categories of parenting. Children of this category engage more in externalizing behaviour, i.e., delinquent acts, ranging from vandalism and petty theft to assault and rape (Hoeve et al., 2009). The following case study is a clear example of uninvolved parenting styles:

Case Study 5

E male, 17 years old, was confused and unsure of which course to take for his undergraduate studies. He consulted his teachers, spoke with his friends and read online, but still remained worried and unable to take such an important decision all by himself. Over dinner, he tried to discuss this matter with his father who is hardly interested in such talks. Throughout the conversation, his father appeared inattentive and uninterested. He was preoccupied with his phone, reading and sending emails related to his job. The conversation didn't last for long, which was soon terminated by his father by asking E to decide by himself. E continues to remain helpless and frustrated due to little input from his father.

(Deb et al., 2020)

Like parenting styles, parenting behaviour such as parental warmth and support, inductive reasoning, and parent–child communication facilitate positive child and adolescent adjustment and in turn, children feel emotionally secure, happy, and become more confident and resilient. Research demonstrates that the socioeconomic background of the family, along with the living environment, determines the parenting behaviours in guiding their children (Conger et al., 2002). Evidence indicates that depressive symptoms of children and adolescents are correlated with exposure to community violence (Ceballo, Ramirez, Hearn, & Maltese, 2003).

(vi) Mental health challenges of parents and its impact on children

The incidences of mental health challenges are increasing at a fast rate and parents with mental health challenges fail to discharge their responsibilities causing child neglect and lack of guidance and support for the education of the children, and other related issues. First-hand experience of the first author in dealing with elderly people with mental health challenges is very disturbing. In most of the cases, the mental health challenge of a person does not get attention and parents arrange the marriage of their child with a person from a distant place, so that they cannot make out the problem. The marriage of a person with mental health challenges is arranged with an expectation that the problem will be resolved automatically after marriage. This is a wrong notion. Rather, the problem aggravates and the spouse becomes the victim of the situation (Maybery, Ling, Szakacs, & Reupert, 2005). Parents of newly married couples often insist that having a new child and caring for it will heal the existing mental health challenges. The reality is that the new born child experiences neglect and is deprived of love and affection as both parents fail to discharge additional responsibilities, i.e., providing quality care to the child due to cognitive distortion.

(vii) Family violence and its impact on child care

Argument and counterargument in a family with small issues are normal since couples often differ in opinion. It is quite unlikely that couples will be compatible in all respects. However, often disagreements cross limits and turn into shouting at each other or fighting. This causes a serious challenge for children and women and they suffer from anxiety and feel insecure (Kashani & Allan, 1998; Kashani, Daniel, Dandoy, & Holcomb, 1992; Levendosky & Graham-Bermann, 2001). Every child expects a happy family environment. Family violence has become a global challenge as it affects the overall growth of a child. Family violence has many adverse effects as highlighted by dozens of previous studies.

(viii) Common childhood disorders and parents' perception about the same

A large number of children across the world suffer from various childhood disorders like learning disability, autism, mental retardation, hyperactivity, attention deficit, etc., and most of them remain unattended since parents and primary school teachers are not aware of the signs and symptoms of the same problems. Every parent expects a normal and a healthy child. Even if parents notice some unusual behaviour during the early days of a child, they prefer to overlook the same with an expectation that over a period of time, it would be fine. Some parents admit their child to schools by paying donations, especially the businessman, despite rejection during the selection process. These children fail to adjust with other children, are unable to respond to teacher's queries, and meet the academic demand and in turn, they experience rejection and suffer from maladjustment. Therefore, all pre-primary and primary school teachers should be trained and given a proper perspective of common childhood disorders during their Bachelor of Education or Masters of Education course, so that they are able to identify the children with similar problems and provide them need-based training or refer them to suitable intervention programmes. At the same time, teachers should also sensitize the parents about the condition of the child and their role in improving the condition and accepting the reality, so that a child does not experience neglect or discrimination within the family.

(ix) Negligence of medical care and its impact

Timely medical attention is essential for avoiding some health problems and recovering from physical ailment. Medical negligence may cause serious health consequences. In the past, children suffered from a range of physical ailments and scientific advancements in the field of medical science came out with effective vaccines as preventive measures. It is expected that every child will receive all the vaccines at appropriate periods, as suggested by the health centre or private practitioners. However, the reality is that a good number of rural children do not receive all the vaccines due to the lack of knowledge about the same facilities and/or myths and misconceptions about vaccination. They remain vulnerable to minor and major physical health problems.

(x) Non-availability of primary and secondary schools in the locality

Although there is tremendous development in the urban areas across the country, there are areas in the rural belt where health, education, and communication facilities are extremely poor. In some states in India, there are places where schools are unavailable within 10–15 kilometres distance and even if there is a primary school, its infrastructure is very poor and/or teachers do not attend the school. Some schools do not have rest rooms or safe drinking water facilities. All these factors are discouraging parents to admit their child in a school.

(xi) Parental high expectation and its consequences

Every parent dreams about their child's future. They dream to see their child becoming a doctor or engineer and fulfil their wishes. They put all their efforts and invest all their life savings to fulfil their wishes. They also love their child unconditionally and in the process, some parents share their dreams with their child and talk about the same frequently, without listening to their child and their interests about their future career. Aptitude of a child is also important in deciding their future career in addition to looking at the job market. Some parents become so obsessed that they put continuous pressure on their child for better academic performance and for pursuing a particular subject. For some children, this pressure becomes unbearable and they suffer from anxiety and depression. In our professional career, we have come across plenty of such cases where a child was forced to study either medical or engineering and after studying the subject for two to three years, they discontinue and even after completion, they want to shift to another subject. This issue is well taken care of in the New Education Policy of, 2020 of the Government of India, wherein more emphasis on multidisciplinary education and with multiple exit options at the undergraduate level is provided, so that a child can switch over to another course if they lose interest in their current one. In most of the developed countries, this system of education is followed.

(xii)Unique characteristics of children

Every child is unique and their interests, intelligence, aptitude, and motivation are also different. So far as the psychological domain is concerned, especially personality characteristics, we find that some children are submissive, while some are dominant. We even find diversity between two siblings. Cognitive capacity of a child is one of the determining factors of intelligence. Deb et al. (2020) remarked that

> school students with high cognitive capacities, which are attention, memory, and learning, attend all the classes with proper attention and gain from the teaching. Generally, the student's with low cognitive competence do not perform well in school examinations. This does not necessarily mean that they will not succeed in life. Some people with low cognitive capacity may succeed because of their high social intelligence and/or emotional intelligence. However, intelligence plays an important role in our life and it takes children in different directions for their career.

Motivation is another psychological aspect of a child. It is the internal drive of an individual to achieve a certain objective in life. Motivation can be assessed by monitoring the nature of engagement of an individual in a particular task.

The motivation of a child in studies depends upon several factors and they include family environment, encouragement from the family members for studies, guidance at home, availability of study materials and school uniform, cultural aspects of a school, school discipline, teachers' punctuality and teaching style, appreciation from teachers for good performance, encouragement from teachers instead of any punishment for poor performance, follow-up of studies, timely completion of syllabus, revision of the syllabus, class tests from time to time, and finally, cooperation of the classmates, as stated by Deb et al. (2020). Positive, encouraging, and supportive academic ambiance of school encourages children in studies. Therefore, every parent and teacher should be supportive in pursuing the child's education at home and in school. Sometimes, children may not perform well in some subjects. It requires discussion with a child to find out his/her difficulties instead of punishing and/or criticizing them and providing them with need-based support. This supportive approach will develop interest in a child towards studies and he/she will perform better.

Referring to the academic performance of another child and comparing it with their own child is a common practice for some parents, which often demotivates a child and at times, some children feel humiliated. Children need guidance, care, love and affection, a congenial family environment, and encouragement for engaging them in studies. Regular monitoring of a child's academic progress and other requirements by the parents are beneficial.

(xiii) Abuse of children and girl child marriage

Abuse of children in different forms is a global challenge. It is more in the developing countries compared to developed countries as a large number of people in the developing countries are not aware of child rights issues and they do not have proper understanding about healthy child upbringing. In India, a large number of children experience neglect and abuse as reported by a series of studies (Deb & Modak, 2010; Deb, Mukherjee, & Mathews, 2011). For example, a Kolkata-based study revealed that

> 52.4%, 25.1%, and 12.7% adolescents suffered psychological, physical, and sexual violence in the last year. Older adolescents (aged 17–18 years) suffered more psychological violence than the younger ones (15–16 years). Sixty nine (18.6%) adolescent students stood witness to violence between adult members in the family. More than three-fifth (61.9%) adolescents experienced at least one type of violence, while one-third (32.7%) experienced physical or sexual violence or both.
>
> (Deb et al., 2016)

Another Puducherry study found that

> 62% of the students reported experiencing school physical/corporal punishment (CP) in the past 12 months, with males and those attending public schools being significantly more likely to report school CP than females and those in private schools. The youth who reported school CP reported more anxiety and depression.
>
> (Deb et al., 2017)

In addition, girl child marriage is another big challenge in India. It deprives girl children from study and career growth and finally they lead a life of poor quality. Neglect and abuse of children have several adverse impacts on their mental health in addition to physical harm. For example, children who experience sexual abuse suffer from anxiety, fear, depression, and adjustment problem (Deb et al., 2017; Deb et al., 2011; Deb & Walsh, 2012).

Sexual abuse has a negative impact on the mental health of a child. A child who experienced sexual abuse suffers from inferiority complex, feeling of shame, and guilt. Therefore, a victim should be given confidence that they are not responsible for the incident and should not feel guilty or ashamed, in

Figure 1.2 Prevention of child abuse.

Source: All figures in this book have been prepared by the authors unless specified otherwise.

addition to extending counselling services and helping the child in delivering justice. The following figure gives an idea about the circle to be created in the community for the protection of children from all forms of abuse (Figure 1.2).

(xiv) **Poverty and lack of support facilities**

About one-fifth of the Indian population live below the poverty line and children from these families do not get basic care and support facilities for their proper upbringing. Most of the parents from this category struggle a lot for their survival. Therefore, sending the children to schools is a luxury for them. Instead, they prefer to engage their child in some economic activities and/or send them to somebody's house to work as a domestic assistant. People below the poverty line do not have proper social networks. Support facility during a crisis is a distant dream for them. The Government of India and other state governments have come up with various poverty alleviation schemes to support the people of lower social strata. Some people enjoy those facilities while many government support facilities do not reach them because of various factors.

(xv) **Lack of knowledge about child rights**

A large number of parents and teachers do not have the basic knowledge about child rights and some of them do not believe in child rights (Deb & Mathews, 2012; Deb et al., 2016). They think children are immature and are unable to think about their welfare so they do not consult them. This sort of an understanding of parents and teachers about children makes them vulnerable to abuse and neglect.

The above case studies are clear examples of neglect of child care and discrimination experienced by them because of various socio-economic factors, poor parenting styles, social myths and misconceptions about child care, and lack of understanding of parents, as well as, primary, middle, and

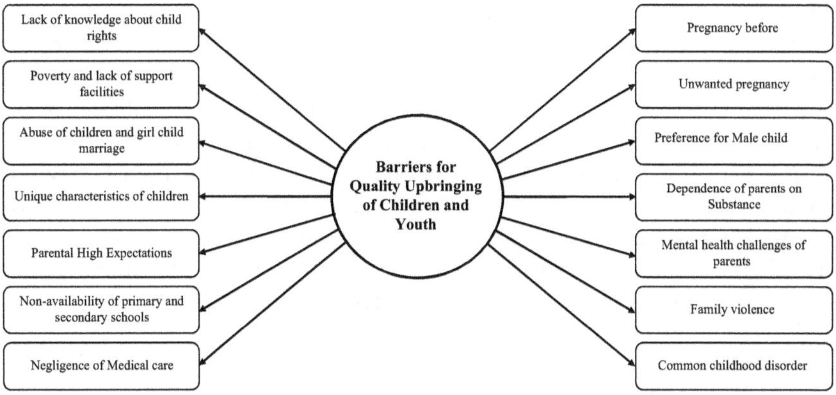

Figure 1.3 Factors influencing early childhood care, safety and overall well-being of children and youth.

secondary school teachers, about healthy child growth and development. A good number of children are in conflict with the law and they live in armed conflict zones. Children from poor families are vulnerable to trafficking and some get engaged in commercial activities in unhygienic conditions, while children of commercial sex workers remain vulnerable to the vicious cycle of abuse and exploitation.

In addition, a large number of children across the society, especially in the rural belt, come across various challenges which adversely affect their social, mental, and career growth and development, and thereby the country loses good human resources. The reality about poor child care emphasizes the need for sensitization of parents, teachers, and the larger society about quality child care, myths and misconceptions about various child care-related issues and protection of children from all adversities. Apart from this, it is essential for respective government officials to implement all the child care-related policies in practice through proper coordination with all allied institutes, including grass-root level organizations. The following model (Figure 1.3) gives an idea about various causal and contributory factors which adversely affect the quality upbringing of children and how a country loses the potentials of a large number of children and youth at later stages:

Socialization process and its necessity

Every society follows certain norms in terms of social code and conduct and every individual is supposed to follow the same. Responsible behaviour of an individual makes a big difference in any system. It helps a system to function effectively by maintaining cordial relationships with others. The fundamental question which arises is, whether every individual behaves in a responsible manner? If not, why? Here lies the role of the socialization process. In a natural process of upbringing, a child gets the basic lessons about the code and conduct from the family members, particularly from the parents. The role of family is very important in the socialization of a child. Socialization starts from the family for a child. One gets the orientation on the socialization process automatically through interaction with the family members, especially parents and siblings. This is called informal socialization training. Children imitate the behaviour of elderly people and practice it. Therefore, parents should be very careful about their behaviour, manners, and lifestyles. Honesty, integrity, humanity, and a positive outlook are very important characteristics of individuals. If a child finds all the characteristics in some of their family members, it will greatly influence them and they will consider them as role models (Deb et al., 2020).

In some cases, parents should orient their child at an early age about the expectations of the society, so that they behave in similar manners, as observed by Deb et al. (2020). This journey is called the socialization process. Through this process, children learn their role as adults that they need to play later in their life. It is a continuous process in the life of human beings when children are familiarized with social norms, customs, and culturally appropriate behaviour and it is practised, generation after generation (Deb et al., 2020).

Orientation on socialization during childhood is very important for familiarizing the children with various social norms, customs, and expectations of the larger society, in order to behave in a responsible manner as an adult and to control impulses. It is a life-long process and one needs formal or informal training at different stages of life for understanding the social and cultural dynamics of a society and behaving accordingly. Finally, the socialization process helps a child to lead a quality life afterwards and contribute towards social development. Keeping this background in mind, this chapter emphasizes the role of family and school in the socialization process, in addition to discussing the child's relationship with peers and other social agents.

Educational institutions are the places for formal socialization training for the children through direct instructions while the family orient children on the socialization process in a non-formal and natural manner. Exposure to language, social norms, customs, and values of the family are some other aspects of the socialization process.

The outcome of the socialization process within the family and institutions are developing good manners, good habits, and developing a good outlook towards life, in addition to developing good qualities like respecting others and their views, acceptance, adjusting in different situations in life, cooperation, tolerance, and responding to different situations in appropriate manners and developing a positive attitude towards interpreting any situation positively which, in turn, helps a child to remain psychologically happy and lead a well-adjusted life (Deb et al., 2020).

Role of family and school in child growth and development

There are parents whose lifestyle and personality adversely impact the child. For example, parents who are dependent on alcohol and/or drugs are often followed by their children from the early stage of life and it becomes a normal behaviour for a child. Slowly, some children try to imitate the same lifestyles and become dependent on alcohol and fail to concentrate on studies. In that case, the parents have no option but to ask their child not to take alcohol. There are parents who earn easy money through manipulation and/or dishonest means and lead a luxurious life and directly or indirectly, they indulge their child by giving more pocket money. Some of the parents save a lot of money for the future of their child and share this information with their child proudly. Financial security makes some children lazy and they do not put much effort for better academic performance. Children of such families do not get proper values from parents except good pocket money. Afterwards, these children struggle in real life in the absence of their parents. There is a popular saying that there are no problematic children, there are problematic parents. According to Deb et al. (2020),

> most of the children from those families are more likely to become maladjusted and problematic, when they grow older. Lack of a role model in the family creates confused states of mind for children. In such situations, children are quite likely to become dependent on outsiders or peer group members. Even by mistake, if they become friendly with some peer group members who are involved in socially undesirable activities, they might get involved in similar tasks and deviate from the mainstream of the society.

Committing mistakes by children is a normal phenomenon. If a child makes a mistake or misbehaves with others in front of parents, it is to be corrected immediately in a friendly manner so that the child understands that they made a mistake and that it is socially not permissible. Some parents correct the mistakes of their child, while some prefer to remain indifferent out of too much affection. Parents' intervention in case of any misconduct of a child will help the child to modify their behaviour, which will be long lasting.

Long clinical experience of the first author in dealing with problematic behaviour of some children states that some parents experienced malhandling and/or disrespect from their child when they tried to correct the misconduct of their child at a later stage. Therefore, it is important to correct children at an early age from committing mistakes.

Deb et al. (2020) remarked that

> parents should lead honest and decent lives and should give more emphasis on human values like good relationships, respecting others and giving more quality time to their children in supervising their studies and creating a happy environment in the family. Children from these families will automatically grow with good values, possess a positive outlook about life, and contribute towards social development. During the process of socialization, in the family, as parents educate their children about their rights, they should also sensitize them about their responsibilities.

Educational institutions are formal platforms to train children on socialization processes in developing good behaviour, growing with good values, and becoming norm-bound. For example, children attend classes on time and complete the homework on a regular basis. This approach makes them disciplined and systematic. Group activities given by the teachers in school help children to develop the skill to work together as a team and accomplish the given task successfully. In every educational institute, there are teachers who are very particular, punctual, knowledgeable as well as friendly. They become role models for students and students develop interest in the subject taught by that particular teacher.

Disciplining children is necessary but it should not be harsh and/or humiliating. If mistakes of a child are corrected by a teacher in a friendly manner, perhaps the same student will never commit the same mistake in the future. At the time of the selection of a teacher in the educational institute, the personality of a teacher should be assessed to avoid recruitment of a candidate with dominating and impulsive nature.

Role of peers and other social agents in the socialization process of children

During the development phase, children develop friendships with other children, mostly with children of the same age, of their neighbourhood and/or in school. School time table does allow children to spend more with peer group members. On the other hand, because of urbanization, children do not get the opportunity to find a friend in the locality as most of the people live in apartments in the urban areas. Most of the parents have one child. As a result, a large number of children suffer from loneliness and gradually become dependent on mobile phones and the internet. Dependence on the virtual world creates a psychological distance among parent–child relationships and makes a child vulnerable to risk behaviour in viewing adult sites in the internet and playing violent games.

Need of the youth and their role

A person aged in the range of 15–29 is referred to as youth as per The National Youth Policy 2017. India is a young nation and is at an advantageous position for its demographic dividend. About 37% of the total population of the country are youth, out of 1.35 billion and this demographic dividend will make a big difference after a decade for a faster economic growth of the country.

Indian youths need quality education, equal opportunity, guidance, encouragement, motivation, and support facilities during any crisis. They should be invited to various decision-making processes related to youth policy and also engaged in community development activities under the able leadership of the community leaders, in addition to identifying their leadership qualities, sports talents, talent in arts and communication, and talents in other creative fields. In turn, the youth would play the role of leaders, academicians, and researchers, and participate in national and international sports events, thus bringing glory to the country. The contribution of Indian youth in the field of information technology is highly significant at the national and international levels.

Therefore, the country needs to pay special attention towards the holistic growth of youth and that is why child protection at an early age is necessary. Only protection of the rights of the children at an early age can ensure that these potentially talented youths will play an important role in society. Potential of every youth is necessary for national growth and prosperity and social transformation. The Government of India has taken various youth development activities in terms of skill building training programmes and training for entrepreneurship, so that the country can achieve the objectives of missions like Atmanirbhar Bharat, Digital India, and Skill India.

The New Education Policy, 2020 (NEP, 2020) will cater to the needs of children and youth of all sections of the society, who belong to diverse backgrounds, potentials, and interest areas. NEP also emphasizes on multidisciplinary education, vocation training, and multiple exit options, so that children can decide to study any subject based on their interest and aptitude. In particular, NEP aims to "ensure equity and inclusion in and through education by addressing all forms of exclusion and marginalization, disparity, vulnerability and inequality in education access, participation, retention and completion and in learning outcomes" (NEP, 2020). Another objective of NEP is to ensure 100% Gross Enrolment Ratio in preschool to secondary levels by 2030.

The adolescent and youth healthy growth model

Adolescence is a transitional phase from childhood to adulthood. During this phase, adolescents experience physical and psychological changes and become curious about physical growth, especially about sexuality. At this stage, they require proper understanding from the adults including parents and teachers and parents should listen to their voices and provide them support and guidance.

Congenial family environment, positive schooling, good parent–child relationships, support for education, and monitoring of social network activities and engagement in the virtual world and proper guidance are very important towards ensuring their healthy growth and development. Adolescents and youth who find a role model in the family are in an advantageous position to follow them. However, all adolescents and youth are not lucky to have a role model in the family. This is a big challenge for a large number of adolescents and youth. Resilience capacity of a youth helps them to deal with any adversity smoothly. The following growth model describes an ideal situation and/or environment for positive growth and development of adolescents and the youth (Deb et al., 2020). In real life, all the situations

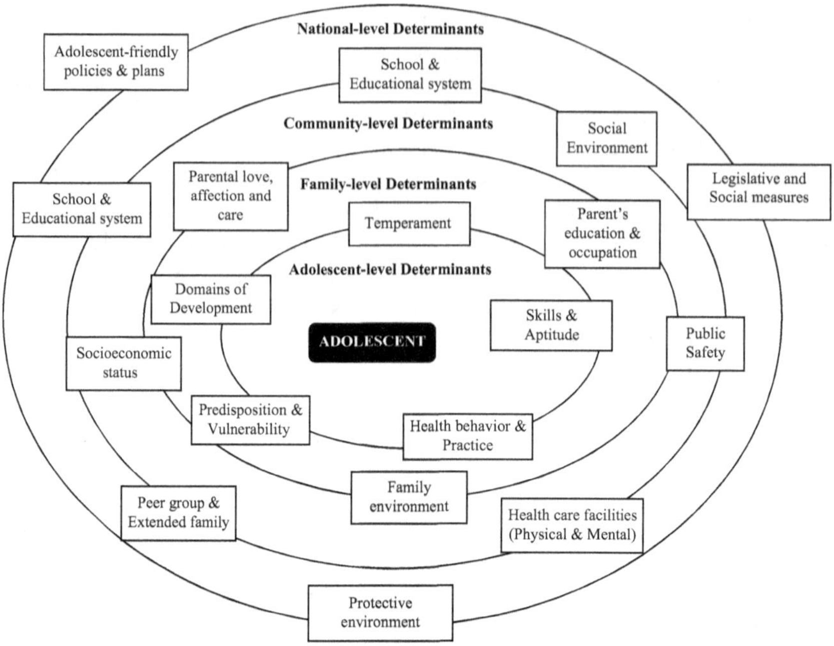

Figure 1.4 The adolescent and youth healthy growth model.

Source: Deb et al. (2020). Childhood to Adolescence: Issues and Concerns, Pearson India Foundation Services Pvt. Ltd.

may not be favourable, but one can deal with them if most of the situations are positive or conductive (Figure 1.4).

The Adolescent Healthy Growth Model is an attempt to create a hypothetical protective shell around the adolescent, with the intention of healthy growth and development. The multi-layered concentric circles model has the adolescent at the centre. Each layer is dynamic in its own nature and the complexity increases proportionate to the radius of the circle. At its first level, the innermost is the 'adolescent-level determinants' which primarily focuses on the factors that would depend directly on the adolescent himself/herself. The second circle is the immediate and the most influencing of all, is the family that can provide access to quality education, food and living conditions, thereby, a quality ground for growth. Status of socioeconomic conditions is also included. It is the community-level determinants that come as the third circle, which includes school, health care facilities, and social environment including peers, neighbours, and extended family. A clean community-social environment is an assurance for the confident growth of an adolescent. The widest of all the circles talk about the surveillance system done at national level that is strengthened through the appropriate adoption of legislative and social measures. Thus, creating a protective and nutritious environment for adolescence should be a joint venture, where responsibility is divided across all the levels.

Conclusion and recommendations

Child protection is about protecting children from all forms of adversities and providing them with basic care and support facilities along with safety, love, and affection. During the developmental phase, children need orientation on the socialization processes to get an idea about social norms, customs, and social expectations and the necessity to follow the same to become a socially well-adjusted person. Socialization is a normal daily life experience gathered through interaction with parents, siblings, and other family members. Children follow the behaviour and manners of elderly people. On and above, academic institutes and interactions with peer group members further familiarize a child about various social customs. Both formal and non-formal training of the socialization processes help children to be socially well-adjusted and responsible individuals in later life. Atrocities and neglect of children and its consequences across the world have drawn the attention of the international policymakers, which necessitated the emergence of the UN Conventions of the Rights of the Child (1989), followed by country-specific legislative and social measures, to ensure safety of the children, so that children enjoy their rights and feel protected. Like other countries, the Government of India has also taken several measures for the protection of children from adversities, abuse, neglect, exploitation, and maltreatment. Evidence highlights that a large number of children across the society experience abuse, neglect, maltreatment, and exploitation owing to several reasons and it affects their mental and physical health as well as career growth and keeps them unskilled. Thereby, the country loses huge human resources. Until children are protected and are safe, youth development is going to be a major challenge. Protection of child rights will ensure healthy growth of a child and will facilitate effective youth development, who will contribute towards national growth and prosperity. Child protection will also facilitate the sustainable development goals as well as the success of various skill development programmes of any country.

The successful implementation of all the measures concerning child protection depends upon cooperation from all concerned persons. Regarding the overall status of the children across the society, it may be stated that the situation has improved substantially. However, many more initiatives need to be taken at the grass-root level, by involving the local NGOs.

Based on sufficient experience of working with children, adolescents, and youth and with available evidence, a number of steps are suggested for protection of child rights for ensuring their quality upbringing, so that the country receives a youth population with a positive outlook and with good academic background:

Child protection committees need to be formed in every educational institution by inviting student representative, to listen to their voices.

Mental health support facilities, mainly individual, family and group counselling facilities, to be arranged in every educational institution, to address the mental health needs of the children.

Both parents and teachers should be involved in various child protection related activities of the institutions.

Special orientation programmes for the primary and secondary school teachers to be organized on common childhood disorders, so that they can identify the children with similar problems and refer them to mental health and other professionals for needful measures.

Sensitization of the larger society about child rights should be a continuous process. In this regard, the media should join hands with the government and NGOs towards disseminating information.

Continuous monitoring and research on the status of children, adolescents, and youths to be carried out by academic institutes to generate more evidence in guiding policymakers for taking appropriate and need-based policy decisions.

Periodic review of government policies and programmes, including legislative measures, are essential while inviting academics, professionals, and grass-root level workers.

Coordination between respective departments of the government, local panchayat, health workers, community leaders, and NGOs working with children are necessary to address the issues and challenges of school dropout children.

Ensuring safe shelter for children in difficult circumstances, i.e., children living on the streets, children of third gender category, abused and trafficked children, and providing them nutrition, medical care, non-formal education, and vocational training, so that they can become independent.

Appropriate preventive measures should be taken so that girl children from poor families do not become a victim of child trafficking and trafficked children are rescued and placed in rehabilitation centres.

Disadvantaged children need special attention from the local administration for protection of their rights in all respects.

Note

1 All case studies in this book are based on field studies by the authors, unless otherwise specified.

References

Abdinia, B. (2014). Knowledge and practice of mothers in the management of children's Diarrhea, in Northwest, Iran. *Archives of Pediatric Infectious Diseases*, 2(4), e17581.

Arnold, F., Choe, M. K., & Roy, T. K. (1998). Son preference, the family-building process and child mortality in India. *Population Studies*, *52*(3), 301–315.

Baumrind, D. (1996). The discipline controversy revisited. *Family Relations* 45, 405–414.

Baumrind, D., Larzelere, R.E., & Owens, E.B. (2010). Effects of preschool parents' Power: assertive patterns and practices on adolescent development. *Parenting*, 10, 157–201.

Behnke, M., Smith, V. C., & Committee on Substance Abuse. (2013). Prenatal substance abuse: short-and long-term effects on the exposed fetus. *Pediatrics, 131*(3), e1009–e1024.

Berisha, M., Hoxha-Gashi, S., Gashi, M., & Ramadani, N. (2009). Maternal practice on management of acute diarrhoea among children under five years old in Kosova. *TAF Preventive Medicine Bulletin*, *8*(5), 369–372.

Bhan, M. K., Bhandari, N., Sazawal, S., Clemens, J., Raj, P., Levine, M. M., & Kaper, J. B. (1989). Descriptive epidemiology of persistent diarrhoea among young children in rural northern India. *Bulletin of the World Health Organization*, *67*(3), 281.

Ceballo, R., Ramirez, C., Hearn, K. D., & Maltese, K. L. (2003). Community violence and children's psychological well-being: does parental monitoring matter? *Journal of Clinical Child and Adolescent Psychology*, 32, 586–592.

Conger, R.D., Wallace, L.E., Sun, Y., Simons, R.L., McLoyd, V.C., & Brody, G.H. (2002). Economic pressure in African American families: a replication and extension of the family stress model. *Developmental Psychology*, 38, 179–193.

Deb, S., Bhandra, S., Sunny, A.M., & Sahay, S. (2020). *Childhood to adolescence: issues and concerns, 1e*. India, Pearson Education.

Deb, S., Kumar, A., Holden, G. W., & Simpson Rowe, L. (2017). School corporal punishment, family tension, and students' internalizing problems: evidence from India. *School Psychology International*, 38(1), 60–77.

Deb, S. & Mathews, B. (2012). Children's rights in India: parents' and teachers' attitudes, knowledge and perceptions. *The International Journal of Children's Rights*, *20*(2), 241–264.

Deb, S. & Modak, S. (2010). Prevalence of violence against children in families in Tripura and its relationship with socio-economic factors. *Journal of Injury and Violence Research*, 2(1), 5.

Deb, S., Mukherjee, A., & Mathews, B. (2011). Aggression in sexually abused trafficked girls and efficacy of intervention. *Journal of Interpersonal Violence*, 26(4), 745–768.

Deb, S., Ray, M., Bhattacharyya, B., & Sun, J. (2016). Violence against the adolescents of Kolkata: a study in relation to the socio-economic background and mental health. *Asian Journal of Psychiatry*, *19*, 4–13.

Deb, S., Strodl, E., & Sun, H. (2015). Academic stress, parental pressure, anxiety and mental health among Indian high school students. *International Journal of Psychology and Behavioral Science*, *5*(1), 26–34.

Deb, S. & Walsh, K. (2012). Impact of physical, psychological, and sexual violence on social adjustment of school children in India. *School Psychology International*, 33(4), 391–415.

Dixit, P., Ram, F., & Dwivedi, L. K. (2012). Determinants of unwanted pregnancies in India using matched case-control designs. *BMC Pregnancy and Childbirth*, *12*(1), 1–12.

Dudeja, P., Singh, A., Jindal, A., & Bhatnagar, N. (2013). Preference for male child in two semi urban communities of Pune. *J Postgrad Med Educ Res*, *47*(3), 144–147.

Ghasemi, A. A., Talebian, A., Masoudi Alavi, N., & Moosavi, G. A. (2013). Knowledge of mothers in management of diarrhoea in under-five children, in Kashan, Iran. *Nurs Midwifery Study*, *1*(3), 158–162.

Ginsburg, G.S. & Bronstein, D. (1993). Family factors related to children's intrinsic/extrinsic motivational orientation and academic performance. *Child Development*, 64, 1461–1474.

Gonzalez, A., Holbein, M., & Quilter, S. (2002). High school students' goal orientations and their relationship to perceived parenting styles. *Contemporary Educational Psychology*, 27, 450–471.

Haider, R., Ashworth, A., Kabir, I., & Huttly, S. R. (2000). Effect of community-based peer counsellors on exclusive breastfeeding practices in Dhaka, Bangladesh: a randomised controlled trial. *The Lancet*, *356*(9242), 1643–1647.

Hajizadeh, M. & Nghiem, S. (2020). Does unwanted pregnancy lead to adverse health and healthcare utilization for mother and child? Evidence from low- and middle-income countries. *International Journal of Public Health*, *65*(4), 457–468.

Hoeve, M., Dubas, J.S., Eichelsheim, V.I., van der Laan, P.H., Smeenk, W., & Gerris, J.R. (2009). The relationship between parenting and delinquency. *Journal of Abnormal Child Psychology*, 37, 749–775.

Integrated Child Development Scheme (ICDS) (1975). The Ministry of Women and Child Development, Government of India.

Janusz, C. B., Frye, M., Mutua, M. K., Wagner, A. L., Banerjee, M., & Boulton, M. L. (2021). Vaccine delay and its association with under-vaccination in children in Sub-Saharan Africa. *American Journal of Preventive Medicine*, *60*(1), S53–S64.

Kashani, J. H. & Allan, W. D. (Eds.). (1998). *The impact of family violence on children and adolescents*. Sage Publications.

Kashani, J. H., Daniel, A. E., Dandoy, A. C., & Holcomb, W. R. (1992). Family violence: impact on children. *Journal of the American Academy of Child & Adolescent Psychiatry*, *31*(2), 181–189.

Knopik, V. S. (2009). Maternal smoking during pregnancy and child outcomes: real or spurious effect? *Developmental Neuropsychology*, *34*(1), 1–36.

Lakshminarayanan, S. & Jayalakshmy, R. (2015). Diarrheal diseases among children in India: current scenario and future perspectives. *Journal of Natural Science, Biology and Medicine*, 6(1), 24.

Law, K. L., Stroud, L. R., LaGasse, L. L., Niaura, R., Liu, J., & Lester, B. M. (2003). Smoking during pregnancy and newborn neurobehavior. *Pediatrics*, *111*(6), 1318–1323.

Levendosky, A. A., & Graham-Bermann, S. A. (2001). Parenting in battered women: The effects of domestic violence on women and their children. *Journal of Family Violence*, *16*(2), 171–192.

Little, R. E. (1977). Moderate alcohol use during pregnancy and decreased infant birth weight. *American Journal of Public Health*, *67*(12), 1154–1156.

Luyckx, K., Tildeley, E.A., Soenens, B., Andrews, J. A., Hampson, S. E., Peterson, M., & Duriez, B. (2011). Parenting and trajectories of children's maladaptive behaviors: a 12-year prospective community study. *Journal of Clinical Child & Adolescent Psychology*, 40, 468–478, doi:10.1080/15374416.2011.563470.

Maccoby, E.E. & Martin, J.A. (1983). Socialization in the context of the family: parent-child interaction. In *Handbook of child psychology*; Mussen, P. H., Ed.; Wiley: New York, NY, 4, 1–103.

Madhu, K., Chowdary, S., & Masthi, R. (2009). Breast feeding practices and new born care in rural areas: a descriptive cross-sectional study. *Indian Journal of Community Medicine: An official publication of Indian Association of Preventive & Social Medicine*, *34*(3), 243.

Maybery, D., Ling, L., Szakacs, E., & Reupert, A. (2005). Children of a parent with a mental illness: perspectives on need. *Australian e-Journal for the Advancement of Mental Health*, 4(2), 78–88.

McLoyd, V. C. (1989). Socialization and development in a changing economy: the effects of paternal job and income loss on children. *American Psychologist*, *44*(2), 293.

McLoyd, V. C. (1990). The impact of economic hardship on Black families and children: psychological distress, parenting, and socio-emotional development. *Child Development*, *61*(2), 311–346.

Millennium Development Goals (MDGs) (2000).

Million Death Study Collaborators. (2010). Causes of neonatal and child mortality in India: a nationally representative mortality survey. *The Lancet*, *376*(9755), 1853–1860.

Mitra, A. (2014). Son preference in India: Implications for gender development. *Journal of Economic Issues*, *48*(4), 1021–1037.

Mutharayappa, R. (1997). Son preference and its effect on fertility in India.

Mutharayappa, K. & Prabhuswamy, P. (2003). Factors and consequences of home deliveries: a study in rural Karnataka. *Journal of Health Management*, *5*(1), 17–35.

National Policy for Children (1994).

Olakunle, J. M., Valentine, U. O., Kamaldeen, A. S., & Buhari, A. S. M. (2012). Assessment of mothers' knowledge of home management of childhood diarrhoea in a Nigerian setting. *International Journal of Pharmaceutical Research and Bio-Science*, *1*(4), 168–184.

Olegård, R., Sabel, K. G., Aronsson, M., Sandin, B., Johansson, P. R., Carlsson, C., ... & Hrbek, A. (1979a). Effects on the child of alcohol abuse during pregnancy: retrospective and prospective studies. *Acta Paediatrica*, *68*, 112–121.

Olegård, R., Sabel, K. G., Aronsson, M., Sandin, B., Johansson, P. R., Carlsson, C., ... & Hrbek, A. (1979b). Effects on the child of alcohol abuse during pregnancy: retrospective and prospective studies. *Acta Paediatrica*, *68*, 112–121.

Ornoy, A. & Ergaz, Z. (2010). Alcohol abuse in pregnant women: effects on the fetus and newborn, mode of action and maternal treatment. *International Journal of Environmental Research and Public Health*, *7*(2), 364–379.

Osonwa Kalu, O., Eko Jimmy, E., & Ema, S. (2016). Utilization of oral rehydration therapy in the management of diarrhoea in children among nursing mothers in Odukpani local government area of cross River State, Nigeria. *American Journal of Public Health Research*, *4*(1), 28–37.

Powers, J. R., McDermott, L. J., Loxton, D. J., & Chojenta, C. L. (2013). A prospective study of prevalence and predictors of concurrent alcohol and tobacco use during pregnancy. *Maternal and Child Health Journal*, *17*(1), 76–84.

Querido, J.G., Warner, T.D. & Eyberg, S.M. (2002). Parenting styles and child behavior in African American families of preschool children. *Journal of Clinical Child and Adolescent Psychology*, 31, 272–277.

Shah, M. S., Ahmad, A., Khalique, N., Afzal, S., Ansari, M. A., & Khan, Z. (2012). Home-based management of acute diarrhoeal disease in an urban slum of Aligarh, India. *The Journal of Infection in Developing Countries*, *6*(02), 137–142.

Stephenson, R., Koenig, M. A., Acharya, R., & Roy, T. K. (2008). Domestic violence, contraceptive use, and unwanted pregnancy in rural India. *Studies in Family Planning*, *39*(3), 177–186.

The Child Labour (Prohibition and Regulation) Act (1986).

The Commissions for Protection of Child Rights Act (2005).

The Guardian and Wards Act (1890).

The Immoral Trafficking Act (1956).

The Indian Constitutions (1949).
The Indian Penal Code (1860).
The Integrated Child Protection Scheme (2009).
The Juvenile Justice (Care and Protection of Children) Act (2015)
The Medical Termination of Pregnancy Act (1971).
The National Charter for Children (2004).
The National Crime Records Bureau, 2018, Ministry of Home Affairs, Government of India.
The National Health Policy (2002).
The National Plan of Action for Children (2005).
The National Policy for Children (2013).
The National Policy for Education (1986).
The National Policy for Empowerment of Women (2001).
The National Youth Policy (2017). The Ministry of Youth Affairs and Sports, Government of India.
The New Education Policy (2020).
The Persons with Disabilities (Equal Opportunities, Protection of Rights and Full Participation) Act (1995).
The Pre-Conception and Pre-natal Diagnostic Technique (Prohibition of Sex Selection) Act (1994).
The Pre-natal Diagnostic Techniques (Regulation and Prevention of Misuse) Act (1994).
The Prohibition of Child Marriage Act (2006).
The Protection of Children from Sexual Offences Act, 2012 (POCSO Act, 2012).
The Protection of Women from Domestic Violence Act (2005).
The Right of Children to Free and Compulsory Education Act (2009).
The UN Convention on the Rights of the Child (1989).
The Young Persons (Harmful Publications) Act (1956).

2 Demographic and socio-economic status of the youth

Population is a source of strength for social and economic prosperity as well as overall development of a country. If a country has proper child development policies and programmes, along with good educational institutions and an inclusive approach, it would help all children to grow healthy with good education and finally, they will become skilled manpower and contribute towards the social and economic prosperity of a country.

Average age of the population is another indicator of the strength of a country. Countries having larger youth populations are considered to be more prosperous as young people would be able to contribute for a longer period. Along with age, factors like educational facilities, quality education, skills of the young population, and employment opportunities make a significant difference in realizing the long-term vision of a country. In terms of demographic dividend, India is in an advantageous position as about 34% of the Indian population are youth, that is, they are between 15 and 29 years of age.

Population of India

The population can contribute significantly towards economic growth and the sustainable development of a nation, if they receive proper care, guidance, and quality education and their rights are protected during childhood. Otherwise, the population might turn into a burden for the nation. As per Census of India 2011, the total population of the country was 1.21 billion – 10,45,96,415 males and 94,985,062 females. India stands second in terms of world population after China. The population growth of India from 2001 to 2011 was 181 million. As per Census of India 2011, the overall literacy rate was 74% and the literacy rates for females and males were 65.46% and 82.10%, respectively. It is one of the most important indicators of social development which facilitates economic growth of a country. It is defined as "the percentage of literates to the total population age 7 years and above".

So far as sex ratio is concerned, it was 940 females against 1000 males. Same gender disparity has been observed in case of children aged 0–6 years, i.e., 914 females against 1000 males. Nevertheless, life expectancy at birth

DOI: 10.4324/9781003170587-2

for both genders was 70.4 years, which is more for females (71.8%) as compared to males (69.2%).

As per the information of United Nations, by mid-2020, the total population of India was projected to be 1,380,004,385 and by 2024 it will surpass China (www.worldometers.info).

Youth population in India and their background

The National Youth Policy (2014) of India defines youth as an individual aged between 15 and 29 years. The growth of the youth population in India is much more than that of the general population of the country. In 1971, the total youth population was 168 million, which increased to 423 million in 2011. Further, if we look at the relative growth of youth with respect to age in 2011, it has been observed that youth aged between 15 and 19 years is more (1,20,526) as compared to youth aged in the range of 20–24 years (111424) and 25–29 years (1,01,414). The World Bank projection of India's youth population by 2021 shows an increasing trend in chronological order. However, by 2031, there will be a sharp decline in the number of youth population aged 15–19 years as compared to the number of same age group in 2021, as projected. In the case of the remaining two age groups, i.e., youth aged 20–24 years and 25–29 years, the increasing trend will continue (Table 2.1). Therefore, it may be stated that India is in an advantageous position over other countries and this youth population will contribute to social transformation and economic growth of the country.

Literacy among the youths

If we look at the literacy status among youths based on Census 2011 data, irrespective of rural and urban location, it has been observed that overall percentage of literacy rate after the Xth and XIIth standard has drastically reduced (Figure 2.1). When comparing rural with urban, the percentage of literacy is decreasing exponentially after XIIth standard in rural, whereas in urban areas, the percentage of literacy is decreasing in a linear manner (Figure 2.1, Figure 2.2, and Figure 2.3). Specifically, the contribution of

Table 2.1 Youths in India: Age and Gender-wise Break-up

Age Groups	*2011**			*2021***			*2031***		
	Male	*Female*	*Total*	*Male*	*Female*	*Total*	*Male*	*Female*	*Total*
15–19	63982	56544	120526	66630	59588	126218	63840	57385	121225
20–24	57585	53840	111424	64793	58149	122942	65454	58689	124143
25–29	51344	50070	101414	61835	55890	117725	65560	58727	124287

* Census of India (2011).
** Population projection by World Bank.

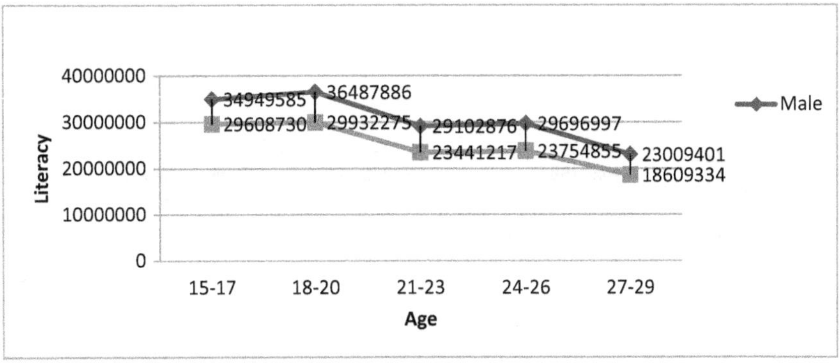

Figure 2.1 Age vs. literacy (overall).

Source: Census of India, 2011. All figures in this chapter have been developed by the authors based on available Census data.

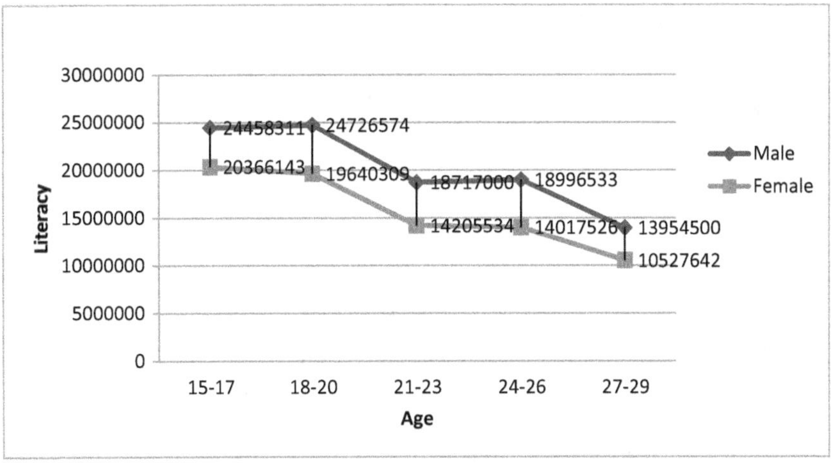

Figure 2.2 Age vs. literacy (rural).

females in the literacy sector is coming down with a sharp drop in value from the rural regions.

Further, it has been noticed that the literacy gap between male and female genders is more in rural areas (11.0%) and less in urban areas (6.0%). However, the overall literacy gap between male and female genders is 10%. The percentage of literate people is more than double of the figure in rural areas, when compared to urban areas.

Illiteracy among the youths

The overall percentage of illiteracy rate after schooling is exponentially increasing (Figure 2.4). When comparing rural and urban areas, the percentage of illiteracy is increasing for both urban and rural areas (Figures 2.5

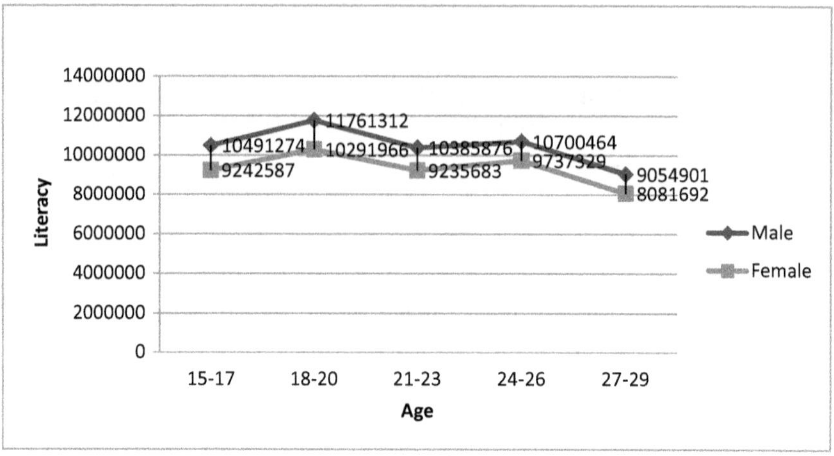

Figure 2.3 Age vs. literacy (urban).

Source: Census of India, 2011.

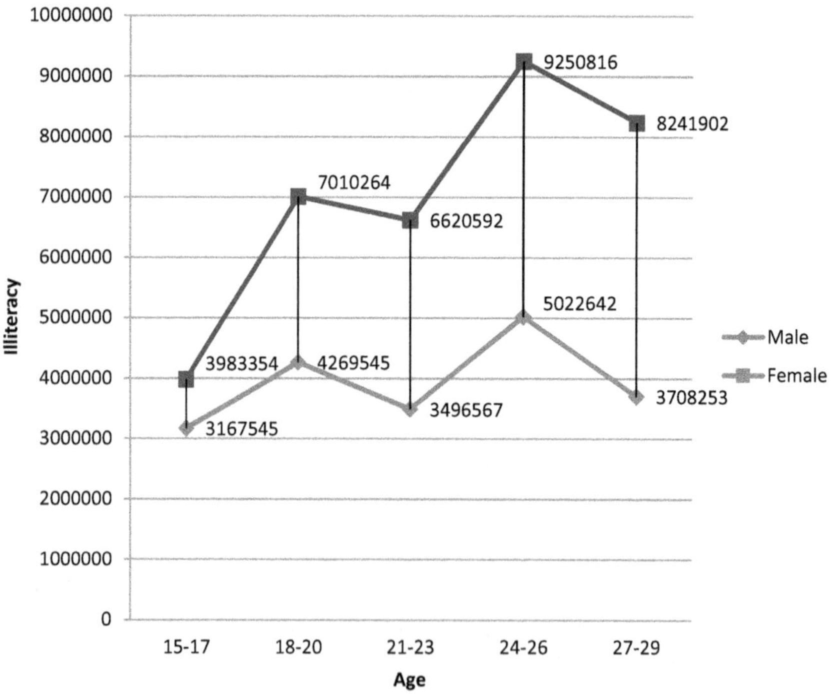

Figure 2.4 Age vs. illiteracy (overall).

Source: Census of India, 2011.

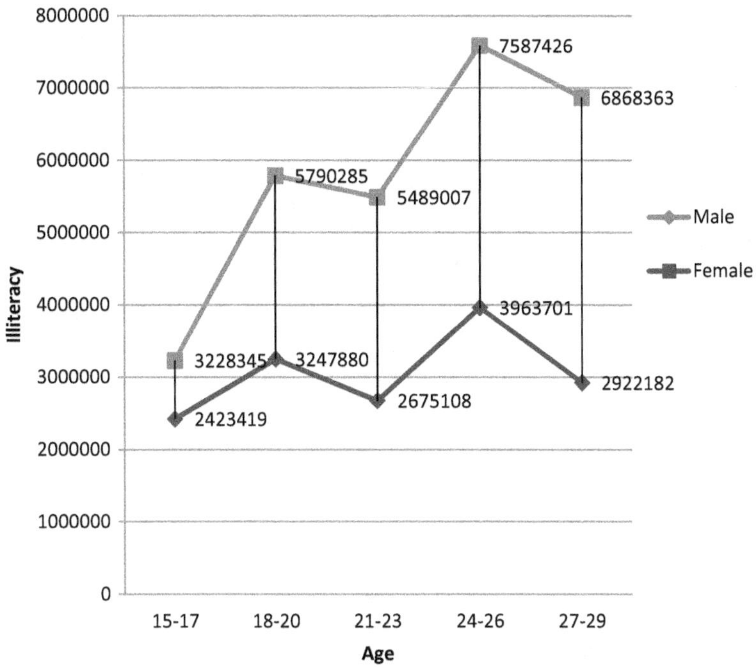

Figure 2.5 Age vs. illiteracy (rural).

and 2.6). The illiteracy gap between male and female genders is widening in the rural region than in the urban area, after schooling. The overall illiteracy gap (in average) between the male and female sexes is above 22%. The illiterate population is more than double in rural areas as compared to urban areas.

Until the age of 26, the literacy rate among males is higher, and after 26, it is higher for females (Figure 2.7).

Figure 2.8 demonstrates the gender-based literacy rate of youth in India, living in both rural and urban areas. Literacy rate of male youths is seven times more than that of females. The percentage of female literacy is less compared to their male counterparts. The percentage of gap between the literacy rate of male and female genders is 10%, whereas the percentage of gap between the illiteracy rate of male and female genders is 30%.

Place of residence of the youths as per census 2011

The places of residence of a majority of the Indian youths are rural areas and with the increase of age, they shift to urban areas for higher studies and/or for jobs (Figure 2.9).

The percentage gap between rural and urban youths is 34%.

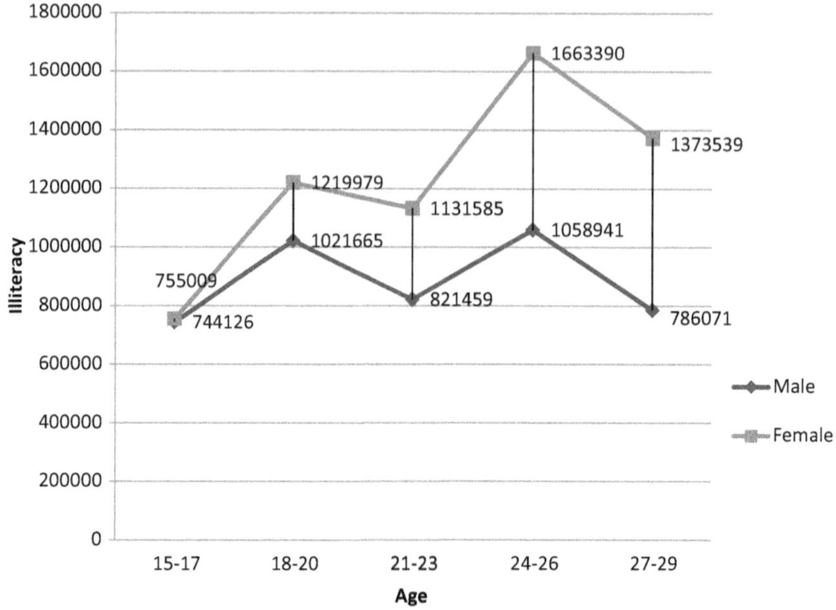

Figure 2.6 Age vs. illiteracy (urban).

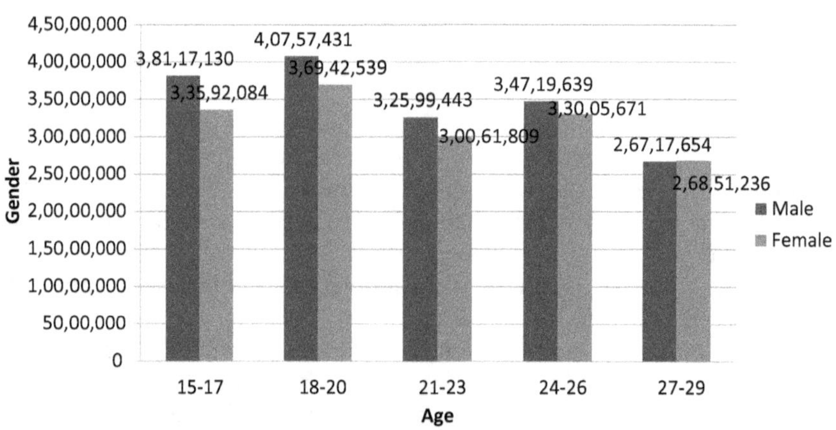

Figure 2.7 Age vs. gender (both literacy and illiteracy).

Source: Census of India, 2011.

Magnitude of disadvantaged youths in India

There are no data regarding the number of disadvantaged youths in India. Disadvantaged youths include those youths who are living below the poverty line, youths living in slum areas and interior villages, trafficked female youths, youths working as labourers, youths living in government observation homes, youths living on the streets, wards of commercial sex workers

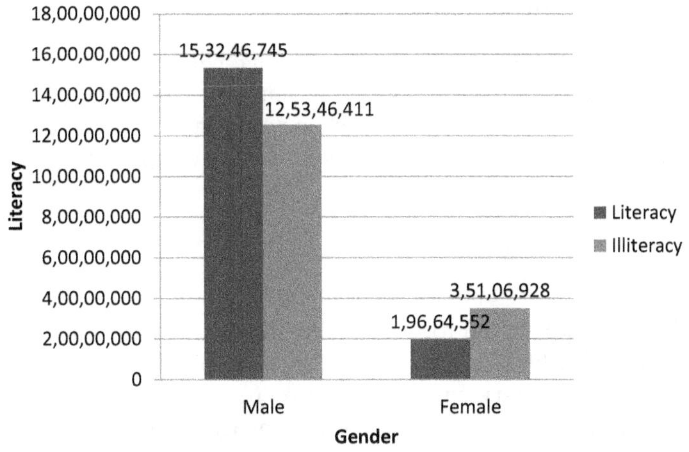

Figure 2.8 Gender vs. literacy.

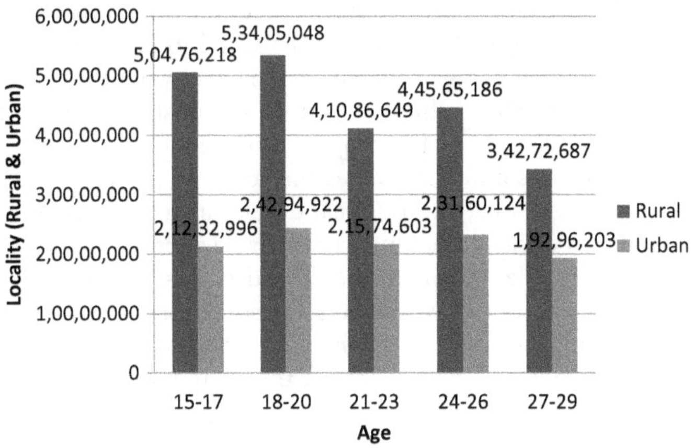

Figure 2.9 Age vs. locality.

and Lesbian, Gay, Bisexual and Transgender (LGBT) youths, and so on. However, their number will be more than a few millions. The majority of the disadvantaged youths are living in underdeveloped areas and in poor conditions without basic facilities.

A large number of disadvantaged youths are deprived of education, healthcare facilities, and there are youths who struggle for survival as most of them are unskilled. There are schemes for welfare of some sections of the disadvantaged youths but most of them are not aware of such schemes. There are NGOs working in different locations for the welfare of disadvantaged children but more and more NGOs should come forward and mobilize the disadvantaged children and bring them under the intervention programmes and provide them skill-based vocational training.

Status of the youths in India

Let us examine the status of youth in India with respect to five broad domains viz., education, health, employment, civic engagement, and migration. The youth's active engagement in socio-political processes, in particular in civic engagement, can ensure sustainable development and economic growth.

Education

Education is very essential for every individual to lead a productive, meaningful, and quality life. Therefore, every child should have access to primary education and necessary support needs to be provided to continue their education up to a certain level. Along with general stream education, skill-based vocational education should also be an option for the youths who wish to join the workforce at an early age, due to family needs. Children and rural youths from marginalized and backward families and remote areas should be encouraged to pursue education as it can help them overcome poverty and hunger. The Right of the Child to Free and Compulsory Education Act (2009), has a provision for the reservation of 25% seats in all schools for marginalized children. School administrators as well as local administration should ensure the proper enforcement of this act.

Education sensitizes and encourages the youth to participate in the processes of social, economic, and political developments of a society. Participation of youth in decision making as well as development processes make them more responsible and inculcate ethical values within them, so that they may act as community volunteers for social development and social transformation and in the process, the issues related to good governance, social inclusion, tolerance, and peace get their attention, and the society at large is benefited in the process.

(i) Highlights of National Sample Survey 75th Round (July 2017–June 2018)
The National Sample Survey Office, under the Ministry of Statistics and Program Implementation, conducted 'Household Social Consumption: Education' 75th round, during July 2017 to June 2018, covering a total of 64,519 rural households from 8097 villages and 49,238 urban households from 6188 blocks across the country. The overall literacy rate among individuals who are seven years and above was 77.7% (73.5% in rural areas while 87.7% in urban areas). NSS 75th round data also highlight gender disparity with respect to literacy (70.3% female against 84.7% male). However, the overall literacy rate in India has increased to 74% in 2011 to 77% during 2017–2018. During the same time, the percentage of female literacy rate has increased from 65.46% to 70.3%, which is a sign of positive social development.

Data provided in Table 2.2 demonstrate that only 5.7% of youth from rural areas go for higher education, i.e., graduation and above, as against 21.7% of urban youth. Lack of higher education facilities like colleges and

Table 2.2 Level of Education among Youth 15 Years and above in India

Status of Education	*Rural (%)*	*Urban (%)*
Illiterate	31.5	13.9
Studied up to primary level	20.9	14.7
Studied up to level upper primary/middle level	17.2	14.0
Studied up to secondary and higher secondary level	24.9	35.8
Graduation and above level	5.7	21.7

Source: NSS 75th Round

universities in rural areas and poor financial conditions are two main factors for the low percentage of rural youth pursuing higher education.

Attendance of educational institutions
Net Attendance Ratio (NAR) in Indian schools at the primary level is 86.8% for males and 85.1% for females. When students get promoted, the NAR goes down. For example, at secondary levels, NARs are 57.9% for males and 57.3% for females with minor attendance variation in rural and urban setups. When we look at attendance ratios of youth aged between 18 and 23 years, it is 32.6% for males and 24.6% for females.

Preference of education
After Class X, the preference for most of the students is to study humanities, followed by science and commerce. An overwhelming percentage of the students (96.1%) studied general education, which is more in female students, while the rest 3.9% were studying technical/professional education, as disclosed by NSS 75th round study.

Free education
Further, NSS 75th round study provides some valuable information about the percentage of students getting free education in India at different levels. For example, 33%, 62%, 72%, 35.5%, and 20% students are receiving free education at pre-primary, primary, upper primary/middle, secondary, and higher secondary levels, respectively. Interestingly, 77% students studying in government institutions at the graduation and postgraduation levels are getting free education. Sadly, the percentage of rural students is much less when compared to urban students, when it comes to free education. This issue requires the attention of the local administration.

Further, NSS 75th round data indicate that about 14% students across the country, who attend formal education, are getting different benefits from the government in terms of scholarship and stipends.

Access to computer and Internet
About one-fifth (23%) of the urban households have computers, while only 4% rural households have the same facility. So far as computer literacy is concerned, among persons aged between 15 and 29 years, about one-fourth (24%) youth in rural areas and more than half in urban areas (56%) are able to operate a computer. Interestingly, about one-third (35%)

Table 2.3 Number of Youths Enrolled at Various Levels in Higher Education (in 000s)

Level	*Male/ Female*	*2010–11*	*2011–12*	*2012–13*	*2013–14*	*2014–15*
Ph. D	Male	48.0	49.3	55.7	64.8	69.6
	Female	29.8	32.1	39.8	43.1	47.7
	Persons	77.8	81.4	95.4	107.9	117.3
M. Phil	Male	12.7	15.9	13.3	13.6	14.1
	Female	12.6	18.2	17.1	17.7	19.3
	Persons	25.3	34.2	30.4	31.4	33.4
Postgraduate	Male	1814.0	1769.3	1769.1	1888.6	1867.1
	Female	1455.7	1597.9	1679.1	1933.6	1986.3
	Persons	3269.7	3367.2	3448.2	3822.2	3853.4
Undergraduate	Male	12117.5	12612.5	12918.8	13574.4	14467.2
	Female	9854.7	10562.4	10971.5	11925.9	12705.1
	Persons	21972.3	23175.0	23890.3	25500.3	27172.3

of youths aged between 15 and 29 reported using the internet across the country (Source: NSS 75th Round). By the time this chapter is published, the percentage of youths using the internet might have gone much higher.

(ii) Higher education among the youth

Available data highlight that enrolment of students for doctorate research is increasing significantly every year, especially among males, although the size of females in research is significant. However, in the case of M.Phil. and postgraduate education, females outnumbered males. There is a sharp decline in the case of postgraduate education for males from 2013–2014 to 2014–2015. But, in the case of undergraduate education, the male students' percentage was more than that of females (Table 2.3).

(iii) Youths' preference for higher studies abroad

Every year, a large number of the Indian youth go abroad for higher studies and most of them are doing well and contributing to the economy of the visiting country after joining the workforce. They also contribute to the national economy by sending money to their family and/or investing money in entrepreneurship activities or in joint ventures with Indians. Data depicted in Figure 2.10 give a clear idea about the total number of Indian students who went abroad during the last six years indicating the upward trend of students' preference for higher studies abroad. However, COVID-19 had a negative impact on students' aspiration to study abroad mainly for safety reasons. The main reasons for choosing foreign universities for higher studies include quality education, prospect for research, job prospect, reputation of the university globally, faculty profile, a desire to settle down abroad, and finally better quality of life.

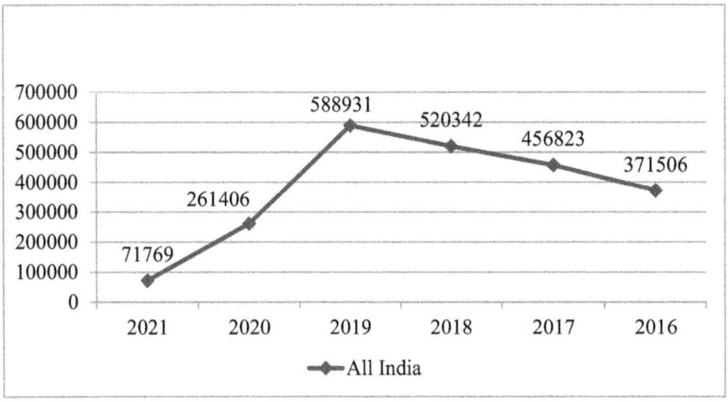

Figure 2.10 Year-wise cumulative details of Indian students pursuing education abroad.

Source: Ministry of External Affairs, Government of India.

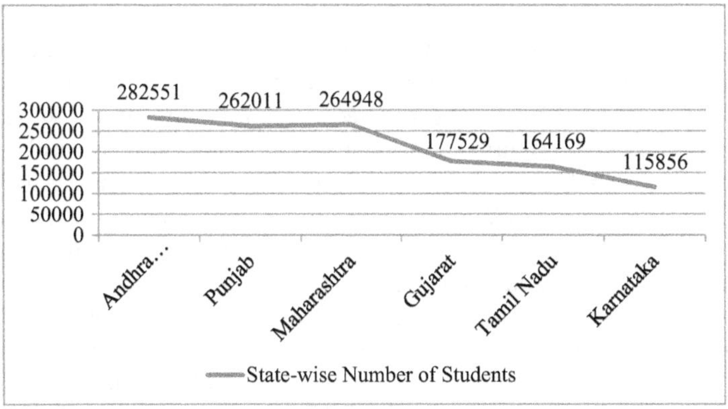

Figure 2.11 State-wise number of Indian students who went abroad for higher education during 2016–2021.

Source: Ministry of External Affairs, Government of India.

Data provided in Figure 2.11 indicate that the maximum number of students who went abroad during the last six years were from Andhra Pradesh, followed by Maharashtra, and Punjab.

In recent years, Canada has become one of the most preferred destinations for higher education for students all over the world, in particular, for the Indian students besides other countries such as the USA, UK, and Australia (Figure 2.12). The key attractions of Canada include its economic immigration gateway and its express entry systems for international students. It has been enumerated by the Immigration, Refugees and Citizenship Canada (IRCC) that the number of Indian students pursuing higher education in Canada rose beyond 40% in the year 2018. Besides, various provinces in Canada promote chances for Indian and international student communities

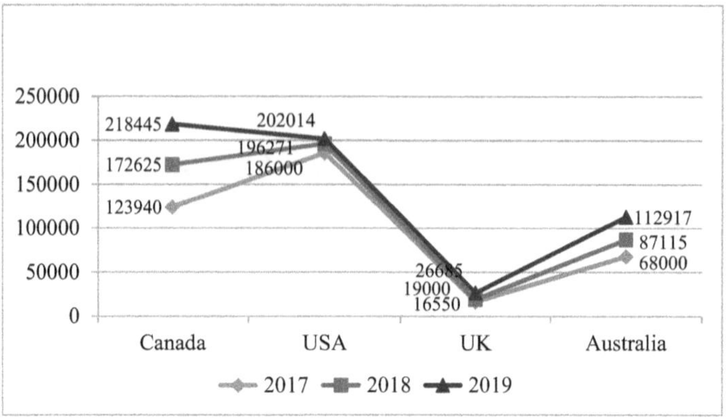

Figure 2.12 Preferred destination of Indian students for education abroad.

Source: Saurabh Arora, India Today, New Delhi, January 9, 2020 (https://www.indiatoday.in/education-today/jobs-and-careers/story/here-s-why-canada-is-a-favourite-destination-for-indian-students-for-higher-studies-1635186-2020-01-09)

to secure permanent residence for those who graduated from the country. Additionally, the other inclining factors for the youth to pursue education in Canada include the cost-effective fee structures with focus on academic excellence, instilling scientific temper and quality standards of skill development that leads to degrees that are internationally accepted and esteemed by multinationals. Canada also is recognized for low living costs with enriching conditions to lead a quality life with peace and tranquillity. The other hallmark is that Canada offers prospective career opportunities and post study work permits for those graduated from Canadian Universities which are not available for international students pursuing education in other preferred countries. With the increase in number of Indian students registering in Canadian Universities and Higher Educational Institutions, the country has instituted supportive policies viz., earn while you learn opportunities, the Study Direct Stream Program, the Post-Graduation Work Permit Program, and immigration opportunities. While Canada has been considered as a country for physical safety and financial security for foreign nationals belonging to diverse cultures to live and pursue studies, careers etc., as the country also records the lowest rates in terms of crime in the entire world.

It is expected that the New Education Policy 2020 will have a significant impact towards the holistic growth and development of children and youth of India as it ensures multidisciplinary education based on the aptitude and interest of the children and youth with multiple exit options.

(iv) Skill-based online training for Indian youths during COVID-19 pandemic

Although COVID-19 disrupted the normal functioning of the educational institutions, the online mode of education replaced the offline mode of education satisfactorily to a great extent. This crisis phase aided both students and teachers and familiarized them with information technology, especially about the basic functioning of online mode of teaching using different virtual platforms. Gradually, people have become acquainted and are comfortable with online modes of teaching. For various academic and research-related activities and for official meetings, the online mode of communication is found to be very beneficial in terms of saving time, cost, and energy. For example, most of the universities are now permitted to conduct PhD viva online mode and this is working well. Besides conducting official meetings online, seminars, conferences, special lectures, and discussions related to research between the supervisor and scholar through online mode is helping all organizations.

Like many other national and international academic institutions, the Rajiv Gandhi National Institute of Youth Development, Ministry of Youth Affairs and Sports, Government of India, conducted several online certificate courses (one week) during the COVID-19 lockdown phase from June 2020 to April 2021, on issues like academic writing, cyber security, artificial intelligence and machine learning, data science, cloud computing, internet of things and automation, and nanotechnology and its implications on the youth studying Computer Science, Mathematics, Commerce, and Pure Science. These courses were free of cost and were meant for the enhancement of their knowledge, clarification of their queries, and familiarizing the youth with the latest advancements in the respective fields. The resource persons for the courses were from Indian Institute of Technology, National Institute of Technology, and other premier institutes. A large number of youths attended all the courses and found it to be very beneficial as indicated by the online feedback of the participants through Google Form after the courses. For example, feedback from 110 participants about one week of Artificial Intelligence and Machine Learning (AI and ML) conducted during September 28, 2020 to October 2, 2020 is highly motivating for the organizers as well for the resource persons as the majority of the participants find the training effective and beneficial (see Figure 2.13, Figure 2.14, Figure 2.15,

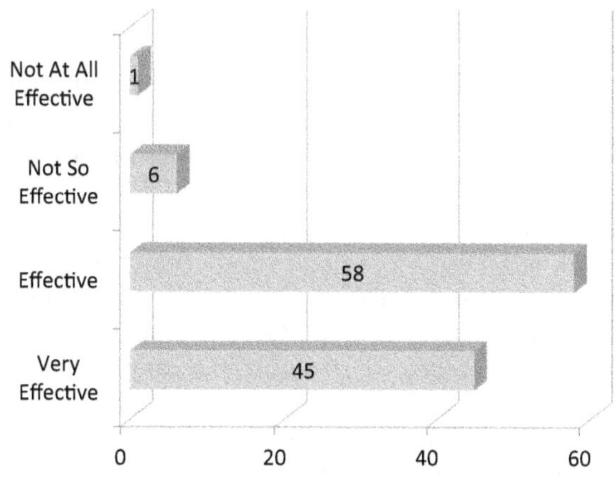

Figure 2.13 Perception about the training on AI and ML (*n*= *110*).

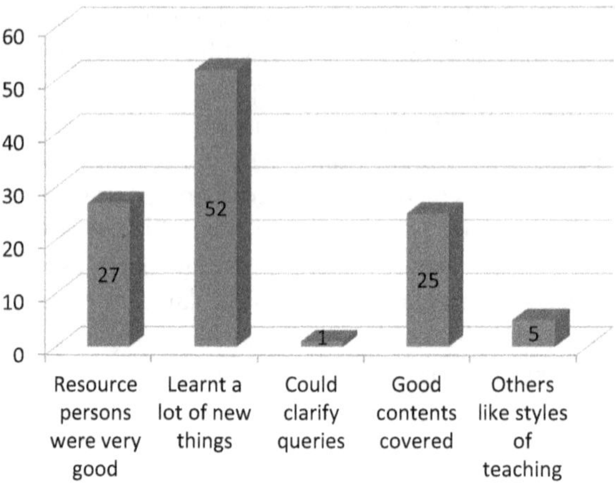

Figure 2.14 Why did you say so? (*n=110*).

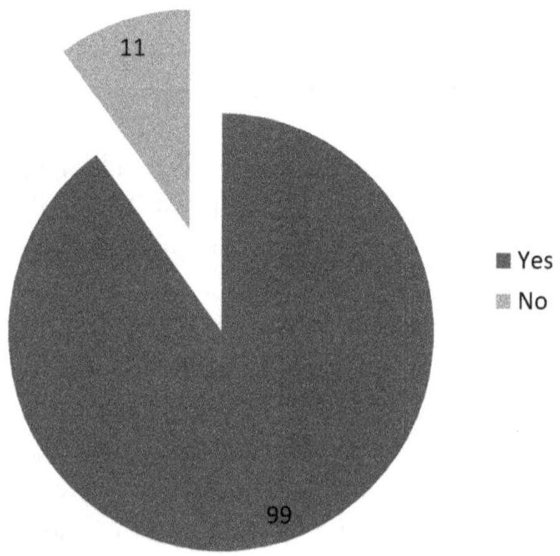

Figure 2.15 Were you able to clarify your queries?

and Figure 2.16). The online academic programmes did not enhance the knowledge and skills of the youth only, it helped them to remain mentally healthy and stress free during the COVID-19 crisis phase.

(v) Major challenge for students and youths

The second phase of COVID-19 caused severe challenges for everyone. Students are the worst categories of sufferers. Given the severity of the COVID-19 situation, i.e., alarming rate of detected COVID cases across the country, the Government of India cancelled CBSE and ICSE Class X final board examinations and postponed the Class XII final examinations and other competitive examinations like National Eligibility Entrance Test (NEET) for admission in medical courses. Similarly, most of the state governments in India also cancelled Class X final board examinations considering the safety of the students.

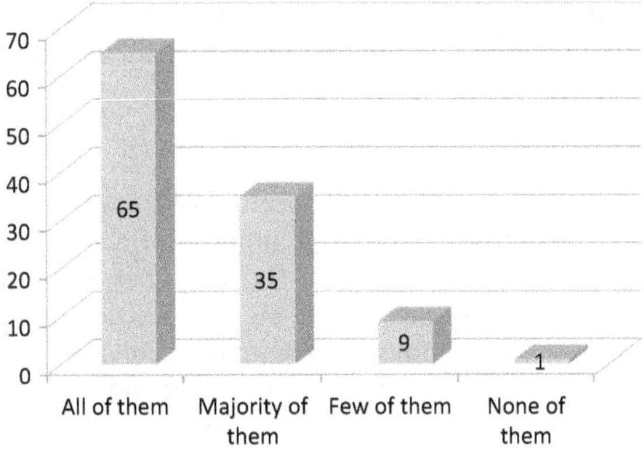

Figure 2.16 Did you find the resource persons knowledgeable and experienced?

Health status of the youths

We all know that health is wealth. But most of us do not lead healthy lifestyles and perform regular exercises, which are prerequisites to remain physically and mentally healthy. Disciplined life with proper care of health and not taking any substances are the key factors for attaining happiness and utilizing time efficiently and effectively for overall personal growth and development. There is no practice of regular or periodic health check-ups in India like in industrial countries. People go for periodic health check-ups only after suffering from some major health problems and on the advice of the doctor after a serious health issue.

In India, immunization is given to every child free of cost and it helps to ensure immunity from certain physical health problems like Hepatitis-B, Hepatitis-A, influenza, tetanus, rotavirus, chicken pox, mumps, typhoid, polio, measles, and so on. During childhood, children get maximum pleasure out of outdoor games and sports. However, these days, urban children and youth hardly get the opportunity for games and sports as there are no playgrounds in most of the urban areas. Games and sports help a child and youth to remain physically fit and psychologically fresh and happy in addition to helping them mingle with other children and to develop a positive outlook to work in a group. Children and youth of today's society found the alternative option to spend time playing games on the mobile and computers or remaining busy on social networking sites or entertainment programmes of the virtual world. As a result, the Ministry of Youth Affairs and Sports, Government of India, has come out with a programme called "FIT INDIA". The objective of the programme is to mobilize the community members including the youth of the country, through regular half an hour to one-hour physical exercise, for remaining physically fit, mentally fresh, and productive.

There are some common physical health problems which adversely affect children and youth and they include anaemia caused by malnutrition, obesity, HIV/AIDS, dependence on substances, and suicide. Every year, about 28 students commit suicide because of academic failure (Crime in India Report, 2020).

(i) Undernutrition among the youths

Anaemia is an issue of concern for the health policymakers as it causes several other health challenges and a large number of children die every year because of anaemia. For example, the latest Global Malnutrition Report 2020 says, "India will miss targets for all four nutritional indicators and these indicators include – Stunting among under-5 children, Anaemia among women of reproductive age, Childhood overweight and Exclusive breastfeeding. According to the data available on stunting and wasting among children in the country, 37.9% of children under five years are stunted and 20.8% are wasted, compared to the Asia average of 22.7% and 9.4% respectively. Additionally, stunting prevalence is 10.1% higher in rural areas compared to urban areas" (Source: https://thecsrjournal.in/india-global-malnutrition-report-2020). Further the report highlights that "the rate of overweight and obesity continues to rise, affecting almost a fifth of the adults, at 21.6% of women and 17.8% of men. There is nearly double as many obese adult females than there are males (5.1% compared to 2.7%). Obesity is a challenge for urban children and youth because of more consumption of fast food while anaemia affects mostly rural youth especially girl children and women mostly because of poverty. Anaemia is also highly prevalent in the country with one in two women of reproductive age being anaemic" (Source:https://thecsrjournal.in/india-global-malnutrition-report-2020). Another report of the State of Food Security and Nutrition in the World (2020) highlights that "14 percent of India's population is undernourished". The report also indicates that 189.2 million people are undernourished in India and 34.7% of the children aged under five in India are stunted (Source: https://www.dailyrounds.org; National Nutrition Month 2020: An Analysis of India's).

Evidence concerning the negative impact of malnutrition is plenty. For example, Martorell (1999) reported that "survivors of malnutrition in early childhood suffer functional disadvantages as adults, including diminished intellectual performance, low work capacity, and increased risk of delivery complications". The author also suggested that "prevention of low birthweight and the promotion of adequate growth and development during early childhood will result in healthier, more productive adults". One Indian study reported that "chronic protein energy malnutrition (stunting) affects the ongoing development of higher cognitive processes during childhood years rather than merely showing a generalized cognitive impairment. Stunting could result in slowing of age-related improvement in certain and not all higher order cognitive processes and may also result in long lasting cognitive impairments" (Kar, Rao, & Chandramouli, 2008). Malnutrition has been found to be significantly associated with more severe pressure ulcers (Iizaka et al., 2010) and an important and strong independent predictor of decreased HRQoL in this dialysis population (Viramontes, Willingham,

Pittman, Selby, & Taal, 2020). In another recent study, it has been observed, "whilst malnutrition results in increased incidence, severity and case fatality of common infections, risks continue beyond acute episodes resulting in significant post-discharge mortality" (Walson & Berkley, 2018). There is some good news for the policymakers. Their efforts to reduce the number of underweight children in India yielded positive results during 2000–2016. The rate of underweight boys has come down to 58.1% from 66.0%, while in the case of girls; it has reduced to 50.1% from 54.2%.

In order to improve the nutrition status of children under six years and adolescents, the Government of India introduced mid-day meals and also Anganwadi Centres, as part of the Integrated Child Development Scheme (ICDS), which provides supplementary nutrition to preschool children. Undoubtedly, both the schemes benefitted a large number of children to overcome undernutrition, but still close monitoring of implementation of the schemes is essential to ensure effective implementation of the schemes across the country through community mobilization.

Müller and Krawinkel (2005) suggested "intervention programs to prevent protein–energy malnutrition through promotion of breast-feeding to food supplementation schemes, whereas micronutrient deficiencies would best be addressed through food-based strategies such as dietary diversification through home gardens and small livestock".

(ii) Substance dependence among the youths

Dependence on alcohol and narcotic drugs among the Indian youths has become another challenge for the public health policymakers. "Alcohol and opioids were the most common drugs of dependence for youth but nicotine and alcohol were found to be the most common initiating drugs in both alcohol and opioid groups", as observed by Saddichha, Sinha, and Khess (2007). One study disclosed that "young drug users with comorbid affective disorders have greater mental health and substance use morbidity than those with substance use problems alone" (Lubman, Allen, Rogers, Cementon, & Bonomo, 2007). Youth with substance dependence are vulnerable to psychosis (Buchy, Perkins, Woods, Liu, & Addington, 2014). It is also found that internalizing disorders and substance use disorders are frequently comorbid among the youths (O'Neil, Conner, & Kendall, 2011). Dependence of educated emerging adults on cannabis and tobacco are highly prevalent in some states of India (Mohanty et al., 2013), while some youth prefer cigarettes, cigars, pipe tobacco, snuff, and chewing tobacco (Chadda & Sengupta, 2002; Preeti & Raut, 2012). A Chennai-based study observed that 41% of the students take tobacco (Madan, Poorni, & Ramachandran, 2006), while another study in Tiruchirapalli slums in Tamil Nadu found alcohol consumption by 70% of the youth (Raj, sAsir, & Tamilenthi, 2013). A study in Bhopal, disclosed high consumption of pans and gutkha among youths (65.3%) (Bathma, Likhar, Agarwal, Mishra, & Shukla, 2015). Similarly, a multi-centric study revealed high prevalence of alcohol consumption among youth, i.e., 60.5% in Arunachal Pradesh, while 22% in Kerala (Tumge, 2009).

Further, research by Mohanan, Swain, Sanah, Sharma, and Ghosh (2014) found that late teens as the initiating age of alcohol consumption. Around 6.14% of youth in rural areas and 0.6% of youth in urban areas are found to be using illicit drugs in West Bengal (Tsering, Pal, & Dasgupta, 2010). Use of illicit drugs is highly prevalent in Punjab as reported by Ambekar et al. (2016). One latest study in Kerala highlights dependence of school going children on Tobacco (more than three times a day by 21.7%), alcohol (more than thrice a week by 13.2%), drugs (psychoactive substances, more than twice in a month by 1.8%), and pan masala (daily) by 10.8% (Thomas, 2017).

Although the incidence of dependence on narcotic drugs among youth has gone down across the country because of intensive community and institute-based intervention programmes, a good number of youths in the north eastern states of India, especially in Manipur, are still victims of the same health problem.

(iii) HIV/AIDS among the youths

HIV/AIDS affected a large number of youths in the country, especially the ones with low level of educational background and the main mode of transmission of the infection is heterosexual contact. However, in Manipur most of the youth got HIV because of intravenous drugs sharing using the same needle. The National AIDS Control Organization (NACO) report, dated June 24, 2016, states that young people are at high risk of contracting HIV (Source: http://naco.gov.in › youth, June 24, 2016). The report also states that youth in the age group of 15–29 years accounts for 31% of AIDS burden in India. In India, people in the age group of 15–29 years comprise almost 25% of the country's population. However, they account for 31% of the AIDS burden. This clearly indicates that young people are at high risk of contracting HIV infection (Source: http://naco.gov.in › youth, June 24, 2016).

Maharashtra is at the top of the list in terms of highest number of new HIV infections in 2019 (8.54 thousand), while Bihar (8.04 thousand) is in the second position, followed by Uttar Pradesh (6.72 thousand), West Bengal (3.97 thousand), Gujarat (3.37 thousand), and Delhi (2.99 thousand), as per the latest report of NACO.

(iv) Age of marriage of the youths

Marriage of youths is a serious issue of concern for all Indian parents. Most of the parents want their male child to get married after getting a job, so that they look after themselves, instead of becoming dependent on the parents. In the case of female children, there is no such bar. Parents are more particular about the marriage of a female child at an early age. Otherwise, it might be difficult to get a match from within the community, as perceived by the majority. Female child marriage before 18 years in the rural areas, is common practice. However, the trend of marriage varies from community to community. Data provided in Table 2.4 indicate that the majority of the youth marry at the age of 25–29 years. About 40 years back, the percentage of early marriage during 15–19 years of age was more than double among female children (i.e., 43.44%) as compared to 19.47% in 2011 (Table 2.4).

Table 2.4 Percentage of Married Females as Revealed by Different Census

Year	*15–19 Years*	*20–24 Years*	*25–29 Years*
1981	43.44	84.46	94.35
1991	35.28	81.81	93.97
2001	24.45	75.73	92.15
2011	19.47	68.50	89.09

Source: Census of India

Table 2.5 Mortality Rate among the Youths

Age Groups	*Urban*	*Rural*
15–19	0.8	1.1
20–24	1.1	1.4
25–29	1.0	1.7

Source: Sample Registration System, Office of the Registrar General of India, 2011.

(v) Age-specific mortality rate among the youths

Age-specific mortality rate gives a clear idea about deaths of youth per year, per 1000 youth. Date provided in Table 2.5 indicates the rural and urban break-up of youth mortality rate, which clearly highlights the disparity in rural and urban setups. It is more in rural setups than in urban setups primarily because of poor health facilities, lack of basic awareness about signs and symptoms of different preventable health problems and remedial measures, and negligence. The issue requires the attention of health policymakers.

Employment of the youths

While most of the youths look for a job after completion of their education, some get engaged in family businesses, while some start their own business. Youths who look for a job in a country like India, face tough competition because of the number of job seekers. There are different competitive examinations at various levels under different ministries and for each post, thousands of youths compete. Very few attends competitive examinations with proper preparation. Most of them apply as their peer group members are applying and they often take it casually. As a result, the youth who work hard, succeed in their mission after a few attempts. Nevertheless, there are examples of success in getting a job through open competition in one attempt. In order to guide and support youths for competitive jobs in government sectors of Indian Administrative Service, Indian Police Service, Indian Revenue Service, different positions in the Indian Railways, Probation Officer Posts for banks, to name a few, a number of professional organizations have come forward to train interested youths. Training from these organizations has helped a large number of the youths of both the genders in getting good jobs through competition.

Other than government jobs, many youths in India are employed in various private organizations, which is relatively easier to procure. However, most of the youth in the Indian society look for a government job since it is safe and secure. Job market is a dynamic system where people keep getting in and out of the system. Jobs in private organizations are not always secure, which causes a lot of anxiety and mental pressure for the youths to ensure continuous good performance. So far as the salary is concerned, private sectors pay much higher salaries to the deserving youths and there is a possibility of faster career growth for youths in the private sectors. However, the hire-and-fire concept is followed in most of the professional organizations.

Employment market is directly associated with the economy of a country. As a result, the rate of employment and unemployment varies from country to country.

Youth participation in labour force

As per NSS 68th round survey during 2011–2012, participation of youths in the labour force was 59.9% for males and 15.9% for females in the urban areas. Interestingly, in the same year, participation of rural youths in the labour force was more, i.e., 63.1% and 18.3% for male and female genders respectively. The data clearly highlight poor participation of females in the labour force, both in rural and urban areas. However, engagement of youth in the workforce, irrespective of gender, is showing a declining trend (Table 2.6).

(i) Unemployment in India

Unemployment rate of youth in India in the last 10 years has gone up from 20.30% in 2010 to 23.75% in 2020. The following table gives a clear idea about the trend of youth unemployment in India (Table 2.7).

Available data pertaining to the unemployment rate among youths in India aged 15–29 years do not indicate a clear trend. It is showing a declining trend for urban females, i.e., 19.9% in 2004–2005 to 15.8% in 2011–2012,

Table 2.6 Youth Employment

Year	*Rural (%)*		*Urban (%)*	
	Male	*Female*	*Male*	*Female*
July 2004–June 2005	75.1	30.9	67.3	17.8
July 2009–June 2010	66.2	23.3	60.4	15.0
July 2011–June 2012	63.1	18.3	59.9	15.9

Source: National Sample Survey Organization

Table 2.7 Year-wise Unemployment Rate in India

Year	*Unemployment Rate (%)*
2010	*20.30*
2011	20.84
2012	21.39
2013	21.85
2014	22.07
2015	22.34
2016	22.58
2017	22.72
2018	22.85
2019	23.34
2020	23.78

Source: https://www.statista.com/statistics/812106/youth-unemployment-rate-in-india

Table 2.8 Unemployment Rate among the Youths in India

Year	*Rural (%)*		*Urban (%)*	
	Male	*Female*	*Male*	*Female*
July 2004–June 2005	5.2	7.6	10.0	19.9
July 2009–June 2010	5.5	6.6	7.9	17.5
July 2011–June 2012	6.1	7.7	8.9	15.8

Source: National Sample Survey Organization

while for urban males it increased from 7.5% in 2009–2010 to 8.9% during 2011–2012. On the other hand, in the rural setups, unemployment has increased from 5.2% (2004–2005) to 6.1% (2011–2012) (Table 2.8).

(ii) COVID-19 and its impact on job market

COVID-19 pandemic contributed adversely to the job market, especially in the private sectors. Notification for jobs in various government departments in 2020 has also gone down significantly. A large number of youths working in private sectors like airline companies, entertainment industries, hotels, and restaurants have lost their jobs.

It is estimated that about 6.1 million youths in the 15–24 age group lost their jobs in 2020 because of COVID-19 lockdown, as indicated in a joint report of the Asian Development Bank (ADB) and International Labour Organization (ILO) (Source: https://www.livemint.com/news/india/6-1-million-indian-youth-may-lose-jobs-in-2020-due-to-covid-19-report-11597763970825.html).

Loss of jobs for youths will cause stress for them and compel them to get engaged in criminal activities for meeting their need, followed by suicidal tendencies. Therefore, efforts should be made by, both the government and entrepreneurs to create jobs for youths during this crisis phase.

Like other countries, youth employment is a priority agenda for the Government of India and accordingly, policy initiative is being taken and more emphasis is given on skill *development of Indian youths, to make India Atmanirbhar*. A detailed discussion about various employment schemes in India is presented in Chapter X of the book.

At the global level, GOAL 8 of the Sustainable Development Goals emphasized on Decent Work and Economic Growth and it is targeted to achieve the same goal by 2030. It is expected that every nation is paying special attention to youth employment through various policies and programmes and partnerships between various government and private organizations.

Civic engagement of the youths

Developing a sense of responsibility among the youth through civic participation has gathered importance among policymakers across the world. It is not only in the cases of youth and child welfare policies, it is also in the cases of social and community development policies and programmes, where youth participation makes a big difference. In addition to youth participation in policy formulation and programme planning and implementation, other areas where civic engagement of youths are necessary include voting, volunteering, participating in group activities, distributing masks during COVID-19 pandemic, creating awareness among the backward communities about safety measures for COVID-19, pond restoration, organizing games and sports in rural areas, taking initiative for cleanliness drives, mobilizing youths for Fit India movement, community gardening, and so on.

Youth participation in civic activities gives them a sense of recognition and in the process, they get the opportunity to showcase their leadership qualities and share their ideas and views about welfare and well-being of the common people of the society. In the last two and half decades, youth civic participation and active engagement in research, draft policy formulation, planning for implementation of various welfare and development programmes, along with other stakeholders at the international level, is visible, especially when international organizations, like various umbrella organizations of the United Nations like ILO, the World Health Organization, UNDP, UNICEF to name a few are brought into consideration.

At the national level, there is a growing trend to listen to children and youth's voices related to various policies and programmes for children and youths. For example, Indian youths were invited to give their feedback in the draft of the National Youth Policy 2021, to ensure that their genuine issues and concerns are addressed in the same policy. Awareness about the rights of children and students has got special attention from the academic administrators and larger society because of youth participation in various bodies of academic institutions. For example, as per the Supreme Court's direction, every academic institute should have a student body that is duly constituted through proper election and there should be a student representative in the sexual harassment committee of an academic institute and/or student redressal committee, which yielded positive developments in the academic institutions, in terms of protection of children and students rights.

Youth civic engagement keeps them engaged in productive activities that are beneficial for the larger society and in the process, they become more experienced and are able to significantly contribute in various community development activities. At the same time, close connection with the local community strengthens their social network and in turn, they feel psychologically happy and self-contained. Further, youth civic engagement keeps them away from risk behaviour, violence, and criminal activities, thus creating a safe environment in the locality. Youths are also able to eradicate myths and misconceptions related to various social and health issues. Engagement of the youth in civic activities at an early age facilitates the development of a future leader who will lead a nation in the right direction. For a dynamic leader, connection with the grassroots is essential to get the pulse of the society.

In the past, elderly people, mainly parents and teachers, did not value the voices of children and youth, and therefore children and youth participation in civic engagement was negligible. Guardians were used to decide everything for the welfare of their children and the youth and community development were based on the understanding of the guardians. There is a paradigm shift now and the earlier views concerning welfare and well-being of children and youth have now changed and the voices of youth and children are now heard by the elderly people. Although this is not a common practice across the society, the situation is changing slowly.

During the COVID-19 pandemic, a large number of Indian youths are engaged in mask distribution, creating awareness about safety measures in the rural areas, helping poor and helpless parents in getting essential items, and assisting people for emergency medical services along with local administration, in different parts of India.

For the social and economic development of a country, every individual's contribution is necessary. India being a country with more than 34% youth population, is in a comfortable position to take the country forward with the active participation of the youth in the development processes and social transformations.

Migration of the youths

Migration from one place to another, whether within the country or from one country to another, has been a normal global phenomenon since time immemorial. Migration is a natural outcome when society faces a shortage of resources or opportunities (Rajan & Sivakumar, 2018). People migrate from one place to another, with the hope of getting better facilities and leading a comfortable life. However, many people migrate to another country out of compulsion, i.e., to escape violence, poverty, and social discrimination. Within the country, rural to urban migration happens mostly for survival. In India, a large number of rural people migrate to urban areas, with their families, in search of livelihood and a good number of them take shelter on the road side or in the slum areas and lead a poor quality of life. Children of such migrant families remain mostly without schooling and grow in a hostile environment with peer group members mostly engaged in socially undesirable activities and they slowly adopt the same.

Majority of youth migrations from rural to urban areas is for the need of higher education and/or for employment. Every year, a large number of rural youths come to urban areas for higher studies and quality education and/or for studying a subject of their choice. The choice of subject and/or institution may not be available in the rural setups. A large number of youths from Northeast India, with low levels of education, migrate to South or North India since there is no work for them in their home state. They mostly work in unorganized sectors like restaurants and/or hotels with low wage.

The reasons for youth migration in India vary from person to person and region to region. Personal considerations, job market, socio-economic circumstances, and the political situation in the state of origin are some of the significant contributing factors towards youth migration in India. Lack of job opportunities, perceived inequalities in the labour market, and gross violation of human rights are often found to be the main causal factors for youth migration.

Moving to foreign countries for higher education, better career growth, and leading a comfortable life are the common aspirations for a large number of Indian youths. Every year, a large number of Indian youths move to foreign countries for higher studies and the trend is increasing steadily. Most of the Indian youths are highly successful in the accomplishment of their academic career and in getting attractive jobs abroad. Contribution of Indian youths in foreign countries in the fields of medical science, engineering, information technology and so on is remarkable, which has been highly acknowledged by the global leaders. A good number of youths are also highly successful as entrepreneurs and acting as job providers.

Participation of the youths in sports

Youth participation in different sports and cultural activities within and outside India is highly appreciable. A good number of youths performed extremely well in different sports events viz., Hockey, Badminton, Cricket, Lawn Tennis, Table Tennis, Swimming, Racing, High Jumping, Football, Cycling, Kabaddi, Boxing, Wrestling, Gymnastics, Shooting and many more, at various international events, and earned good appreciation and fame for the country. At present, some of the sports like cricket, lawn tennis, and football are highly rewarding.

Sports should be promoted at every educational institution as it helps in improving physical fitness and mental health. It also enhances concentration during studies. The Sports Authority of India, under the Ministry of Youth Affairs and Sports, Government of India, has created good infrastructure facilities and encouraged the youth of the country to take advantage of the same facilities for better performances.

Youth diversity in terms of intelligence, aptitude, interest, creativity, and motivations

When one is studying the background and status of the youths, one should also look at them from psychological and/or mental health perspectives also. Every youth is creative as well as unique in terms of physical and psychological characteristics. In terms of their psyche, especially personality characteristics, we find some youths are submissive while some are dominant. Diversity is even found between two siblings. One child is very studious and intelligent while another one is not at all interested in studies, although both of them were born and brought up in the same family with equal care, guidance, and opportunities (Deb et al., 2020). According to psychologists, individual differences indicate distinctiveness and variations in the individual's characteristics and behaviour patterns. Nevertheless, intelligence, aptitude, interest, creativity, and motivation of youths vary and they act as per their personal psychological traits. There is a need to identify similar traits of every youth through proper assessment and channelize them in the right direction for their career growth and development. Administrators of educational institutions, for example, school authorities should pay special attention to this issue and engage qualified psychologists in every institution for the same purpose.

Status of youths in different states and union territories in India as per India Youth Development Index and Report, 2017

In order to have some idea about the status of Indian youths, it is worth referring here to the India Youth Development Index and Report, 2017 (YDI 2017) with reference to six domains, i.e., education, health, work, political participation, civic participation, and social inclusion. In particular, YDI is a combined index of 19 indicators which examine the holistic growth and development of youths in 20 major states and 10 minor states of India. YDI values range between 0 and 1. A score of 1 indicates highest youth development while 0 indicates no youth development. For capturing the status of gender, the Youth Gender Development Index has been calculated separately for each state. YDI 2017 was prepared by the Rajiv Gandhi National Institute of Youth Development (RGNIYD) under the Ministry of Youth Affairs and Sports, Government of India. RGNIYD also published the YDI 2010. YDI gives comprehensive information about the region-wise status of Indian youths.

YDI also helps researchers, policymakers, and various agencies engaged in youth welfare activities in assessing the present status and needs of the youth to take up need-based policies and intervention programmes for their holistic development. The broad framework of YDI is based on Global YDI created by the United Nations, except the inclusion of an additional domain of India YDI, i.e., social inclusion. The social inclusion domain is included in India's YDI to examine the inclusiveness of societal progress since structural inequalities have existed in India for a long time.

Overall and domain-wise India youth development index across states

YDI facilitates monitoring the progress of the youth development process in different states and taking need-based measures in terms of proper policy and programmes for interventions. In India, the nation-wide YDI value is 0.569 with wide variation across the states. While the YDI value of Himachal Pradesh is 0.689, it was 0.466 for Bihar, among the major states. On the other hand, in the case of minor states, the YDI value for Pondicherry and Goa were more than the value of Himachal Pradesh (Table 2.9).

Based on the scores, the Global YDI report of the United Nations grouped different countries into four broad categories viz., Low, Medium, High, and Very High. Following the same classification at the global level, India belongs to the Medium category with a score of 0.548 and ranked 133 out of 179 countries.

However, at the national level, the India YDI 2017 classifies different States and Union Territories on the basis of seven parameters. These include Low (0–0.494), Medium (>0.494–0.607), High (>0.607–0.671), and Very High (>0.671–1). Two Union Territories and one State (i.e., Himachal Pradesh, Goa, and Puducherry) fall in the Very High category while Bihar stood last in the Low category. Further, YDI data indicates that 10 States/ Union Territories belong to the high category and they include Gujarat, Kerala, Maharashtra, Punjab, Tamil Nadu, Uttarakhand, Delhi, Meghalaya, Mizoram, and Sikkim (Figure 2.17).

Youth gender development index

Gender disparity in every aspect of life is a big challenge as India is still considered to be a patriarchal society. It is the mindset of common people that male children must be provided better care and facilities as they will carry forward the family tradition. Preference for a male child is unconsciously imbibed by a large number of parents and even grandparents, who blame their sons-in-law for delivering a female child. Nutrition, education, medical care, civic participation, and participation in the political process are some of the prominent areas where gender discrimination exists to a great extent. It is more in the rural areas than the urban areas. However, research highlights that there is a change in urban areas in terms of better care for girl children as disclosed by a Kolkata-based study (Deb &

Table 2.9 Domain-wise and Overall Youth Development Index across Indian States – 2017

Major States	*Education*	*Health*	*Work*	*Political Participation*	*Civic Participation*	*Social Inclusion*	*Youth Development Index*	*Rank*
Andhra Pradesh	0.560	0.596	0.582	0.427	0.219	0.759	**0.572**	13
Assam	0.527	0.533	0.372	0.397	0.182	0.938	**0.515**	19
Bihar	0.353	0.609	0.458	0.249	0.112	0.687	**0.466**	20
Chhattisgarh	0.575	0.548	0.611	0.572	0.190	0.851	**0.590**	11
Gujarat	0.545	0.671	0.669	0.431	0.142	0.803	**0.610**	7
Haryana	0.566	0.655	0.517	0.529	0.296	0.826	**0.592**	10
Himachal Pradesh	0.716	0.778	0.619	0.275	0.495	0.881	**0.689**	1
Jammu & Kashmir	0.565	0.683	0.503	0.515	0.330	0.796	**0.592**	9
Jharkhand	0.396	0.596	0.501	0.565	0.186	0.784	**0.520**	18
Karnataka	0.572	0.676	0.629	0.354	0.228	0.755	**0.602**	8
Kerala	0.735	0.759	0.403	0.226	0.358	0.879	**0.624**	3
Madhya Pradesh	0.470	0.638	0.593	0.407	0.219	0.720	**0.557**	14
Maharashtra	0.625	0.668	0.630	0.381	0.171	0.766	**0.614**	6
Odisha	0.519	0.619	0.578	0.300	0.159	0.734	**0.552**	15
Punjab	0.600	0.719	0.595	0.364	0.394	0.759	**0.623**	5
Rajasthan	0.439	0.667	0.622	0.585	0.157	0.763	**0.576**	12
Tamil Nadu	0.651	0.697	0.571	0.369	0.287	0.868	**0.632**	2
Uttar Pradesh	0.465	0.597	0.562	0.501	0.110	0.799	**0.547**	16
Uttarakhand	0.621	0.736	0.512	0.393	0.368	0.852	**0.624**	4
West Bengal	0.521	0.503	0.532	0.381	0.108	0.807	**0.524**	17

(Continue)

Table 2.9 (Continued)

Major States	*Education*	*Health*	*Work*	*Political Participation*	*Civic Participation*	*Social Inclusion*	*Youth Development Index*	*Rank*
Minor States								
Arunachal Pradesh	0.525	0.487	0.486	0.535	0.395	0.906	**0.548**	9
Delhi	0.606	0.723	0.536	0.480	0.212	0.900	**0.625**	6
Goa	0.661	0.809	0.635	0.253	0.744	0.884	**0.701**	2
Manipur	0.657	0.589	0.471	0.345	0.481	0.863	**0.591**	7
Meghalaya	0.590	0.591	0.785	0.415	0.349	0.884	**0.652**	4
Mizoram	0.752	0.622	0.514	0.318	0.778	0.959	**0.663**	3
Nagaland	0.667	0.669	0.211	0.303	0.355	0.953	**0.550**	8
Pondicherry	0.724	0.700	0.751	0.272	0.978	0.806	**0.724**	1
Sikkim	0.648	0.571	0.604	0.329	0.795	0.842	**0.633**	5
Tripura	0.596	0.579	0.274	0.341	0.337	0.900	**0.520**	10
Total	0.513	0.632	0.572	0.436	0.191	0.785	**0.569**	

Source: India Youth Development Index and Report, 2017.

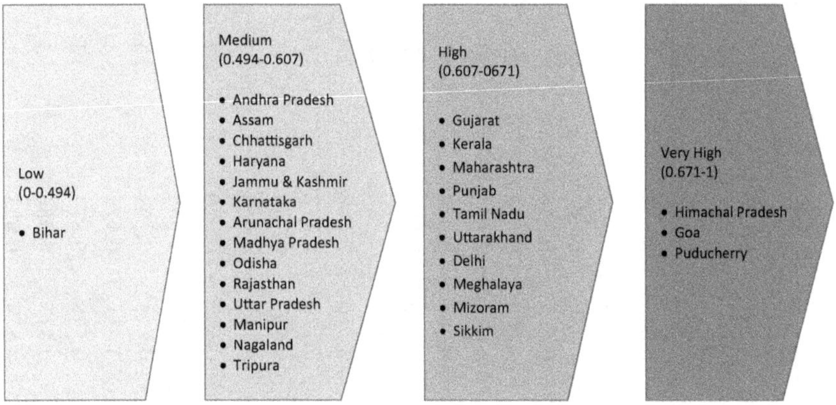

Figure 2.17 Classification of states according to YDI values.

Source: India Youth Development Index and Report, 2017.

Chatterjee, 2008). In the urban belt of Kolkata, a good number of parents feel that a female child will provide better support during old age than a male child. Various initiatives taken by the government to eradicate gender disparity and gender discrimination in India paid good results. However, more concerted efforts need to be made to bring permanent changes in the mind of common people about gender issues. Gender disparity varies from state to state as implementation of policies and programmes of the central government depends upon the state machinery and in particular, the respective minister and his/her officials. A sensitive minister can bring a miraculous change in the community if he or she wishes to do so. Let us examine the status of youths in terms of gender inequality, with respect to three parameters viz., education, health, and work. Information pertaining to the status of gender with respect to political participation, civic participation, and social inclusion are not available.

Interestingly, Punjab is at the top of the list among the major states of India in terms of better care for female children, followed by Himachal, as indicated by the overall score of the Youth Gender Development Index (see Table 2.10). However, if we look at the score of education and work of male youth in both Punjab and Himachal Pradesh, they are in an advantageous position as compared to female youths. In terms of health care, female youths receive better scores in both the states as compared to their counterparts.

On the other hand, Bihar, Jharkhand, and Rajasthan score the least, highlighting high gender disparity. Pondicherry, Arunachal Pradesh, and Meghalaya score the highest in the Youth Gender Development Index from amongst the minor states and union territories. Surprisingly, Nagaland, Tripura, and Goa show poor performance. Nevertheless, the Youth Gender Development Index provides a very interesting picture that female youths receive better health care in most of the states and union territories in India.

Table 2.10 Gender Development Index across Indian States

	Youth Development Indicators for FEMALES				*Youth Development Indicators for MALES*					
Major States	*Education*	*Health*	*Work*	*YDI-F*	*Education*	*Health*	*Work*	*YDI-M*	*Youth Gender Development Index*	*Rank*
Andhra Pradesh	0.599	0.741	0.528	0.617	0.699	0.635	0.601	0.643	**0.959**	5
Assam	0.482	0.630	0.343	0.470	0.589	0.513	0.420	0.503	**0.936**	7
Bihar	0.184	0.622	0.265	0.312	0.476	0.582	0.524	0.526	**0.593**	20
Chhattisgarh	0.549	0.543	0.603	0.564	0.732	0.477	0.611	0.597	**0.944**	6
Gujarat	0.549	0.652	0.530	0.574	0.737	0.633	0.732	0.699	**0.822**	16
Haryana	0.601	0.613	0.481	0.562	0.732	0.633	0.576	0.644	**0.872**	13
Himachal Pradesh	0.774	0.796	0.556	0.700	0.785	0.629	0.646	0.683	**1.024**	2
Jammu & Kashmir	0.476	0.639	0.385	0.489	0.681	0.599	0.557	0.610	**0.802**	17
Jharkhand	0.301	0.604	0.379	0.410	0.556	0.570	0.585	0.570	**0.720**	19
Karnataka	0.602	0.691	0.524	0.602	0.716	0.720	0.694	0.710	**0.848**	15
Kerala	0.848	0.854	0.332	0.622	0.862	0.692	0.609	0.714	**0.872**	14
Madhya Pradesh	0.406	0.686	0.599	0.551	0.616	0.584	0.627	0.609	**0.904**	10
Maharashtra	0.689	0.668	0.580	0.644	0.767	0.661	0.668	0.697	**0.924**	8
Odisha	0.480	0.747	0.490	0.560	0.688	0.512	0.642	0.609	**0.920**	9
Punjab	0.686	0.729	0.603	0.670	0.743	0.575	0.637	0.648	**1.034**	1
Rajasthan	0.308	0.664	0.601	0.498	0.656	0.663	0.643	0.654	**0.761**	18
Tamil Nadu	0.736	0.711	0.489	0.635	0.811	0.561	0.617	0.655	**0.970**	4
Uttar Pradesh	0.375	0.578	0.593	0.504	0.599	0.532	0.607	0.578	**0.873**	12
Uttarakhand	0.651	0.717	0.484	0.609	0.739	0.609	0.524	0.617	**0.986**	3
West Bengal	0.530	0.618	0.395	0.506	0.644	0.502	0.597	0.578	**0.875**	11

Minor States										
Arunachal Pradesh	0.442	0.545	0.451	0.477	0.582	0.276	0.495	0.430	**1.109**	2
Delhi	0.709	0.763	0.533	0.661	0.766	0.549	0.580	0.625	**1.057**	5
Goa	0.773	0.812	0.530	0.693	0.801	0.712	0.736	0.749	**0.925**	8
Manipur	0.621	0.663	0.414	0.554	0.704	0.461	0.517	0.552	**1.005**	7
Meghalaya	0.577	0.678	0.787	0.675	0.581	0.483	0.807	0.610	**1.108**	3
Mizoram	0.669	0.729	0.449	0.602	0.711	0.455	0.558	0.565	**1.066**	4
Nagaland	0.682	0.714	0.118	0.386	0.737	0.549	0.245	0.463	**0.835**	10
Pondicherry	0.831	0.721	0.833	0.793	0.840	0.536	0.685	0.676	**1.174**	1
Sikkim	0.641	0.627	0.522	0.594	0.689	0.415	0.632	0.565	**1.051**	6
Tripura	0.602	0.642	0.233	0.448	0.662	0.551	0.374	0.515	**0.870**	9
Total	0.502	0.660	0.462	0.535	0.670	0.588	0.618	0.625	**0.856**	

Source: India Youth Development Index and Report, 2017

Efforts should be taken while bringing out the next YDI, in order to generate data with regard to political participation, civic participation, and social inclusion of the youth of the country, to get a better picture of the status of youths in India.

Youth and education

Education is essential for every child to lead a quality life. It helps a child gain knowledge and skills that are required to become a responsible and productive citizen. Education also brings rationality in the minds of people. It is a fundamental right of every child, as indicated in the Indian Constitution. With proper education, one can become a potential citizen for social development and social transformation. The Right of Children to Free and Compulsory Education Act, 2009 emphasizes on free and compulsory education for all children up to 14 years of age. The same Act also has a provision of 25% seat reservation for marginalized children. In order to promote school education and create a safe school environment the Act "prohibits all kinds of physical punishment and mental harassment, discrimination based on gender, caste, class and religion, screening procedures for admission of children capitation fee, private tuition centres, and functioning of unrecognised schools".

The Millennium Development Goals of the United Nations also emphasized on education. Although literacy rate has increased significantly in India over a period of time, 100% literacy needs to be targeted, irrespective of gender and social class.

Let us look at the Youth Education Index (YEI) of the YDI for having a better idea about the education of youths across the country. It is measured by combining the scores of education expenditure (as a percent of GSDP with 20% weight), youth literacy rate (with 40% weight), youth education level (with 40% weight). At the national level, the score of YEI is 0.513. With respect to the education domain, Kerala, Himachal Pradesh, and Tamil Nadu are found to be the best performers among the major states of India. On the other hand, Bihar is found to be the least performer in youth education, followed by Jharkhand and Rajasthan (Table 2.11).

Similarly, Mizoram stood out as the best performer in youth education within the minor states category while Puducherry is in the second position. Sadly, youth education in Arunachal Pradesh and Meghalaya is found to be dissatisfactory (Source: National Youth Development Index, 2017).

Gender Development Index (GDI) concerning education highlights gender disparity across the states and union territories in India with some variations. It was assessed based on two parameters – Literacy rate and education level – with equal weightage, since data pertaining to other parameters were not available. The composite score for females in GDI is 0.502 against 0.670 for males.

Table 2.11 Youth Education Index – 2017

	Indicator Indices				
Major States	*YEDU_ EXP*	*YLIT_RATE*	*YEDU_ LEVEL*	*Education Index*	*Rank*
Andhra Pradesh	0.401	0.669	0.550	0.560	11
Assam	0.497	0.616	0.454	0.527	13
Bihar	0.408	0.399	0.279	0.353	20
Chhattisgarh	0.308	0.707	0.576	0.575	7
Gujarat	0.123	0.759	0.542	0.545	12
Haryana	0.142	0.774	0.571	0.566	9
Himachal Pradesh	0.463	0.912	0.647	0.716	2
Jammu & Kashmir	0.486	0.621	0.547	0.565	10
Jharkhand	0.256	0.540	0.322	0.396	19
Karnataka	0.217	0.776	0.545	0.572	8
Kerala	0.259	0.978	0.731	0.735	1
Madhya Pradesh	0.284	0.624	0.411	0.470	16
Maharashtra	0.199	0.855	0.606	0.625	4
Odisha	0.268	0.694	0.469	0.519	15
Punjab	0.136	0.771	0.661	0.600	6
Rajasthan	0.231	0.583	0.398	0.439	18
Tamil Nadu	0.165	0.887	0.658	0.651	3
Uttar Pradesh	0.358	0.583	0.402	0.465	17
Uttarakhand	0.326	0.810	0.580	0.621	5
West Bengal	0.258	0.715	0.460	0.521	14
Minor States					
Arunachal Pradesh	0.574	0.575	0.450	0.525	10
Delhi	0.069	0.846	0.634	0.606	7
Goa	0.156	0.912	0.664	0.661	4
Manipur	0.631	0.746	0.580	0.657	5
Meghalaya	0.635	0.670	0.489	0.590	9
Mizoram	1.000	0.869	0.512	0.752	1
Nagaland	0.498	0.760	0.660	0.667	3
Pondicherry	0.281	0.932	0.739	0.724	2
Sikkim	0.577	0.866	0.466	0.648	6
Tripura	0.451	0.876	0.388	0.596	8
Total	0.210	0.687	0.492	0.513	

P – Education expenditure as % of GSDP; YLIT_RATE – Youth Literacy Rate; YEDU_LEVEL – Education Level

Source: India Youth Development Index and Report, 2017

Health status of the youths

Understanding the health status of youths is essential since they are the future of the country and potential parents. Therefore, the National Youth Policy 2014 emphasized on healthcare services with special reference to preventing diseases, promoting medical pluralism, and building a knowledge base for better health services, in addition to creating awareness among youths about adverse impacts of substance dependence and HIV/AIDS.

All India Youth Health Index (YHI, 2017) score is 0.632. State- and union territory-wise comparison of YHI indicates that Himachal Pradesh and Kerala are the best performers followed by Uttarakhand. In this regard, the performance of states like West Bengal, Assam, and Chhattisgarh is the worst among the major state categories. Similarly, Goa, Delhi, and Pondicherry – three union territories, are the best performers among minor states, with regard to health parameters, while Arunachal Pradesh, Sikkim, and Tripura could not do well in providing healthcare services to the youth. In all the states and union territories, the female health status is better than that of the males, except Haryana and Karnataka, as indicated by the India Youth Development Index and Report, 2017.

Engagement of the youths in economic activities

Engagement in economic activities after the completion of education is the desire for every youth of a nation. Parents also wish to see that their child is employed. In turn, it contributes to national economic growth by making optimal utilization of human resources. However, scarcity of suitable employment opportunities is an issue for a country like India, which causes unemployment. Let us examine the Youth Work Index (YWI). All India YWI score is 0.572. State- and union territory-wise comparison highlights that Gujarat, Maharashtra, and Karnataka did well in this regard among the major state categories while the situation is worse in Assam, Kerala, and Bihar. Lack of industries in the abovementioned three states is responsible for the same situation and most of the youths from these three states move out for employment. On the other hand, the status of work for youth is better in Meghalaya, Pondicherry, and Goa among the minor categories while Nagaland, Tripura, and Manipur belong to the other end of the scale. Among the three poor performing states, in addition to lack of government job opportunities, the tourism industry fails to attract tourists from other states.

For improving the economy of the country, female participation in the workforce is helpful. The composite score of Youth Gender Work Index at the national level is 0.747, indicating a positive picture. In some of the states, women participation in the workforce is appreciable and those include Chhattisgarh, Uttar Pradesh, and Punjab.

Youths participation in political process in terms of casting votes and contesting elections

Youths' participation in the political processes, in terms of voting and candidature for election is an opportunity for them to raise their voice for their cause. Although youth participation in voting has increased substantially as indicated in the last assembly election in five states of India, i.e., West Bengal, Assam, Tamil Nadu, Puducherry, and Kerala in April 2021, their participation while contesting elections is very minimal. It seems that the youth are the major deciding factors for forming the government because of their percentage of share in the voting process. As per the YDI 2017, "Youth Political Participation Index (YPPI) at the national level score 0.436 implying that there is more scope for the youth to be politically active". The information provided by YDI 2017 gives a clear picture of reasonably less participation of youths from the southern states in the political process, as compared to other states. Youth participation in the political process, i.e., casting votes, is higher in Rajasthan, Chhattisgarh, and Jharkhand, among the major categories of the states.

Youth participation in civic activities at the community level

Engagement of youths in civic activities is important towards community development and for creating a healthy and safe society. Youths can hasten changes in the society through community mobilization. Youth engagement in Nehru Yuva Kendra Sangathan (NYKS), National Service Scheme (NSS), and National Cadet Corps (NCC) does not help the community only, it also makes them more disciplined and they develop a sense of belongingness and thereby at times of crisis, youth act as active members of any rescue team. At the national level, the Youth Civic Participation Index (YCPI) score is 0.191. Himachal Pradesh, Punjab, and Uttarakhand are among the good performers in terms of youth civic participation, while some of the states with a large number of youth population are found to be poor performers and those states include West Bengal, Uttar Pradesh, and Bihar. Authorities of those states must take care of the issue for better engagement of the youth in civic participation to create human resources for facing any future challenge. Again, Puducherry is found to be a good performer in terms of youth civic engagement, followed by Sikkim and Mizoram. Surprisingly, youth in Delhi are not much engaged in civic activities along with Tripura and Meghalaya.

Social inclusion of the youths

For faster growth of a society, the inclusive approach should be adopted by the administration. Every youth has potential, irrespective of their socio-economic and community backgrounds. What is needed is to identify their strength and accordingly, they need to be channelized. The Constitution of India guarantees equality. Despite several measures to remove social barriers, they still exist and block the growth and career development of youths in some sections of the society. Therefore, there is a necessity to examine the ground reality with respect to social equality and inclusion of youths from marginalized communities in different development activities, for their career growth. Youth Social Inclusion Index (YSII) provides a clear picture about the issue. It is measured by combining the Social Inequality index (with 75% weightage) and the Share of youth with Disability (with 25% weightage).

According to YDI-2017, "YSII at the national level scores is 0.785 indicting the extent of social inclusivity of marginalized sections in various social indicators of development". In this regard, Assam, Himachal Pradesh, and Kerala performed better among the major states. Bihar is again the least performer, followed by Madhya Pradesh, and Odisha. Interestingly, the performance of all the minor states in regard to social inclusion is better than that of major states. However, the performance of Mizoram, Nagaland, and Arunachal Pradesh among the minor states is extraordinary. Pondicherry is found to be the worst performer in social inclusion.

YDI provides a very clear picture about the progress of youth development in different states and union territories of India. The states which have been performing well and have been taking appropriate measures for overall youth development include Himachal Pradesh, Tamil Nadu, Kerala, Uttarakhand, and Punjab, among the major states and Puducherry, Goa, Mizoram, Meghalaya, and Sikkim, among the minor states. The states which could not create proper ambiance for youth development with respect to all the domains, with little variations are Bihar, Assam, Jharkhand, West Bengal, Uttar Pradesh, Odisha, Madhya Pradesh, Andhra Pradesh, and so on. The authorities of the poor performing states and union territories need to pay attention towards the improvement of the situation so that optimal potentials of the youth across the country could be tapped for faster economic growth and social development of the country.

Conclusion and recommendations

The youth population in India is about 34% of the total population of the country as per Census 2011 report. It is projected to be 34.33% by 2020 and by 2031 there will be a sharp decline of the youth population in India. Most of the youths live in the rural areas and the percentage of literacy and higher education is much higher among urban youths. Gender-wise disparity is observed in terms of education among the youth. So far as the status of the youth is concerned, youth are vulnerable to some physical health problems like malnutrition, unprotected sexual behaviour, dependence on substances, HIV/AIDS, and so on. Youth participation in civic activities and in the political process is increasing gradually. In terms of social inclusion, latest policies of the Government of India are found to be facilitating. Any information about disadvantaged youths is scanty.

YDI 2017 provides a fair picture about the status of youths in different states and union territories. As per YDI 2017, Himachal Pradesh (0.689) is at the top of the list among the major states in terms of overall performance, followed by Tamil Nadu (0.632), Kerala (0.624), Uttarakhand (0.624), and Punjab (0.623), while among the minor states Puducherry tops the list with a total score of 0.724, followed by Goa (0.701), Mizoram (0.663), Meghalaya (0.663), and Sikkim (0.633). However, domain-wise performance varied across states and union territories. For example, as far as health, education, and civic participation are concerned among the major states, Himachal Pradesh performed best with 0.716, 0.778, and 0495 scores respectively. Rajasthan was the best performer in terms of political participation (0.585), while Assam did extremely well in case of social inclusion with a 0.938 score. The states which lag in youth development include Bihar (0.466) with the least development, followed by Assam (0.515), Jharkhand (0.520), West Bengal (0.524) and others.

Under the category of minor states, Mizoram performed the best with respect to education (0.725) and social inclusion (0.959), while Goa did well in the domain of health and work with 0.809 and 0.635 scores respectively. The performance of Arunachal Pradesh was best among the minor states in the domain of political participation. In terms of youth engagement in civic activities, Puducherry scored the highest (0.978).

For improving the status of youth across the country, there is a need to carry out research in every location to understand the issues and challenges faced by the youth in terms of education, health, civic engagement, engagement in political processes, and social inclusion.

Relevant government officials at all levels need to be sensitized about various schemes related to youth development so that they can act as catalysts to implement every programme effectively in association with allied organizations and NGOs working with children and the youth. Ensuring quality education, organizing effective skill development training programmes, ensuring accessibility to healthcare facilities, and inclusive approach require the attention of the states and union territories, especially the states which performed poorly in the same domains. Periodic monitoring of all youth welfare-related activities is necessary to ensure a smooth implementation of the programmes and taking corrective measures, if needed.

References

Ambekar, A., Rao, R., Agrawal, A., Mishra, A., Kumar, R., & Kumar, M. (2016). *Punjab opioid dependence survey: brief report*. New Delhi: SPYM and NDDTC, AIIMS.

Bathma, V., Likhar, S., Agarwal, S., Mishra, M., & Shukla, U. (2015). Tobacco use among adolescents: a burning issue in Bhopal city. *National Journal of Community Medicine*, 6(1), 103–107.

Buchy, L., Perkins, D., Woods, S. W., Liu, L., & Addington, J. (2014). Impact of substance use on conversion to psychosis in youth at clinical high risk of psychosis. *Schizophrenia Research*, *156*(2–3), 277–280.

Chadda, R. & Sengupta, S. (2002). Tobacco use by Indian adolescents. *Tobacco Induced Diseases*, 1(2), 111.

Deb, S., Bhadra, S., Sunny, A.M., & Sahay, S. (2020). *Childhood to adolescence: issues and concerns*, New Delhi, PEARSON.

Deb, S. & Chatterjee, P. (2008). *Styles of parenting adolescents: the indian scenario*. New Delhi, Akansha Publishing.

India Youth Development Index and Report (2017). *Rajiv Gandhi National Institute of Youth Development, Ministry of Youth Affairs and Sports*, Government of India.

Kar, B. R., Rao, S. L., & Chandramouli, B. A. (2008). Cognitive development in children with chronic protein energy malnutrition. *Behavioral and Brain Functions*, *4*(1), 1–12.

Lubman, D. I., Allen, N. B., Rogers, N., Cementon, E., & Bonomo, Y. (2007). The impact of co-occurring mood and anxiety disorders among substance-abusing youth. *Journal of Affective Disorders*, *103*(1–3), 105–112.

Madan, K. P., Poorni, S., & Ramachandran, S. (2006). Tobacco use among school children in Chennai city, India. *Indian Journal of Cancer*, 43(3), 127–131.

Martorell, R. (1999). The nature of child malnutrition and its long-term implications. *Food and Nutrition Bulletin*, *20*(3), 288–292.

Mohanan, P., Swain, S., Sanah, N., Sharma, V., & Ghosh, D. (2014). A study on the prevalence of alcohol consumption, tobacco use and sexual behaviour among adolescents in urban areas of the Udupi District, Karnataka, India. *Sultan Qaboos University Medical Journal*, 14(1), e104.

Mohanty, S., Tripathy, R., Palo, S. K., & Jena, D. (2013). Socioeconomic, demographic study on substance abuse among students of professional college in a southern town, Berhampur of Odisha state (India). *Journal of forensic and legal medicine*, *20*(8), 1057–1062

Müller, O., & Krawinkel, M. (2005). Malnutrition and health in developing countries. *Cmaj*, *173*(3), 279–286.

NSS 75th round (July 2017–June 2018). *Survey on Household Social Consumption: Education, National Statistical Office, Ministry of Statistics and Programme Implementation*, Government of India.

O'Neil, K. A., Conner, B. T., & Kendall, P. C. (2011). Internalizing disorders and substance use disorders in youth: Comorbidity, risk, temporal order, and implications for intervention. *Clinical Psychology Review*, *31*(1), 104–112.

Preeti, S. & Raut, D. (2012). Prevalence and pattern of tobacco consumption in India. *International Research Journal of Social Sciences*, 1(4), 36–43.

Raj, R.S., Asir, R.M. and Tamilenthi, S (2013). A study on alcoholism among youth residing in Trichirappalli slums, Tamil Nadu, India. *African Journal of Science and Research*, 2(2), 1–7.

Rajan, S. I. & Sivakumar, P. (Eds.) (2018). *Youth migration in emerging india: trends, challenges and opportunities*. Orient Black Swan.

Saddichha, S., Sinha, B. N. P., & Khess, C. R. J. (2007). The role of gateway drugs and psychosocial factors in substance dependence in Eastern India. *The International Journal of Psychiatry in Medicine*, *37*(3), 257–266.

Thomas, S. (2017). Emerging Adults Risk Behaviour: Its Association and Impact. Unpublished Doctoral Dissertation, submitted to Pondicherry University.

Tsering, D., Pal, R., & Dasgupta, A. (2010). Licit and illicit substance use by adolescent students in eastern India: prevalence and associated risk factors. *Journal of Neurosciences in Rural Practice*, 1(2), 76–81.

Tumge, L. (2009). Prevalence and patterns of alcohol use among college students: comparing scenario in Arunachal Pradesh and Kerala (Msters Dissertation), SCTIMST.

Viramontes, Horner. D., Willingham, F., Pittman, Z., Selby, N., & Taal, M. (2020). P1474 impact of malnutrition on health-related quality of life in dialysis patients: a prospective study. *Nephrology Dialysis Transplantation*, *35*(Supplement_3), gfaa142-P1474.

Walson, J. L. & Berkley, J. A. (2018). The impact of malnutrition on childhood infections. *Current Opinion in Infectious Diseases*, *31*(3), 231.

3 Role of family and its culture in child upbringing and youth development

> At the international level, the family is appreciated but not prioritized in development efforts. The very contribution of families to the achievement of development goals continues to be largely overlooked, while there seems to be a consensus on the fact that, so far, the stability and cohesiveness of communities and societies largely rest on the strength of the family. In effect, the very achievement of development goals depends on how well families are empowered to contribute to the achievement of those goals. Thus, policies focusing on improving the well-being of families are certain to benefit development.
>
> Ban-Ki-Moon (Report of the United Nations Secretary-General, 2010, p. 4)

Very few institutions in society have as critical an impact on the development of the youth as the family. Despite its many variations around the world, and the many changes in the structure and culture of families across the ages, the family has been understood as the institution formed of people connected by biological or conjugal bonds rather than business interests or informal pleasure, with implications for protection, nurturance, and mutual responsibility towards each other and to the unit (Smock & Schwartz, 2020; Van Hook, 2019). Again, across the ages, one consistent role of the family has been to nurture the next generation, born out of conjugal union or adopted into the family. Families provide children and youth their legal, cultural, social, and religious identity, and are the architects of their socialization into the human world. Families add the building blocks of food, dressing, manners, language, information, and basic life skills that are later honed and sculptured into finer shapes by educational institutions, workplaces, socio-cultural organizations, religious entities, and interpersonal relationships. Families are also the core institutions through which individuals share resources such as property, income, or means of daily sustenance, and care for the elderly and the sick (UN Women, 2020).

Positive youth development consists of viewing the youth as resources, as having the potential to develop for the future (Lewin-Bizan, Bowers, & Lerner, 2010; Ye, Wen, Wang, & Lin, 2020). Because of its almost universal presence in the society, the family's role in youth development has often received inadequate policy attention. However, it is increasingly being

DOI: 10.4324/9781003170587-3

recognized that the family's role is paramount to empower a youth to access and make use of various policy resources available. Further, the family provides the youth the resilience to combat various shocks arising through the life stages (Zolkoski & Bullock, 2012).

With globalization, technological advances, and other socio-demographic changes, the concept of the family in India and the rest of the world has undergone significant changes over the years. Nevertheless, it remains the core institution dedicated to child and youth development for humankind. We explore the role of the family in youth development, the challenges that a less than optimal family environment may add to the youth's upbringing, and possible policy interventions to empower and enable families to bring up their youths to be productive citizens of the society.

Changing nature of families across the world

Goldenberg and Goldenberg (2012) identify several critical features of a family: a shared history and sense of purpose, power structure and defined roles for its members often backed by socio-religious and legal contracts, reciprocal and durable loyalties and emotional attachments spanning across generations, and complex but shared patterns of communication, problem solving, and perceptions of the world. Coontz (2005) proposed that the evolution of family was based on the division of labour between men and women, where the role of the man as a provider and the woman as a nurturer needed to coexist closely to be possible. However, as the world moved towards greater women empowerment, inclusion of women in the workplace, and liberal culture, the nature of families changed drastically. Only 38% of families in the world follow the conventional pattern of a couple and at least one child (UN Women, 2020). 27% of the families in the world are extended families, including biological and conjugal relatives other than those related as spouses, parents, or children. Women empowerment and recognition of the rights of women have also been correlated with rise in divorce rates (Härkönen, 2014) and cohabitation (Posel, Rudwick, & Casale, 2011). Households with a single parent are becoming increasingly common, of which 84% are run by single mothers (UN Women, 2020).

The Progress of the World's Women 2019–2020 (UN Women, 2020) report identifies four major changes in the family form:

1. End of the exclusive male breadwinner model
2. Diverse forms of partnerships – ranging from marriage to cohabitation
3. Delinking of partnerships from biological reproduction
4. Decreased cohabitation of multiple generations

The changes in the family structure and culture in India have important implications for the way the family's role has been understood across the ages in the upbringing of the children. In many cases, the change provides more impetus for an open democratic microculture within families and greater emphasis on positive parenting – focusing on the strengths of the youth (Jarvis & Georgeson, 2018). At the same time, in many cases, the changes have deprived families of the support of a wider network, such as extended family consisting of grandparents, relatives, and cousins, clan, society, or religious groups, or legal protection that in many countries is limited only to traditional family structures built on legal heterosexual unions (Capaldi, 2019).

Indian families and the youths

Traditionally, the Indian subcontinent is characterized by a close-knit social structure, with the family playing an important role in the life of a person throughout the lifespan. Hofstede, in his global cultural framework, found India to be high on collectivism (placing the collective's interest over that of the individual) and on power distance (characterized by respect for authority) (Hofstede, 2009). These values make the family assume a special importance in the Indian culture. The Indian family ethos has traditionally been one characterized by respect for parents and other elders (Alexander & Chauhan, 2020). At the same time, elders in the family are responsible for providing for their youngsters, providing them with education and values, and preparing them as suitable citizens of the society. The ancient scriptures of India, such as the Ramayana and Mahabharata provided illustrations of the responsibilities of family members towards each other and their roles in the family structure (e.g., Mullaiti, 1995). Further, multigenerational ties form a critical part of the Indian family ethos. 25% of Asian families have grandparents staying with the children. While in many parts of urban India, work-related migration has led to the rise of nuclear family units, close ties with grandparents and extended family members are common in the Indian milieu (UNGAESC, 2020).

Another important characteristic that separates the Indian family ethos from that of the West is the extended connection between parents and children throughout the lifespan of the individuals (Kõu, Mulder, & Bailey, 2017). Unlike the West, the pressure on the youth to eke out a separate identity as soon as they come of age is low. So, it is not unusual to find adult children staying with parents till they land a job, till marriage, or even after marriage. This provides the Indian youth with an extended support framework even into the late years of young adulthood, in terms of shelter, nutrition, social and emotional support, vocational and financial support, and buffer against crisis (Rajan & Balagopal, 2017; Sadruddin et al., 2019). Presence of grandparents has been associated with greater prosocial behaviour, resilience, and positive mental health among the youth (Kim, 2020). However, at the same time, it may lead to the limitation of choices for the Indian youth as an individual and suppress the development of autonomy and independent decision-making skills (Scott, 2021). Multigenerational cohabitation may also lead to the escalation of intergenerational conflicts, leading to mental stress, financial strains, and in worse cases, domestic violence against family members, such as aged parents or daughters-in-law (Yeung, Desai, & Jones, 2018).

While the presence of a strong close-knit family structure is of considerable benefit to the Indian youth, families are not closed systems, and are therefore open to influences of the environment on its culture and values and its access to resources. Thus, the effectiveness of the family environment in positive youth development is also determined and limited by socio-economic conditions in the environment. In 2020, India was ranked 59 among 80 nations of the world when it comes to suitability for raising children, ranking beneath US and China (both ranked 43). This ranking came based on factors such as the extent to which the society is considered family-friendly and happy, concern for human rights, gender equality upheld by the society, and the state of public healthcare and education. Although India's 2020 performance is seen as an improvement from rank 65 in 2019, it indicates the importance of the variety of factors that determine the efficacy of families in youth development (US News, 2020).

Family's role in child development across different stages of youth

Several researchers have explored the family's influence on youth development through the perspective of parenting. Parents or caregivers are the first persons with whom an infant establishes an extended relationship. Erikson (1963) proposed that the extent to which caregivers pay attention to the infant's needs in the very early months of life builds in the child an assurance of support and an attitude towards the world and problems. This basic trust, in turn, leads to the first of the virtues – hope (Erikson, 1959; Plakun, 2017). Responses and reinforcement from the caregivers are therefore critical in building the child's attitude towards itself, towards other people in the environment, and towards the world and its functioning.

Nutrition, shelter, and basic life amenities

The family is the single most important source of the basic life amenities to a child – food, shelter, clothing, and enculturation into the ways of living. While the role of the family in helping a child survive the early years is well-recognized, its importance does not diminish even as the child enters adolescence and youth. Until one reaches young adulthood and is earning an independent living, the youth in India remain heavily dependent on the family structure for the basic amenities for survival – food, clothing, and shelter. Family units enable transfer of resources from earning members of the population to dependent members of the family, enabling the youth in the formative years of their lives, to focus on education and skill development, without spending energy on earning a living or managing a household (Beckmeyer & Russell, 2018; Kim, 2004). The family has been recognized as one of most important sources of nursing in sickness (e.g., Pilapil, Coletti, Rabey, & DeLaet, 2017) – making homecare for the sick an important part of health policy interventions in India. Fully functioning family units in a country take the load off governmental interventions to provide nutrition, health care, and shelter to citizens, and also channelize the flow of resources to the most vulnerable members of the society.

Education and work

One of the most critical roles that the family plays in positive youth development in India is providing the youth access to education and vocational skills. The family is the first source of education for the child. If a family has literate members, they play the critical role of introducing a child to the building blocks of education – alphabets and numbers, and basic reading, writing, and arithmetic (Apostu, 2017; Green, 2006). The individualized attention to primary education provided by the family enormously eases the work of the school as the child enters the formal education system. It helps smoothen the child's grasp of concepts and knowledge even in the group environment of the classroom (Belley & Lochner, 2007). Even where the family members are not literate, they contribute to informal schooling of the child through stories about history of the land, mythology, religion, and national values, socializing the child for effective adjustment in the society (Kemple & Nissenberg, 2000).

When the child enters youth, the role of the family somewhat diminishes in the education of the child. However, the family still plays a critical role in providing the youth with resources for learning – such as books and other educational equipment, tuition fees, and fees for additional educational support, certifications, and examinations. Home support with schoolwork has also been found to be valuable in helping the youth survive the pressure of the education system (Polo, Zychinski, & Roundfield, 2012; Sheppard, 2009). Family is one of the most important sources of unpaid mentoring and schooling received by the youth in India, and transfer of skills from one generation to the next.

An important area where the Indian family makes a valuable contribution in youth development is vocational skilling of the youth. Perhaps, the most prominent way in which families contribute to vocational empowerment of the youth is through induction in the family businesses. Since ancient times, family businesses have been the single-most important influencer for a person to earn his/her vocational identity. In India, the traditional practice of social class had been heavily dependent on vocational specialization, leading to early skilling of the youth in specific trades that would make them productive members of the society (Lee, 2006; Munshi, 2019). In family businesses, youth have an opportunity to gain valuable experience as apprentices, in a relatively safe and friendly work condition. Family businesses also provide the youth with a comfortable launchpad and a secure entry into the vocational world. Indian youth joining family trades, bank on the experience of elders to take their careers forward and utilize family funds and goodwill to expand their business or to rescue it from difficult situations (Bajpai, 2017; Rhodes, 1990).

Even in the absence of an established family business, the family may assist vocational skilling of the youth in several other ways. Firstly, a family may fund the youth's access to vocational education and internship opportunities, empowering them to develop vocational skills and access to jobs. Secondly, family provides early enculturation into different vocational roles by providing exposure to the work roles of the adult members of the family. This contributes to the tendency of youths entering the vocation of their parents or significant other family members, even when there is no fixed family trade, as a way of self-expression and building of one's professional identity (Lindstrom, Doren, Metheny, Johnson, & Zane, 2007). Thirdly, families provide the youths with a vocational network and connection that helps the youth in establishing credibility in the job market and obtain professional exposure. Again, family funds and heirlooms remain one of the most exploited resources in India for funding of startups launched by the youth. Even when it comes to business loans, family members are prized as guarantors, providing the youth access to funds for building their professional identities (e.g., Escolar-Llamazares et al., 2019; Farrukh, Khan, Khan, Ramzani, & Soladoye, 2017).

Development of character and values

Family as a social unit is a constant to a person during the formative years. This makes the family emerge as the biggest influencer in the individual's character and values. The family provides the child the first lessons in enculturation and socialization, providing them the needed lessons to adjust with the society, including language, dressing, food habits, art, religion, and culture (Bales & Parsons, 2014). Family's inputs shape a child's early thinking and perception of the world, and what to expect from it, while later experiences in schools build on these ideas. Therefore, it is of great importance that this early experience is positive and builds ideas consistent with a positive self-image and empathy for others (Baferani, 2015).

The family also plays a critical role in shaping the youth's attitude towards the self and other people. Dewanggi, Hastuti, and Herawati (2015) found that the mother's behaviour is correlated with positive strengths in a child. For instance, positive parenting (built on encouragement, care, and mutual respect) is seen to contribute to the youth's well-being, self-esteem, and satisfaction with life (Jiang, Huebner, & Hills, 2013).

A particularly potent form of parenting for youth development is strength-based training. Strength-based training involves identification of the areas in which a youth is talented and providing them increased opportunities in areas where they are proficient, instead of focusing primarily on their deficiencies (Jach, Sun, Chin, & Waters, 2017). Strength-based training has been associated with lower risk of depression and anxiety, and higher self-esteem in adolescents (Jach et al., 2017), as well as psychological harmony and school performance (Duan, Zhang, Li, Tang, & Duan, 2012).

Family's role is also critical in developing values such as gender sensitivity in the youth (McHale, Crouter, & Whiteman, 2003). In most Indian households, housework is primarily the responsibility of women and girls. Such a system puts young girls at a disadvantage when it comes to education or skilling and sets up a poor example for the next generation (UN Women, 2020). Non-egalitarian family roles also push Indian girls into early marriages. Approximately 650 million girls are married in childhood in the world, with one in every three child brides living in India (United Nations Children Fund, 2019).

Buffer against crisis

An important role of the family is to provide a buffer against crises that may affect a person in his or her lifetime. At a microscopic level, families assist youth to cope with the vulnerabilities of adolescence, emotional stress, legal conflicts, illnesses, accidents, and other challenges such as unemployment or closure of business ventures (Manczak, Skerrett, Gabriel, Ryan, & Langenecker, 2018; Turagabeci, Nakamura, Kizuki, & Takano, 2007). The safety net provided by the close-knit family system in India, both in terms of emotional support, physical care, as well as financial resources such as inheritance and family infrastructure, ensure that the youth can cope with the crises and bounce back without significant damage to reputation or well-being.

Families also provide children, youth, and other vulnerable sections of the society physical and mental support against unexpected crises that can emerge owing to wars, pandemics, or natural disasters. Supportive family environments and strong relational ties have been proven to be effective in providing protection to the dependent population in an economy during times of major disturbances (Walsh, 2016).

The evolutionary and socio-cultural role of the family in nurturing and supporting the dependent members of the population has led to the legal recognition of family ties and responsibilities in human society in various forms. Social and legal frameworks defining family processes have been common since ancient times in India – defining the roles and responsibilities of family members towards each other, permissible relationships among them, and modes through which tangible wealth would transfer from one generation to another (Cretney, 2003). In the modern society, such socio-religio-cultural obligations have given rise to legal statutes in India, in the form of property and inheritance laws, laws governing marriage, divorce, permissible relationships, and cohabitation, laws governing custody and childcare, and provisions for protection and support for the elderly and other dependent family members.

Challenging family conditions for youth development

The family has a close connection with the well-being of the youth, being the primary source of tangible and intangible resources. However, families differ in the extent to which they are empowered to provide the youth a positive developmental experience. Many families lack access to the resources, which limits the youth's opportunities to develop self optimally (Orth, 2018). Again, the family environment may not be optimally suited for nurturing of children and youth, leading to exploitation and deprivation. Youth growing up in a deprived environment are not able to utilize resources later in life even if they are made accessible to them. Thus, the efficacy of the family system often determines the extent to which other policy interventions for sustainable development are effective in empowering the vulnerable sections of the population.

Poverty and its impact on youth development

Recognized as the first concern to be addressed through the SDGs (UNDP, 2019), poverty remains one of the most pressing problems for many Indians even in the 21st century. A significant percentage of the world population lives in extreme poverty, and a significant other section live in impoverished conditions that limit their access to the basic amenities for living (UNDESA, 2020).

Poverty also correlates highly with certain other environmental challenges, putting families from sections of the society at a systematic disadvantage when it comes to sustainable living and growth. Mokomane (2013) reported that in developing countries, families of migrants, families located in rural areas or urban slums, families headed by women, and families headed by unskilled parents are particularly prone to poverty.

Poor families in India are often ill-equipped to raise their children for a variety of reasons. Owing to lack of education about healthy living and lack of access to contraceptives and other medical facilities, poor parents tend to have more children (e.g., Jacobson, 2018). This in turn contributes to less attention to each child while growing up, affecting the latter's physical and mental health. Several researchers have shown evidence of higher child mortality in poor families (e.g., Spencer, 2018), owing to lack of access to medical facilities, poor nutrition, and unhygienic conditions of living. Children and youth growing up in poverty are also less likely to have access to education and vocational skilling opportunities, as well as wholesome entertainment opportunities, significantly stalling their overall development (De Lannoy, Leibbrandt, & Frame, 2015).

Poverty is also one of the powerful predictors for the early entry of children and youth in the labour force in India. Income from children and adolescents tend to make up for as much as 25% of the family income for many poor families, disincentivizing sending children and youth to schools or skilling them for vocation (Anker & Melkas, 1996). The earning potential of youth encourages poorer sections of the society to have large families, further aggravating the problem. Diwan (2017) reported that families with 5–10 children contribute 58% of the child labourers in India. There have also been instances of children and youth from poor families being pushed into bonded labour to pay off ancestral debts or pushed into family trade early in life. Underprivileged children in India also drop out of schools in agricultural seasons to help adults with harvesting for family trades (Diwan, 2017). Poverty thus deprives the youth of the opportunity for skilling, thus limiting access to high-earning professions later in life (Emerson & Souza, 2011). Early entry into the workforce in hazardous work conditions also affects the youth's physical health and productivity, damaging their productive potential for the entire lifespan.

Migration of family

Closely correlated with poverty is the phenomenon of migration. Migration consists of relatively long-term relocation of individuals or families from one location to another in search of resources for living (Cohen, 2016). In 2011, India reported having 139 million internal migrants on the average every year (Wanchuk, 2019). The most common cause of migration in India is economic migration where families relocate in search of jobs or means of earning a livelihood. Economic migration in India mostly corresponds to urban migration, where people from rural India move to urban locations in search of a living (Panda & Mishra, 2018). Mass migration may also arise from uncertain environmental conditions such as political violence, riots, civil war, or cross-border warfare, and terrorist activities (Schwartz, 2018).

Migrant families face several challenges when it comes to child upbringing and youth development. Migration is often unplanned and performed under duress, leaving the migrant families financially weak and devoid of the resources for a productive living. Again, since they are removed from their original ecosystems, migrant families are often denied the benefits of a supportive community and stability of shelter and lifestyle (UNDESA, 2019). These affect the development of youth in migrant families as they must live in uncertainty, with less-than-optimal resources, and often under hostile and alien conditions. Frequent relocations deprive children of education or health benefits from the government (Fellmeth et al., 2018). Also, migrant homes also have both parents working to make ends meet. Without the support mechanism of childcare available, the youth, typically young girls are relegated to housework and childcare. Domestic responsibilities lead to early dropouts from schools and the workforce for the adolescents and the youth in India (Roy, Singh, & Roy, 2015), affecting their productive potential for a lifetime. Migrant homes, particularly those in the slums, leave the youth vulnerable to hostile ecosystems, making them easy targets for sexual predators, crimes, and illegal activities such as drug peddling, arson, gang activities, and violence (e.g., Curtis, Miller, & Berry, 2000).

Broken homes and violent families

A condition that affects the well-being of rich and poor families alike is family culture. Toxic family environments significantly affect child rearing and youth development, leaving the children and youth vulnerable to emotional stress, instability, and physical violence. Violence in families may arise from multiple situations such as marital discord, property disputes, addiction and drug abuse by earning members or heads of the family, and gender discrimination (Garbarino, 1998).

Violent homes affect adolescents and youth in multiple ways. Violent and abusive role models affect the youth's attitude towards violence, making them more prone to abusive behaviour later in life. Martin et al. (2002) reported a generational pattern of violence at home in India, transmitted through vicarious learning. They also leave the youth vulnerable to physical or sexual abuse or mental stress, affecting their well-being, self-confidence, and life skills. Young girls are also at an increased risk of sexual violence at home or in the neighbourhood and forced or underage marriages (Rehel, 2014).

Abusive home environments deny the youth the opportunity to benefit from the guidance and mentoring of significant others in the family (Ozer, Lavi, Douglas, & Wolf, 2017). It also affects the likelihood of engaging in productive pursuits such as skilling, education, or entertainment. Violent home environments caused by drug or alcohol abuse of family members deplete the family of financial resources that could have been devoted to fruitful purposes. This causes early dropouts from the educational system, lack of access to health care, and lack of capital and securities for entrepreneurial ventures for the youth in low- and middle-income countries such as India (Fellmeth et al., 2018). Such youths also have an early exposure to substance abuse, causing the bane to be carried forward to the next generation (Rusby, Light, Crowley, & Westling, 2018). Divorces, poor family functioning, and poor communication at home have been related to modern-day maladies such as Problematic Internet Use and addiction with video games in the youth (Chen, Chen, & Gau, 2015; Yu & Shek, 2013).

Violent environment at home and instability has also been correlated to early induction into the workforce. In India, adolescents and youths from families with domestic violence, alcoholic or drug addiction tend to start earning early to satisfy their basic needs of food and clothing (Habib, 2017; Laing, McWhirter, Templeton, & Hannah-Russell, 2019; Singh & Parihar, 2016). Research on Indian child labourers also shows that children from broken homes or those with stepparents enter the workforce early (Singh & Parihar, 2016).

Lack of parental education

Educated parents are more efficient in giving children a meaningful childhood, because of their awareness about various opportunities, their openness to positive parenting practices, and their dedication to the upbringing of the next generation over immediate gratification of superficial needs (Monaghan, 2017). Uneducated parents tend to view education as an opportunity cost, leading to early dropouts (e.g., Adonteng-Kissi, 2018; Kielland & Tovo, 2006). Also, they cannot help the children with studies, making it particularly difficult for first-generation learners to keep up with the system (Guio, Choi, & Escardíbul, 2018). Reddy and Sinha (2010) reported lack of formal education in parents as one of the prime predictors that made children likely to enter the workforce early.

Lack of education in parents also reduces the likelihood of protective parenting, resulting in ineffective supervision and monitoring of the youth. Educated parents and caregivers are aware of the potential benefits and threats from various options for engagement that are available in the environment, making them vigilant in case of problematic behaviour and proactive in providing access to important resources. Low parental education has been found to have a positive correlation with Problematic Internet Use in adolescents and youth (Ang, Chong, Chye, & Huan, 2012).

The impact of the family in child rearing and youth development has been presented in Figure 3.1.

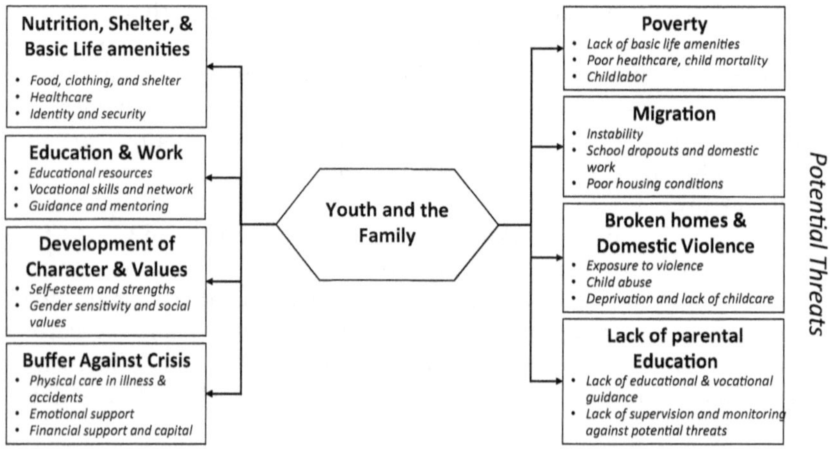

Figure 3.1 Youth and the family: impact and challenges.

Family and the New Normal: Implications for youth development

The COVID-19 pandemic hitting the world in December 2020 disrupted life in a way that has been unfamiliar for the past few decades. The communicable nature of the COVID-19 infections led to a nationwide lockdown in India – severely impeding daily life, occupational endeavours, and educational pursuits. The aftershock of these restrictions hit millions of working people and in turn, the family dependent on their income for living. At the same time, the pandemic confined Indians in close quarters of their homes with their family members, making the family's role immensely critical to compensate for the gaps being created in the medical, educational, and social and mental health needs of a person (Sahoo et al., 2020). Homecare during the COVID-19 pandemic provided by the family members of the sick person has been crucial in taking the load of public health facilities for less severe health conditions. Caregivers at home have also compensated for the role of the teacher at home, helping the children and youth to catch up with instructional materials and keep up with the lost school and college days (Morgan, 2020).

The 2020 Substantive Report of the United Nations General Assembly and Security Council (UNGAESC, 2020) focused on the role of family in building resilience in children and youth in times of crisis such as the COVID-19 pandemic. The UNGAESC 2020 report states that families across the world are likely to be driven into poverty due to the pandemic, with 80–115 million people likely to enter extreme poverty. Poverty accompanied by lack of employment, and lack of access to health care, education, and wholesome entertainment is likely to deprive many vulnerable families of an adequate environment to nurture the youth. In India, closing down of schools and colleges due to the pandemic left millions of children dependent on the online mode of education – leading to the digital divide due to lack of connectivity or access to digital devices (Sambuli & Magnoli, 2019). Again, migration of hundreds of families from one part of India to another due to closure of their places of work during the lockdown has left many children and youth vulnerable to the disruption caused by relocation (Breman, 2020).

The COVID-19 pandemic had serious implications for working parents in India, particularly those from low-income families working in essential industries, as they are likely to be missing in childcare facilities as well as adequate facilities for isolation (Gupta & Sahoo, 2020). Families with teleworking parents also face the additional trouble as parents must juggle between extended work hours and children and adolescents at home. Social isolation during the COVID-19 pandemic has deprived many Indian families of the support network of extended families, grandparents, neighbourhood, and communities. This has been related to increased cases in India of parental burnout and child mental health problems, violence and altercations within the family, and straining of relationships (Maiti, Singh, Innamuri, & Hasija, 2020). The pandemic has also seen increased domestic violence against women and girls in India (Malathesh, Das, & Chatterjee, 2020). COVID-19 has also deprived 1.3 billion children of educational access, increasing the stress on already strained families to compensate for the loss (UNICEF, 2020). Only one-third of the nations is working for children, elderly, and differently abled people, further increasing the pressure on the family systems for the support of the vulnerable (UNGAESC, 2020).

Policy and legal interventions for family and youth

Children and the youth are one of the most important resources for humankind for its continued survival, as effective upbringing will ensure that the new generations are equipped to deal with the challenges of the future and create a better world for tomorrow. They are also one of the most vulnerable sections of the society in their formative years, as deprivation of critical resources during this time may translate into irreparable loss for them going ahead. Hence, there have been legislation and statutory measures across the world protecting the interest of children and young people. One of the most significant interventions in this area has been the UN Convention on the Rights of the Child, 1989 (UNO, 1989). The Child Rights Convention (CRC) guidelines speak of the rights of young people aged below 18 across various areas – such as the right to nutrition and living conditions conducive to survival; the right to be protected from abuse, inhuman treatment, and exploitation; the right to receive education, care, social security, and opportunities to play; the right to practise one's religion and culture; and right to freedom of expression and access to information, among others. The CRC guidelines are binding on the member states of the United Nations Organization and are expected to guide the spirit of policies and legislations at the United Nations and its member states.

Child rights are intricately related to the welfare of the family. In 1994, the United Nations celebrated the International Year of the Family, to bring attention to the role of the family in the welfare of individuals, and the importance of preserving family as an institution through access to resources, support, and protection against exploitation. Coupled with the CRC guidelines, the focus on the family led to significant policy decisions to protect and empower the family units across the world. The SDGs were launched in 2012 to "meet the urgent environmental, political and economic challenges" that assail the world (UNDP, 2019). The SDGs of the United Nations uphold the rights of the women and gender equality, a goal that incorporates egalitarian practices in the family settings (UN Women, 2020), such as sharing of household work and child-rearing responsibilities, property rights for women, and equal treatment in family in terms of access to education, nutrition, entertainment, and other resources. Other SDGs having implications for family empowerment are goals pertaining to education, nutrition, vocation for the youth, and end of violence (Richardson et al., 2020).

In India, there have been several policy measures aimed at strengthening the family's ability to fend for its members. India has the largest food security system in the world known as the Public Distributions System (PDS). The PDS implements distribution of available staple food grains and other essentials to Indian citizens at a controlled price, with specific focus on those living below or immediately above the poverty line (Department of Food and Public Distribution, 2018). The PDS serves a person right from the birth until death, by ensuring that the family can fulfil the nutritional needs of its children. In several states of India, the access to food grains through PDS is being replaced by direct cash transfer, giving poor families the flexibility to spend on their biggest necessities.

To ensure the upbringings of healthy children, the Government of India has also launched several other programmes. The Integrated Child Development Scheme (ICDS) was launched in 1975, focusing on the holistic physical, mental, and social development of the child (Ministry of Woman and Child Development, 2018). The ICDS has led to the establishment of 0.13 billion Anganwadi Centres (AWCs), across India, that serve as centres for child welfare, outreach, and linkages in rural India. Another significant initiative is the Midday Meal Program that provides school-going children one balanced meal at school daily.

A programme recently launched by the Government of India is the POSHAN (PM's Overarching Scheme for Health and Nutrition) Abhiyaan also called the National Nutrition Mission (NMM) (*POSHAN Abhiyaan – PM's Overarching Scheme for Holistic Nourishment*, 2018). This programme aims to provide nutrition, immunization, and monitoring to children growing up in less-endowed households. Launched in 2017, the POSHAN Abhiyaan aims to reduce child malnutrition rate in the country and prevent child mortality (PIB, 2019). Again, the Ayushman Bharat Yojana is a government-funded programme providing healthcare benefits for economically disadvantaged citizens of India. Ayushman Bharat is presently the world's largest programme of its kind. Improved access to health care in rural India has significantly enhanced health-seeking behaviour in 22 states of India (Tripathi, 2019). The Government of India also has launched several schemes for maternal and child health, such as the Family Planning Program, Janani Suraksha Yojana, and the Universal Immunization Program. The Global Childhood Report (Save the Children, 2019), states that owing to economic growth and other interventions relating to child nutrition, there is a 30% decline in stunting and 57% decline in child mortality in India in recent times.

Apart from nutrition and health care, there have been other initiatives in India in recent times, to empower families and to provide a holistic environment to their children and youth. One important initiative in this regard is the Atal Mission for Rejuvenation and Urban Transformation (AMRUT) (Ministry of Housing and Urban Affairs, 2019). Launched in 2015, this programme provides for healthy and sanitary urban conditions and provision of parks and open areas for the recreation of the youth. Another one is the Pradhan Mantri Gramin Awas Yojana, providing homes at affordable rates for economically challenged sections of the society.

Role of observation homes as per the Juvenile Justice (Care and Protection) Act 2000 in case of orphan and destitute children

The family being one of the most revered socio-cultural units of the Indian society, there have been several legal provisions protecting the sanctity of the institution and the rights and responsibility of the family members towards each other. Care of dependent children is a legal responsibility of the parents. Further, in India, the age of dependency extends into late adulthood, with sons aged below 25, non-earning sons, and unmarried daughters of any age irrespective of their earning status qualified to be considered dependants (Muthukumar, 2020). This provides the youth an extended safety net into adulthood from their family, which helps them to have access to security, care, and resources, within the structure of the family. Laws governing marriage and divorces in India have special provisions for the custody well-being of the dependent children, so that the latter's security and access to the critical resources are not sacrificed (Singh, 2008).

Despite the close-knit family system of India, there are thousands of children in the subcontinent who grow up without a shelter or live in extreme situations where the family's security is negligible. These include abandoned children and youth, orphans, trafficked children and youth, and destitute who live without shelter on the streets. Again, there are children who are rescued from violent or broken homes due to divorce, abusive parenting, domestic disturbances, or natural disasters. In 2000, The Juvenile Justice (Care and Protection) of Children Act was passed aimed at ending the malpractices leading to abuse of children and youth and helping the children return to mainstream living (The Ministry of Law and Justice, GoI, 2016). The Juvenile Justice Act provides for equitable compassionate treatment of children and underage youth showing deviant behaviour, and shelter for youths found without protection. In addition, it also prevents hiring of children in hazardous occupations and rehabilitation of the deviant youth.

One of the most important provisions of the Juvenile Justice Act is the setup of government-run children homes – for sheltering homeless children and youth, or those living in dangerous conditions. Shelter homes provide night stay facilities for homeless youths as well as relatively long duration stay facilities ranging from a few weeks to one year. The shelter homes, set up separately for boys and girls, provide food, clothing, sanitation, and health care, as well as facilities for education, vocational training, and recreation. Shelter homes also work for providing linkages to corporate or social organizations for vocational opportunities, or gainful employment of the sheltered children and youth.

Despite the multiple interventions for the protection of children and youth and the empowerment of the family units where they grow up, there still exists a significant scope for improvement of the situation. The challenges partly arise from the large size of the population in India, which creates procedural challenges in providing universal coverage. At the same time, often families are not equipped to access the various educational and nutritional resources available for the children and the youth. Need-based interventions are therefore required to address the critical problems faced by the families in youth development.

Recommendations: Creating an ideal family environment for nurturing children and youth

Worldwide, government and non-governmental organizations are launching hundreds of programmes and interventions to address the issue of youth development – trying to devise a plan that would empower the youth and ensure their holistic and sustainable well-being. However, it is important to recognize that most of these interventions aim to supplement the role of the family or compensate for the gaps that less-than-optimal family environments leave in the process of youth development. Thus, a healthy and empowered family would probably turn many of these supplementary interventions redundant and reduce the burden on policy intervention plans. Secondly, despite multiple resources made available to the individual for youth development, a healthy family environment is critical to allow youth and children to access and meaningfully use these resources. Thus, healthy family functioning is as critical for well-being as any of the goals of food, education, health care, or freedom of expression and action.

Recommendations for family welfare in the context of youth development are presented in Figure 3.2.

Educational interventions for parenting, child rearing, and youth development

Rather than being something ingrained in the genetic makeup of humans, effective child-rearing practices are often seen as a reflexive, complex process that needs to be learnt to be effectively executed. However, little

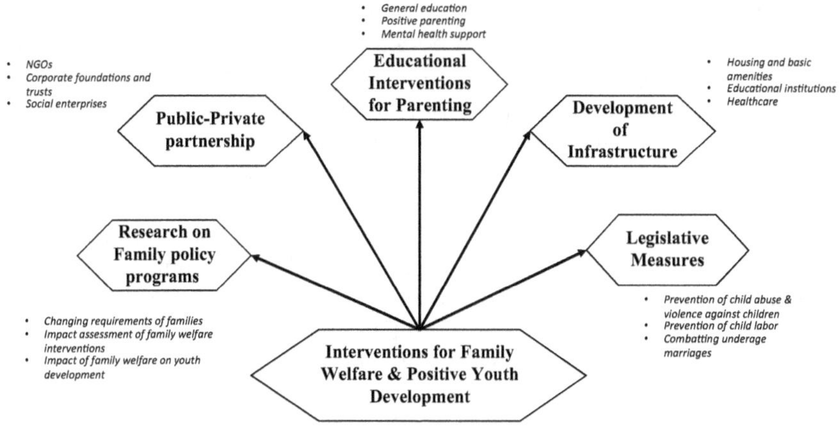

Figure 3.2 Interventions for family welfare and positive youth development.

instruction is available to a person when it comes to child rearing, making the caregivers dependent on ancestral and cultural knowledge on child-rearing practices. This knowledge, although valuable in most cases, may need to be adapted with the demands of the changing times. For instance, India traditionally values child-rearing ethos based on care and responsibility and power distance, to the extent of attributing divine prestige to parents and caregivers. While this ensures a bond of strong emotional attachment and moral obligation towards the family, it may stand in contrast with the increased individualistic bent of cultural values that is becoming common in India with globalization, and the heightened exposure to information that has come with the internet (Sahithya, Manohari, & Vijaya, 2019; Sondhi, 2017). Further, the new generation is often well-versed in digital technology, while the older generation is not, reversing the traditional mentor–mentee roles of caregivers and children (Livingstone & Byrne, 2018; Vogel, 2019). All these require the traditional parenting, as it is understood, needs to be modified to meet the demand of the changing times.

In recent times, there has been an increased emphasis on development of positive parenting skills among caregivers. Positive parenting comprises respect for the youth's autonomy as well as adequate supervision and monitoring, respect, encouragement, unconditional positive regard, and opportunities for development of the youth's strengths (Neppl, Jeon, Diggs, & Donnellan, 2020; UNGAESC, 2020). Focus on the strengths rather than the weaknesses of the youth helps build self-esteem and empower the youth to solve problems on their own. Positive parenting has been found to enhance mental well-being and creativity among the youth and decrease depressive symptoms and deviant behaviour (Piarnau, 2020).

Parenting education programmes have been recommended for familiarizing parents with the developmental stages of children and youth and their specific requirements (ECLAC, 2020). Such programmes also familiarize parents with the challenges of each stage, the opportunities, and the various methods of disciplining the youth without resorting to punitive measures or violence (Nelsen, Bill, & Marchese, 2018). Increased access to positive parenting programmes in both rural and urban areas, and IEC on positive parenting practices targeted at caregivers and other family members may be highly useful in adapting parenting styles to the requirements of modern times. Further, such programmes need to involve both parents to ensure consistent egalitarian practices at home (Alemann, Garg, & Vlahovicova, 2020).

In addition to emphasis on parenting education, there is need for further emphasis on general education on parents and other adult members of the family, through universal access to primary and secondary education, increased vocational skilling opportunities, and grants and scholarships for higher education, wherever needed. Parental education correlates highly with the youth's likelihood of receiving vocational and general education, living in a supervised environment, and receiving adequate nutrition, care, and emotional support (Guryan, Hurst, & Kearney, 2008). Thus, universal access to education in one generation passes on the benefits to the next generations as well. Educational interventions must also relate to specific areas relevant to care and upbringing such as child and youth development, nutrition, basic home-based health care, healthy habits, and best practices for living (Alderman & Headey, 2017; Petersson, Petersson, & Håkansson, 2004). Such information, disseminated either through formal setups or through various IEC media, can help in building awareness about the role of the family in child and youth development and the best practices in this regard.

Parents and other caregivers also need to be familiarized with mental health issues that may affect the youth and possible interventions. Youth is a time of emotional turmoil and many times; the family is the first to sense the crisis. However, stigma associated with going to a mental health expert and lack of awareness about mental health issues cause such problems to be trivialized and ignored (Chandra & Minkovitz, 2006; Turner, Jensen-Doss, & Heffer, 2015). This may lead to aggravation of the problem and in worst cases, self-harm and suicide. India has one of the highest rates of suicide among the youth in the world (Garai, 2020). It is critical that parents are educated in the common signs of mental illness such as depression, so that they can address the problem through support and seek professional help for the youth, whenever needed. Parents and guardians to be brought under the intervention programme to bring change in their perception about various myths and misconceptions related to child rearing and disciplining of children and youth.

Legislations banning exploitation of children and encouraging positive discipline

Family violence is another issue which adversely affects the mental health and education of children and youth needs community intervention and/or school-based counselling.

Family units being close-knit structures, events inside the family often escape the monitoring of the society (Bryce, Robinson, & Petherick, 2019). This is particularly true for a country like India, where mild corporal punishment for the youth is traditionally accepted and even encouraged at places. This leaves children and youth vulnerable to violence or systematic abuse by family members. Such exploitation is also normalized in different strata of the society across the world, making them escape the spotlight of curative measures (Lokot, Bhatia, Kenny, & Cislaghi, 2020). Discipline in the form of corporal punishment may often reach severe proportions and cause fatal physical damage to the child as well as mental trauma. Children exposed to regular corporal discipline suffer from lack of self-esteem, are more prone to bullying others, and are likely to show violent streaks themselves later in life (Taquette & Monteiro, 2019; Winstok, 2015. There is a need for increased attention to the promotion of positive discipline that encourages healthy behaviour in the children without resorting to punitive measures (Lustick, 2017; Nelsen, 2011). Positive discipline practices need to be popularized through parental education interventions as well as through IEC materials and popular media, so that more and more families become aware of the effective ways of children and youth development (Carroll & Brown, 2020; UNGAESC, 2020).

Families are often places for sexual abuse of children and youth. Research shows that in a significantly large number of cases of sexual abuse of young people, the offender is a family member, relative, or someone who has regular access to the family home (WHO, 2003). The power asymmetry and complexities of emotional ties in families make the survivor less likely to speak up in case of abuse (Kiser et al., 2014). Even in cases where the survivor struggles to break free, the complaints are usually hushed up for fear of damage to family reputation, destruction of family ties, or dependence on the abuser financially and socially. This is accompanied by victim blaming, making it even more difficult for the survivor to escape (Assink et al., 2019; Masilo, 2018). Stringent laws are needed to combat child and youth abuse inside families, along with support structures to provide the survivor immediate protection, shelter, justice, and continued support. Active presence of institutions such as Child Protection Services and Child Helplines can help in providing children and youth security against abuse in family settings (Wilson, Hean, Abebe, & Heaslip, 2020). The Juvenile Justice Act of India provides for such support services in the form of Child Helpline (1098), POSCO e-box facilitating online filing of anonymous complaints of abuse against children, foster homes, institutional care, and adoption services (PIB, 2019; Seth & Srivastava, 2017). Increased effort needs to be made to improve the efficacy of these institutions and to spread awareness about their presence among young people as well as adults, so that people in need can access them on time. Schools can be valuable in transmission of such knowledge to children and caregivers (Münger & Markström, 2019). Teachers may also be made aware of the legal provisions against abuse and trained to detect signs of abuse and exploitation in children and youth.

Effective legal provisions are also needed to combat other forms of exploitation of children and youth such as underage marriage, malnutrition, exposure to violent family environments even without active physical abuse of the child, and denial of rights to education and freedom of expression. In India, a major challenge in this area is the early induction of the youth in the family trade and domestic duties as an unpaid helping hand, severely impeding the youth's access to formal skilling, and resulting in school dropouts (Diwan, 2017; Gamlin, Camacho, Ong, & Hesketh, 2015; Save the Children, 2016). The Child Labour (Prohibition and Regulation) Amendment Act 2016 prohibits underage employment for children in hazardous occupations (Ministry of Law and Justice, 2016). In India, child marriage continues to be a major problem too, despite legal provisions to nullify and penalize underage marital unions of young people (Ray, 2019; Save the Children, 2019). More efforts are needed to spread the message through popular media, schools, and government bodies to prevent such atrocities. The ICDS, with the Anganwadi workers as its forerunners, plays an important role in such outreach and can also assist in monitoring of condition of children and youth, particularly in rural areas and in urban slum settings (Ministry of Woman and Child Development, 2018).

Development of infrastructure for family well-being

Positive youth development is not the work of the family alone. Several factors contribute to raising children such as physical safety, availability of quality education and health care, family-friendly environment, gender egalitarianism, and income equality (US News, 2020). Therefore, there is a need to develop environmental conditions that help the family provide its members a fulfilling experience and satisfy the needs of the dependent members. Such interventions may range from finding employment for adult family members so that families do not have to depend on limited governmental support to fulfil their basic needs, to proper housing facilities so that families have a secure shelter to protect themselves. Since salaried jobs are too few to cater to the needs of the entire Indian population, in recent years, India has adopted several interventions to promote small entrepreneurships, such as the Start Up India and Atmanirbhar Bharat (Gandhi, Batra, & Gupta, 2019; Massand, Lodi, & Ambreen, 2020). Such programmes ensure easy availability of capital, simplified business laws, tax benefits, and access to new markets. Increase in entrepreneurial opportunities help families become self-dependent in providing for their basic and aspirational needs and provide the youth with a conducive environment to grow.

Safe and accessible housing has also been a concern of successive Indian governments for long. Overpopulation, poverty, and migration lead to the rise of slums, makeshift human settlements that are usually characterized by poor infrastructure and hygiene, lack of basic amenities such as internet, electricity, and water, and exposure to violence, drugs, and other illegal activities (PWC & Save the Children, 2015; UN-Habitat, 2014; UNICEF, 2012). Poor makeshift shelters are also prone to destruction in natural disasters such as floods, earthquakes, or forest fires, leading to loss of life and property, and uncertainty for the Indian youth (Malhotra, 2018). The Pradhan Mantri Gramin Awas Yojana and AMRUT are some of the interventions adopted in India to ensure affordable housing to families from disadvantaged backgrounds, (Gohil & Gandhi, 2019; Ministry of Housing and Urban Affairs, 2019). Similarly, improvement of infrastructure for electricity, water, and internet has been made possible in India through various other schemes such as the Jal Jeevan Mission (targeted at functional household tap connection to every rural household) (All India Radio, 2021), and the National Optic Fibre Network (NOFN) scheme backed by the National Digital Communication Policy 2018 (BBNL, 2021; NDCP, 2018). India has one of the world's least expensive internet access that enables families to provide digital education to their children, that has become of particular importance in the pandemic times (Roy, 2019). Similarly, interventions such as the Ujjwala Yojana, that has led to access of LPG cooking gas cylinders in 99% of the poor households, have worked to drastically improve the air quality and safety inside homes that were earlier using pollution-causing fossil fuels (PTI, 2021; Swain & Mishra, 2020).

While interventions exist, it is important to ensure that more and more families come within the scope of these interventions and there is minimal slippage from the safety net. For this, it is important to have close monitoring of the existing interventions and their efficacy and their adequate implementation on the field.

Public–private partnerships in family welfare

Despite the multiple interventions adopted by the Government of India and the state governments from time to time, the efforts fall short when it comes to the scope of the work afforded by the population size and diversity of India (Kaur, 2019). This makes public–private partnerships involving non-governmental organizations, philanthropic enterprises, corporate trusts, and social enterprises critical for the transmission of human resources, financial resources, and management expertise to address the problem at hand. The United Nations Organization encourages the participation of non-governmental social for-profit and not-for-profit enterprises to supplement government efforts and provide the last mile coverage (Hege & Demailly, 2018). In India too, several organizations provide family welfare and outreach in collaboration with the government to strengthen and enable the families and enable them for positive youth development (Chanani et al., 2019).

Research on family welfare needs and impact of interventions

The world is undergoing change at a rapid pace, and families too are changing in keeping with the demands of the changing times. Family processes that lend resilience to family structures against crises include positive belief systems that regard crises as challenges, flexibility, management of resources, open communication, mutual trust, and shared decision-making (Walsh, 2003). There is need for extensive research to ensure how these values may be developed within the family settings and be communicated to the future generations.

The requirements of the Indian youth from the family today have gone beyond basic education, nutrition, and health care, to digital skill building and access, information about dynamic work opportunities, and mental support to deal with the challenges of the complex world. Similarly, changes are coming about in family laws and human rights, with increased acceptance of flexible family structures, same-sex relationships and marriages, increased liberalization of the societal norms, and freedom of speech and expression (Trask, 2009). The needs of the families are therefore changing in terms of the challenges they must face and the resources they need to cope with these challenges. There needs to be continued research on the changing nature and needs of families, to know the specific needs of families from different cultures, religious groups, political identities, or social class. This needs to be accompanied by documentation and sharing of good practices on parenting, so that they may be disseminated widely and adopted by other families living with children and youth (Zepeda, Varela, & Morales, 2004).

Along with research on the changing natures of families, there needs to be a concentrated impact assessment of the various government, public, and private interventions targeted at family welfare in India, specifically those that have implications for the youth. Apart from nationwide assessment of well-being such as the National Family Health Surveys (Ministry of Health and Family Welfare, 2017), impact assessment of each intervention is critical to understand how far the targeted beneficiaries benefit from the interventions and what interventions are needed to enable them to access these benefits. Such assessments need to specifically study the impact on specific groups such as the children and the youth to see if the intended impact is reached.

To understand the complicated family dynamics in India because of cultural diversity and its impact on children and youth, there is a need to conduct research in different geographic locations covering families from different cultural backgrounds. The findings of the study would help to understand the family dynamics from cultural perspectives and prescribe appropriate measures to local administration for addressing issues and challenges which hinder healthy growth and development of children and youth.

Conclusion and recommendations

Few other institutions of the world assume such epic importance in the upbringing of children and youth as the family does. Experiences gained in the family colour the perception of the youth about the self and the world. Therefore, it is essential that the experience and exposure a youth gathers from the family enrich the youth and help them develop into empowered adult members of the society. While the increased focus on individualism, independent living, and modernization has weakened the ties of traditional family systems (e.g., Kalmijn & Saraceno, 2008), families remain of critical importance in India in passing traditional knowledge and values from one generation to another (Albanese, De Blasio, & Sestito, 2016), protecting the vulnerable, combatting crisis, and providing the sustained and unconditional human connect that makes life meaningful for an individual. When it comes to the youth, empowerment of the family leads to direct empowerment of the youth. It is therefore necessary that increased policy interventions in India focus on strengthening the most natural bonds available to human beings to nurture and grow productive members of the future society.

References

Adonteng-Kissi, O. (2018). Causes of child labour: perceptions of rural and urban parents in Ghana. *Children and Youth Services Review*, *91*, 55–65. doi:10.1016/j.childyouth.2018.05.034

Albanese, G., De Blasio, G., & Sestito, P. (2016). My parents taught me. Evidence on the family transmission of values. *Journal of Population Economics*, *29*(2), 571–592. doi:10.1007/s00148-015-0574-8

Alderman, H., & Headey, D. D. (2017). How important is parental education for child nutrition?. *World Development*, 94, 448–464. doi:10.1016/j.worlddev.2017.02.007

Alemann, C., Garg, A., & Vlahovicova, K. (2020). *The role of fathers in parenting for gender equality*. Retrieved March 9, 2021 from https://www.un.org/development/desa/family/wp-content/uploads/sites/23/2020/06/Parenting-education-the-role-of-fathers.Alemann.pdf

Alexander, A. J., & Chauhan, V. (2020). Parents and emerging adults in India. In B. Ashdown & A. Faherty (Eds.) *Parents and caregivers across cultures* (pp. 217–230). Springer, Cham. doi:10.1007/978-3-030-35590-6_15

All India Radio (2021, March 13). *Nearly four crore water connections provided to rural households since the launch of Jal Jeevan Mission*. Retrieved March 9, 2021 from http://www.newsonair.com/News?title=Jal-Shakti-Minister-to-chair-Conference-of-Ministers-of-States%2C-UTs-on-Jal-Jeevan-Mission-today&id=411781

Ang, R. P., Chong, W. H., Chye, S., & Huan, V. S. (2012). Loneliness and generalized problematic Internet use: parents' perceived knowledge of adolescents' online activities as a moderator. *Computers in Human Behavior*, *28*(4), 1342–1347. doi:10.1016/j.chb.2012.02.019

Anker, R., & Melkas, H. (1996). *Economic incentives for children and families to eliminate or reduce child labour*. Geneva: International Labour Office.

Apostu, O. (2017). Family's role in sustaining the educational trajectory of children from socially and economically disadvantaged communities. *Revista Românească pentru Educaţie Multidimensională*, *9*(2), 93–107.

Assink, M., van der Put, C. E., Meeuwsen, M. W., de Jong, N. M., Oort, F. J., Stams, G. J. J., & Hoeve, M. (2019). Risk factors for child sexual abuse victimization: a meta-analytic review. *Psychological Bulletin*, *145*(5), 459. doi:10.1037/bul0000188

Baferani, M. H. (2015). The role of the family in the socialization of children. *Mediterranean Journal of Social Sciences*, 6(6 S6), 417–417. doi:10.5901/mjss.2015.v6n6s6p417

Bajpai, A. (2017). *Child rights in India: law, policy, and practice*. New Delhi: Oxford University Press.

Bales, R. F., & Parsons, T. (2014). *Family: socialization and interaction process*. Oxon: Routledge.

BBNL (2021). *GPs to which OFC connected & equipment installed*. Retrieved March 9, 2021 from www.bbnl.nic.in

Beckmeyer, J. J., & Russell, L. T. (2018). Family structure and family management practices: associations with positive aspects of youth well-being. *Journal of Family Issues*, *39*(7), 2131–2154. doi:10.1177/0192513X17741921

Belley, P., & Lochner, L. (2007). The changing role of family income and ability in determining educational achievement. *Journal of Human Capital*, *1*(1), 37–89.

Breman, J. (2020). The pandemic in India and its impact on footloose labour. *The Indian Journal of Labour Economics*, *63*(4), 901–919. doi:10.1007/s41027-020-00285-8

Bryce, I., Robinson, Y., & Petherick, W. (Eds.). (2019). *Child abuse and neglect: forensic issues in evidence, impact and management*. London: Academic Press.

Capaldi, R. (2019). *21st century parenting: a guide to raising emotionally resilient children in an unstable world*. Central Recovery Press.

Carroll, P., & Brown, P. (2020). The effectiveness of positive discipline parenting workshops on parental attitude and behavior. *The Journal of Individual Psychology*, *76*(3), 286–303. doi:10.1353/jip.2020.0030.

Chanani, S., Waingankar, A., Shah More, N., Pantvaidya, S., Fernandez, A., & Jayaraman, A. (2019). Effectiveness of NGO-government partnership to prevent and treat child wasting in urban India. *Maternal & Child Nutrition*, *15*, e12706. doi:10.1111/mcn.12706

Chandra, A., & Minkovitz, C. S. (2006). Stigma starts early: gender differences in teen willingness to use mental health services. *Journal of Adolescent Health*, *38*(6), 754-e1-e8. doi:10.1016/j.jadohealth.2005.08.011

Chen, Y. L., Chen, S. H., & Gau, S. F. S. (2015). ADHD and autistic traits, family function, parenting style, and social adjustment for Internet addiction among children and adolescents in Taiwan: a longitudinal study. *Research in Developmental Disabilities*, *39*, 20–31. doi:10.1016/j.ridd.2014.12.025

Cohen, R. (2016). *Migration and its enemies: global capital, migrant labour and the nation-state*. London: Routledge. doi:10.4324/9781315595313

Coontz, S. (2005). *Marriage, a history: from obedience to intimacy or how love conquered marriage*. New York: Viking.

Cretney, S. M. (2003). *Family law in the twentieth century: a history*. New York: Oxford University Press.

Curtis, T., Miller, B. C., & Berry, E. H. (2000). Changes in reports and incidence of child abuse following natural disasters. *Child Abuse & Neglect*, *24*(9), 1151–1162. doi:10.1016/S0145-2134(00)00176-9

De Lannoy, A., Leibbrandt, M., & Frame, E. (2015). A focus on youth: an opportunity to disrupt the intergenerational transmission of poverty. *South African Child Gauge*, 22–33.

Department of Food and Public Distribution. (2018). *Annual report 2017–18*. Retrieved March 9, 2021 from http://dfpd.nic.in/lwb3ahiaaqb0aguacgblageaza-bkageadabhac8auabvahiadabhagwalwbnageazwbhahoaaqbuagualwbeag8ayw-b1ag0azqbuahqalwa=1_141_1_annualreportenglish.pdf

Dewanggi, M., Hastuti, D., & Herawati, T. (2015). The influence of attachment and quality of parenting and parenting environment on children's character in rural and urban areas of Bogor. *Jurnal Ilmu Keluarga & Konsumen*, *8*(1), 20–27. doi:10.24156/jikk.2015.8.1.20

Diwan, V. (2017). Child labour: a chronic problem. *Social Science and Humanities Journal*, 250–255.

Duan, T. T., Zhang, W. J., Li, Y. H., Tang, T. Y., & Duan, X. Q. (2012). Influence of parenting style and character strength on psychology harmony. *Psychological Exploration*, *32*(2), 183–187.

ECLAC (2020). *Economic Commission for Latin America and the Caribbean: Contribution to the Secretary-General Report*. Retrieved March 9. 2021 from https://www.un.org/development/desa/family/wp-content/uploads/sites/23/2020/08/ECLAC.pdf

Emerson, P. M., & Souza, A. P. (2011). Is child labor harmful? The impact of working earlier in life on adult earnings. *Economic Development and Cultural Change*, *59*(2), 345–385.

Erikson, E. H. (1959). *Identity and the life cycle: selected papers*. New York: W.W. Norton & Company.

Erikson, E. (1963). *Childhood and society*. New York: Norton.

Escolar-Llamazares, M. C., Luis-Rico, I., de la Torre-Cruz, T., Herrero, Á., Jiménez, A., Palmero-Cámara, C., & Jiménez-Eguizábal, A. (2019). The socio-educational, psychological and family-related antecedents of entrepreneurial intentions among Spanish Youth. *Sustainability*, 11(5), 1252. doi:10.3390/su11051252

Farrukh, M., Khan, A. A., Khan, M. S., Ramzani, S. R., & Soladoye, B. S. A. (2017). Entrepreneurial intentions: the role of family factors, personality traits and self-efficacy. *World Journal of Entrepreneurship, Management and Sustainable Development*, *13*(4), 303–317. doi:10.1108/WJEMSD-03-2017-0018

Fellmeth, G., Rose-Clarke, K., Zhao, C., Busert, L. K., Zheng, Y., Massazza, A., … & Devakumar, D. (2018). Health impacts of parental migration on left-behind children and adolescents: a systematic review and meta-analysis. *The Lancet*, *392*(10164), 2567–2582. doi:10.1016/S0140-6736(18)32558-3

Gamlin, J., Camacho, A. Z., Ong, M., & Hesketh, T. (2015). Is domestic work a worst form of child labour? The findings of a six-country study of the psychosocial effects of child domestic work. *Children's Geographies*, *13*(2), 212–225. doi: 10.1080/14733285.2013.829660

Gandhi, D., Batra, N. K., & Gupta, T. (2019). Startup India: opportunities and challenges. *Invertis Journal of Management*, 11(2), 97–104.

Garai, S. (2020, January 29). Student suicides rising, 28 lives lost every day. *The Hindu*. Retrieved March 9. 2021 from https://www.thehindu.com/news/national/student-suicides-rising-28-lives-lost-every-day/article30685085.ece

Garbarino, J. (1998). Raising children in a socially toxic environment. *Family Matters*, *50*, 53–55.

Gohil, J., & Gandhi, Z. H. (2019). Pradhan Mantri Awas Yojana (PMAY) Scheme—an emerging prospect of affordable housing in India. *International Research Journal of Engineering and Technology*, *6*(12), 2546–2550.

Goldenberg, H., & Goldenberg, I. (2012). *Family therapy: an overview*. Belmont: Cengage.

Green, N. C. (2006). Everyday life in distance education: one family's home schooling experience. *Distance Education*, *27*(1), 27–44. doi:10.1080/01587910600653132

Guio, J., Choi, Á., & Escardíbul, J. O. (2018). Labor markets, academic performance and school dropout risk: evidence for Spain. *International Journal of Manpower*, *39*(2), 301–318. doi:10.1108/IJM-08-2016-0158

Gupta, S., & Sahoo, S. (2020). Pandemic and mental health of the front-line healthcare workers: a review and implications in the Indian context amidst COVID-19. *General Psychiatry*, *33*(5). doi:10.1136/gpsych-2020-100284

Guryan, J., Hurst, E., & Kearney, M. (2008). Parental education and parental time with children. *Journal of Economic Perspectives*, *22*(3), 23–46. doi:10.1257/jep.22.3.23

Habib, F. (2017). Causes of homelessness among children. *Biomedica*, *26*(2), 109–113.

Härkönen, J. (2014). Divorce: trends, patterns, causes, and consequences. In J. Treas, J. Scott, & M. Richards (Eds.). *The Wiley Blackwell companion to the sociology of families* (pp. 303–322). London and New York: Wiley-Blackwell.

Hege, E., & Demailly, D. (2018). NGO mobilisation around the SDGs. *IDDRI Study*. Retrieved March 9, 2021 from https://www.issuelab.org/resources/29778/29778.pdf

Hofstede, G. (2009). *Geert Hofstede cultural dimensions*. Retrieved March 9. 2021 from http://taylortraining.com/clients/mcc/Hofstede_Cultural_Dimension_Explained(external).pdf

Jach, H. K., Sun, L, Chin, T. C., & Waters, L. E. (2017). Strengths and subjective well-being in adolescence: strength-based parenting and the moderating effect of mindset. *Journal of Happiness Studies*, *19*, 567–586. doi:10.1007/s10902-016-9841-y

Jacobson, J. L. (2018). Women's health: The price of poverty. In M. Koblinsky, J. Timyan, & J. Gay (Eds.) *The health of women* (pp. 3–32). New York: Routledge.

Jarvis, P., & Georgeson, J. (2018). Parenting and the family in the 21st century. In *BERA-TACTYC Early Childhood Research Review 2003–2017* (pp. 30–48). London: British Educational Research Association.

Jiang, X., Huebner, E. S., & Hills, K. J. (2013). Parent attachment and early adolescents' life satisfaction: the mediating effect of hope. *Psychology in the Schools*, *50*(4), 340–352. doi:10.1002/pits.21680

Kalmijn, M., & Saraceno, C. (2008). A comparative perspective on intergenerational support: Responsiveness to parental needs in individualistic and familialistic countries. *European Societies*, *10*(3), 479–508. doi:10.1080/14616690701744364

Kaur, B. (2019, July 4). Economic Survey 2018–19: Healthcare still inaccessible in rural India. *Down to Earth*. Retrieved March 9. 2021 from https://www.downtoearth.org.in/news/health/economic-survey-2018-19-healthcare-still-inaccessible-in-rural-india-65443

Kemple, K. M., & Nissenberg, S. A. (2000). Nurturing creativity in early childhood education: families are part of it. *Early Childhood Education Journal*, *28*(1), 67–71.

Kielland, A., & Tovo, M. C. (2006). *Children at work: child labor practices in Africa*. Boulder, CO: Lynne Rienner Publishers.

Kim, H. J. (2004). Family resources and children's academic performance. *Children and Youth Services Review*, *26*(6), 529–536. doi:10.1016/j.childyouth.2004.02.008

Kim, S. (2020). *Grandparenting: Focus on Asia*. Retrieved March 9. 2021 from https://www.un.org/development/desa/family/wp-content/uploads/sites/23/2020/06/EGM2020.Grandparenting-in-Asia.SK_.pdf

Kiser, L. J., Stover, C. S., Navalta, C. P., Dorado, J., Vogel, J. M., Abdul-Adil, J. K., ... & Briggs, E. C. (2014). Effects of the child–perpetrator relationship on mental health outcomes of child abuse: it's (not) all relative. *Child Abuse & Neglect*, *38*(6), 1083–1093. doi:10.1016/j.chiabu.2014.02.017

Kõu, A., Mulder, C. H., & Bailey, A. (2017). 'For the sake of the family and future': the linked lives of highly skilled Indian migrants. *Journal of Ethnic and Migration Studies*, *43*(16), 2788–2805. doi:10.1080/1369183X.2017.1314608

Laing, K., McWhirter, J., Templeton, L., & Hannah-Russell, C. (2019). M-PACT+: supporting families affected by parental substance misuse. *Health Education*, *119*(1), 63–82. doi:10.1108/HE-08-2017-0043

Lee, J. (2006). Impact of family relationships on attitudes of the second generation in family business. *Family Business Review*, *19*(3), 175–191. doi:10.1111/j.1741-6248.2006.00069.x

Lewin-Bizan, S., Bowers, E. P., & Lerner, R. M. (2010). One good thing leads to another: cascades of positive youth development among American adolescents. *Development and Psychopathology*, *22*(4), 759–770. doi:10.1017/S0954579410000441

Lindstrom, L., Doren, B., Metheny, J., Johnson, P., & Zane, C. (2007). Transition to employment: role of the family in career development. *Exceptional Children*, *73*(3), 348–366. doi:10.1177/001440290707300305

Livingstone, S., & Byrne, J. (2018). Parenting in the digital age: the challenges of parental responsibility in comparative perspective. In G. Mascheroni, C. Ponte, & A. Jorge (Eds.) *Digital parenting: the challenges for families in the digital age, yearbook 2018* (pp. 19–30), Gothenburg: Nordicom, University of Gothenburg.

Lokot, M., Bhatia, A., Kenny, L., & Cislaghi, B. (2020). Corporal punishment, discipline and social norms: a systematic review in low-and middle-income countries. *Aggression and Violent Behavior*, *55*, 101507. doi:10.1016/j.avb.2020.101507

Lustick, H. (2017). Making discipline relevant: toward a theory of culturally responsive positive school-wide discipline. *Race Ethnicity and Education*, *20*(5), 681–695. doi:10.1080/13613324.2016.1150828

Maiti, T., Singh, S., Innamuri, R., & Hasija, A. D. (2020). Marital distress during COVID-19 pandemic and lockdown: a brief narrative. *International Journal of Indian Psychology*, *8*(2), 426–433. doi:10.25215/0802.257

Malathesh, B. C., Das, S., & Chatterjee, S. S. (2020). COVID-19 and domestic violence against women. *Asian Journal of Psychiatry*, *53*, 102227. doi:10.1016/j.ajp.2020.102227

Malhotra, A. (2018, September 5). Devastated and destroyed: delhi slums struggle to recover from frequent fires. *The Guardian*. Retrieved March 9, 2021 from https://www.theguardian.com/cities/2018/sep/05/devastated-destroyed-delhi-slums-recover-fires

Manczak, E. M., Skerrett, K. A., Gabriel, L. B., Ryan, K. A., & Langenecker, S. A. (2018). Family support: A possible buffer against disruptive events for individuals with and without remitted depression. *Journal of Family Psychology*, *32*(7), 926–935. doi:10.1037/fam0000451

Martin, S. L., Moracco, K. E., Garro, J., Tsui, A. O., Kupper, L. L., Chase, J. L., & Campbell, J. C. (2002). Domestic violence across generations: findings from northern India. *International Journal of Epidemiology*, *31*(3), 560–572. doi:10.1093/ije/31.3.560

Masilo, D. T. (2018). Prevention of child sexual abuse within the family system: guidelines for an educational social group work program. *Journal of Child Sexual Abuse*, *27*(4), 335–346. doi:10.1080/10538712.2018.1430089

Massand, A., Lodi, M. K., & Ambreen, L. (2020). Atmanirbhar Bharat: economic, legal, and social aspects. *International Journal of Management (IJM)*, *11*(6), 1038–1046. doi:10.34218/IJM.11.6.2020.092

McHale, S. M., Crouter, A. C., & Whiteman, S. D. (2003). The family contexts of gender development in childhood and adolescence. *Social Development*, *12*(1), 125–148. doi:10.1111/1467-9507.00225

Ministry of Health and Family Welfare (2017). *National Family Health Survey – 4: 2015 – 2016*. International Institute of Population Sciences. Retrieved March 9. 2021 from http://rchiips.org/NFHS/NFHS-4Reports/India.pdf

Ministry of Housing and Urban Affairs (2019). *Handbook of Urban Statistics 2019*. Retrieved March 9. 2021 from http://mohua.gov.in/pdf/5c80e2225a124Handbook%20of%20Urban%20Statistics%202019.pdf

Ministry of Law and Justice (2016). *The Child Labour (Prohibition and Regulation) Amendment Act, 2016*. Retrieved March 9. 2021 from https://pencil.gov.in/THE%20CHILD%20LABOUR%20(PROHIBITION%20AND%20REGULATION)%20AMENDMENT%20ACT,%202016(1).pdf

Ministry of Woman and Child Development (2018, July 30). *INTEGRATED CHILD DEVELOPMENT SERVICES (ICDS) SCHEME. 13.63 lakh Anganwadi Centres (AWCs) of the 14 lakh AWCs sanctioned across the country are operational as on 01.06.2018*. Press Information Bureau, Government of India. Retrieved March 9. 2021 from https://pib.gov.in/newsite/PrintRelease.aspx?relid=181218

Mokomane, Z. (2013). Social protection as a mechanism for family protection in sub-Saharan Africa. *International Journal of Social Welfare*, *22*(3), 248–259. doi:10.1111/j.1468-2397.2012.00893.x

Monaghan, D. (2017). Does college enrollment and bachelor's completion by mothers impact children's educational outcomes? *Sociology of Education*, *90*(1), 3–24. doi:10.1177/0038040716681054

Morgan, H. (2020). Best practices for implementing remote learning during a pandemic. *The Clearing House: A Journal of Educational Strategies, Issues and Ideas*, *93*(3), 135–141. doi:10.1080/00098655.2020.1751480

Mullaiti, L. (1995). Families in India: beliefs and realities. *Journal of Comparative Family Studies*, *26*(1), 11–25. doi:10.3138/jcfs.26.1.11

Münger, A. C., & Markström, A. M. (2019). School and child protection services professionals' views on the school's mission and responsibilities for children living with domestic violence–tensions and gaps. *Journal of Family Violence*, *34*(5), 385–398. doi:10.1007/s10896-019-00035-5

Munshi, K. (2019). Caste and the Indian economy. *Journal of Economic Literature*, *57*(4), 781–834. doi:10.1257/jel.20171307

Muthukumar, S. (2020, March 6). *How much money can a child make and still be claimed as a dependent?* Retrieved March 9. 2021 from https://vakilsearch.com/advice/how-much-money-can-a-child-make-and-still-be-claimed-as-a-dependent/

NDCP (2018). *National Digital Communications Policy 2018*. Retrieved March 9. 2021 from https://dot.gov.in/sites/default/files/EnglishPolicy-NDCP.pdf

Nelsen, J. (2011). *Positive discipline: the classic guide to helping children develop self-discipline, responsibility, cooperation, and problem-solving skills*. New York: Ballantine Books.

Nelsen, J., Bill, K., & Marchese, J. (2018). *Positive Discipline for today's busy (and overwhelmed) parent: how to balance work, parenting, and self for lasting well-being*. New York: Harmony Books.

Neppl, T. K., Jeon, S., Diggs, O., & Donnellan, M. B. (2020). Positive parenting, effortful control, and developmental outcomes across early childhood. *Developmental Psychology*, *56*(3), 444–457. doi:10.1037/dev0000874

Orth, U. (2018). The family environment in early childhood has a long-term effect on self-esteem: a longitudinal study from birth to age 27 years. *Journal of Personality and Social Psychology*, *114*(4), 637–655. doi:10.1037/pspp0000143

Ozer, E. J., Lavi, I., Douglas, L., & Wolf, J. P. (2017). Protective factors for youth exposed to violence in their communities: a review of family, school, and community moderators. *Journal of Clinical Child & Adolescent Psychology*, *46*(3), 353–378. doi:10.1080/15374416.2015.1046178

Panda, S. S., & Mishra, N. R. (2018). Factors affecting temporary labour migration for seasonal work: a review. *Management Research Review*, *41*(10), 1176–1200. doi:10.1108/MRR-04-2017-0104

Petersson, K., Petersson, C., & Håkansson, A. (2004). What is good parental education? *Scandinavian Journal of Caring Sciences*, *18*(1), 82–89. doi:10.1111/j.1471-6712.2004.00260.x

Piarnau, I. S. (2020). *Positive parenting: concept and applications*. Retrieved March 9. 2021 from www.un.org/development/desa/family/2020/06/09/impact-of-covid19/ignaciosociaspositiveparenting/.

PIB (2019, January 17). *Ministry of Women & Child Development-Year End Review 2018*. Press Information Bureau, Government of India. Retrieved March 9. 2021 from https://pib.gov.in/newsite/PrintRelease.aspx?relid=187560

Pilapil, M., Coletti, D. J., Rabey, C., & DeLaet, D. (2017). Caring for the caregiver: supporting families of youth with special health care needs. *Current Problems in Pediatric and Adolescent Health Care*, 47(8), 190–199. doi:10.1016/j.cppeds.2017.07.003

Plakun, E. M. (2017). *Ideas and identities: the life and work of Erik Erikson*. Madison: International Universities Press.

Polo, A. J., Zychinski, K. E., & Roundfield, K. E. (2012). The parental schoolwork support measure–youth: Development and psychometric evaluation. *Cultural Diversity and Ethnic Minority Psychology, 18*(3), 297–306. doi:10.1037/a0028729

Posel, D. R., Rudwick, S., & Casale, D. (2011). Is marriage a dying institution in South Africa? Exploring changes in marriage in the context of illobolo payments. *Agenda: Empowering Women for Gender Equality*, *25*(1), 102–111. doi:10.1080/10130950.2011.575589

POSHAN Abhiyaan – PM's Overarching Scheme for Holistic Nourishment (2018, October 22). Retrieved March 9. 2021 from https://www.india.gov.in/spotlight/poshan-abhiyaan-pms-overarching-scheme-holistic-nourishment

PTI (2021, March 31). Domestic LPG to be cheaper by Rs 10 per cylinder from April 1. *Business Standard*. Retrieved March 9. 2021 from https://www.business-standard.com/article/economy-policy/domestic-lpg-to-be-cheaper-by-rs-10-per-cylinder-from-april-1-121033101117_1.html#.

PWC & Save the Children (2015). *Forgotten Voices: The World of Urban Children in India*. Retrieved March 9. 2021 from https://www.pwc.in/assets/pdfs/publications/urban-child/urban-child-india-report.pdf

Rajan, S. I., & Balagopal, G. (2017). Caring India: an introduction. In S. Irudaya Rajan & G. Balagopal (Eds.) *Elderly Care in India* (pp. 1–36). Singapore: Springer. doi:10.1007/978-981-10-3439-8_1

Ray, U.K. (2019, April 16). Child marriage rampant in West Bengal's Malda, but parties believe addressing social evil would be political suicide. *Firstpost*. Retrieved March 9. 2021 from https://www.firstpost.com/india/child-marriage-rampant-in-west-bengals-malda-district-but-parties-believe-addressing-social-evil-would-be-political-suicide-6457521.html

Reddy, A. N., & Sinha, S. (2010). *School Dropouts or Pushouts? Overcoming Barriers for the Right to Education. CREATE Pathways to Access. Research Monograph No. 40*. Retrieved March 9. 2021 from https://eric.ed.gov/?id=ED512268

Rehel, E. M. (2014). When dad stays home too: Paternity leave, gender, and parenting. *Gender & Society*, *28*(1), 110–132. doi:10.1177/0891243213503900

Report of the United Nations Secretary-General (2010). *United Nations General Assembly Economic and Social Council*. Retrieved March 9, 2021 from https://unctad.org/system/files/official-document/a66d64_en.pdf

Rhodes, V. J. (1990). *Child labor in India: Some historical aspects*. Retrieved March 9, 2021 from https://archives.columbusstate.edu/gah/1990/101-107.pdf

Richardson, D., Dugarova, E., Higgins, D., Hirao, K., Karamperidou, D., Mokomane, Z., & Robila, M. (2020). *Families, family policy and the Sustainable Development*

Goals (No. inorer1092). Retrieved March 9, 2021 from https://www.unicef-irc.org/publications/pdf/Families%20family%20policy%20and%20the%20SDGs.pdf

Roy, P.K. (2019, March 18). Mobile data: why India has the world's cheapest. *BBC*. Retrieved March 9, 2021 from https://www.bbc.com/news/world-asia-india-47537201

Roy, A. K., Singh, P., & Roy, U. N. (2015). Impact of rural-urban labour migration on education of children: a case study of left behind and accompanied migrant children in India. *Space and Culture, India*, 2(4), 17–34. doi:10.20896/saci.v2i4.74

Rusby, J. C., Light, J. M., Crowley, R., & Westling, E. (2018). Influence of parent–youth relationship, parental monitoring, and parent substance use on adolescent substance use onset. *Journal of Family Psychology*, *32*(3), 310–320. doi:10.1037/fam0000350

Sadruddin, A. F., Ponguta, L. A., Zonderman, A. L., Wiley, K. S., Grimshaw, A., & Panter-Brick, C. (2019). How do grandparents influence child health and development? A systematic review. *Social Science & Medicine*, 239, 112476. doi:10.1016/j.socscimed.2019.112476

Sahithya, B. R., Manohari, S. M., & Vijaya, R. (2019). Parenting styles and its impact on children–a cross cultural review with a focus on India. *Mental Health, Religion & Culture*, 22(4), 357–383. doi:10.1080/13674676.2019.1594178

Sahoo, S., Rani, S., Parveen, S., Singh, A. P., Mehra, A., Chakrabarti, S., … & Tandup, C. (2020). Self-harm and COVID-19 Pandemic: an emerging concern–A report of 2 cases from India. *Asian Journal of Psychiatry*, *51*, 102104. doi:10.1016/j.ajp.2020.102104

Sambuli, N. & Magnoli, S. (2019, April 29). What is digital equality? An interview with Nanjira Sambuli. *World Economic Forum*. Retrieved March 9, 2021 from https://www.weforum.org/agenda/2019/04/digital-equality-interview-nanjira-sambuli/

Save the Children (2016). *Every last girl: Free to live, free to learn, free from harm*. Retrieved March 9, 2021 from https://www.savethechildren.org.uk/content/dam/global/reports/advocacy/every-last-girl.pdf

Save the Children (2019). *Global Childhood Report 2019*. Retrieved March 9, 2021 from https://reliefweb.int/sites/reliefweb.int/files/resources/global-childhood-report-2019-pdf%20%281%29.pdf

Schwartz, S. (2018). *Homeward bound: return migration and local conflict after civil war*. Columbia Academic Commons. Retrieved March 9, 2021 from https://academiccommons.columbia.edu/doi/10.7916/D8ZK706X

Scott, A. F. (2021). Economic development and self-determination. *Studies in Humanities and Social Sciences*, *25*(2), 51–70p.

Seth, R., & Srivastava, R. N. (2017). Child sexual abuse: management and prevention, and protection of children from Sexual Offences (POCSO) Act. *Indian Pediatrics*, *54*(11), 949–953. doi:10.1007/s13312-017-1189-9

Sheppard, A. (2009). Research Section: school attendance and attainment: poor attenders' perceptions of schoolwork and parental involvement in their education. *British Journal of Special Education*, *36*(2), 104–111. doi:10.1111/j.1467-8578.2009.00413.x

Singh, K. (2008). Child custody cases in the context of international migration. In R. Palriwala & P. Uberoi (Eds.) *Marriage, migration and gender*, New Delhi: Sage Publications India Ltd.

Singh, S. K., & Parihar, A. (2016). *Child labour in India: a study of Saharsa district of Bihar. Advances in Economics and Business Management (AEBM)*, 2(11), 1121–1123.

Smock, P. J., & Schwartz, C. R. (2020). The demography of families: a review of patterns and change. *Journal of Marriage and Family*, *82*(1), 9–34. doi:10.1111/jomf.12612

Sondhi, R. (2017). Parenting adolescents in India: a cultural perspective. In M. H. Maurer (Ed) *Child and adolescent mental health* (pp. 91–108). Rijeka: InTech.

Spencer, N. (2018). *Poverty and child health*. London: CRC Press.

Swain, S. S., & Mishra, P. (2020). Determinants of adoption of cleaner cooking energy: experience of the Pradhan Mantri Ujjwala Yojana in rural Odisha, India. *Journal of Cleaner Production*, *248*, 119223. doi:10.1016/j.jclepro.2019.119223

Taquette, S. R., & Monteiro, D. L. M. (2019). Causes and consequences of adolescent dating violence: a systematic review. *Journal of Injury and Violence Research*, *11*(2), 137. doi:10.5249/jivr.v11i2.1061

Trask, B. (2009). *Globalization and families: accelerated systemic social change*. London: Springer Science & Business Media.

Tripathi, D. (2019, July 25). Government's thrust on healthcare pays off in rural India. *Livemint*. Retrieved March 9, 2021 from https://www.livemint.com/politics/policy/government-s-thrust-on-healthcare-pays-off-in-rural-india-1563992840042.html

Turagabeci, A. R., Nakamura, K., Kizuki, M., & Takano, T. (2007). Family structure and health, how companionship acts as a buffer against ill health. *Health and Quality of Life Outcomes*, *5*(1), 1–9. doi:10.1186/1477-7525-5-61

Turner, E. A., Jensen-Doss, A., & Heffer, R. W. (2015). Ethnicity as a moderator of how parents' attitudes and perceived stigma influence intentions to seek child mental health services. *Cultural Diversity and Ethnic Minority Psychology*, *21*(4), 613–618. doi:10.1037/cdp0000047

UN News (2020). *Best Countries for Raising Kids*. Retrieved March 9, 2021 from https://www.usnews.com/news/best-countries/best-raising-children

UN Women (2020). *Progress of the World's Women 2019–2020: Families in A Changing World*. Retrieved March 9, 2021 from https://www.unwomen.org/-/media/headquarters/attachments/sections/library/publications/2019/progress-of-the-worlds-women-2019-2020-en.pdf?la=en&vs=3512

UNDESA (2019). *International Migration 2019*. Retrieved March 9, 2021 from https://www.un.org/en/development/desa/population/migration/publications/migrationreport/docs/InternationalMigration2019_Report.pdf

UNDESA (2020, March 27). *Special issue on COVID-19 and Youth*. Retrieved March 9, 2021 from https://www.un.org/development/desa/dspd/wp-content/uploads/sites/22/2020/04/YOUTH-FLASH-Special-issue-on-COVID-19-1.pdf

UNDP (2019). *Sustainable development goals: Background on the goals*. United Nations Development Program. Retrieved March 9, 2021 from https://www.undp.org/content/undp/en/home/sustainable-development-goals/background.html

UNGAESC (2020, November 23). *Implementation of the objectives of the International Year of the Family and its follow-up processes: Report of the Secretary-General*. United Nations General Assembly Economic and Social Council. Retrieved March 9, 2021 from https://www.un.org/development/desa/family/publications/un-reports-and-resolutions.html

UN-Habitat (2014). *A practical guide to designing, planning, and executing city-wide slum upgrading programs*. Retrieved March 9, 2021 from https://unhabitat.org/wp-content/uploads/2015/A%20Practical%20Guide%20low%20res.pdf

UNICEF (2012). *The State of the World's Children 2012: Children in an Urban World*. United Nations Children's Fund. Retrieved March 9, 2021 from https://www.unicef.org/publications/files/SOWC_2012-Main_Report_EN_13Mar2012.pdf

UNICEF. (2020). *How many children and young people have internet access at home?: estimating digital connectivity during the COVID-19 pandemic*. UNICEF. Retrieved March 9, 2021 from http://202.1.196.69/jspui/bitstream/123456789/8093/1/How%20many%20children%20and%20young%20people%20have%20internet%20access%20at%20home%3F%20%3A%20estimating%20digital%20connectivity%20during%20the%20COVID-19%20pandemic.pdf

United Nations Children's Fund (2019). *Ending Child marriage: a profile of child marriage in India*. New York: UNICEF.

UNO (1989). *Convention on the Rights of the Child*. United Nations Organization Retrieved March 9, 2021 from https://www.ohchr.org/en/professionalinterest/pages/crc.aspx

Van Hook, M. P. (2019). *Social work practice with families: a resiliency-based approach*. New York: Oxford University Press.

Vogel, P. (2019). Millennials and digital natives. In *Generation jobless?* (pp. 45–56). London: Palgrave Macmillan. doi:10.1057/9781137375940_2

Walsh, F. (2003). Family resilience: a framework for clinical practice. *Family Process*, 42(1), 1–18. doi:10.1111/j.1545-5300.2003.00001.x

Walsh, F. (2016). Family resilience: a developmental systems framework. *European Journal of Developmental Psychology*, *13*(3), 313–324. doi:10.1080/17405629.2016.1154035

Wanchuk, R.N. (2019, May 23). Their future was a brick kiln, but top cop and NGO ensure 800 kids bag a new destiny. *The Better India*. Retrieved March 9, 2021 from https://www.thebetterindia.com/183256/ips-hero-education-telangana-mahesh-bhagwat-odisha-migrant-children/

WHO (2003). Sexual violence: prevalence, dynamics and consequences. *Guidelines for medico-legal care for victims of sexual violence*. World Health Organization. Retrieved March 9, 2021 from https://www.who.int/violence_injury_prevention/resources/publications/en/guidelines_chap2.pdf

Wilson, S., Hean, S., Abebe, T., & Heaslip, V. (2020). Children's experiences with Child Protection Services: a synthesis of qualitative evidence. *Children and Youth Services Review*, *113*, 104974. doi:10.1016/j.childyouth.2020.104974

Winstok, Z. (2015). Effects of childhood experience of violence between parents and/or parent-to-child violence on young Israeli adults' global self-esteem. *Violence and Victims*, *30*(4), 699–713. 10.1891/0886-6708.VV-D-13-00126

Ye, Z., Wen, M., Wang, W., & Lin, D. (2020). Subjective family socio-economic status, school social capital, and positive youth development among young adolescents in China: a multiple mediation model. *International Journal of Psychology*, *55*(2), 173–181. doi:10.1002/ijop.12583

Yeung, W. J. J., Desai, S., & Jones, G. W. (2018). Families in southeast and South Asia. *Annual Review of Sociology*, *44*, 469–495. doi:10.1146/annurev-soc-073117-041124

Yu, L., & Shek, D. T. (2013). Internet addiction in Hong Kong adolescents: a three-year longitudinal study. *Journal of Pediatric & Adolescent Gynecology*, 26(3 Suppl), S10–S17. doi:10.1016/j.jpag.2013.03.010

Zepeda, M., Varela, F., & Morales, A. (2004). Promoting Positive Parenting Practices through Parenting Education. Retrieved March 9, 2021 from https://eric.ed.gov/?id=ED496882

Zolkoski, S. M., & Bullock, L. M. (2012). Resilience in children and youth: a review. *Children and Youth Services Review*, *34*(12), 2295–2303. doi:10.1016/j.childyouth.2012.08.009

4 Role of teachers and other important influencers in youth development

During the formative years of development, every child needs care and guidance. The mother is considered to be the most important care provider for healthy mental and psychical growth of a child. A child gets basic lessons on socialization processes from the mother, followed by father, siblings, and other family members. The role of family for quality child upbringing is immense. Thereafter, a child gets admitted in the pre-school, which helps in social adjustment with other children and develops a habit of attending school. Once a child goes to primary school, he/she does not face much problem in adjusting with the school environment as he/she is already oriented with the similar system at the pre-primary level.

Role of teachers in the youth development

In the school, the role of teachers is very important in disciplining a child, to shape their behaviour, to improve their adjustment capacity, to develop a positive outlook about life, and to develop good habits in terms of attending classes on time with proper uniform and doing the homework and attending classes obediently and finally producing a responsible and skilled manpower who can play an active role in social and economic development of the country. A teacher not only teaches the students in the class, but also he/she acts as a friend and philosopher and supports the students as and when required and even outside the classroom. Therefore, the bond between a teacher and a student is very crucial for creating a non-threatening psychological environment in an academic institution for effective learning. A non-threatening school environment encourages the children to attend school on a regular basis and they find learning joyful. Bundick and Tirri (2014) carried out a cross-cultural study covering students from the United States and Finland to understand student perceptions of the role of teachers in fostering youth development in the mid and late adolescent years. Results of the study supported the role of teachers in fostering youth development positively.

Some students are engaged in risk behaviour under the peer group influence or many other reasons. Teachers' positive relationships with the

DOI: 10.4324/9781003170587-4

students help them to come out of the problem. In this regard, a longitudinal study by Sanders, Munford, and Liebenberg (2016), revealed that:

> positive relationships with teaching staff were inversely related to student risks, they enhanced resilience and positive outcomes for both groups. At-risk students reported better outcomes when teachers took account of the impact that risks had on student performance and when teachers worked respectfully with them and provided opportunities to exercise personal agency. The results suggest that schools constitute an important protective asset for at-risk students.

A teacher with a good academic background, effective methods of teaching with updated knowledge and good communication skills, and a pleasing personality becomes popular among the students. As a result, students become interested in the subject and never miss any class of the same teacher. Regarding this issue, Armstrong and Hope (2016) conducted a cross-sectional study to examine the relationship between teacher communication and student motivation in completing specific technical college courses. Findings disclosed that "student motivation was correlated with challenging, encouragement and praise, nonverbal support, understanding and friendly teacher communication".

Punctuality of a teacher is also important to bring seriousness to the teaching and learning process. If a teacher is punctual, every student will be attending the class on time and this habit will help the student succeed in the future. The following case study is a bright example of the dedication of a knowledgeable teacher who guided a large number of youths of the country, with his individual capacity, for preparing them for the all-India level entrance examination for admission in the Indian Institute of Technology (IIT). Anand Kumar's passion for teaching and helping underprivileged youth is a source of inspiration for a large number of youths across the society.

Case Study 1

Anand Kumar, aged 48 years, living in Bihar, runs a private non-profit coaching centre to guide youth for IIT entrance examination. The name of the centre is Super-30. He is a mathematics teacher. Every year, he takes 30 underprivileged youths and prepare them for the IIT entrance examination with personal care. He develop a passion for teaching. Most of the students are able to qualify the IIT entrance examination under his guidance and become a successful professional. Now, most of his students are highly established and work across the world. In 2018, 422 of 510 students succeeded in getting admission to the IITs. The Discovery Channel presented his work in the form of a documentary. He has received several national and international awards in recognition of his significant contribution for youth development.

A teacher should be available outside the classroom for clarifications of any query and they should also give a space to the students to share their personal problems. In turn, it helps strengthen the teacher–student relationship and facilitates better outcomes in terms of the teaching–learning process. Wang, Brinkworth, and Eccles (2013) reported that

> positive teacher–student relationships protected adolescents against depression and misconduct throughout ages 13–18. In addition, positive teacher–student relationships moderated the negative influences of adolescents' early poor effortful control and conflictive parents–adolescent relationships on misconduct and helped such at-risk adolescents to attain less behaviourally delinquent developmental trajectories over time.

Mental support from teachers at times of crisis helps students to regain self-confidence to overcome the crisis. Guidance from teachers for the future career of the students helps a large number of students to reach their goals in life. Encouragement of the students towards good performance and/or improvement at some level of performance are highly motivating for the students. There are several examples of the high impact of positive words of a teacher towards the students. Positive words from a teacher can transform a less motivated student to a highly motivated one, which is called extrinsic motivation. The following case study is one such bright example of the positive impact of a teacher's friendly gesture towards a student.

Case Study 2

F, aged 45 years, is an English teacher of a government higher secondary school in Chennai. She is a very simple and open-minded teacher with a pleasing personality. She goes to class on time and teaches the subject in an interesting manner, which generates interest among the students. She always enters the class with a smiling face despite her work pressure. Students are fond of her and they have access to her for discussion about any personal issues and problems. She always encourages students for better performance and in fact, most of the students in English get high marks. Most of the students are in touch with her even after passing out of the school.

There are teachers with short temperament. They never exchange smiles with the students and always underestimate and demean them. These types of teachers neither encourage students to come out with their queries nor allow them to ask questions for clarifications. As a result, students prefer not to open their mouth in the class and they lose interest in the same subject. So, the personality of a teacher and their capacity for effective teaching matters a lot while teaching. This issue requires the attention of the academic administration while recruiting a teacher and also during the service period for mental health intervention needs. Based on the findings of a study, Bastian, McCord, Marks, and Carpenter (2017) suggested that "administrators of schools should consider using personality trait measures, along with other valid indicators, as a way to improve teacher hiring decisions". A latest study by Harding et al. (2019) reported that:

> better teacher wellbeing was associated with better student well-being and lower student psychological distress Teacher presenteeism and the quality of the teacher-student relationship appeared to be on the pathway of these relationships. Higher levels of teacher depressive symptoms were associated with poorer student wellbeing and psychological distress.

Teachers are always perceived to be a motivating force for the youth, to aid in their career growth and development. Most of the teachers are really committed to quality teaching and guiding the students/youth for studies.

Sometimes students' challenging behaviour, viz., inattention, internalizing, and externalizing disruptive and aggressive behaviours, is responsible for strained relationships with their teachers, bringing punishment for the students. In addition, students' greater dissatisfaction with the school environment, poor teaching methods, and lack of engagement of teachers in the classroom further deteriorates teacher–student relationships. This issue requires the attention of school counsellors and/or psychologists for support services. Parents should be involved in the process to resolve the issue with their support.

Unfortunately, there are some teachers in most of the educational institutes who use students as a weapon to organize strikes, highlighting silly issues in the name of students' welfare and thus disturbing the normal functioning of an institute. They mostly indulge in these types of negative activities to divert the attention of the authorities so that their incapability in terms of academic engagement and research-based output is not exposed. Therefore, students and youths should be able to judge between guidance and misguidance and behave accordingly in the academic institutes.

Role of community leaders in mobilizing youth for community development activities

For any community development-related activity, leadership is required, who will come out with a formal structure and engage different allied organizations, local people, and youth for their contribution towards sustainable development. A community leader should develop a shared vision and carry out a need assessment and develop a strategic plan for initiating community development activities. Fund-raising process is to be initiated for meeting the expenses. Educating and/or sensitizing the local community about the issues and challenges with the help of local youth, by taking their suggestions and engaging them in the process of development activities will result in positive outcomes. In the end, there is a need to carry out the process and evaluate the outcomes and the community mobilization efforts.

Community leaders are those who engage in various community development activities for the benefit of the common people and help people in terms of giving advice and/or suggestions as and when they are approached. They support people at times of crisis and make a difference in the locality. They are highly respected and people listen to their voices and respond positively. In every community, there are people, irrespective of age, gender, and socio-economic background, who are directly or indirectly considered as community leaders for their contributions. Their activities inspire common people and youth. In many places, community members and youths join for sustainability of welfare activities. Let us look at the activities of some of those people and the influence of their activities.

Welfare of slum children

The total number of slums in India is beyond the exact estimation. Maharashtra has the maximum number of slums in India and the biggest slums of Asia are located there. Life in slums is totally different from other developed areas. Basic facilities such as electricity, safe drinking water, proper road, sanitation facilities, playground, and so on are hardly available, like urban developed areas. People from different cultural backgrounds live in the slums and the overall social and psychological environment is not conducive for a healthy growth and development of children and youth. People living here survive doing odd jobs and/or casual work and some of them are involved in anti-social activities. As a result, children brought up in such areas follow the profession of elderly people and some get engaged in anti-social activities unconsciously under the influence of peer group members. There are different organizations and individuals working there for the welfare of children. The following case study is highly inspiring for the larger society where an individual's dedication motivated the youth of the same locality for community development activities.

Case Study 3

G, aged 54 years and a graduate, is married with two girl children and has been living with his family in a slum area opposite to Salt Lake, Kolkata for the last 10 years. Prior to shifting to a slum area,

G was working in a private company and living with his family in a developed area. G came from a well-off family and from childhood, he had interests in social welfare activities, especially providing educational care and guidance to disadvantaged children. Along with his normal day-to-day activities, he was giving voluntary services to the children of the same slum for about 10 years. Afterwards, he felt like moving to the slum to deliver better services to the children of the same community and their family. Most of the people in the same slum are engaged in sewage cleaning jobs and the majority of the male members are alcoholics. For a positive growth, education, and career development of children and the youth of the same locality, G preferred to shift in the same slum so that he could spend more time with the elderly people to change their lifestyles and the children could enjoy congenial and violence-free home environments. His wife also joined him in educating the women of the locality about health and hygiene, sensitizing them about the value of education and the need for savings. Activities of G helped children to get admission in the neighbouring schools, continue their education with his guidance, staying away from anti-social activities and changing the lifestyles of elderly people as well as mobilizing the youth of the locality for community development activities and creating a healthy psychological environment, in addition to ensuring cleanliness of the slum.

Welfare of CSWs

Commercial sex workers (CSWs) across the society experience discrimination, oppression and are denied of their rights to a great extent. They hardly get recognition in any platform of the society. Limited organizations are working for their welfare across the society. However, there are examples of individual contribution to protect the CSWs from atrocities, exploitation, and threat. For example,

Case Study 4

H, aged 45 years and graduate, has been living in a Red Light Area of Kolkata for the last 20 years. He is a government employee and is also involved in politics. He has a special concern for the welfare of commercial sex workers (CSWs) and their children. From time to time, he organizes sensitization programmes on health and hygiene and the need of using condoms by the CSWs while entertaining the clients. His presence in the locality safeguarded the CSWs from the pimps and anti-socials. Utilizing his political contacts, he arranged to bring some projects for welfare of the children of CSWs and for organizing health camps for CSWs, as they are vulnerable to various health problems. He could attract the local youth to join him for the welfare of CSWs and their children. Some of the local youths are engaged in providing guidance to children for studies in the evening when their mothers remain busy entertaining the clients.

Cleaning of the environment

Environmental hazard has become a global challenge. Safe and clean environment makes a big difference in the lives of people. People remain less vulnerable to various health problems and psychologically feel happy. Their irresponsible behaviour causes environmental problems. Every individual's contribution and responsible behaviour can make the environment neat and clean. The government of India's Swach Bharat Abhiyaan made a significant difference for the cleanliness of the environment. However, cleanliness drives should be strengthened by involving the people of all sections of the society and youths from educational institutions should play an active role in this regard. Cleanliness drives are not one-time activities; it should be regularized to ensure complete and sustainable cleanliness of every locality. Individual initiatives by the youth have also made a great difference in some localities.

Providing food, medicine, and clothes to disadvantaged children

Sadly, about one-fifth of the people of India live below the poverty line. They cannot afford medical expenses and a good number of them do not have proper clothes. The postgraduate students from the social work departments of universities carry out field visits to different backward or underdeveloped areas for having first-hand experience of the struggle of the poor people. Inspired by first-hand experience, one student, after completion of the Master Degree, decided to deliver free medicine, food, and old clothes to the people of backward villages of South 24 Parganas of West Bengal. He and some of his friends collected medicines from the medical representatives, biscuits from the bakeries, and old clothes from urban apartments. His work drew the attention of the local youth and they also assisted him in delivering his services to the poor. For example,

Case Study 5

I, aged 35 years, post-graduate in social work from Kolkata, is working in a non-government organization for 10 years. He developed a special interest in serving the underprivileged children and their family as he was exposed to the sufferings of underprivileged people while working in a NGO. Every Sunday, he visits different villages in South 24 Parganas of West Bengal and distributes free medicines, old clothes, and food to the children of poor families. He is assisted by one of his friends, who is a doctor. Medicines and old clothes are collected from different sources. He collects biscuits, free of cost from different bakeries. He mobilizes the youth of different villages to help him deliver the services. Local youths are also active in helping him for such a good cause.

Medical care

Medical care is a distant dream for many in the rural areas. Visiting a qualified doctor is a luxury for most rural people. Although Primary Health Care Centres are available in the rural areas, services are not good and encouraging. Every year, a good number of people from the lower social strata die without proper medical care. An individual initiative has shown the larger society that if one wishes one can make a difference with his/her dedication.

Case Study 6

Subasini Mistry, a vegetable seller, established Humanity Hospital in Hanspukur village, West Bengal on March 9, 1996 with small support from different local people and with her little savings for offering free medical services to the poor. Her husband – a vegetable seller – died on April 13, 1971 from preventable health problems because of poverty which motivated Subasini Mistry to establish a hospital. She struggled a lot after the death of her husband in bringing up her four children, two sons and two daughters. Elder son works in the agricultural field while the younger one has become a doctor and is helping the mother to run the hospital. A good number of people visit the same hospital everyday with different health problems. Now it is one of the better medical institutes outside Kolkata, catering the needs of medical care for poor people. In recognition of her contribution to the society, she was awarded Padma Shri in 2018 – India's fourth-highest civilian award. She is an example before the youth of the county that education and poverty cannot be a barrier for doing something extraordinary for the benefit of the larger society. It requires will and determination. (Source: https://humanityhospital.org/)

Role of spiritual leaders in youth development

It is difficult to define spirituality in a single sentence. In simple terms,

> spirituality is a worldview and a way of life based on the belief that there is more to life than what meets the senses, more to the universe than just purposeless mechanics, more to consciousness than electrical impulses in the brain, and more to our existence than the body and its needs.
>
> (Source: https://liveanddare.com/what-is-spirituality)

Some of the examples of spiritual behaviour are volunteerism, optimism, contributing to society, connectedness with others, feeling of belonging/being part of a group, and love of self/reason to care for self. Recent studies have found that spirituality may serve as a psychological and social resource for coping with stress (Koenig, 2010).

The role of spiritual leaders in inculcating values among the youth and engaging them in positive community-based activities, like other categories of leaders, is immense. The lifestyles and vision about life related to various spiritual models of spiritual leaders are inspiring and motivating. For example, Gautam Buddha's thoughts and vision about life had inspired thousands of youths across the society. The ethical ideologies of the Buddhist Philosophy include (i) *Sila* – which encompass virtues, good conduct and morality; (ii) *Samadhi* – which includes concentration, meditation, and mental development, which strengthens and controls the human mind, besides helping individuals to maintain good conduct; and finally, (iii) *Prajna* – which embraces discernment, insight, wisdom, and enlightenment, which are imperative to maintain a pure and a calm mind.

The Buddhist traditions teach youth not to harm others (like *ahimsa*), desiring for a contented life, leading a decent life, abstaining from being unkind to others, and refraining from abusive practices. These will not only cultivate morality in youth but will also infuse a sense of conviction to lead a purposeful and meaningful life. The youth must be responsibly mindful of their thoughts, feelings, and actions, which will have future consequences (similar to *karma*) and will convert as the determining influences in the cycle of rebirth (*samsara*).

The modern age is being described as an increasingly "secular age" (Tacey, 2016), where the importance of religion and spirituality is diminishing when it comes to laws, policymaking, and societal values – at least in the non-theocratic countries of the world. This has led to diminishing attention on the influences of spirituality and spiritual leaders on youth development. The youth is perceived to be rebellious and attracted to rationality. Hence, their interest in traditional religious and spiritual beliefs and values is perceived to be low (Cusack, 2011). Despite the increased popularity of the secular spirit, research shows surprising trends when it comes to spiritual influence on the youth. Benson and Roehlkepartain (2008) reported that most of the youths surveyed have considered spirituality as an important part of their development. All these reinstate the importance of spiritual influence on youth development and consequent positive outcomes.

Research on theological influences draws a clear distinction between religion and spirituality. Religion refers to the concepts, rituals, and practices associated with one's understanding of a supreme power and means of accessing the same. Religion thus is a socially derived identity and institution, handed over from one generation to another across the ages. Spirituality on the other hand has been defined as the "personal and private beliefs that transcend the material aspects of life and give a deep sense of wholeness, connectedness, and openness to the infinite" (Myers, Sweeney, & Witmer, 2000, p. 265). In the words of Pargament (1999), religion encompasses rituals and processes related to what is considered sacred while spirituality transcends the rituals and concerns with the sacred itself. Worthington, Hook, Davis, and McDaniel (2011) associated spirituality with hope, compassion, ethics, and purpose in life.

Spirituality has significant implications in youth development. According to King and Boyatzis (2004), adolescence is "an age period of intense ideological hunger, a striving for meaning and purpose, and desire for relationships and connectedness" (p. 2). Spirituality helps in compensating for the ideological vacuum in the youth, providing them a sense of purpose, ethics, and community feeling. Religion and spirituality also fulfil the dual purpose of passing down traditions and symbols from one generation to another and orienting the youth to the larger belief system of the society (Bengtson, 2017).

Socialization about religion and spirituality comes to the youth chiefly from the parents. According to the spiritual modelling perspective, the religious acts of parents serve as the model for the religious pursuits of adolescents (Regnerus, Smith, & Smith, 2004). Again, the religious understanding of the parents influences the religious exposure of the children and the youth. However, the youth also gather their religious influences from a variety of other sources such as the peer group, neighbourhood, as well as from the media (Martin, White, & Perlman, 2003). Thus, influences external to the home environment may play a significant role in the spiritual development of the youth. An important role in this regard is played by spiritual mass leaders, who serve as the mouthpiece of different religious/

spiritual sects and disseminate the messages of that school of thought, in order to mobilize people towards specific beliefs.

Lippman and McIntosh (2010), in a survey, found that over 94% of the youth in India believed in God, and most of the youth surveyed, regarded religion as very important in their life. A major pathway through which the youth encounter spirituality outside their homes is through educational institutions. Almost all major religions would have educational wings targeted at spiritual development of the youth. In the Indian subcontinent, these majorly include the Christian Missionary schools and colleges, the Madrassas dedicated to Islamic studies, and various Hindu Vedic schools and educational institutes run by trusts such as the Rastriya Swayamsevak Sangh (RSS), Ramakrishna Mission, Arya Samaj, and others (e.g. Husni, 2020; Woodward & Kimmons, 2019). In addition to education, such institutes are also renowned for their emphasis on spiritual development, with prayers, moral education, and spiritual pursuits forming a significant part of their curricula. In addition, religious institutions have dedicated youth wings for the young people to have a simplified understanding of their traditional religious beliefs and engage in community service. Famous examples include the Young Men and Women's Christian Associations (YMCAs and YWCAs), or the Akhil Bhartiya Vidyarthi Parishad of RSS. Another influential group with a worldwide presence is the ISKCON (International Society of Krishna Consciousness), whose youth wing FOLK (Friends of Lord Krishna) connects with thousands of youths worldwide to spread the message of non-violence, duty, and service.

The importance of spiritual leaders in youth development in India is attested by the fact that the birth anniversary of the great spiritual leader, Swami Vivekananda, is celebrated as the National Youth Day in India. The Hindu ascetic Swami Vivekananda is renowned for the revival of the pride of ancient Indian learnings and spiritual achievements, and also for his many works directed to the youth, where he urged the youth to be active, dedicated to self-development, and service the humankind (Rani, 2017). His works are regarded as among the prime inspirations for the freedom struggle in India, inspiring young revolutionary nationalists, and iconic leaders like Netaji Subhas Chandra Bose.

Case Study 7

Swami Vivekananda is a role model for thousands of youths across the world and he believed that the youth are highly potent and they can bring positive changes in the society and eradicate social myths and misconceptions and aid in creating a better society. He considered youth as the greatest asset and wealth of India. He was of the opinion that youths were full of energy, idealism, enthusiasm, hope, optimism, and adventurous spirit. For eradication of myths and misconceptions from the society, youth can play a crucial role as role models for others. By organizing rallies, the youth can create social awareness about contemporary social and health issues related to the adverse effects of drug addiction, alcoholism, girl child marriage, dowry system, crime against children and women, and corruption.

He stated that "it is the young, the strong, and healthy, of sharp intellect that will reach the Lord". In just 39 years, his thoughts about a healthy, prosperous, and discrimination-free society impressed the larger society, including the youth. In one of his addresses for the youth, Swami Vivekananda stated that

> teach yourself, teach everyone, his real nature, call upon the sleeping soul, and see how it awakes. Power will come, glory will done, goodness will come, purity will come, and everything that is excellent will come when this sleeping soul is roused to self-conscious activity.

Character building is very important for every youth to play a responsible role in society. He urged the youth to build up their character, and manifest their real nature, which is ever pure. "Neither money pays, nor name, nor fame, nor learning, it is character that can cleave through adamantine walls of difficulty - bear this in mind" was his earnest advice to the youth. Every year the National Youth Day is celebrated on January 12 to honour the birth anniversary of Swami Vivekananda.

India has also been home to several world-renowned spiritual leaders in recent times, such as the Buddhist leader and Nobel Peace Prize recipient Dalai Lama (the Head of the Tibetan Government in Exile in Dharamshala, India), Maharishi Mahesh Yogi (proponent of the Transcendental Meditation and followed by celebrities such as the Beatles), Osho Rajneesh, Sadhguru Jaggi Vasudev, Sri Sri Ravi Shankar (founder of the Art of Living), and BK Shivani, to name a few (Bhattacharya, 2021). Although their teachings span across different religions and schools of thoughts, these leaders are remarkable for their simplification of the complex tenets of religious philosophy and the popularization of lifestyles and activities promoting physical and mental health, such as yoga, meditation, and abstinence from drugs and violence, and emphasis on social upliftment as well as environmental conservation. Millions of people across India and the rest of the world follow Indian spiritual leaders, a substantial part of which are formed by the youths, who volunteer in their various outreach programmes, participate in their workshops and trainings, and spread their message in the society (Peltonen, 2017).

Several researchers have found a relationship between spiritual development and life outcomes. Wong (2012) reported that spiritual beliefs lead to greater meaning in life which, in turn, leads to greater well-being and lower chances of mental illnesses. Similar findings were reported by Wong, Rew, and Slaikeu (2006). The collectivistic activities and initiatives promoted by various religious and spiritual organizations for the youth are effective in promoting a sense of purpose and belongingness among the youth (Bruce & Cockreham, 2004). Again, such initiatives are valuable in teaching values such as empathy, forgiveness, fellow-feeling, and independence (Hui & Ho, 2004). Spiritual development in adolescents has been associated with academic, physical, psychological, and social well-being (Scales, Syvertsen, Benson, Roehlkepartain, & Sesma, 2014).

While the role of spiritual leadership in youth development is undeniable, there is also a possibility that spirituality and religious adherence would escalate into dogmatism, cult followership, and negativity among the youth. There are multiple instances around the world of radical extremism, which is promoted in the name of religion and spirituality. They promote violence, anti-social activities, self-destructive behaviour, and lawlessness. Being gullible, the youths are often targets of such radical agenda online or offline, which gradually influence them to become foot soldiers in violent socio-political activities. A recent example is that of ISIS (Islamic State of Iraq and Syria), which has been found to recruit hundreds of young men and women from Europe, the USA, and Asia, for their terrorist activities. Several other radical religious organizations have also been reported to affect the lives of thousands of youths through the spreading of false news of religious crises, hatred against plurality, and providing them arms to rebel against the state (Ramakrishna, 2017). At the other end of the spectrum, the growing impetus of secular values often causes religion and spirituality to be viewed with suspicion (Tacey, 2016), denying the youth access to the support of spiritual nurturance. Increased secularization of curricula at schools often lead to the denial of traditional knowledge and values among the youth, thus creating an ideological vacuum, and causing them to fall prey to false propaganda later (Inglehart, 2020).

Political leadership and its influence on the youths

While political consciousness and activism is not as pervasive as religious and spiritual cognizance among the youth in India, it nevertheless forms a critical part of coming of age for the youth in democratic nations. India practices universal adult franchise, making the youth aged 18 and above a lucrative target segment for political narratives and influence. India also has a multi-party system, providing exposure for the youth to a plurality of thoughts and ideologies from various national and regional parties. Political awareness and ideology significantly influence the way the youth see his or her role in the developmental trajectory of the nation, the responsibility the youth feel towards the country and its people, and the steps the youth take to create an envisioned world (Farthing, 2010; Miller, 2013).

Like religion and spirituality, political awareness and influence also stems primarily from parents and other family members. Research shows that youths are likely to adhere to the political beliefs of their significant family members, owing to selective exposure to ideologies and institutionalization from a young age. Other influences tend to be peer groups and media (Pasek, Kenski, Romer, & Jamieson, 2006). Student politics further initiate the youth into political activities on a miniature scale in colleges and universities. India has a thriving ecosystem of student political parties such as the Akhil Bhartiya Vidyarthi Parishad (ABVP), Student Federation of India (SFI), and the National Student Union of India (NSUI), to name a few. Most of the student political parties are youth wings of national or regional political parties, causing student politics to be viewed as a stepping stone to a full-fledged political career. Political activities run by student unions are pervasive across most higher education institutes in India, particularly those running on public funds, including many Institutes of National Importance (Pathania, 2018).

The pervasiveness of political parties in student politics and the system of adult franchise adds to the importance of the role of political leadership of the nation on youth development in India. Research shows that the section of Indian youths who have high political awareness often tend to follow political leaders regularly on social media platforms such as Twitter and Facebook, and actively engage in political discourses, activities, and outreach endeavours as volunteers or party cadres. For example, the 2019 Youth Connect Survey indicates that 73.16% of the Indian youth surveyed regularly follow political news and updates and 81% look forward to voting in the next elections (Youth Elect, 2019). Further, global political leaders are often among the top influencers among the youth. Leaders such as the Indian Prime Minister Narendra Modi, ex-US President Barack Obama, or the Canadian President Justin Trudeau, are among the most-followed people on social media worldwide, the bulk of whose followership comes from the youths around the world (Sharma, 2016). Shri Kiren Rijiju, Minister, Ministry of Youth Affairs and Sports, Government of India is also a dynamic leader who is a source of inspiration for many youths for his positive role in motivating young people in sports and motivating Indian youth for physical fitness.

Political leadership in India plays a significant role in youth development in multiple ways. The first is the direct influence of the political leadership of a country on creating conditions conducive to positive youth development. The political leadership of a country, whether in a democracy or in an autocracy, is responsible for setting the national as well the regional policies for governance, resource allocation, and developmental endeavours in health, education, and job generation (Flanagan, 2004). Leadership with a positive, pro-development agenda and a vision for the future helps in putting the nation forward through the creation of valuable infrastructure that the youth may access for education, work, or wholesome entertainment. Political leadership also sets the national agenda of India during wars, pandemics, terrorist activities, civil wars, or natural disasters, by diverting resources where it is deemed necessary, and deciding strategic moves of engagement, disengagement, and alliances (Kaarbo, 2018). Thus, they have an important role in ensuring the peace and stability that is critical for youth development and in cutting down the negative influences on the youth in the form of radicalism and anti-national and anti-humanitarian propaganda. Further, the political leadership sets the international relations for India, ensuring that the country is protected from cross-border aggression, and the youth of the country has access to global resources. In all this, the political leadership, at the national and regional levels, plays important roles to ensure that the Indian youth can keep up their pace with the changing times. The political opposition also has an important role to play here, by acting as a watchdog, offering constructive criticism, and offering alternative leadership in a lawful and democratic manner (Shrivastava & Dwivedi, 2021). In India, the agenda for youth development in education, jobs, access to resources, and national growth form essential parts of election manifestos and engage significant parts of various resources in policymaking.

The other way in which the political leadership of the country influences the youth is by promoting and preserving the humanitarian spirit, the nationalistic sentiments, and respect for the political ideology of a nation. The political leadership of a democratic nation sets the tone for democratic decision-making, healthy dissent, and hearing the voice of the people by making the citizens aware of the ground realities and alternatives available, their power to make the destiny of the nation, and their responsibilities as citizens (e.g. Sørensen & Torfing, 2018). This contributes to youth development through active political participation, voting, and providing the voice of the youth a forum for influencing policy making. Along with ensuring that the interest of the youth is protected in the national agenda, this also provides the youth with exposure in political decision-making and prepares them to pick up the baton for the political leadership in the future.

The pervasive influence of political leadership on resource allocation, laws, and international relations also implies that political power must be used with discretion, responsibility, and a long-term agenda. There have been instances around the world where the youth have been incited by the political leaders to engage in dissents and protests, often of a violent nature and provoking them to destroy life and property, breaking the law and in the process, jeopardizing their own lives. The banned People's War or the Naxal Movement in India is a sad example of such a political movement that was primarily fuelled by the youth (Puri, 2019). Other examples include the SIMI (Arosoaie, 2018), whose activities have been restricted on the Indian soil due to evidence of their active participation in terrorism. Even at the local level, political parties often engage in violence, where the youth members and volunteers often become the cannon fodder. It is essential that the political leadership in India behave in a responsible manner, by putting national interests over their own personal agenda, to promote the well-being of the nation and the youth. It is also critical that the youth is seen as more than a vote bank by the political parties, who need to engage in active attempts to hear the voices of the youth, provide them the resources to grow, and tap their ideas and energy for building the nation's future (Kumar, 2014).

Business leadership and its influence on the youth

Economic activities form the backbone of a nation. Countries that are considerably self-sufficient in meeting their own needs for consumption and can engage in profitable cross-border trade with indigenous products. Such services are formidable in their international standing and will fare well in terms of well-being and quality of living of the citizens and the progress of the nation. Businesses play an important role in this regard, by being the source of economic activities, converting raw materials into consumables, and generating employment and wealth for the nation (Nuruzzaman, Singh, & Pattnaik, 2019). Whether they are from the organized or the unorganized sector, businesses contribute to national well-being through the generation of employment and value and generating taxes for the implementation of policies and for governance.

In India, the advent of modern industries happened as a reaction against the British rule, the pioneering path set by Shri JRD Tata in 1906 with his Tata Iron and Steel Factory. The legacy of Shri JRD Tata and his successors in nation-building has made their name one of the most well-recognized brands across various industries. Post-independence, similar impactful business contributions have made business leaders from the business families of Ambanis, Mittals, Bajajs, and Adanis. At the same time, stalwarts such as Narayana Murthy and Azim Premji have become household names across India. The influential role of businesses in nation building in the open-market economies today has relegated the position of importance of business leaders across the world. Along with Indian business tycoons, founders of global business giants such as Elon Musk (Tesla), Steve Jobs (Apple), Mark Zuckerberg (Facebook), and Jeff Bezos (Amazon) are enormously popular among the youth in India today. Young business leaders heading start-ups such as Ritesh Agarwal (Oyorooms), Adar Poonawala (Serum Institute of India), Sachin Bansal (Flipkart), Nandan Reddy (Swiggy), or Bhavish Agarwal (Olacabs) are remarkably popular for their contribution to the growth trajectory of India in the twenty-first century.

The role of the businesses in employment and resource generation attests their importance in youth development. Businesses provide employment to the youth of the country by keeping them gainfully engaged and making them productive citizens of India. A thriving business ecosystem provides quality products and services at affordable prices and in regular supply to the citizens, thus ensuring healthy standards of living for the youth and opportunities for growth. Finally, business leaders spearheading successful entrepreneurial ventures and family businesses serve as role models for the Indian youth in being enterprising and progressive, while also being socially productive (Bowers, Rosch, & Collier, 2016). Further, business leaders often make their mark through corporate social responsibilities and philanthropic activities, guiding the youth in leaving a positive impact on the society and the environment, along with the Indian economy.

The impact of business leadership on youth development comes from both direct and indirect sources. This, however, also necessitates that the business leadership is conscious about leaving a positive influence on the youth with its activities. Unethical actions on the part of business leaders, particularly if not immediately followed by negative consequences, serve to encourage unethical behaviour among the youth. Further, profiteering overtakes the social spirit of business ventures, leading to long-term impacts on the well-being of the citizens of the country, specifically the youth. It is important that the Indian business leadership is cognizant of the impact of its actions on the youth and acts accordingly, so that, along with profit-making, the interests of the nation and its citizens and humanity are preserved (Mea & Sims, 2019). At the same time, it is important that the corporate setup of India provides fair employment terms to the youth and provides them an opportunity to thrive at work.

Art and music and its impact on mind and behaviour of the youths

Music has a positive impact on the mental health of common people. Popular songs and/or music are not only refreshing, they give happiness and people feel psychologically calm and comfortable. It also helps to enhance good parent-child relationships and make a child communicative and aids their overall social development. In this regard, Nicholson, Berthelsen, Abad, Williams, and Bradley (2008) undertook a study to examine the effectiveness of music in improving the parent-child relationships and found significant improvements after 10 weeks of group music therapy for marginalized parents and their children. Based on the findings from individual randomized trials Maratos, Gold, Wang, and Crawford (2008) suggest "that music therapy is accepted by people with depression and is associated with improvements in mood". In another study, Daykin, De Viggiani, Pilkington, and Moriarty (2013) undertook a secondary study to examine the impact of music on the health, well-being, and behaviour of young offenders and those considered at risk of offending young offenders. It was observed that music had positive impacts on the behaviour and thought of young offenders. Evidence also suggests that "listening to music can reduce anxiety, blood pressure, and pain as well as improve sleep quality, mood, mental alertness, self-esteem and memory" (Maratos et al., 2008). For prevention of suicide, music is found to be very effective.

However, too much listening to music causes distraction from studies for the youth and listening to music on high volume, during festivals, causes disturbance to others and sick people. Using earphones for listening to music for longer durations causes headache and sometimes, one becomes vulnerable to road accidents. Therefore, the youth should judiciously engage in listening to music for personal comfort and ensuring that others are not disturbed. According to the Council on Communications and Media (2009),

> the popular music has profound influence on adolescents' behaviour and emotions and is also a serious concern for the parents as lyrics have become more explicit in their references to drugs, sex, and violence over the years, particularly in certain genres. A teenager's preference for certain types of music could be correlated or associated with certain behaviours. As with popular music, the perception and the effect of music-video messages are important, because research has reported that exposure to violence, sexual messages, sexual stereotypes, and use of substances of abuse in music videos might produce significant negative changes in behaviours and attitudes of young viewers.

Film and film personalities

The role of film and film personalities such as Amitabh Bachchan, Shah Rukh Khan, Salman Khan, Rani Mukherjee, Amir Khan, Akshay Kumar, to name a few, in inspiring youth and defence personnel at times of crisis is worth mentioning here. For example, in order to rejuvenate and refresh the minds of young defence personnel of the army in high altitude and in border areas, many popular Indian film personalities visited and entertained them. Films are mostly made based on social interpretation of real life, to entertain the audience and to convey positive messages leading to social transformation. The films based on patriotic themes and on humanity inculcate a feeling of nationalism among the youth and motivate them for volunteering. For example, movies like "Three Idiots" directed by Rajkumar Hirani, released in 2009, portrayed a very pertinent issue through the film, i.e. aptitude and interest of the youth should be given priority in guiding them for selection of subjects for future career. Another recent film titled "Hindi Medium" (released in 2017) directed by Saket Chaudhry presented a very good picture of the manipulation of parents' identity for ensuring admission of children in schools under the reservation category.

Some of the film personalities have been playing a crucial role in helping disadvantaged children, the elderly, and needy people in different ways. During the COVID-19 pandemic support from some of the film personalities in sending migrant labourers to their hometown and providing food and shelter, was highly motivating for the younger generations. For example, to name a few, actor Salman Khan has been providing food to the front-line workers in Mumbai while Akshay Kumar donated money to Gautam Gambhir's Foundation to help COVID victims. On the other hand, Sonu Sood, with his team, arranged to send back thousands of migrant labourers to their hometown and arranged buses since the COVID-19 lockdown in Mumbai, in addition to providing food and water. According to Sonu Sood, "Migrant workers have helped build our roads, homes, and offices. We cannot stand and watch them be homeless".

Sports personalities

Games and sports not only keep the youth physically fit and psychologically fresh, but also enhance self-confidence and help them in socializing, while playing with others as a team member. Evidence demonstrates that youth engaged in games and sports have higher self-esteem, stronger connections with their school, better peer relationships, and fewer behavioural problems, in addition to developing leadership qualities.

Indian youth are highly talented and they are performing extremely well both in various national sports events and also at the international level. The performance of Indian sports personalities greatly motivates young people to work hard and perform well in their areas of interest. Some of the sports personalities who highly inspired the youth of the country and internationally include Sunil Gavaskar, Kavid Dev, Mohammed Azharuddin, Sachin Tendulkar, Sourav Ganguly, Gautam Gambhir, Mahendra Singh Dhoni to name a few from the group of retired cricket players. Among the current cricket players, Virat Kohli, Rohit Sharma, Hardik Pandya, are very popular among cricket fans, inspiring young people of the country. Mary Kom (Boxing), Sania Mirza (Lawn Tennis), Saina Nehwal (Badminton), Dipa Karmakar (Gymnastics), and Hima Das (Athletics), are considered some of the most successful female Indian sportspersons who performed well at the national and international levels, earning appreciation and raising the image of the country at the international level and also inspire a large number of youth across geographical boundaries. Some of them came from the lower social strata and financially poor families. However, poverty and lack of sports facilities could not stop them from reaching higher levels and performing extraordinarily. The key message for the youth of the country is to set the goal in life, work hard continuously and remain firm in one's decision and ultimately reach the goal in life. Hard work and determination always pays. The Ministry of Youth Affairs and Sports, Government of India is continuously encouraging the youth of the country towards physical fitness and their participation in games and sports, providing support in different forms and creating good infrastructure in Sports Authority of India campuses.

Evidence suggests that motivation of the youth by different role models and community leaders engage them and youth organizations in civic activities, resulting in the welfare and well-being of community members through collaborative efforts by youth and adults, for attaining long-term success of community development efforts (Barnett & Brennan, 2006; Christens & Dolan, 2011; Iwasaki, 2016). For example, one study by Christens & Dolan, 2011 found that:

> model for youth organizing is effective at producing impacts at multiple levels because it weaves together youth development, community development, and social change into a unified organizing cycle. The initiative encourages participants by promoting psychological empowerment, leadership development, and socio-political development. Simultaneously, youth organizing produces community-level impacts including new program implementation, policy change, and institution building.

The findings of a study by Barnett and Brennan (2006) provide insights into the factors that most directly shape youth attitudes and involvement in their communities, as well as presenting direct implications for applied use. According to Iwasaki (2016), "youth civic engagement is an important means of overcoming disrespect and marginalization of young people that, when done right, can contribute to positive change for all of society". Zeldin (2004) found that:

> engaging youth in decision making secured the commitment of young people to their organizational communities, and additionally, contributed positively to youth development. Further, the adult leaders reported that the experience of working with youth had a positive effect on their own development and contributed to the overall efficacy of their organizations.

Brennan, Barnett, and McGrath (2009) observed that:

> by considering an interactive and dynamic relationship between community and youth development, stronger communities can emerge. Based on the findings, as well as other emerging research authors suggested that youth and community development specialists will need to more clearly identify roles and responsibilities for youth in the community building process.

However, youth should be empowered to take any positive initiatives for community development and they should be involved in the decision-making process (Richards-Schuster, 2012). McLaughlin (2000) remarked that community involvement is essential for the success of any activity initiated by community-based organizations (CBOs).

Conclusion and recommendations

Children and youth are innocent as well as easily influenced. They require guidance from the senior members of the family and society, whether the parents, teachers, community leaders, spiritual leaders, political leaders, sports personalities, film personalities, music and arts, or entrepreneurs, so that they do not engage in risk behaviour and remain focussed in career growth with full motivation and engage in productive and social development activities as Swami Vivekananda strongly believed that the youth can bring positive changes in the society.

In fact, youth development does not happen in a vacuum. While immediate family members, peers, teachers, and other acquaintances play a major role in youth development, a lot of influence is also exerted by individuals and institutions of national and international importance (Mea & Sims, 2019). Leadership in spiritual domains, politics, and business, influence the youth both directly and indirectly, by fulfilling their ideological needs, providing them a sense of purpose and direction and at the same time, ensuring that conditions exist so that they can achieve their full potential. Hence, it is critical that public figures in various domains are cognizant of their role and impact as influencers of the youth and take precautions to play a predominantly positive role in the development of the youth of the country. Secondly, it is important that leadership in politics and business recognize the youth as their stakeholders and actively adopt policies that promote the youth or prevent their exploitation for political gains or business profits. Again, it is critical to provide the youth an opportunity to craft the offerings of such influential institutions, through youth wings and participatory management. Early exposure to responsible roles in institutions that are dedicated to spirituality, business, or politics, will prepare the youth to take on more responsible roles later on, while benefiting from the mentoring of existing leaders. At the same time, this will infuse fresh thoughts, modern ideas, and an experimental spirit in such institutions, leading to their transformation in a direction that is suitable for the world of the future.

There are many instances of positive influence of different leaders on youth, as discussed before, for bringing change in their outlook and mobilizing them for social transformation. Evidence also demonstrates that music has a positive impact on the mental health of the youth. The role of business leaders like Ratan Tata and film personalities like Sonu Sood to name a few, as well as some social and spiritual groups, as mentioned before, during the COVID-19 pandemic, is highly inspiring for the youth. In different parts of the country, a large number of youths were also actively involved in creating awareness about safety measures and helping elderly people get the essential items during the lockdown phase.

From the first-hand field experience of the authors in working with the youth, teachers, and other influencers, a number of steps are suggested and they include,

- In general, teachers should be very sensitive in dealing with the students and the youth in the educational institutions. They should understand the youths' perspectives on various issues and guide them accordingly in the right direction.
- Teachers should meet the youth outside the classroom and create a friendly psychological ambiance, so that students come out with their issues and concerns and discuss the same with the teachers for finding solutions to various issues and concerns that affect students' mental health and career growth.
- Teachers should discuss the dos and don'ts with the students and youth openly and empower them to make appropriate decisions in life.
- Efforts should be made by all categories of community leaders to reach out to unreached youths out of the school or college and to support and mobilize them for good causes and also help and guide them in their career growth.
- Elderly people playing the role of leaders at different levels and in different spheres of life should lead a decent and honest life with integrity so that the youth can follow them and are guided in the right direction by their activities.

References

Armstrong, S. W., & Hope, W. C. (2016). Technical college teachers' communication and its impact on student motivation. *Journal of Education and Human Development*, *5*(1), 24–33. doi:10.15640/jehd.v5n1a3

Arosoaie, A. (2018). Understanding the creation and radicalisation of the Students Islamic Movement of India (SIMI) and the Indian Mujahideen (IM). *South Asia: Journal of South Asian Studies*, *41*(3), 519–534. doi:10.1080/00856401.2018.1469205

Barnett, R. V., & Brennan, M. A. (2006). Integrating youth into community development: implications for policy planning and program evaluation. *Journal of Youth Development*, *1*(2), 5–19. doi:10.5195/jyd.2006.382

Bastian, K. C., McCord, D. M., Marks, J. T., & Carpenter, D. (2017). A temperament for teaching? Associations between personality traits and beginning teacher performance and retention. *AERA Open*, *3*(1), 2332858416684764. doi:10.1177/2332858416684764

Bengtson, V. L. (2017). *Families and faith: how religion is passed down across generations*. New York: Oxford University Press.

Benson, P. L., & Roehlkepartain, E. C. (2008). Spiritual development: a missing priority in youth development. *New Directions for Youth Development*, *2008*(118), 13–28. doi:10.1002/yd.253

Bhattacharya, D. (2021, January 2). Spiritual Gurus Of India And Their Teachings/Ye Hai India. Retrieved July 1, 2021 from https://yehaindia.com/spiritual-gurus-of-india-and-their-teachings/

Bowers, J. R., Rosch, D. M., & Collier, D. A. (2016). Examining the relationship between role models and leadership growth during the transition to adulthood. *Journal of Adolescent Research*, *31*(1), 96–118. doi:10.1177/0743558415576570

Brennan, M. A., Barnett, R. V., & McGrath, B. (2009). The intersection of youth and community development in Ireland and Florida: building stronger communities through youth civic engagement. *Community Development*, *40*(4), 331–345. doi:10.1080/15575330903279630

Bruce, M. A., & Cockreham, D. (2004). Enhancing the spiritual development of adolescent girls. *Professional School Counseling*, 7(5), 334–342.

Bundick, M. J., & Tirri, K. (2014). Student perceptions of teacher support and competencies for fostering youth purpose and positive youth development: perspectives from two countries. *Applied Developmental Science*, *18*(3), 148–162. doi:10.1080/10888691.2014.924357

Christens, B. D., & Dolan, T. (2011). Interweaving youth development, community development, and social change through youth organizing. *Youth & Society*, *43*(2), 528–548. doi:10.1177/0044118X10383647

Council on Communications and Media. (2009). Impact of music, music lyrics, and music videos on children and youth. *Pediatrics*, *124*(5), 1488–1494. doi:10.1542/peds.2009-2145

Cusack, C. M. (2011). Some recent trends in the study of religion and youth. *Journal of Religious History*, *35*(3), 409–418. doi:10.1111/j.1467-9809.2011.01078.x

Daykin, N., De Viggiani, N., Pilkington, P., & Moriarty, Y. (2013). Music making for health, well-being and behaviour change in youth justice settings: a systematic review. *Health Promotion International*, *28*(2), 197–210.

Farthing, R. (2010). The politics of youthful anti-politics: representing the "issue" of youth participation in politics. *Journal of Youth Studies*, *13*(2), 181–195. doi:10.1080/13676260903233696

Flanagan, C. A. (2004). Volunteerism, leadership, political socialization, and civic engagement. In R. M. Lerner & L. Steinberg (Eds.), *Handbook of adolescent psychology* (pp. 721–745). John Wiley & Sons Inc.

Harding, S., Morris, R., Gunnell, D., Ford, T., Hollingworth, W., Tilling, K., ..., & Kidger, J. (2019). Is teachers' mental health and wellbeing associated with students' mental health and wellbeing?. *Journal of Affective Disorders*, *242*, 180–187.

Hui, E. K. P., & Ho, D. K. Y. (2004). Forgiveness in the context of developmental guidance: implementation and evaluation. *British Journal of Guidance and Counselling*, 32(4), 477–492. doi:10.1080/03069880412331303286

Husni, H. (2020). The effectiveness of the social responsibility program for Islamic religious education through the participatory action research method. *The Social Studies: An International Journal*, 6(1), 103–116.

Inglehart, R. F. (2020). Giving up on God: the global decline of religion. *Foreign Affairs*, *99*, 110.

Iwasaki, Y. (2016). The role of youth engagement in positive youth development and social justice youth development for high-risk, marginalised youth. *International Journal of Adolescence and Youth*, *21*(3), 267–278.

Kaarbo, J. (2018). Prime minister leadership style and the role of parliament in security policy. *The British Journal of Politics and International Relations*, *20*(1), 35–51. doi:10.1177/1369148117745679

King, P. E., & Boyatzis, C. J. (2004). Exploring adolescent spiritual and religious development: current and future theoretical and empirical perspectives. *Applied Developmental Science*, *8*(1), 2–6. doi:10.1207/S1532480XADS0801_1

Koenig, H. G. (2010). Spirituality and mental health. *International Journal of Applied Psychoanalytic Studies*, 7(2), 116–122. doi:10.1002/aps.239

Kumar, S. (2014). *Indian youth and electoral politics: an emerging engagement*. New Delhi: Sage Publishing.

Lippman, L. H., & McIntosh, H. (2010). The demographics of spirituality among youth: international and U.S. Patterns. *Child Trends: Research Brief*, 1–15.

Maratos, A., Gold, C., Wang, X., & Crawford, M. (2008). Music therapy for depression. *Cochrane Database of Systematic Reviews*, (1).

Martin, T. F., White, J. M., & Perlman, D. (2003). Religious socialization: a test of the channeling hypothesis of parental influence on adolescent faith maturity. *Journal of Adolescent Research*, 18(2), 169–187. doi:10.1177/0743558402250349

McLaughlin, M. W. (2000). Community counts: how youth organizations matter for youth development, Public Education Network, North America.

Mea, W. J., & Sims, R. R. (2019). Human dignity-centered business ethics: a conceptual framework for business leaders. *Journal of Business Ethics*, *160*(1), 53–69. doi:10.1007/s10551-018-3929-8

Miller, W. J. (2013). Show me, tell me: social media and the political awareness of American youth. *Afro-Americans in New York Life and History*, *37*(1), 75.

Myers, J. E., Sweeney, T. J., & Witmer, J. M. (2000). The wheel of wellness counseling for wellness: a holistic model for treatment planning. *Journal of Counseling & Development*, 78(3), 251–266. doi:10.1002/j.1556-6676.2000.tb01906.x

Nicholson, J. M., Berthelsen, D., Abad, V., Williams, K., & Bradley, J. (2008). Impact of music therapy to promote positive parenting and child development. *Journal of Health Psychology*, *13*(2), 226–238.

Nuruzzaman, N., Singh, D., & Pattnaik, C. (2019). Competing to be innovative: foreign competition and imitative innovation of emerging economy firms. *International Business Review*, *28*(5), 101490.

Pargament, K. I. (1999). The psychology of religion and spirituality? Yes and no. *The International Journal for The Psychology of Religion*, *9*(1), 3–16.

Pasek, J., Kenski, K., Romer, D., & Jamieson, K. H. (2006). America's youth and community engagement: how use of mass media is related to civic activity and political awareness in 14-to 22-year-olds. *Communication Research*, *33*(3), 115–135.

Pathania, G. J. (2018). *The university as a site of resistance: identity and student politics*. Oxford, UK: Oxford University Press.

Peltonen, T. (2017). *Spirituality and religion in organizing: beyond secular leadership*. Springer.

Puri, S. (2019). 7 India's two-track response to the Naxalite movement. In *Countering insurgencies and violent extremism in South and South East Asia*. (pp. 153–167). Routledge.

Ramakrishna, K. (2017). The growth of ISIS extremism in Southeast Asia: its ideological and cognitive features—and possible policy responses. *New England Journal of Public Policy*, *29*(1), 6.

Rani, V. (2017). Swami Vivekananda: the eternal youth icon and national resurgence. *Asian Journal of Multidimensional Research (AJMR)*, 6(7), 14–18.

Regnerus, M. D., Smith, C., & Smith, B. (2004). Social context in the development of adolescent religiosity. *Applied Developmental Science*, 8(1), 27–38.

Richards-Schuster, K. (2012). Empowering the voice of youth: the role of youth advisory councils in grant making focused on youth. *New Directions for Evaluation*, *2012*(136), 87–100.

Sanders, J., Munford, R., & Liebenberg, L. (2016). The role of teachers in building resilience of at risk youth. *International Journal of Educational Research, 80*, 111–123.

Scales P.C., Syvertsen A.K., Benson P.L., Roehlkepartain E.C., Sesma A. (2014) Relation of spiritual development to youth health and well-being: evidence from a global study. In: Ben-Arieh A., Casas F., Frønes I., Korbin J. (eds) *Handbook of child well-being*. Dordrecht: Springer.

Sharma, A (2016). Can PM Modi top Barack Obama on social media? *The Economic Times*. Retrieved July 1, 2021 from https://brandequity.economictimes.indiatimes.com/news/digital/can-pm-modi-top-barack-obama-on-social-media/53568671

Shrivastava, A., & Dwivedi, R. (2021). The role of opposition in a democracy: a bibliometric analysis. *Library Philosophy and Practice*, 1A-24.

Sørensen, E., & Torfing, J. (2018). The democratizing impact of governance networks: from pluralization, via democratic anchorage, to interactive political leadership. *Public Administration*, *96*(2), 302–317.

Tacey, D. (2016). Spirituality, religion and youth in scular times. In P. Daughtry and S. Devenish (Eds.) *Spirituality for youth-work* (pp. 3). Newcastle: Cambridge Scholars Publishing.

Wang, M. T., Brinkworth, M., & Eccles, J. (2013). Moderating effects of teacher–student relationship in adolescent trajectories of emotional and behavioral adjustment. *Developmental Psychology*, *49*(4), 690.

Wong, P. T. P. Ed. (2012). *The human quest for meaning: theories, research, and applications*. London, UK: Routledge.

Wong, Y. J., Rew, L., & Slaikeu, K. D. (2006). A systematic review of recent research on adolescent religiosity/spirituality and mental health. *Issues in Mental Health Nursing*, 27(2), 161–183.

Woodward, S., & Kimmons, R. (2019). Religious implications of social media in education. *Religion & Education*, 46(2), 271–293.

Worthington, E. L., Hook, J. N., Davis, D. E., & McDaniel, M. A. (2011). Religion and spirituality. *Journal of Clinical Psychology*, 67, 204–214.

Youth Elect (2019, March 6). *Youth Ki Awaaz Survey Reveals What Young India Is Thinking This Election*. Youth ki Awaz. Retrieved July 1, 2021 from https://www.youthkiawaaz.com/2019/03/youth-ki-awaaz-survey-reveals-interesting-things-on-what-young-india-wants-this-election/

Zeldin, S. (2004). Youth as agents of adult and community development: mapping the processes and outcomes of youth engaged in organizational governance. *Applied Developmental Science*, *8*(2), 75–90.

5 Changing socio-economic and political scenario and youth development

Instability and the vulnerable: Youth in a transitioning world

> With just 10 years to go, an ambitious global effort is underway to deliver the 2030 promise—by mobilizing more governments, civil society, businesses and calling on all people to make the Global Goals their own...2020 needs to usher in a decade of ambitious action to deliver the Goals by 2030. The Decade of Action calls for accelerating sustainable solutions to all the world's biggest challenges — ranging from poverty and gender to climate change, inequality and closing the finance gap.
>
> United Nations (2020)

The capacity to evolve and advance is what sets humanity apart from other known species on the planet. However, the last few decades have been remarkable even for human standards for the rapid rate of advancement and the paradigm shifts happening in the way life was known before. Many of these changes are remarkably positive. The world has not seen a nuclear warfare or a truly global conflict for the last 70 years, economies have opened to an era of peaceful co-existence and free markets, and human rights and popular opinion across the globe are being viewed with far more importance than ever before. Johan Norberg, the celebrated Swedish academician, shared data in 2019 to show that the bygone decade had been the most fruitful in showing a steady decline in extreme poverty, hunger, illiteracy, child mortality, and deaths due to pollution and AIDS (Chandy, 2020).

While the advancements in quality of life are extraordinary for several sections of the human society, many have observed the rate of change to be too slow to meet the targeted sustainable development goals set by the United Nations by 2030 (United Nations, 2019). At the same time, advancement in technology, globalization, and proliferation of digital communication is creating new challenges for the world. As some gaps owing to disproportionate privileges are closing, new divides are coming up owing to lopsided access to the currencies of the new world order. India, too, is witnessing significant changes in social structures, demography, culture, resources, and privileges – with increased access to electricity, water, nutrition, and healthcare across classes on the one hand and digital divide dividing urban centres

DOI: 10.4324/9781003170587-5

and rural lands on the other. The youths are the primary stakeholders of this evolving national canvas, as they are slated to inherit the changes with their advantages and challenges. At the same time, the youths are particularly vulnerable to flux in the environment, and the uncertainty it brings.

Coming of age across the ages

> Our capability to thrive, in harmony with all the other species, as well as to achieve a better life and a better world, depends on our ability to embrace change, break the status quo and evolve. It's when we are young that we have the energy, the courage, and the ambition to question things and change them...when we are old, we tend to accept things as they are and preserve the existing.
>
> Emanuele Musa, Co-Founder & CEO, Babele (Sustainable Development Solutions Network – Youth, 2020, p. 2)

Youth has been regarded as the formative years of human life, where the skills and experiences acquired, in many ways, determine a person's life trajectory for the rest of their existence (e.g. Carr, Martins, Stingel, Lemgruber, & Juruena, 2013). The traditional Indian perspective defines the youth as a period of *Bramhacharya* – ranging from early adolescence to the mid-twenties, where the youth lived a life of austerity away from regular living, receiving education and training from the Guru, to transform oneself into a skilled professional and a valued citizen of the society (Plant, 2014; Sarda, Deshpande, Deo, & Karanjkar, 2018). Youth has been traditionally looked upon as a phase of gradual induction into adult life – when the carefree pleasures of childhood are slowly replaced by adult responsibilities and tasks. However, even the exposure to the adult world is expected to happen in a protected environment, to prevent overwhelming the youth with the novelty and the associated challenges.

It is interesting to note that the understanding of childhood, adolescence, and youth as a period requiring protection, special attention, and privileges is a relatively modern phenomenon. Prior to the modern medical miracles, shorter life expectancies made societies opt for an early induction of the youth into adult living and activities. The practice of early marriage started adult responsibilities early for young people, limiting the scope for self-development, empowerment, and vocational upliftment (Côté & Levine, 2015; Walker, 2012). Again, low levels of mechanization of industries and high mortality rates raised the requirement for a regular flow of human resources in the workforce. Well into the twentieth century, young adolescents, particularly those born to working-class parents or less-privileged sections of the society, were absorbed into trade and commerce as apprentices in various vocations (Frenette, 2015; Gessler, 2017). For the youth from the more privileged classes, adolescence was a time for education, skilling, and grooming oneself for the chosen career path ahead, decided either by family trade or by one's abilities and interests.

Since the World War II, the world has seen an increase in life expectancy due to modern medicine and relative political stability. This has replaced the need for early induction of the youth into adult life with an increased emphasis on the skilling and empowerment of the youth and a gradual and smooth transition into the adult world. The modern understanding of youth encompasses the dual necessities of training and skilling of the youth in the early years as well gradual transition into adult opportunities and responsibilities, such as having a career, starting one's family, building a political voice, and participating in social development (Roberts, 2019).

The role of the society in youth development is substantial. Socio-economic conditions in which the youth grow up determine the gender and professional roles and limits for the youth. While an open and liberal socio-economic milieu grants autonomy to the youth, lack of opportunities may severely stunt the potential of the youth capital of a nation (Benson & Saito, 2001). Exposure to violence, crimes, and unstable conditions may deviate the youth to delinquency, exploitation, and destructive behaviour, particularly when protection and mentoring is absent (Antunes & Ahlin, 2017; Ozer, Lavi, Douglas, & Wolf, 2017). All these result in the weakening of the youth potential of the nation and the future of the country.

Changing times and the youth: Social and economic opportunities

Globalization and open economies

The rapid opening up of the regional markets in the new millennium has redefined the economic landscape of the modern world. Globalization of trade and commerce helps in two ways. First, it helps firms find new markets for their products. This, in turn, generates a need for skilled and unskilled labour, and leads to economic empowerment. Global value chains, where the production process is distributed across many countries rather than one, have ensured new jobs and industries in developing nations that have an inexpensive supply of labour or raw materials (World Bank, 2020). Second, globalization brings the offerings and resources previously available within constricted geographical boundaries to the rest of the world, improving the quality of living across different nations of the world. Globalization also leads to exchange of information, knowhow, and ideas, which lead to liberalization of ideas, awareness among people, and improvement in governance (Glatzer, 2012; Simplice, 2013).

The most critical things for the development of the youth are education, employment, and access to basic citizenship rights. Globalization and opening of economies have important implications for the youth of the world. Opening of economies has created a massive volume of jobs, particularly in the developing countries. Global giants, such as Unilever, Amazon, Microsoft, Dell, and the like, have set up subsidiaries across the world to add efficiency to the supply chain, employing thousands of local citizens in the process (Rama, 2003). Again, support functions for these booming industries have led to the rise of more specialized jobs and industries around the world (Linden, Dedrick, & Kraemer, 2011).

Home to the second-largest youth population of the world, India had traditionally been known as an agricultural land, with most of the people employed in agriculture. However, in 2019, although the agricultural sector employed more than 42.6% of the workforce in India, it generated only 18.325% of the Gross Domestic Product (GDP) (Statista, 2021c; Statista, 2021d). After the liberalization of the economy in 1991, India emerged as one of the global hubs of Information Technology Enabled Services (IteS) and is likely to emerge as the world's biggest hub of analytics by 2025 (Bhatia, 2019). Presently, the service sector in India employs 32% of the workforce and contributes about 50% of the GDP of the nation (Statista, 2021b). Along with strengthening the indigenous service and manufacturing sectors, India has also opened the economy to Foreign Direct Investment (FDI) in many sectors, leading to significant job generation for the youth of the nation (e.g. Basu & Ghosh, 2017). As of April 2020, India has 124 registered foreign companies operating in India (Statista, 2021a). With the wake of the COVID-19 pandemic, global FDI fell by 42%, whereas in India, FDI rose by 13% in the same period, backed by investment in the digital sector (Mathew, 2021). This is critical to divert the workforce from the agriculture sector – and end disguised unemployment for a vast section of the population (Bhattacharyya & Mukherjee, 2019; Cho, 2020). At the other end, Indian entrepreneurs have benefited from globalization by setting up their businesses across the world. A 2020 CII report showed that as many as 155 Indian firms presently operate in the USA, investing nearly 20 billion USD (Singh, 2020). Indian firms also have a dominating presence in other parts of the world such as Europe, Africa, the Middle East, and other parts of Asia. Globalization of Indian firms again creates lucrative job opportunities for the Indian youth abroad and in India (Anand, 2015; Arora & Gambardella, 2005).

The second major advantage of globalization is the improved access to global standards in goods, services, and customer experiences. With globalization, access to the latest offerings in information and communication technology, healthcare, sports, mobility, education, and entertainment are becoming accessible across the world. This leads to a vast improvement in the standards of living of the local population of a region as they no longer must depend solely on indigenous production capacity for their consumption (Jorda & Sarabia, 2014; Perlas, 2019). Further, open economies inspire competition in the market, ending monopolistic market structures, and forcing local players to up their game to survive and thrive (Coşar, Guner, & Tybout, 2016).

In the context of youth development, open market structures bring significant benefits in the context of education and skill development. For instance, with collaboration among premier educational institutions of the world, satellite campuses, and opportunities for distance learning, world-class educational interventions, and vocational training opportunities are accessible to the youth from less-advantaged sections of the globe (Schumann, 2018; Spring, 2014). India is presently mulling FDI in the educational sector, which is likely to open up the Indian youth to international school and college curricula, and global teaching and research practices (Nanda & Mishra, 2020). Similar choices are opening for healthcare, sports, communication, digital technology, and entertainment. Almost all the dominant brands among the Indian youth when it comes to IT technology and mobile phones, entertainment in the form of social media or Over-The-Top (OTT) platforms, fashion, and sports happen to be global brands, such as Amazon, Netflix, Google, Samsung, or Nike, that provide tough competition to indigenous brands. Globalization also introduces the youth to knowhow and best practices from across the globe, creating in them awareness about and acceptance for different cultures, diversity, and plurality (Buckingham & Kehily, 2014).

The digital age

What comes the closest to globalization in its transformational impact on youth development is the rapid digitalization of the world. Digital technology and its advanced forms, such as artificial intelligence, machine learning, Internet of Things, and robotics is changing life as it is known today in multiple ways and at a rapid pace. Digitalization is transforming occupations considerably through extensive automatization of the menial components and the repetitive grunt work, making the jobs of the future more cerebral and strategic in nature (Girasa, 2020). This is making the jobs for the youth today less hazardous and more engaging in terms of experience and impact (Buck & Morrow, 2018). Secondly, the use of technology has promoted remote working, where people physically located in distant places can come together to work in virtual teams. Remote working has afforded unprecedented flexibility to the new-generation workers as they are able to work from convenient locations at a suitable time without having to relocate to the location of their offices. It also helps organizations find suitable employees overcoming geographical constraints and has allowed employees to work in global roles without expensive relocation (Choudhury, Foroughi, & Larson, 2020). During the Covid-19 pandemic, the ability of organizations to move their operations almost entirely to the online mode, wherever feasible, helped businesses across the world to survive (Wang, Liu, Qian, & Parker, 2021). Remote working has also been a major impetus to the gig economy, where workers are working flexibly across many organizations in projects fitting with their interest (Thompson, 2018). India has been no different in this regard. The COVID-19 pandemic has been a major impetus for the proliferation of the gig economy in India (PTI, 2020).

Digitalization has also made available to the Indian youth several vocations that were previously unknown. The youth today are not limited to the traditional jobs of a banker, a teacher, or a businessman. The digital economy has brought up new roles of software engineer, digital marketing managers, social media influencers, digital animators, graphic designers, and online content creators (Manyika, 2017). According to the Future of Work report 2018, 21% of the presently known jobs are going to vanish, and 27% of the job roles are going to be new by 2022 (Centre for the New Economy and Society, 2018). While this requires significant reskilling on the part of the Indian workforce, growing up as digital natives, the millennial youth have a definite advantage in absorption of the new skills and etiquettes of the digital world.

Beyond the professional world, digitalization is fast transforming most aspects of living as it is known today. Low-cost ubiquitous access to high-speed Internet has impacted education substantially. Online, remote classes, digital certifications and training, and Massive Online Open Courses enable the youth to access education from anywhere, and even juggle education with work (Tyner, 2014). Online learning platforms such as Udemy, Coursera, edX, and SWAYAM enable the Indian youth to skill themselves continuously at low investment of time and money (Funes & Mackness, 2018; Palvia et al., 2018). Online learning platforms also enable the youth to turn into trainers themselves and share their skills with interested others to make a living. Youth-run courses and educational content are among the most frequented ones on online learning platforms and social media platforms such as YouTube (Hidalgo-Mari & Segarra-Saavedra, 2017; Karampampas, 2020).

Social media is one of the most influential transformations that have come about because of the digital age. The youth form the largest proportion of the users of social media platforms such as Facebook, Twitter, Instagram, and Quora (Ortiz-Ospina, 2019). Data from the Indian subcontinent reveals that social media has transformed the way the youth connect to the world, letting their group of acquaintances and influencers extend beyond those they know personally and build networks around the world with like-minded individuals (Akram & Kumar, 2017; Bhardwaj, Avasthi, & Goundar, 2017). The internet has also transformed daily living through online banking and financial investment, online shopping, and e-commerce through websites such as Amazon or eBay, entertainment through OTT platforms such as Netflix and Amazon Prime, and online digital gaming activities. Some of these businesses have also undergone massive Indianization, such as the Amazon "Smart Stores", to build trust among the Indian consumers. Digital connectivity also has impacted healthcare for the youth. Numerous health applications such as step counters and calorie counters, as well as apps providing mental health guidance, and training for meditation, relaxation, and time management, find the youth among their greatest users (Buttazzoni, Brar, & Minaker, 2021; Kwok, Leung, Hui, & Wong, 2021).

The transformational impact of digital technology is not limited to the youth. Rather, it affects all sections of the society who encounter such technology from time to time. However, the youth, being digital natives (exposed to and using the digital technology consistently from an early age), have an edge over people from other age groups when it comes to adoption, learning, and building such technology (International Telecommunication Union, 2017; Kesharwani, 2020). Thus, the youth are becoming increasingly likely to be employees of choice in the changing workforce of today (e.g. Ghobadi & Mathiassen, 2020).

Civic awareness and political activism

While youth has been popularly seen as a time of self-development and skilling, away from the demands of the adult world, it is also a time marked by increased interest in the operations of the institutions that run the human society – government, legal order, and civic networks. As one enters adolescence, greater free movements away from parental supervision necessitate that the youth is familiar with the structures and norms of the society – the rules of governance, law and justice, politics, and social welfare. At the same time, youth leads to an exposure to structural inequalities embedded in the society – arising out of race, gender, class, or socio-economic conditions. Across the world, youths form one of the most vociferous voices when it comes to politics, civic awareness, and social welfare. 55% of the youth across OECD countries do not trust the government (Gallup, 2019). The characteristic willingness of the youth to question the order and experiment with the unknown, as well as the desire to break free from parental control and traditional patterns to carve out one's own identity make this age particularly ripe for activism (Keating & Melis, 2017; Mohanty, Middaugh, Bowyer, & Kahne, 2017).

The participation of the youth in social causes, even for those who have not yet reached the voting age, is increasingly being viewed as being important and desirable (Middaugh, Clark, & Ballard, 2017). As most significant policies having an impact horizon of minimum 5–10 years, the youth of today are the primary stakeholders and beneficiaries of the policies adopted. Again, lacking the structural securities of a job, savings, assets, or educational degrees, the youth are particularly vulnerable to the impact of policies adopted in education, economic activities, healthcare, financial support, and international relations (Fothergill, 2017; Sukarieh & Tannock, 2018). Finally, the perspective of the youth is often expected to introduce novel means of addressing an existing problem, due to a relative absence of entrenched priorities and sense of privilege, and a greater willingness to disturb the status quo by moving out of the comfort zone (Nieuwelink, ten Dam, & Dekker, 2019). The energy and enthusiasm of the youth population is also what makes them particularly attractive as political foot-soldiers, to popularize different political ideologies in educational institutions and organizations (e.g. Fisher, 2012).

The advent of the digital age in India, marked by the democratization of smartphones, access to cheap, high-speed internet, and popularization of social media has transformed the role of the youth in India from passive observers of global politics to active influencers. Social media has afforded young people a means of broadcasting their thoughts to the entire world and finding an audience of like-minded peers they would not have met otherwise (Gordon & Taft, 2011; Vromen, Loader, Xenos, & Bailo, 2016). Further, social media sites such as Facebook and Instagram have afforded the opportunity to craft one's identity as adhering to causes and communicating one's beliefs in a creative way – using memes, hashtags, short videos, and slogans (Way & Redden, 2017). Youth influencers such as Greta Thunberg, Malala Yousufzai, or Emma Thompson are increasingly having an impact on global perspectives on climate change, child rights, women's rights, education, violence against the youth, and racism (Burney, 2019; Kemp, 2016). Recent protests such as the #BlackLivesMatter in the United States have generated massive online support from the youth (Maqbool, 2020). In India, too, social media has emerged as a political tool for the millennials. A 2019 report by ADG Online revealed that more than one-third of first-time voters in India were influenced by political messages on social media (PTI, 2019). The relatively low-investment, high visibility forum of social media has led to a spurt in youth activism, resulting in greater understanding of political and social concerns around the world, and formation of opinion and awareness from an early age (Smith, Krishna, & Al-Sinan, 2019; Vie, 2014). Social media and the internet also afford greater access to divergent viewpoints, global news, and policy concerns across nations, which is expected to lead to a more realistic and nuanced understanding of one's own privileges and rights and priorities for the new order (Gillespie, 2018; Petray & Collin, 2017).

The potential of the youth to have a fresh perspective on global problems and their orientation towards finding a solution have also has led to the incorporation of the voice of the youth in policy matters to a greater extent than before. Global organizations such as the United Nations and the European Union organize youth parliaments and youth conferences, where young leaders are encouraged to express their opinions on global matters of importance (e.g. United Nations Department of Economic and Social Affairs [UNDESA], 2020). Across the world, nations are also encouraging the participation of young leaders in politics to bring about a better connection with young voters and better reflection of the sentiment of the youth in the election manifestos (Pruitt, 2017). In India, participation of the youth in policy matters is being encouraged in recent times through interactive portals such as MyGov.in (where citizens can share their opinions, ideas, and solutions for issues of governance), youth parliaments, and internship opportunities of youth with Members of Parliament, District Collectors, and other representatives of the government.

Challenges for the youth in the emerging world order

> Globalization has had both positive and negative impacts, and the winners have not compensated the losers.
>
> (Atalla, 2020)

In the last two decades, the world has seen dramatic improvements in access to resources, human rights, climatic awareness, and improvement in general standards of living. However, many experts point out that the improvement comes at a slower rate than desired. For instance, more than one billion people in the developing world lack access to electricity (United Nations, 2016). In many cases, the structural inequalities have taken a new form but have the same impact on the well-being of global citizens. Further, while many of inequalities of earlier times have been eradicated to some extent, they have been replaced by systematic discrimination arising out of the new currencies of today's world – digital access and proficiency (Scheerder, van Deursen, & van Dijk, 2017; Van Dijk, 2020). The youth, lacking in resources and social influence, are particularly vulnerable to the malaise of the new world order.

Globalization and open economies have been touted as a "double-edged sword" (Janssens, Maddux, & Nguyen, 2019; Nolan, 2018). While vastly improving global standards of living and access to resources, globalization has also been found to disrupt traditional ways of living and institutions at a rapid pace, depriving many of the safety net they provided (Lund & Tyson, 2018; Wilding, 2018). Many of the challenges that assail the youth in the new world order arise out of an increasingly open economic model that leaves nations vulnerable to influences from faraway corners of the world.

Aftershocks in a connected world: recessions, trade disruptions, and pandemics

Open economies with their multiple benefits have the critical disadvantage of making local markets heavily dependent on foreign presence. When giant multinational corporations across the world enter a new market, they manage to capture the major share of the customer base – owing to their ability to provide a competitive price due to economies of scale, greater power to negotiate favourable trade terms from the government, superior product quality due to larger investments in research and development, and gigantic marketing budgets, flooding the viewers with positive brand communication (e.g. Fuerst-Bjeliš & Leimgruber, 2020; Kim & Milner, 2019; Stiglitz, 2017). This makes it particularly difficult for local business initiatives to thrive or grow big. In India, the market for digital devices and phones as well as many other electronic goods and cosmetics is almost entirely dominated by non-Indian MNCs. While such ventures bring investments, jobs, and competitive prices and quality for the consumers, in many nations, open market has led to the virtual annihilation of local small businesses, leaving countries under the almost monopolistic control of global firms (Ballor & Yildirim, 2020). The result is a transfer of wealth in the form of profit from the developing nations to the developed nations. Secondly, highly competitive markets make it difficult for local industries to grow. This makes developing nations heavily dependent on imports of finished foods, and thereby on the currency dynamic of powerful nations (Caldentey & Vernengo, 2017). Devaluation of powerful currencies of the world such as the US Dollar has spiralled major economic disruptions in smaller nations (Atalla, 2020). A critical recent example has been the global economic meltdown of 2008, where the disruption of the housing bubble in the USA had major repercussions for smaller economies around the world, dependent on the USA for trade and commerce (Bhattacharyya & Ghosh, 2020; Davies, 2020). Unstable economic conditions vulnerable to global influences have negative implications for youth development. While global value chains bring jobs to developing nations, in many cases the jobs are low value in nature, such as the manufacturing sweatshops in Bangladesh or Thailand, or the IT backend services in India and China (e.g. Aguiar de Medeiros & Trebat, 2017; Bair, Anner, & Blasi, 2017). It also leaves the country vulnerable to global political influences in the form of economic sanctions, curtails, and economic blockades, leading to sudden job losses for the youth in the economy (McGowan, 2018). International sanctions and trade treaties also prevent developing nations from adopting agricultural, manufacturing, or environmental policies that benefit the youth of the nation, if they happen to hurt the interest of foreign firms operating in the country (Belova, 2018; Lv & Xu, 2019).

Open borders also are leaving countries painfully vulnerable to disruptive influences from elsewhere in the world, affecting the life of the citizens, and especially the vulnerable sections, such as the children and the youth. Many advanced nations are shifting their carbon footprint to the developing nations by moving their production and processing departments to these low-cost locations. While this is contributing to job generation, it is also leading to environmental hazards such as air and water pollution, groundwater depletion, and exposure of the young workforce to hazardous work conditions and wastes. Coca Cola has been under severe criticism in India for lowering the water table, whereas brands of cosmetics have come under the fire for using the hazardous mineral mica mined by child labourers in various parts of India (Berglund, 2017; Bliss, 2017).

One of the most severe impacts of open borders came in 2020 with the COVID-19 pandemic that started from a laboratory in Wuhan, China (World Health Organization, 2020). The highly permeable international borders have led to disease to spread almost instantly to different corners of the world. The resulting disruption has been unprecedented in terms of loss of lives, physical and mental health hazards, shutdown of economic activities and daily living, and opportunity lost for skilling and vocation. According to a 2020 UNDESA report, the youth has been the worst affected by the pandemic (UNDESA, 2020). The COVID-19 pandemic has led to what has been called a "lost generation". Millions of children and young people have dropped out of education, lost their vocations, and are facing acute malnutrition or economic exploitation (UNICEF, 2020). A total of 167 countries declared closure of educational institutions in the wake of the COVID-19 pandemic, affecting more than 1.5 billion children and adolescents (UNESCO, 2020). The UNICEF report on the impact of COVID-19 on mental health of Latin American youths revealed feelings of pessimism, anxiety, and depression, with the symptoms being more frequent among women than among men exploitation (UNICEF, 2020).

Home to a population of over 1.3 billion people, India has responded to the pandemic with nationwide as well as partial, localized lockdown of economic and social activities, closure of schools and colleges and shifting education online, phenomenal spending on healthcare and development of vaccines, execution of the largest vaccination drive in the world, and massive economic packages for the economically weaker sections of the society and businesses to survive the market conditions. Nevertheless, the impact of the pandemic has been substantial on the nation. India has over 250 million students whose education has been disrupted by the pandemic, and research suggests that a significant portion of them are dropping out of education owing to lack of access to digital technology, denial of perks such as mid-day meals, and increased pressure to join the workforce to add to the family income (The Hindu, 2021). A decline in the income of 97% of Indian households has affected the youth directly in terms of resources available for skilling, nutrition, entrepreneurship, and healthcare. Again, the second wave of the COVID-19 in 2021 alone saw 10 million job losses, a substantial number of which left young employees out of jobs (Business Today, 2021). Statista's (2021b) report shows that Indian employees aged between 15 and 39 are the worst hit by pandemic attrition, with those aged between 25 and 29 years accounting for as much as 46% of all job losses. The lethal second wave also claimed a substantial number of young lives in India, who had to step out of homes for professional reasons, without vaccination (The Times of India, 2021a). Although 88% of COVID related fatalities in India are still made up by those aged 45 years and above, the vulnerability of the young population to new strains of the virus has led to irreparable losses for families, many robbed of their sole bread-earners (The Times of India, 2021a).

War and mass migration

Although the world has avoided nuclear war or global combat, the number of countries involved in armed conflict has reached the peak since the 1990s (UNICEF, 2021). A 2016 estimate stated that one-third of the youth in the world lives in countries affected by conflict and lack of peace (Commonwealth Secretariat, 2016). South Asia is particularly notable for cross-border conflicts, insurgency, and terrorism, making the Indian youth vulnerable to uncertainties. Unrest concerning the Rohingyas in Myanmar and their illegal settlement in India, insurgency and terrorist activities in Jammu and Kashmir in India, Taliban threats in Afghanistan, Maoist activities in parts of central India, and the rise of ISIS in Kerala have been of significant concern for youth development in recent times – as they disrupt normal living, including access to the basic minimal requirements such as nutrition, healthcare, education, and vocation. Another major threat is youth being absorbed into armed violence as foot-soldiers. Reports of mass recruitments of Indian youths into ISIS for terrorist activities in Syria and other Middle-Eastern countries have alerted the country to the danger of radicalization of young people (Philip, 2019; PTI, 2018) Civil unrest within the national borders, in the forms of political or communal violence, has also been of concern. Political violence at a regional level is not uncommon in parts of India, leading to more deaths than what is caused by terror attacks, with the youth as the chief casualty in such conflicts (Kharat, 2021).

Mass migration is one of the defining challenges of the modern world, arising out of unequal distribution of resources, climatic hazards, prolonged disturbance and lawlessness, and search for opportunities. Civil unrest and wars are also some of the major causal factors of mass displacement or mass migration – where substantial portions of the populace move to locations of greater stability in search of shelter and living. Legal migration that happens in search of vocation can happen across national borders or within it. India has the largest number of international immigrants, followed by Mexico and China (IOM, 2020). Indian youth migrate abroad for work in substantial numbers (Chavan & Taksa, 2017; Khadria, 2009). At the same time, India witnesses a substantial amount of internal migration, as people move from less privileged states to the more privileged ones in search of vocation. Migration also happens due to water scarcity in India, or at the end of the agricultural season, as farmhands move to the urban areas in search of a parallel means of living (Singh, Osbahr, & Dorward, 2018). India also receives migrants from all the neighbouring states of Pakistan, Bangladesh, Nepal, and Sri Lanka – who come either in search of jobs or to escape political or religious persecution. According to the UN Migration Report 2020 (IOM, 2020), South Asia has seen close to 3.3 million displacements in 2018 alone, owing to natural hazards and civil unrest.

Migration is an issue that affects the youth disproportionately. 70% of the migrants of the world are aged below 30 (OECD, 2019; UNDESA, 2019). Migrants live in dangerous conditions that make them particularly vulnerable to environmental changes such as natural disasters or the pandemic. For instance, the COVID-19 pandemic saw the major displacement of migrant workers from different parts of India to their home states as they lost their means of livelihood and shelter in their places of work (Siegfried, 2020). Migrants are also often deprived of the social securities and safety net of the community and affirmative government policies that would have been available to them in their home soil. To address this, in 2020, the

Government of India launched the One Nation One Ration Card (ONORC) scheme, allowing nationwide portability of the Ration Card, and providing migrant workers access to the Public Distribution System of affordable or free food grains wherever they are (The Times of India, 2021b).

Migration also causes undue pressure on the public resources of Indian cities, such as educational facilities, places of residence, healthcare, and nutrition, depriving many youths of the basic minimum requirements for a healthy living. Migrant youths are vulnerable to the threats of homelessness, early dropouts from schools, and violence and crime to survive (UNDESA, 2019). Children and youth are particularly vulnerable in this alien environment, as they strive to adjust to the alien and often hostile situations with little or no social and financial capital.

Unemployment

The youth potential of India is among its strengths – because the youth form the future workforce of a nation and ensure a steady supply of energetic young workers in the labour pool. Despite this, the youth are three times more likely to be unemployed than other members of the employable age of 25 to 64 (ILO, 2020a). According to ILO (2019), youth unemployment rate worldwide (both in terms of vocational and educational activities) stands at 22.1% and is as high as 30% among women and 15% among men. Further, there is a need for 600 million jobs to be generated over the next 15 years to meet the current need of employment for the youth (ILO, 2020a). India's unemployment rate during the first and second COVID waves had peaked to as much as 23% and 12%, respectively, a substantial portion of which were made up of the youth unemployment (CMIE, 2021).

The reasons why unemployment of the youth is such a critical problem are complex and varied. The first reason for this is the unequal concentration of the youth population across countries. The "youth bulge", or a high concentration of the youth population, is far more common in the less developed countries of the world than in the economically advanced nations (Vanderwey, 2019). These nations often lack the resources for education and employment of their entire youth population, leading to a substantial increase in unemployment. Secondly, lack of adequate resources for skilling and mentoring lowers the employability of the youth, making it difficult for them to find substantive means of income. The relative inexperience of the youth makes them particularly likely to take up vocations in hazardous conditions in the low pay sector. Approximately 96.8% of the youth in developing countries work in the informal and the vulnerable sector, characterizing their work with instability, unhealthy work conditions, and possibilities of exploitation (ILO, 2020b). The relatively low bargaining power of the youth and their less seniority make them particularly vulnerable to layoffs. One in six youths lost their jobs during the pandemic (ILO, 2020b), which also cut out the access to formal insurance programmes, for which employment is needed (UNDESA, 2020).

The youth have been traditionally associated with entrepreneurship, owing to their high appetite for risks, interest in novelty, and low sunk costs in a given career path. However, even when it comes to youth entrepreneurship, several challenges make it particularly difficult for the youth to set up a business and sustain it. The UNDESA 2018 report stated that the major challenges for entrepreneurship ventures for youths include access to finance, education and skills development, awareness raising and networking, and lack of visibility. Thus, while entrepreneurship could solve the problem of youth unemployment in India to a considerable extent, the youth is often overlooked when it comes to the resources that are critical for entrepreneurship.

The digital divide

The digital divide refers to unequal access to digital technology, unequal skills in exploiting digital technology, and unequal benefits accrued out across different sections of humanity (Scheerder et al., 2017). With the rapid digitalization of the modern world in the last two decades, access to and knowledge of digital technology and means to use it for education, business, and communication has become almost imperative. This creates a gaping divide between the youth who are growing up as digital natives and their contemporaries who have little or no access to digital technology and education to exploit it.

What makes the digital divide a particularly problematic condition in India and elsewhere is that it correlates closely with other privilege gaps such as that of wealth, education, social class, race, and gender (UNDESA, 2018). For instance, 90% of youth without internet access live in Africa or Asia (International Telecommunication Union, 2017). Indian youths with inadequate access to digital technology are inadequately prepared for the demands of an IT-driven work world and deprived of many resources that are increasingly becoming available primarily on the online mode. One example of this was the COVID-19 induced lockdown, where reports showed as many as 50% of Indian students not having access to online classes (FE Bureau, 2021). Lack of familiarization with digital technology affects their readiness for the modern workplace and for entrepreneurial ventures. Lack of digital access and training also deprive the digitally challenged Indian youth in rural India of educational and vocational linkages available online, such as scholarships, seed funds, professional networks, job postings, and mentoring, severely affecting their employability. It is important that in addition to shifting focus to the latest technology, the basic need of universal internet access to all is satisfied (Sambuli & Magnoli, 2019).

Destabilization of traditional institutions

Much of the negative impact of the emerging new world order understandably falls on the less privileged youth, who are vulnerable to instability and not resourceful enough to withstand the shocks. However, the complex impact of open economies, digitalization, and globalized perspectives is transformational across all sections of human society, including youth from the privileged classes. With the increasing opening up of economies, the youth today have access to the resources and consumer experiences available across different corners of the world. However, this access is not limited to material resources alone, but extends to philosophies, political, social, and religious beliefs, understanding of human rights and values, and goals of existence. Such influence is not new to a nation such as India that has been open to international exposure and cross-border exchange of knowhow since ancient history. However, the pace of change today is rapid, flooding the youth's consciousness with information, opinions, and values that are often contradictory to one another. At the same time, changing economic and social conditions have brought about changes in lifestyles and societal structures, impacting the way newer generations seek support, adjust, and deal with the challenges of life.

India has traditionally been a nation high on collectivism and power distance, with importance attached to family ties, community networks, religious and ethical values, and nationalism (e.g. Engelhard & Garg, 2018). However, with the advent of the social media with global social networks, easy access to creative content from the western world (such as books, films, and music), and promotion of western values of consumerism, hedonism, and individualism in product placements, the values of the new generations are found to be tilting towards greater individualism and consumerism (Suchday, Santoro, Ramanayake, Lewin, & Almeida, 2018). This is often leading to a significant gap in the cultural values across generations. In many cases, it is even causing a gradual decline of traditional art, trade forms, and practices, even vernacular languages. India is estimated to have lost about 250 languages since 1961, and another 197 languages spoken in India are endangered (Mohanty, 2020).

The importance of the family and close ties in the development and well-being of the youth cannot be overemphasized. In a poll during the COVID-19, the youth reported seeking help primarily from family members, friends, and close community members to deal with the stress of COVID-19 (UNICEF, 2020). However, with the open economy changing the nature of jobs available, there has been a massive disruption in the traditional family systems in India, with the joint families replaced by nuclear units who must live away from the extended family systems owing to vocational demands. This has significantly changed the perspective of children and youth toward the importance of family ties, and the support available to them in case of crisis (McMurphy, 2020). Similarly, the advent of the social media and the increasing fear of "missing out" make the youth spend a significant amount of their time seeking online validation, cutting them off from social ties of actual relationships with friends, neighbours, and community members (Blackwell, Leaman, Tramposch, Osborne, & Liss, 2017). While in many cases, the changing values are welcome drifts towards human rights, empathy, environmental sensitivity, and justice, in many cases, it also is leading to the alienation of the youth from traditional strengths and knowledge of a race, owing to unwarranted vilification of what does not fit with the accepted western model of living. Breakdown of traditional family structures and community relationships is also likely to draw the youth into violence (ILO, 2020a).

Politicization of the youth

Political participation of the youth is not a novelty. Across history, youth have been the primary spearheads in revolutions, armed conflicts, and social transformations. Political participation, till very recent times, involved active physical participation for causes of one's liking – involving youth in activities such as demonstrations, voting, agitation, and social transformations. However, since political and civic involvement necessitated major investment of time and energy, it tended to be limited to only a small, dedicated section of the youth population having interest and passion for the issue. With the advent of social media in India, there has been a vast transformation in the ways in which youth engage politically. Social media being a low investment forum, it engages a lot more youths than before to voice a political opinion, support dissenting voices, and movements, and participate in trending issues. The emergence of the Indian youth as a primary influencer in policy issues and as opinion leaders is becoming common – granting the youth the voice and the power to influence policy decisions, draw attention to issues of importance, and stop harmful trends. However, research shows that in many cases, the voices of youth in politics, social issues, and civic awareness building are ill-informed, based on half-baked understanding of political and social complexities. For instance, the popularity of memes and satire in youth political commentary has often been found to lead to trivialization of issues and inadequate and oversimplified understanding of real issues (Penney, 2020). Youth voices on social media are also vulnerable to the proliferation of fake news, leading to major unrest and hate campaigns based on unverified claims (Westerlund, 2019).

Political activism on social media makes the youth vulnerable to other negative influences as well. Research relates the expression of dissatisfaction on social media, with the risk of exposure to extremist groups such as the ISIS and other terrorist organizations, who use the social media for gradual induction of the youth in their fold (Costello, Barrett-Fox, Bernatzky, Hawdon, & Mendes, 2020). Activism on social media has escalated in many cases to cyberbullying, leading to harassment and even loss of life of the victims (e.g. Aboujaoude, Savage, Starcevic, & Salame, 2015). Youth activism has also been connected to severe social disruptions as influential groups try to sway the gullible youth to forward their own political agenda. A recent example is the "Toolkit" fiasco in India, where a document inciting open civil disobedience and public disruption on the Indian Independence Day was shared on social media by the popular youth climate activist Greta Thunberg, drawing major criticisms nationwide

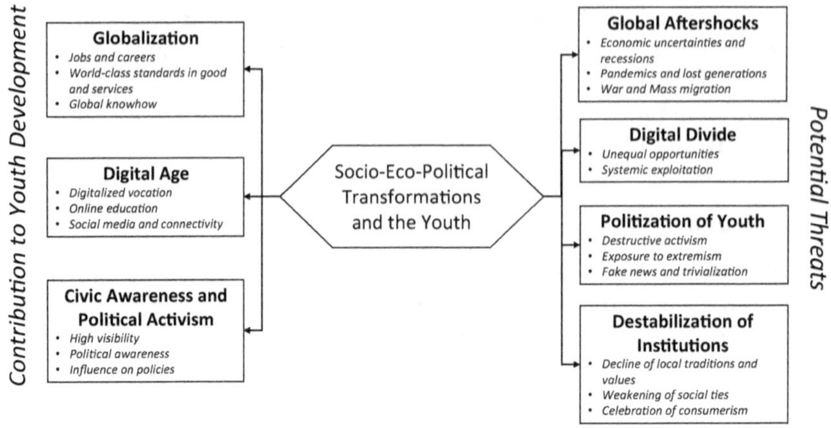

Figure 5.1 Changes in the social, economic, and political environments and impact on youth development.

and accusations of external interference in India's policy decisions (Joshi, 2021) Similar escalations of youth-backed movements into violence and destruction of public property was witnessed during the BLM protests in the USA. While the core issues are critical and merit discussion and awareness, youth movements on social media have been found in recent times to be frequently escalating into uncontrollable forms, with little tangible benefits emerging out of them. Further, digital footprint on social media, reflecting strong political biases and potentially disruptive and even illegal thoughts and opinions, have been found to interfere with the career aspirations for the youth, as firms are cyber-vetting applicant profiles to find matches in professional values and weed out potentially disruptive elements (Jeske & Holland, 2019).

Youth Development in the Changing Times: The Indian Scenario

When it comes to the context of the subcontinent, India has one of the largest vocational training systems in the world – running in parallel to the formal education system. However, many youths drop out of education and vocational training early owing to poverty, migration, civil unrest and war, and occupational demands. India has attempted to address this through free basic minimum education in childhood in government schools and provision of midday meals in schools to support the child's nutritional needs. However, with migration, pandemic, and poverty affecting a substantial number of youths in India, efforts need to be upped in this direction. Apart from a large network of engineering, medicine, and other professional education institutes, India also has a network of Industrial Training Institutes (ITIs), where the youth can get certified in technical and vocational skills and earn a stipend while receiving training. The National Education Policy of 2020 has further emphasized on vocational skilling of the youth, with Technical and Vocational Education (TVET) proposed to be a part of secondary education, allowing the youth an early induction into training for a career of their choice (Ministry of Human Resource Development, 2020).

A critical part of the training of the youth today is digital education. India has the least expensive internet connectivity in the world, coupled with access to inexpensive digital devices in an open market (Roy, 2019). But nevertheless, the digital divide is prominent. Again, for those who have access, entertainment remains the chief reason for using the internet rather than productive outputs. For most children in India, school is the only place to get a structured exposure to digital devices, digital media, and its utility in education, vocation, and networking. The Government of India has recently adopted the "Responsible AI for Youth" programme, the National Program for Government Schools as a part of the Digital India initiative. This programme aims at introduction of digital training and access in government schools (NeGD, 2021). In addition, the Government of India has adopted policies of providing free Wi-Fi in public spots such as railway stations, digital kiosks and internet cafes, and universal connection to electricity that would enable the youth to access the digital world and benefit from it (Rituraj, 2018).

Income inequality, unstable conditions, and poverty are likely to increase the chances of the youth not being gainfully employed (UNDESA, 2020). Therefore, there is an increased emphasis on providing stable conditions to the youth of the country while they train and equip themselves for the world. India has the world's largest public distribution system, providing a safety net to every citizen of the country for basic nutrition and life needs. Similarly, the MNREGA guarantees employment for hundreds of days a year to the working population from the rural areas (Department of Food and Public Distribution, 2018). Youths remain significant beneficiaries of these programmes across different states of the nation. In addition, there are several policies targeting specific groups of youth such as women and girls and differently abled youth, and youth from economically and socially backward communities, helping them to find stability and progress well in the world (Ministry of Youth Affairs and Sports, 2014).

One of the major initiatives adopted by the Government of India in recent years is the encouragement for entrepreneurship for the youth. In 2016, the Government of India launched the StartUp India programme, encompassing initiatives for easy loans and seed fund for starting new businesses, incubation and mentoring, and infrastructural support for the entrepreneurs – in terms of eradication of red tapism and procedural hassles in business registration and taxation (Gandhi, Batra, & Gupta, 2019; Manshani & Dubey, 2017). India has shown a steady climb in the Ease of Doing Business parameters in recent years (Seth Sharma, 2019). In addition, the Aatmanirbhar Bharat drive encouraging Indian business is also leading to employment generation for the youth in organic ways through expansion of the manufacturing sector (Massand, Lodi, & Ambreen, 2020). This is accompanied by specific policies targeting employment generation and trade promotion in handloom, small and medium scale industries, and women-led businesses, positively contributing to youth empowerment across the nation.

The importance of the youth in raising civic awareness and bringing transformational impact to the society has been recognized for long. For this, there have been efforts to channelize the voice of the youth in constructive ways for the development of society. The government-run digital portal MyGov.in invites the citizens to contribute their opinions in policy matters and to build awareness about various government initiatives and schemes to empower the people. These portals are important means through which the youth can reach the policymakers, make their voices heard, and leave an impact on future government decisions (Kaur & Mehta, 2017; Mishra, 2020).

Cushioning the impact of a transitioning world

As the world has entered the third decade of the twenty-first century, globalization and digitalization has brought about a surge of opportunities, opening new markets and vocations across nations. Increasing awareness for human rights and dignity, climate change, and the peaceful coexistence of plurality is exerting influences on nations to protect the rights of the citizens, to offer them the freedom of choice and rule of law, and to promote environmentally sustainable policies. At the same time, the changing times also bring about rapid flux in the traditional institutions, value and support systems, and security nets, leaving the youth vulnerable to several damaging consequences. It is important that nations plan ahead to arrest the damaging consequences owing to rapid changes in social and economic orders and draw the maximum benefits out of the opportunities available.

Policy measures to safeguard the youth: Education, employment and healthcare

Right to Education has been recognized as one of the key Rights of the Child in the UN Declaration of Child Rights (Tobin, 2019). Passage through a standardized and formalized education system allows the youth to have a level playing field when it comes to meeting the challenges of the adult world. To this end, India, like many other nations of the world, is attempting to ensure education to their children and youth. However, while universal coverage is common in the advanced nations, the school dropout rate is high in the developing nations. It is important to ensure that the children and youth in India have access to quality education on a regular basis. To this end, researchers have recommended the importance of public-private partnerships. Involvement of social entrepreneurs and NGOs in the educational initiatives for the underprivileged ensure provision of quality education to young people beyond the government-funded network (Verger, Moschetti, & Fontdevila, 2020). There is also an increased recognition of the importance of global standardization of educational content and practices, empowering the youth to keep up with the employment demands in an increasingly boundaryless world (Schumann, 2018). Welcoming foreign direct investment in the educational space and partnership of Indian universities with global institutes of repute can promote global insemination of best practices in education and research.

Connecting education with vocational training has been recognized as one of the critical components of youth empowerment by making them employable. To this end, the TVET systems have been the focal point for many nations. In India too, along with secondary education, the youth is inducted into vocational training. However, major challenges in this regard have been the connection of TVET education with employment opportunities. In many cases, TVET is seen as inferior to mainstream education, and TVET graduates are seen as unemployable. Nations such as Germany are trying to combat this problem by making internships a critical component of TVET education, where the youth learn while they earn. Similar student internship model may be fruitful in the Indian context. It is important to make technical education in India industry-oriented and to update curriculum according to industry demands. This would enhance the employability of the youth and make them productive members of the workforce (Okolie et al., 2020; Remington, 2018).

Along with mainstream and vocational education, there needs to be an impetus towards entrepreneurship so that the youths can emerge as job-generators for many others. The United Nations (UNDESA, 2018) identifies entrepreneurship, particularly social entrepreneurship, as a potent sector to find meaningful employment for the youth and to empower them while adding structural improvements to the civic order. Many nations around the world provide capital to the youth to launch independent businesses. Startup India, too, is a potent step in this direction. However, it is important that, along with capital, the youth is provided training in utilizing the capital. Further, continued mentoring is needed for the young Indian entrepreneurs, to combat the various challenges of the entrepreneurial journey. The various initiatives for entrepreneurs in India need to emphasize on financial education for the youth to enable them to plan and launch their own businesses without being dependent on salaried work. Again, entrepreneurial education, quotas, tax breaks, seed funds, and incentives that would encourage youth-led start-up ideas are critical at this stage (UNDESA, 2018, 2020). Similarly, assistance in the form of incubation, training in digital literacy, business regulations, and management knowledge is important to ensure that the youth-driven ventures in India are successful.

Along with education and training, it is essential to have a peaceful environment and adequate infrastructure to promote youth employment. According to World Bank data, rise in the ease of doing business brings down the NEET rate for youth (unemployment in terms of vocation and education) (UNDESA, 2020). Between 2014 and 2019, India has improved its Ease of Doing Business ranking by 79 points and is presently ranked 63 in the world. Other interventions include policies promoting FDI, nationwide internet connectivity, promotion of literacy and basic education, tax benefits, infrastructure building, ICT connectivity, and governance ensuring stability and rule of law (World Bank, 2020).

Policy interventions are also needed in areas where the youth is vulnerable to the impact of a transitioning world. For instance, it has been found that the youth can often be overlooked when it comes to health initiatives. The priority of the youth, perceived as more resilient in terms of health, takes a backseat while attending to the needs of young children or senior citizens. Further, the youth often lack the capital to self-fund the required healthcare. The UNDESA Report of COVID-19 interventions recommends universal health insurance and public security systems for the youth (UNDESA, 2020). Health initiatives should incorporate not only physical health but also mental health of the youth in India, helping them to combat depression, feelings of hopelessness and helplessness, anxiety, and isolation.

Along with the general initiatives, special attention needs to be paid to the disadvantaged youth, who are subject to migration, natural disasters, civil unrest, political violence, economic crisis, or poverty. Special efforts need to be made to create welfare funds to aid such youth so that they can gain stability in their environment through shelter, relocation, skilling, and financial support. It is also important to provide them with affirmative policies to compensate for the lost opportunity. An example of this is the reservation offered in education and jobs for Kashmiri Hindu youth refugees who are the victims of religious and political violence in Kashmir (Johar, 2018).

Digital empowerment and new age career skills

The rapid digitalization of the modern world and the widespread impact of digital technology make it important that the youth are empowered in the access and use of digital contrivances. The challenges of a growing digital divide have made governments across the world adopt interventions to bring access to digital facilities to all. The Digital India initiatives in recent years are timely steps in this direction. In this regard, public-private partnership is of critical importance to ensure that the governmental efforts to provide access are supplemented till the last mile (Scheerder et al., 2017). This is not a difficult target either, since digital empowerment also translates for profitability for businesses who stand to benefit from the network presence of the youth and transactions on e-commerce sites. Digital access needs to be accompanied by targeted delivery of digital and non-digital education, so that the youth is able to explore the digital world and enjoy its benefits without being drawn into unproductive side of the internet, such as passive consumption of content, social browsing, and games, as well as the dark internet with its threat of crimes, hate content, and cyberbullying (Corrales, Fenwick, & Forgó, 2018; Tynes, 2006).

Digital empowerment also necessitates the training of the youth in vocational skills using digital technology and the latest innovations in the IT world. The youth need to be provided exposure to advanced AI, robotics, and other state-of-the-art innovations, so that they are familiarized with the demands of the new work environment by the time they enter the workforce. Simultaneously, there needs to be regulations to protect the youth from potential threats in the digital world. The world, as well as India, has recently woken up to the importance of legislation for cybercrimes and ethical responsibilities in AI-driven work, and several legislations are coming about to protect the privacy of the user, curbing online internet-based crimes, and establishing ethical responsibilities when it comes to employing artificial intelligence and humanized for critical actions (Chander, 2012).

Another important concern for the Indian policymakers is digital and social media and the content of the youth. While freedom of expression is the essence of democracy, in many cases, the content available on digital media, shared and popularized by the youth are found to go against the sovereignty and legal boundaries set by citizenship laws, human rights, and cultural heritage of a land. India has recently witnessed several outrages and cases filed in courts against OTT platforms for showing content that are offensive to communities and insulting to institutions of national importance. Further, owing to the potency of social media to reach a very large audience within a short period of time, social media can be powerful tools of causing civic disruptions. The recent cases of government actions against Twitter for problematic tweets are an example of how restraints on social media practices are going to be critical for the future (Bhargava, 2021). At the same time, India, like several other nations, have implemented restrictions against harmful online content such as pornography, TikTok, or addictive online games, chiefly out of concern for their impact on the youth (Singal, 2021). It is important that with increased access to resources for education, entertainment, activism, and broadcasting, there is awareness of the need for responsible conduct on the social media and other digital platforms, and regulations set to protect the interests of the users and national integrity (Gorwa, 2019).

Channelizing youth activism: Role of youth for changing social stigma and creating good social ambience

While a lot is being said about the importance of regulating youth activism and political behaviour, the potential of the youth in bringing about social transformation is relatively understated. The youth is characterized by energy and fresh perspectives about the world, making them more open to ideas of transformation than older adults, more willing to learn new skills and processes, and more flexible about challenging existing notions (Rexhepi, Filiposka, & Trajkovik, 2018). This makes the youth particularly valuable when it comes to bringing about social change. Across the world, the youth have been traditionally seen as powerful agents of change in art, culture, lifestyles, political opinions, and civic orders, and have been the driving forces behind major social changes. In the twenty-first century, a connected world and the open forum of social media have democratized the access to the spotlight. A person, no matter how inexperienced or insignificant in stature, can reach out to millions and become viral in minutes if he or she has something novel, outstanding, or disruptive to offer. This is of tremendous importance to youth development, as the youth now can serve both as a fountainhead of new ideas and as a watchdog for the interests of the society threatened by vested interests. The 2020 OECD report on COVID-19 responses recommends involving youth in finding solutions to recovery measures (OECD, 2020).

India has traditionally seen the youth as a period of enculturation and development, where the youth is taught the values, rules, and principles of the existing order. With the advent of the digital platforms, the induction of the youth into the adult role is happening much earlier, where from early adolescence, the youth being flooded with controversies and narratives in matters of socio-political interests, forcing them to take a stand and choose a side, often without a clear understanding of all the concerns at stake (Darden, 2019; Rossini, Stromer-Galley, Baptista, & Veiga de Olivéira, 2020). This indicates a need for a well-defined process by which the energy of the youth can be channelized in socially constructive directions. Figure 5.2 presents a framework for channelizing the energy of the youth for sustainable social solutions:

The first step of inducting the Indian youth into socially transformational roles is to build in them an *awareness* of the many social issues concerning humankind, the challenges that assail India and the world, and

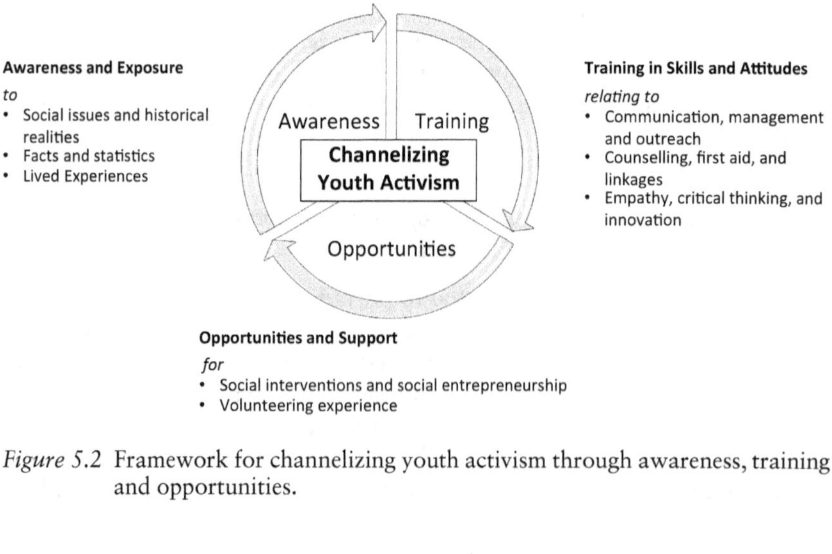

Figure 5.2 Framework for channelizing youth activism through awareness, training and opportunities.

the solutions that have been explored. While many traditionally prefer to shelter the adolescent and the youth from frustrating issues and concerns, it needs to be realized that it is difficult to insulate the youth of today from politics, social concerns, hate, and propaganda. Gradual induction under controlled and safe conditions on the other hand helps in developing a reasoned perspective in the matters without overwhelming the youth with contradictions and outrages. At the same time, it helps in setting the narrative that is consistent with the values of justice, human rights, and empathy. Gradual awareness also helps in building an understanding of complex issues such as war, racism, and systematic exploitation in simple, youth-friendly ways, using factually correct data and perspectives. This, in turn, helps the youth to detect fake narratives and propaganda going ahead and make an informed decision about which side to take (Chandra & Liang, 2017). Awareness may be built about one's cultural and social heritage, and important socio-cultural issues of India through educational curricula, awareness drives, webinars and seminars specifically targeted at the youth, newspapers, newsletters, and magazines with attractive infographics and youth-friendly languages, and digital content on social media platforms that the youth visit (Killen, 2019).

Along with awareness, it is also important to provide the Indian youth, especially those coming from the privileged classes, first-hand *exposure* to different lived realities, to build in them empathy for human beings under different conditions, and an appreciation of diversity, structural inequalities, and privilege gaps. The youth needs to be inducted to different living conditions, experiencing challenges as they affect millions of citizens in India and worldwide, and witnessing the effectiveness of existing solutions, This would clarify in the minds of the youth the challenges of executing theoretical solutions on the ground, the dynamics of human emotions and experiences, and the impact of exploitation and unequal privileges on life and growth (Khan, Ahmad, & Khan, 2019). Such exposure may again come from carefully inducted programmes in the educational curricula, where the youth is provided with immersive experiences in the lived experiences of slum dwellers, rural population, migrants, and victims of violence. Exposure under controlled environments protects the youth from threats of such encounters while building in them a clear understanding of the issues and perceptions involved.

Awareness and exposure may still leave the Indian youth passive witnesses of social inequalities unless they are also empowered with actual *skills and attitudes* that will take them beyond simply sharing a post on social media to express discontent. Research shows that skills in providing professional assistance make people more likely to offer help when others are in trouble (e.g. Carpenter & Myers, 2010). The youth in India need systematic training in basic skills of outreach and social service, such as public communication, developing IEC materials, counselling, first aid, and event management. In addition, they need to be provided with an understanding of the laws and regulations of the nation and the governance structure, linkages to major institutions that may assist in their social outreach activities, and a clear understanding of their rights and responsibilities. The Indian youth also need to be trained in important attitudes needed for social upliftment and change, such as empathy and compassion, critical thinking, healthy scepticism, creativity, tenacity, and cooperation (Koprowska, 2020). All these may be developed through school and college curricula, and through community and family efforts, that build in the youth a sense of self-efficacy about leading social transformation (Beesley, Watts, & Harrison, 2017; Blakemore & Agllias, 2019). Again, it is important to develop the communication skills needed to express their thoughts in a concise and readable manner, and critical viewing skills, so that they do not passively consume information but actively dissect it to find logical inconsistencies and problematic implications (Wilkins & Godfred, 2013).

Perhaps the most important thing that may convert digital activism to meaningful impact on the ground is frequent *opportunities for social interventions* for the youth, to participate in issues close to their heart in real life. This is possible through creating forums for interventions by the youth and allowing youth volunteers to participate in actual social work on the ground to combat stigma, end inequalities, and close privilege gaps. Social interventions also need to be made a compulsory part of curricula to provide a greater number of youth systematic exposure to important issues. Along with volunteering opportunities, policies should be encouraged to fund and flourish social entrepreneurship ventures spearheaded by the youth dealing with important issues such as climate change, pollution, digital empowerment, racism, and preservation of heritage. The Government of India incentivizes flow of corporate social responsibility funds into social entrepreneurship ventures that address the UN Sustainable Development Goals (Jain, Kansal, & Joshi, 2020). Similar efforts need to be made to fund youth-driven social entrepreneurship ventures, provide them mentoring and incubation support, and promote them to work on the ground (UNDESA, 2018). Further, such support should be provided on a sustained basis to set up an ecosystem of social ventures by the youth, where the youth previously trained through the system may now serve as *mentors* for the future generations of Indian youth (Chigunta, Gough, & Langevang, 2016). Continuous interaction with youth and mentoring them would help to guide them in the right direction for career growth and development. There is also a need for open discussion with youth about various issues so that their queries are clarified. Youth should be sensitized about their roles and responsibilities towards community development in addition to sensitizing them about opportunities for career growth.

Conclusion and recommendations

The situation of India, like the rest of the world in the twenty-first century, is one marked by rapid changes in technology, lifestyles, rhetoric, and institutionalized values. This puts the Indian lives in a state of relative uncertainty and turmoil, more so for the youth, who are in the formative years of their lives, and are vulnerable to the shocks of the system. However, the changing times also offer the Indian youth opportunities like never before, to transcend national boundaries and have a global impact, to pursue their interests beyond traditional limits of resources, and to make their voices heard, even when not backed by institutional support. The need of the hour is to defend the youth from the challenges of the changing times and empower them to make the most out of what the new age has to offer. At the same time, efforts need to be made to channelize the newfound voice of the youth in sustainable interventions that would benefit the country and humankind for the ages to come.

References

Aboujaoude, E., Savage, M., Starcevic, V., & Salame, W. (2015). Cyberbullying: review of an old problem gone viral. *Journal of Adolescent Health*, *57*, 10–18. doi:10.1016/j.jadohealth.2015.04.011.

Aguiar de Medeiros, C., & Trebat, N. (2017). Inequality and income distribution in global value chains. *Journal of Economic Issues*, *51*(2), 401–408. doi:10.1080/00213624.2017.1320916.

Akram, W., & Kumar, R. (2017). A study on positive and negative effects of social media on society. *International Journal of Computer Sciences and Engineering*, *5*(10), 347–354.

Anand, B. (2015). Reverse globalization by internationalization of SME's: opportunities and challenges ahead. *Procedia-Social and Behavioral Sciences*, *195*, 1003–1011. doi:10.1016/j.sbspro.2015.06.359.

Antunes, M. J. L., & Ahlin, E. M. (2017). Youth exposure to violence in the community: towards a theoretical framework for explaining risk and protective factors. *Aggression and Violent Behavior*, *34*, 166–177. doi:10.1016/j.avb.2017.01.015.

Arora, A., & Gambardella, A. (2005). The globalization of the software industry: perspectives and opportunities for developed and developing countries. *Innovation Policy and The Economy*, *5*, 1–32.

Atalla, P. (2020, February 24). How globalization is being redefined for a new generation. *EY*. Retrieved March 7, 2021 from https://www.ey.com/en_gl/government-public-sector/how-globalization-is-being-redefined-for-a-new-generation

Bair, J., Anner, M., & Blasi, J. (2017). Sweatshops and the search for solutions, yesterday and today. In R. Prentice & G. De Neve (Ed.) *Unmaking the global sweatshop: health and safety of the world's garment workers* (pp. 29–56). Philadelphia, PA: University of Pennsylvania Press. doi:10.9783/9780812294316-003.

Ballor, G. A., & Yildirim, A. B. (2020). Multinational corporations and the politics of international trade in multidisciplinary perspective. *Business and Politics*, *22*(4), 573–586. doi:10.1017/bap.2020.14.

Basu, S., & Ghosh, S. (2017). FDI in India: understanding the implications for growth and job creation. *Journal of Management & Public Policy*, 9(1), 5–16. doi:10.5958/0976-0148.2017.00005.1

Beesley, P., Watts, M., & Harrison, M. (2017). *Developing your communication skills in social work*. Los Angeles: Sage.

Belova, T. N. (2018). The art of agrarian policy: protectionism or free trade? *Problems of Economic Transition*, *60*(4), 325–339. doi:10.1080/10611991.2018.1497279.

Benson, P. L., & Saito, R. N. (2001). The scientific foundations of youth development. In: P. L. Benson & K. J. Pittman (Eds.) *Trends in youth development. Outreach scholarship*, vol 6. (pp. 135–154). Boston, MA: Springer. doi:10.1007/978-1-4615-1459-6_5

Berglund, H. (2017). Civil society and political protest in India – The case of Coca-Cola in Kerala. *India Review*, *16*(3), 324–343. doi:10.1080/14736489.2017.1348086

Bhardwaj, A., Avasthi, V., & Goundar, S. (2017). Impact of social networking on Indian youth-A survey. *International Journal of Electronics and Information Engineering*, 7(1), 41–51. doi:10.6636/IJEIE.201709.7(1).05

Bhargava, Y. (2021, February 10). Indian laws must be followed: government to Twitter. *The Hindu*. Retrieved March 7, 2021 from https://www.thehindu.com/news/national/indian-laws-must-be-followed-government-to-twitter/article33798461.ece

Bhatia, R. (2019). Analytics and data science industry in India: study 2019. *Analytics India Mag*. Retrieved March 7, 2021 from https://analyticsindiamag.com/analytics-data-science-industry-in-india-study-2019-by-aim-praxis-business-school/

Bhattacharyya, R., & Ghosh, S. (2020). Effect of the global financial meltdown on India's aggregate export volumes. *Applied Economics*, *52*(23), 2460–2471. doi:10.1080/00036846.2019.1691714

Bhattacharyya, S., & Mukherjee, A. (2019). Importance of skill development in Indian agriculture. In O. Prakash, A. Mukherjee, & P. Joshi (Eds.) *ICT and social media for skill development in agriculture* (pp. 47–62). New Delhi: Today & Tomorrow's Printers and Publishers.

Blackwell, D., Leaman, C., Tramposch, R., Osborne, C., & Liss, M. (2017). Extraversion, neuroticism, attachment style and fear of missing out as predictors of social media use and addiction. *Personality and Individual Differences*, *116*, 69–72. doi:10.1016/j.paid.2017.04.039

Blakemore, T., & Agllias, K. (2019). Student reflections on vulnerability and self-awareness in a social work skills course. *Australian Social Work*, *72*(1), 21–33. doi:10.1080/0312407X.2018.1516793

Bliss, S. (2017). Natural resources: child labour in India's mica mines: the global beauty industry. *Geography Bulletin*, *49*(3), 23–31.

Buck, B., & Morrow, J. (2018). AI, performance management and engagement: keeping your best. *Strategic HR Review*, *17* (5), 261–262. doi:10.1108/SHR-10-2018-145

Buckingham, D., & Kehily, M. J. (2014). Introduction: rethinking youth cultures in the age of global media. In D. Buckingham, S. Bragg, & M.J. Kehily (Eds.) *Youth Cultures in The Age Of Global Media* (pp. 1–18). London: Palgrave Macmillan. doi:10.1057/9781137008152_1

FE Bureau (2021, February 22). *Over half Indian students don't have internet access*. Retrieved July 2, 2019 from https://www.financialexpress.com/education-2/over-half-indian-students-dont-have-internet-access/2199250//

Burney, E. (2019). 4 Gen Z Political Influencers Taking On The Status Quo – And Winning. *Vogue*. Retrieved March 7, 2021 from https://www.vogue.co.uk/news/article/gen-z-political-influencers

Business Today (2021, June 1). *10 million lost jobs in Covid 2nd wave, 97% households' income declined: CMIE*. BusinessToday.in, Retrieved July 2, 2021 from https://www.businesstoday.in/latest/economy-politics/story/income-of-97-households-declined-since-covid-19-pandemic-began-cmie-298381-2021-06-01

Buttazzoni, A., Brar, K., & Minaker, L. (2021). Smartphone-based interventions and internalizing disorders in youth: systematic review and meta-analysis. *Journal of Medical Internet Research*, *23*(1), e16490. doi:10.2196/16490

Caldentey, E. P., & Vernengo, M. (2017). Wage-led, debt-led growth in an open economy. *Review of Keynesian Economics*, *5*(3), 307–335. doi:10.4337/roke.2017.03.02

Carpenter, J., & Myers, C. K. (2010). Why volunteer? Evidence on the role of altruism, image, and incentives. *Journal of Public Economics*, 94(11–12), 911–920. doi:10.1016/j.jpubeco.2010.07.007

Carr, C. P., Martins, C. M. S., Stingel, A. M., Lemgruber, V. B., & Juruena, M. F. (2013). The role of early life stress in adult psychiatric disorders: a systematic review according to childhood trauma subtypes. *The Journal of Nervous and Mental Disease*, 201(12), 1007–1020. doi:10.1097/NMD.0000000000000049

Centre for the New Economy and Society (2018). *The Future of Jobs Report 2018*. World Economic Forum. Retrieved March 7, 2021 from http://www3.weforum.org/docs/WEF_Future_of_Jobs_2018.pdf

Chander, H. (2012). *Cyber laws and IT protection*. New Delhi: PHI Learning Pvt. Ltd.

Chandra, Y., & Liang, S. (2017). Social enterprise as a mechanism of youth empowerment. *The Hong Kong Journal of Social Work*, *51*(01n02), 115–144. doi:10.1142/S0219246217000080

Chandy, L. (2020, January 27). *New Insights: Best decade ever? Measuring success – comparing the progress of global development in relative vs. absolute terms*. Retrieved March 7, 2021 from https://www.unicef.org/globalinsight/stories/new-insights-best-decade-ever

Chavan, M., & Taksa, L. (2017). Shifts in intergenerational mobility of indian immigrant entrepreneurs. *International Migration*, 55(1), 99–127.

Chigunta, F., Gough, K. V., & Langevang, T. (2016). Overcoming constraints through ingenuity and social entrepreneurship. Young entrepreneurs in sub-Saharan Africa. In K.V. Gough & T. Langevang (Eds.) *Young entrepreneurs in sub-Saharan Africa* (pp. 67–88). New York: Routledge.

Cho, Y. S. (2020). *"Disguised unemployment" in underdeveloped areas*. University of California Press. doi:10.1525/9780520311305

Choudhury, P., Foroughi, C., & Larson, B. Z. (2020). Work-from-anywhere: the productivity effects of geographic flexibility. In *Academy of Management Proceedings* (Vol. 2020, No. 1, p. 21199). Briarcliff Manor, NY 10510: Academy of Management. Retrieved March 7, 2021 from https://journals.aom.org/doi/pdf/10.5465/AMBPP.2020.225

CMIE (2021). *Unemployment rate for India*. Retrieved July 2, 2021 from https://unemploymentinindia.cmie.com/

Commonwealth Secretariat (2016). *Global Youth Development Index and Report 2016*. London. Retrieved March 7, 2021 from http://cmydiprod.uksouth.cloudapp.azure.com/sites/default/files/2016-10/2016%20Global%20Youth%20Development%20Index%20and%20Report.pdf.

Corrales, M., Fenwick, M., & Forgó, N. (Eds.). (2018). *Robotics, AI and the future of law*. Singapore: Springer.

Coşar, A. K., Guner, N., & Tybout, J. (2016). Firm dynamics, job turnover, and wage distributions in an open economy. *American Economic Review*, *106*(3), 625–663. doi:10.1257/aer.20110457

Costello, M., Barrett-Fox, R., Bernatzky, C., Hawdon, J., & Mendes, K. (2020). Predictors of viewing online extremism among America's youth. *Youth & Society*, *52*(5), 710–727. doi:10.1177/0044118X18768115

Côté, J. E., & Levine, C. (2015). *Identity formation, youth, and development: a simplified approach*. New York: Psychology Press. doi:10.4324/9780203767047

Darden, J. T. (2019). *Tackling Terrorists' Exploitation of Youth*. American Enterprise Institute. Retrieved March 7, 2021 from https://www.un.org/sexualviolenceinconflict/wp-content/uploads/2019/05/report/tackling-terrorists-exploitation-of-youth/Tackling-Terrorists-Exploitation-of-Youth.pdf

Davies, W. (2020). The last global crisis didn't change the world. But this one could. *The Guardian*. Retrieved March 7, 2021 from https://www.theguardian.com/commentisfree/2020/mar/24/coronavirus-crisis-change-world-financial-global-capitalism#

Department of Food and Public Distribution (2018). *Annual Report 2017–18*. Retrieved March 7, 2021 from http://dfpd.nic.in/LwB3AHIAaQB0AGUAcgBlAGEAZABkAGEAdABhAC8AUABvAHIAdABhAGwALwBNAGEAZwBhAHoAaQBAGUALwBEAG8AYwB1AG0AZQBuAHQALwA=1_141_1_annualreportenglish.pdf

Engelhard, F., & Garg, R. (2018). The influence of intra-cultural diversity on self-efficacy beliefs: evidence from India. *International Journal of Indian Culture and Business Management*, *16*(2), 131–155. doi:10.1504/IJICBM.2018.090086

Fisher, D. R. (2012). Youth political participation: bridging activism and electoral politics. *Annual Review of Sociology*, *38*, 119–137. doi:10.1146/annurev-soc-071811-145439

Fothergill, A. (2017). Children, youth, and disaster. In *Oxford Research Encyclopedia of Natural Hazard Science*. doi:10.1093/acrefore/9780199389407.013.23

Frenette, A. (2015). From apprenticeship to internship: the social and legal antecedents of the intern economy. *Triple C – Communication, Capitalism & Critique: Open Access Journal for a Global Sustainable Information Society*, *13*(2), 351–360. doi:10.31269/triplec.v13i2.625

Fuerst-Bjeliš, B., & Leimgruber, W. (2020). Marginalization–the dark side of globalization. In B. Fuerst-Bjeliš & W. Leimgruber (Eds.) *Globalization, Marginalization and Conflict: Perspectives on Geographical Marginality*, vol 6. (pp. 3–11). Cham: Springer. doi:10.1007/978-3-030-53218-5_1

Funes, M., & Mackness, J. (2018). When inclusion excludes: a counter narrative of open online education. *Learning, Media and Technology*, *43*(2), 119–138. doi:10.1080/17439884.2018.1444638

Gallup (2019), Gallup World Poll. Retrieved March 9, 2021 from https://www.gallup.com/analytics/232838/world-poll.aspx.

Gandhi, D., Batra, N. K., & Gupta, T. (2019). Startup India: opportunities and Challenges. *Invertis Journal of Management*, *11*(2), 97–104.

Gessler, M. (2017). The lack of collaboration between companies and schools in the German dual apprenticeship system: historical background and recent data. *International Journal for Research in Vocational Education and Training (IJRVET)*, *4*(2), 164–195. doi:10.13152/IJRVET.4.2.4

Ghobadi, S., & Mathiassen, L. (2020). A generational perspective on the software workforce: precocious Users of social networking in software development.

Journal of Management Information Systems, *37*(1), 96–128. doi:10.1080/07421222.2019.1705508

Gillespie, T. (2018). *Custodians of the Internet: platforms, content moderation, and the hidden decisions that shape social media*. New Haven: Yale University Press.

Girasa, R. (2020). Applications of AI and projections of AI impact. In *Artificial intelligence as a disruptive technology* (pp. 23–67). Cham: Palgrave Macmillan. 10.1007/978-3-030-35975-1_2

Glatzer, W. (2012). Cross-national comparisons of quality of life in developed nations, including the impact of globalization. In K. Land, A. Michalos, & M. Sirgy (Eds.) *Handbook of social indicators and quality of life research* (pp. 381–398). Dordrecht: Springer. doi:10.1007/978-94-007-2421-1_18

Gordon, H. R., & Taft, J. K. (2011). Rethinking youth political socialization: teenage activists talk back. *Youth & Society*, *43*(4), 1499–1527. doi:10.1177/0044118X10386087

Gorwa, R. (2019). The platform governance triangle: conceptualising the informal regulation of online content. *Internet Policy Review*, 8(2), 1–22. doi:10.14763/2019.2.1407

Hidalgo-Mari, T., & Segarra-Saavedra, J. (2017). The YouTuber phenomenon and its transmedia expansion. *Analysis of youth empowerment in social media*. Retrieved March 7, 2021 from https://core.ac.uk/download/pdf/288436878.pdf

ILO (2019). *World Employment Social Outlook*. Retrieved March 9, 2021 from https://www.ilo.org/wcmsp5/groups/public/---dgreports/---dcomm/---publ/documents/publication/wcms_670542.pdf

ILO (2020a). *Global Employment Trends for Youth 2020: Technology and the Future of Jobs*. Retrieved March 9, 2021 from https://www.ilo.org/wcmsp5/groups/public/---dgreports/---dcomm/---publ/documents/publication/wcms_737648.pdf

ILO (2020b, May 27). *ILO Monitor: COVID-19 and the world of work. Fourth edition Updated estimates and analysis*. Retrieved March 9, 2021 from https://www.ilo.org/wcmsp5/groups/public/---dgreports/---dcomm/documents/briefingnote/wcms_745963.pdf

International Telecommunication Union (2017). *Measuring the Information Society Report Volume 1*. Retrieved March 9, 2021 from https://www.itu.int/en/ITU-D/Statistics/Documents/publications/misr2017/MISR2017_Volume1.pdf

IOM (2020). *World Migration Report 2020*. Retrieved March 9, 2021 from https://publications.iom.int/books/world-migration-report-2020

Jain, A., Kansal, M., & Joshi, M. (2020). New development: corporate philanthropy to mandatory corporate social responsibility (CSR) – a new law for India. *Public Money & Management*, 1–3. doi:10.1080/09540962.2020.1714280

Janssens, M., Maddux, W. W., & Nguyen, T. (2019). Globalization: current issues and future research directions. *Negotiation and Conflict Management Research*, 12(2), 174–185. doi:10.1111/ncmr.12149

Jeske, D., & Holland, P. (2019). Employer and employee vetting: reputation management challenges in the information age. In P. Holland (Ed.) *Contemporary HRM issues in the 21st century* (pp. 145–157). Bingley: Emerald Publishing Limited. doi:10.1108/978-1-78973-457-720191018

Johar, P. (2018). The caste of migrants: affirmative action and the case of Kashmiri Pandits. *Prabuddha: Journal of Social Equality*, *1*(1), 45–56.

Jorda, V. & Sarabia, J.M. (2014). Well-being distribution in the globalization era: 30 years of convergence. *Applied Research in Quality of Life*, *10*, 123–140. doi:10.1007/s11482-014-9304-8.

Joshi, M. (2021, February 22). Explained: why is Delhi Police probing a farmers' protest "toolkit" tweeted by Greta Thunberg? *The Indian Express*. Retrieved March 9, 2021 from https://indianexpress.com/article/explained/greta-thunberg-toolkit-farmers-protest-fir-delhi-police-7176187/

Rajagopal, K. (2021, March 4). Supreme Court for screening of OTT content, says some show pornography. *The Hindu*. Retrieved March 7, 2021 from https://www.thehindu.com/news/national/sc-for-screening-of-ott-content-says-some-show-pornography/article33987361.ece

Karampampas, P. (2020). Goth YouTubers and the informal mentoring of young goths: peer support and solidarity in the Greek goth scene. *Journal of Youth Studies*, 23(8), 989–1003. doi:10.1080/13676261.2019.1646892

Kaur, S., & Mehta, S. (2017). Content analysis of e-Government site Mygov.in: sociological perspective. *Asian Journal of Research in Social Sciences and Humanities*, 7(7), 12–20.

Keating, A., & Melis, G. (2017). Social media and youth political engagement: preaching to the converted or providing a new voice for youth? *The British Journal of Politics and International Relations*, 19(4), 877–894. doi:10.1177/1369148117718461

Kemp, N. (2016, June 23). *Rise of the anti-blogger: how the influence model is changing. Campaign*. Retrieved March 9, 2021 from https://www.campaignlive.co.uk/article/rise-anti-blogger-influence-model-changing/1399333

Kesharwani, A. (2020). Do (how) digital natives adopt a new technology differently than digital immigrants? A longitudinal study. *Information & Management*, 57(2), 103170. doi:10.1016/j.im.2019.103170

Khadria, B. (2009). The future of South Asian migration: a look at India, Pakistan and Bangladesh. *OECD Journal: General Papers*, 2009(4): 26–49. doi:10.1787/gen_papers-v2009-art9-en

Khan, R. A., Ahmad, M. S., & Khan, R. U. (2019). Service-Learning for youth leadership. *Applied Research in Quality of Life*, 1–4. doi:10.1007/s11482-019-09766-5

Kharat, R. S. (2021, May 14). The culture of political violence in India is not new. *The Pioneer*. Retrieved July 2, 2020 from https://www.dailypioneer.com/2021/columnists/the-culture-of-political-violence-in-india-is-not-new.html

Killen, M. (2019). Developing inclusive youth: how to reduce social exclusion and foster equality and equity in childhood. *American Educator*, 43(3), 8–12.

Kim, I. S., & Milner, H. V. (2019). *Multinational corporations and their influence through lobbying on foreign policy*. Retrieved March 7, 2021 from https://www.brookings.edu/wp-content/uploads/2019/12/Kim_Milner_manuscript.pdf

Koprowska, J. (2020). *Communication and interpersonal skills in social work*. London: Sage.

Kwok, R. C. W., Leung, A. C. M., Hui, S. S. C., & Wong, C. C. K. (2021). Virtual trainer system: a tool to increase exercise participation and work productivity. *Internet Research*, *31*(3), 892–910. doi:10.1108/INTR-04-2020-0236

Linden, G., Dedrick, J., & Kraemer, K. L. (2011). Innovation and job creation in a global economy: the case of Apple's iPod. *Journal Of International Commerce & Economics*, 3, 223.

Lund, S., & Tyson, L. (2018). Globalization is not in retreat: digital technology and the future of trade. *Foreign Affairs*, *97*, 130.

Lv, Z., & Xu, T. (2019). Do economic sanctions affect protectionism? Evidence from agricultural support. *Economics & Politics*, 31(1), 27–42. doi:10.1111/ecpo.12124

Manshani, S., & Dubey, A. (2017). Startup women in Startup India: a study of women entrepreneurs in India. *International Journal of Business Management (IJBGM)*, *6*(4), 91–100.

Manyika, J. (2017). *Technology, Jobs, And the Future of Work. McKinsey Global Institute.* Retrieved March 7, 2021 from http://fs2.american.edu/dfagel/www/Class%20Readings/Marx/Technology,%20jobs,%20and%20the%20future%20of%20work%20_%20McKinsey%20&%20Company.pdf

Maqbool, A. (2020, July 10). Black Lives Matter: from social media post to global movement. *BBC World.* Retrieved from https://www.bbc.com/news/world-us-canada-53273381

Massand, A., Lodi, M. K., & Ambreen, L. (2020). Atmanirbhar Bharat: economic, legal, and social aspects. *International Journal of Management (IJM)*, *11*(6), 1038–1046. doi:10.34218/IJM.11.6.2020.092

Mathew, J. C. (2021, January 25). India bucks global decline in FDI; grows 13% against world's 42% fall in 2020. *Business Today*. Retrieved March 7, 2021 from https://www.businesstoday.in/current/economy-politics/india-bucks-global-decline-in-fdi-grows-13-against-world-42-fall-in-2020/story/428959.html

McGowan, S. (2018). *Economic sanctions as tools of economic imperialism.* University of Central Oklahoma. ProQuest Dissertations Publishing, 2018. 10815170. Retrieved March 7, 2021 from https://shareok.org/bitstream/handle/11244/325081/McGowanS2018.pdf?sequence=1

McMurphy, L. (2020). *It takes a village: alternatives to the nuclear family and how the traditional model fails us.* (Unpublished thesis). Texas State University, San Marcos, Texas. Retrieved March 7, 2021 from https://digital.library.txstate.edu/bitstream/handle/10877/13129/MCMURPHY-HONORSTHESIS-2020.pdf?

Middaugh, E., Clark, L. S., & Ballard, P. J. (2017). Digital media, participatory politics, and positive youth development. *Pediatrics*, 140(Supplement 2), S127–S131. doi:10.1542/peds.2016-1758Q

Ministry of Human Resource Development (2020). *National Educational Policy 2020.* Retrieved March 7, 2021 from https://www.education.gov.in/sites/upload_files/mhrd/files/NEP_Final_English_0.pdf

Ministry of Youth Affairs and Sports (2014). *National Youth Policy 2014.* Retrieved March 7, 2021 from https://yas.nic.in/sites/default/files/National-Youth-Policy-Document.pdf

Mishra, S. S. (2020). Testing the antecedents to e-democracy towards citizens' happiness: a structural equation modelling approach to "MyGov" initiative, India. *International Journal of Public Administration*, *43*(15), 1293–1303. doi:10.1080/01900692.2019.1669051

Mohanty, A. (2020, August 26). Seven decades after independence, many tribal languages in India face extinction threat. *Down To Earth.* Retrieved March 9, 2021 from https://www.downtoearth.org.in/blog/governance/seven-decades-after-independence-many-tribal-languages-in-india-face-extinction-threat-73071

Mohanty, A. Middaugh, E., Bowyer, B., & Kahne, J. (2017). U suk! Participatory media and youth experiences with political discourse. *Youth & Society*, *49*(7), 902–922. doi:10.1177/0044118X16655246

Nanda, P.K., & Mishra, A.R. (2020, February 10). Govt plans to ease rules on foreign investment in education sector. *LiveMint.* Retrieved March 7, 2021 from https://www.livemint.com/education/news/govt-plans-to-ease-rules-on-foreign-investment-in-education-sector-11581358606272.html

NeGD (2021). *Responsible AI for Youth: a national programme for government schools.* Retrieved March 7, 2021 from https://responsibleaiforyouth.negd.in/home

Nieuwelink, H., ten Dam, G., & Dekker, P. (2019). Adolescent citizenship and educational track: a qualitative study on the development of views on the common good. *Research Papers in Education*, *34*(3), 373–388. doi:10.1080/02671522.2018.1452958

Nolan, P. (2018). The two-edged sword of capitalist globalization. *Challenge*, 61(1), 92–103. doi:10.1080/05775132.2018.1423668

OECD (2019). *2019 International Migration and Displacement Trends and Policies Report to the G20.* Retrieved March 7, 2021 from https://www.oecd.org/migration/mig/G20-migration-and-displacement-trends-and-policies-report-2019.pdf

OECD (2020, June 11). *OECD Policy Responses to Coronavirus (COVID-19): Youth and COVID-19: Response, recovery and resilience.* Retrieved March 7, 2021 from https://www.oecd.org/coronavirus/en/policy-responses

Okolie, U. C., Elom, E. N., Igwe, P. A., Nwajiuba, C. A., Binuomote, M. O., & Igu, N. (2020). How TVET teachers foster employability skills: insights from developing countries. *International Journal of Training Research*, 1–19. doi:10.1080/14480220.2020.1860301

Ortiz-Ospina, E. (2019, September 18). The rise of social media. *Our World in Data.* Retrieved March 7, 2021 from https://ourworldindata.org/rise-of-social-media

Ozer, E. J., Lavi, I., Douglas, L., & Wolf, J. P. (2017). Protective factors for youth exposed to violence in their communities: a review of family, school, and community moderators. *Journal of Clinical Child & Adolescent Psychology*, 46(3), 353–378. doi:10.1080/15374416.2015.1046178

Palvia, S., Aeron, P., Gupta, P., Mahapatra, D., Parida, R., Rosner, R., & Sindhi, S. (2018). Online education: worldwide status, challenges, trends, and implications. *Journal of Global Information Technology Management*, *21*(4), 233–241, doi:10.1080/1097198X.2018.1542262

Penney, J. (2020). "It's so hard not to be funny in this situation": memes and humor in US youth online political expression. *Television & New Media*, 21(8), 791–806. doi:10.1177/1527476419886068

Perlas, N. (2019). *Shaping globalization: civil society, cultural power, and threefolding.* Forest Row: Temple Lodge Publishing Ltd.

Petray, T. L., & Collin, R. (2017). Your privilege is trending: confronting whiteness on social media. *Social Media+Society*, 3(2), 2056305117706783. doi:10.1177/2056305117706783

Philip, S. (2019, December 5). Explained: Kerala's Islamic State connection. *The Indian Express.* Retrieved July 2, 2021 from https://indianexpress.com/article/explained/simply-put-keralas-isis-connection-islamic-state-afghanistan-6149447/

Plant, P. (2014). Green guidance. In G. Arulmani, A. Bakshi, F. Leong, A. Watts (Eds.) *Handbook of Career Development. International and Cultural Psychology* (pp. 7–17). New York: Springer. doi:10.1007/978-1-4614-9460-7_17

Pruitt, L. (2017). Youth, politics, and participation in a changing world. *Journal of Sociology*, *53*(2), 507–513. doi:10.1177/1440783317705733

PTI (2018, July 14). Four Indian youth planning to join ISIS held in Syria. *The Economic Times.* Retrieved July 2, 2021 from https://economictimes.indiatimes.com/news/defence/four-indian-youth-planning-to-join-isis-held-in-syria/articleshow/50572961.cms?from=mdrRajagopal.

PTI (2019, May 12). Social media plays key role in influencing first-time voters: report. *The Economic Times*. Retrieved July 2, 2021 from https://economictimes.indiatimes.com/news/elections/lok-sabha/india/social-media-plays-key-role-in-influencing-first-time-voters-report/articleshow/69295605.cms?utm_source=contentofinterest&utm_medium=text&utm_campaign=cppst

PTI (2020, October 18). COVID-19 prompts workers, corporates to adopt gig economy. *ET Auto.com*. Retrieved March 7, 2021 from https://auto.economictimes.indiatimes.com/news/industry/covid-19-prompts-workers-corporates-to-adopt-gig-economy/78732889

Rama, M. (2003). *Globalization and workers in developing countries*. World Bank Policy research working paper, (2958). Retrieved March 7, 2021 from https://openknowledge.worldbank.org/bitstream/handle/10986/19177/multi0page.pdf

Remington, T. F. (2018). Public–private partnerships in TVET: adapting the dual system in the United States. *Journal of Vocational Education & Training*, *70*(4), 497–523. doi:10.1080/13636820.2018.1450776

Rexhepi, A., Filiposka, S., & Trajkovik, V. (2018). Youth e-participation as a pillar of sustainable societies. *Journal of Cleaner Production*, 174, 114–122. doi:10.1016/j.jclepro.2017.10.327

Rituraj, V. (2018). Making of e-India through the "Digital India" e-Governance Plan: impact and challenges. In P. Kumar, V. K. Jain, K.S. Pareek (Eds.) *The stances of e-government: policies, processes and technologies*. Chapman & Hall: CRC. doi:10.1201/9780203731451

Roberts, K. (2019). *Youth and leisure*. London: Routledge. doi:10.4324/9780429024528

Rossini, P., Stromer-Galley, J., Baptista, E. A., & Veiga de Oliveira, V. (2020). Dysfunctional information sharing on WhatsApp and Facebook: the role of political talk, cross-cutting exposure and social corrections. *New Media & Society, Jume* 2020. doi:10.1177/1461444820928059

Roy, P.K. (2019, March 18). Mobile data: why India has the world's cheapest. *BBC*. Retrieved March 7, 2021 from https://www.bbc.com/news/world-asia-india-47537201

Sambuli, N. & Magnoli, S. (2019, April 29). *What is digital equality? An interview with Nanjira Sambuli*. World Economic Forum. Retrieved March 7, 2021 from https://www.weforum.org/agenda/2019/04/digital-equality-interview-nanjira-sambuli/

Sarda, M., Deshpande, B., Deo, S., & Karanjkar, R. (2018). A comparative study on maslow's theory and indian ashrama system. *International Journal of Innovative Technology and Exploring Engineering*, *8*(2), 48–50

Scheerder, A., van Deursen, A., & van Dijk, J. (2017). Determinants of Internet skills, uses and outcomes. A systematic review of the second-and third-level digital divide. *Telematics and Informatics*, *34*(8), 1607–1624. doi:10.1016/j.tele.2017.07.007

Schumann, C. (2018). Cosmopolitanism and globalization in education. In P. Smeyers (Ed) *International handbook of philosophy of education* (pp. 821–831). Springer, Cham. doi:10.1007/978-3-319-72761-5_59

Seth Sharma, Y. (2019, October 24). India jumps to 63rd position in World Bank's Ease of Doing Business 2020 report. *The Economic Times*. Retrieved March 7, 2021 from https://economictimes.indiatimes.com/news/economy/indicators/india-jumps-to-63rd-position-in-world-banks-doing-business-2020-report/articleshow/71731589.cms?from=mdr

Sherif, M. & Sherif, C.W., (2009). *Problems of Youth Transition to Adulthood in a Changing World*. Chicago: Aldine Pub. Co.

Siegfried, K. (2020, March 11). *The Refugee Brief*. Retrieved March 7, 2021 from https://www.unhcr.org/refugeebrief/the-refugee-brief-11-march-2020/

Simplice, A. (2013). Globalization and Africa: implications for human development. *International Journal of Development Issues*, 12(3), 213–238. doi:10.1108/IJDI-10-2012-0064

Singal, N. (2021, January 25). India bans TikTok permanently; App evaluates notice. *BusinessToday.in*. Retrieved March 7, 2021 from https://www.businesstoday.in/technology/news/india-bans-tiktok-permanently-app-evaluates-notice/story/429086.html#

Singh, C., Osbahr, H., & Dorward, P. (2018). The implications of rural perceptions of water scarcity on differential adaptation behaviour in Rajasthan, India. *Regional Environmental Change*, 18(8), 2417–2432. doi:10.1007/s10113-018-1358-y

Singh, P. (2020, June 16). 155 Indian companies create nearly 125K jobs in US: CII report. *Hindustan Times*. Retrieved March 7, 2021 from https://www.hindustantimes.com/indians-abroad/155-indian-companies-create-nearly-125k-jobs-in-us-cii-report/story-UvESpZD7jRbZ2TGxDCMtJJ.html

Smith, B. G., Krishna, A., & Al-Sinan, R. (2019). Beyond slacktivism: examining the entanglement between social media engagement, empowerment, and participation in activism. *International Journal of Strategic Communication*, *13*(3), 182–196. doi:10.1080/1553118X.2019.1621870

Spring, J. (2014). *Globalization of education: an introduction*. New York: Routledge. doi:10.4324/9781315795843

Statista (2021a, March 19). *Number of registered foreign companies in India FY 2020 by state*. Retrieved March 7, 2021 from https://www.statista.com/statistics/1009251/india-number-of-registered-foreign-companies-by-state/

Statista (2021b, May 26). *Impact on job loss and gain due to the coronavirus (COVID-19) lockdown in India between April and July 2020, by age group*. Retrieved July 2, 2021 from https://www.statista.com/statistics/1125798/india-covid-19-impact-on-job-loss-by-age-group/

Statista (2021c, July 23). *Distribution of gross domestic product (GDP) across economic sectors in India 2019*. Retrieved October 14, 2021 from https://www.statista.com/statistics/271329/distribution-of-gross-domestic-product-gdp-across-economic-sectors-in-india/

Statista (2021d, July 23). *India: distribution of the workforce across economic sectors from 2010 to 2020*. Retrieved October 14, 2021 from https://www.statista.com/statistics/271320/distribution-of-the-workforce-across-economic-sectors-in-india/

Stiglitz, J. E. (2017). The overselling of globalization. *Business Economics*, 52(3), 129–137. doi:10.1057/s11369-017-0047-z

Suchday, S., Santoro, A. F., Ramanayake, N., Lewin, H., & Almeida, M. (2018). Religion, spirituality, globalization reflected in life beliefs among urban Asian Indian youth. *Psychology of Religion and Spirituality*, 10(2), 146–156. doi:10.1037/rel0000161

Sukarieh, M., & Tannock, S. (2018). The global securitisation of youth. *Third World Quarterly*, 39(5), 854–870. doi:10.1080/01436597.2017.1369038

Sustainable Development Solutions Network – Youth (2020). *Youth Solutions Report 2020*. New York: Sustainable Development Solutions Network - Youth. Retrieved March 7, 2021 from https://www.undp.org/content/undp/en/home/librarypage/democratic-governance/youth-solutions-report-2020.html

The Hindu (2021, January 10). *Education Ministry calls for action plan to stop school drop-outs*. Retrieved July 2, 2021 from https://www.thehindu.com/news/national/education-ministry-draws-up-plans-to-support-students-hit-by-pandemic/article33543296.ece

The Times of India (2021a, May 22). *'Young people with no comorbidities at risk in 2nd wave'*. Retrieved July 2, 2021 from https://timesofindia.indiatimes.com/india/young-people-with-no-comorbidities-at-risk-in-2nd-wave/articleshow/82849169.cms

The Times of India (2021b, June 30). *One Nation, One Ration Card scheme: All you need to know*. Retrieved July 2, 2021 from https://timesofindia.indiatimes.com/india/one-nation-one-ration-card-scheme-all-you-need-to-know/articleshow/83978697.cms

Thompson, B. Y. (2018). Digital nomads: employment in the online gig economy. *Glocalism, Journal of Culture, Politics and Innovation*, *1*, 1–26.

Tobin, J. (Ed.). (2019). *The UN convention on the rights of the child: a commentary*. Oxford: Oxford University Press.

Tyner, K. (2014). *Literacy in a digital world: teaching and learning in the age of information*. New York: Routledge. doi:10.4324/9781410601971

Tynes, B. (2006). Children, adolescents, and the culture of hate online. In N. Dowd, D. Singer & R. F. Wilson (Eds.). *Handbook of children, culture, and violence*. Thousand Oaks: Sage.

UNDESA (2018). *World Youth Report: Youth and the 2030 Agenda for Sustainable Development*. United Nations Department of Economic and Social Affairs. Retrieved March 7, 2021 from https://www.un.org/development/desa/youth/wp-content/uploads/sites/21/2018/12/WorldYouthReport-2030Agenda.pdf

UNDESA (2019). *International Migration 2019*. Retrieved March 7, 2021 from https://www.un.org/en/development/desa/population/migration/publications/migrationreport/docs/InternationalMigration2019_Report.pdf

UNESCO (2020, March 24). *COVID-19 Educational Disruption and Response*. Retrieved March 7, 2021 from https://en.unesco.org/news/covid-19-educational-disruption-and-response

UNDESA (2020, March 27). *Special issue on COVID-19 and Youth*. Retrieved March 7, 2021 from https://www.un.org/development/desa/dspd/wp-content/uploads/sites/22/2020/04/YOUTH-FLASH-Special-issue-on-COVID-19-1.pdf

UNICEF (2020). *The impact of COVID-19 on the mental health of adolescents and youth*. Retrieved March 7, 2021 from https://www.un.org/development/desa/dspd/wp-content/uploads/sites/22/2020/04/YOUTH-FLASH-Special-issue-on-COVID-19-1.pdf

UNICEF (2021). *Children Under Attack*. Retrieved March 7, 2021 from https://www.unicef.org/children-under-attack

United Nations (2016). *Report on the World Social Situation 2016 – Leaving No One Behind: The Imperative of Inclusive Development*. Produced by the Department of Economic and Social Affairs, Division for Social Policy and Development. Sales No. E.16.IV.1. Retrieved March 7, 2021 from https://www.un.org/esa/socdev/rwss/2016/full-report.pdf.

United Nations (2019). *The Sustainable Development Goals Report 2019*. Retrieved March 7, 2021 from https://unstats.un.org/sdgs/report/2019/The-Sustainable-Development-Goals-Report-2019.pdf

United Nations (2020). *Decade of Action: Ten years to transform our world.* Retrieved March 7, 2021 from https://www.un.org/sustainabledevelopment/decade-of-action/

United Nations Department of Economic and Social Affairs [UNDESA] (2020). *The United Nations Guide to the Youth Delegate Programme.* Retrieved from https://www.un.org/development/desa/youth/wp-content/uploads/sites/21/2020/05/Youth-Delegates-Guide_May-20200-WEB-1.pdf

United Nations Youth (2013). *Definition of Youth.* Retrieved March 7, 2021 from https://www.un.org/esa/socdev/documents/youth/fact-sheets/youth-definition.pdf

Van Dijk, J. (2020). *The digital divide.* John Wiley & Sons.

Vanderwey, H. (2019, February 1). *Turning youth unemployment into entrepreneurship.* Pacific.UNDP.org. Retrieved March 7, 2021 from https://www.pacific.undp.org/content/pacific/en/home/blog/2019/turning-youth-unemployment-into-entrepreneurship.html

Verger, A., Moschetti, M. C., & Fontdevila, C. (2020). How and why policy design matters: understanding the diverging effects of public-private partnerships in education. *Comparative Education*, 56(2), 278–303.

Vie, S. (2014). In defense of "slacktivism": the Human Rights Campaign Facebook logo as digital activism. *First Monday.* Retrieved March 7, 2021 from https://firstmonday.org/article/view/4961/3868

Vromen, A., Loader, B., Xenos, M. and Bailo, F. (2016) Everyday making through Facebook engagement: young citizens' political interactions in Australia, the United Kingdom and the United States. *Political Studies*, 64(3), 513–533. doi:10.1177/0032321715614012

Walker, J. A. (2012). Early marriage in Africa–trends, harmful effects, and interventions. *African Journal of Reproductive Health*, 16(2), 231–240.

Wang, B., Liu, Y., Qian, J., & Parker, S. K. (2021). Achieving effective remote working during the COVID-19 pandemic: a work design perspective. *Applied Psychology*, *70*(1), 16–59. doi:10.1111/apps.12290

Way, A. K., & Redden, S. M. (2017). The study of youth online: a critical review and agenda. *Review of Communication*, 17(2), 119–136. doi:10.1080/15358593.2017.1293838

Westerlund, M. (2019). The emergence of deepfake technology: a review. *Technology Innovation Management Review*, 9(11), 40–53. http://doi.org/10.22215/timreview/1282

Wilding, R. (2018). *Families, intimacy and globalization.* London: Macmillan International Higher Education.

Wilkins, D., & Godfred, W. D. B. (2013). *Critical analysis skills for social workers.* Berkshire: McGraw-Hill Education.

World Bank (2020). *World Development Report 2020: Trading for Development in the Age of Global Value Chains.* Retrieved March 7, 2021 from https://www.worldbank.org/en/publication/wdr2020

World Health Organization (2020, January 14). *Laboratory testing for 2019 novel coronavirus (2019-nCoV) in suspected human cases.* Retrieved March 7, 2021 from https://apps.who.int/iris/bitstream/handle/10665/332300/WHO-2019-nCoV-laboratory-2020.2-eng.pdf

6 Adversities experienced by youth and their risk behaviour

Human civilization is undergoing a phase of transition across the world in terms of technological advancements. Technological advancements have impacted the lifestyles of people of all sections of the society. Children and youths are greatly influenced by the virtual world. Virtual world has both positive and negative impacts on children and youths. Positive impact includes access to all information and connecting with people of larger society, while negative impact is dependence on the Internet and/or mobile and access to adult information resulting in waste of valuable time and distraction in studies. Risk behaviour of a large number of youths is greatly influenced by adult sites of the Internet in addition to other social and psychological factors.

Challenges and/or adversities in life are a normal phenomenon. In fact, without challenge, life is boring or dull. Challenges in various phases of life motivate us to remain active and creative, to make better progress, and achieve our target. We keep on making every effort to overcome the challenges by adopting situation-specific best strategies. Most of the time we are successful in overcoming the challenges while in some cases we fail because of various reasons. Nevertheless, failure is also an experience to overcome similar challenges in future. If one maintains good interpersonal relationships with different social agents one will be more likely to enjoy social support at times of crisis and psychologically one feels much stronger and confident.

However, challenges and/or adversities in the case of children, adolescents, and youth during the development phase are also a normal phenomenon owing to various life challenges. They are more vulnerable to adversities since they are minor, voiceless and mentally and physically are not stronger like adults to overcome the challenges and/or adversities on their own. Therefore, it is the responsibility of the biological parents to protect children, adolescents, and youth from all adversities, teach them how to deal with life challenges, and provide them mental support. Children and adolescents should also be encouraged to share the problems faced by them like sexual abuse and blackmailing by anybody and trust them instead of blaming them. The UN Convention on the Rights of the Child (1989) emphasized on the same issue. If parents fail to provide basic care and

DOI: 10.4324/9781003170587-6

protection to the children, it is the responsibility of the local government to take care of overall healthy growth and development of the children.

Nature of adversities experienced by youth

Youths experience a range of adversities during their development phase and it varies from individual to individual. The perception of an individual about adversity has many implications. For example, poverty is one such adversity that has many interpretations. To some individuals and/or youth poverty is not an issue and they do not consider it as an adversity, while some youth may consider it as a serious challenge in life, irrespective of the nature of poverty. In the following section, a brief description of each adversity is provided.

Abuse

It is an act that affects a child and youth physically, psychologically, sexually, and/or commercially. Broadly, youths and children experience physical abuse and/or corporal punishment, psychological abuse, sexual abuse, and abuse for commercialized vices. Children and youths mostly experience psychological abuse, followed by physical abuse, sexual abuse, and/or abuse for commercialized vices. For example, one recent cross-sectional study carried out in one city of Kerala selecting 6957 adolescents randomly observed that

> the one-year prevalence of any abuse was 89.9% suggesting that child maltreatment was widespread. Physical and emotional abuses were also very common as compared to sexual abuse (16.7%). However, lifetime prevalence of sexual abuse was 19.9%. Boys reported more abuse than girls across all the categories of abuse (including sexual abuse). Abuse was more frequent in the higher age groups and classes at school. Abuse was also more frequent in nuclear families and families that reported alcohol use. Children who reported an abusive experience usually faced more than one category of abuse; abuse in one category was significantly associated with abuse in other categories.
>
> (Kumar, Kar, & Kumar, 2019)

Another study conducted in Tripura covering Grate 8 and 9 students disclosed that 21.9%, 20.9%, and 18.1% experienced physical, psychological, and sexual abuse while 29.7% witnessed family violence. Findings also disclosed that male children were more often victims of physical and psychological violence while female children were more often victims of sexual violence (Deb & Walsh, 2012). One Kolkata-based study revealed that

> 52.4%, 25.1%, and 12.7% adolescents suffered psychological, physical, and sexual violence in the last year. Older adolescents (aged 17–18 years)

> suffered more psychological violence than the younger ones (15–16 years) ($p < 0.05$). Sixty-nine (18.6%) adolescent students stood witness to violence between adult members in the family. More than three-fifth (61.9%) adolescents experienced at least one type of violence, while one-third (32.7%) experienced physical or sexual violence or both.
>
> (Deb, Ray, Bhattacharyya, & Sun, 2016)

Neglect

It is common among children from lower socio-economic strata, i.e. parents from poor families fail to provide adequate nutrition to their children, medical care, and education. It may not be intentional. It is the social condition because of discriminatory social policies and social inequalities. However, neglect of children is a global phenomenon with some variation in terms of form and extent. Some countries have child protective services while it is absent in most of the developing countries. Neglect has been recognized as a form of maltreatment. Prevention- and intervention-related services are somehow inadequate even in high-income countries (Kobulsky, Dubowitz, & Xu, 2020).

Poverty

A large number of youths come from very poor families and as a result they are unable to pursue their education, get involved in economic activities for survival and remain unskilled labour for life long and finally lead a poor quality of life. Geographical location of residence of youths and children, i.e. interior villages with poor educational and communication facilities is one of the contributing factors for low education among youth (Connell, 1994; Tilak, 2002).

Unemployment

A large number of youths remain unemployed for a number of reasons and this is a big challenge for a country. The main reasons for unemployment include lack of job opportunity, lack of demand for the subject studied by a student, poor educational performance, poor communication skills, and so on (Amani, 2017). In a patriarchal society like India, every parent expects their child to become economically independent and take the responsibility of a family. If a youth remains unemployed for a longer period it not only causes psychological distress to them, it affects their social status and their potentials remain unutilized. And in turn, it is a national loss.

One study carried out in South Africa found that the lack of soft skills of youth, particularly, their communication ability or their levels of pragmatic language usage is the barrier to get a better job (Kaburise, 2016). The researcher emphasized on improving the communication skills of youth while undergoing higher education.

Sudden death of the main earning member of the family

A good number of children and youths face a serious crisis because of the sudden death of a main earning member of the family or loved one with whom they shared strong emotional relationships. This sort of situation causes discontinuation of education for some children and youths to take care of family immediate needs engaging in economic activities especially in the case of an elder child of a family.

Lack of social support

Crisis in life may come any time in anybody's life. However, at times of any crisis social support is found to be very beneficial. The children and youths who enjoy better social support can cope with any adversities easily compared to their counterparts with much social support. Social support gives a lot of mental strength to an individual.

Natural calamities and pandemics

Natural calamities occur suddenly even sometimes without giving much warning signs. It has a tremendous adverse impact on the overall life of children and youths and their family. A large number of children and youths who experience national calamities suffer from post-traumatic stress disorder. Natural calamities cause physical injury and even death of people, destroy their houses, and upset the normal life of a community.

Like other natural calamities, COVID-19 pandemic adversely affected the global population causing loss of life of lakhs and lakhs of people. It also affected the education and career of youth across the globe. A large number of youths working in private sectors lost their jobs during the lockdown phase.

Victim of circumstances

Becoming a victim of circumstances is quite common in any society. Therefore, one has to be alert so that nobody can take advantage of the simplicity of a person. A person with poor locus of control is more vulnerable to victim of circumstances, i.e. misguidance or doing something wrong under instigation.

Accident

Rush driving of bike and car without following the traffic rules is the main cause of accidents among youth across the society for which parents are partially responsible. A good number of parents give bikes to their children at an early age to make them happy.

Chronic physical health problem (self or family member)

Any serious health problem of any member of the family causes unprecedented problems for a youth from middle- or lower middle-class family as it involves personal and special care as well as money for treatment. It is very hard for a middle-class or poor family to bear all health-related expenditures especially for a family with poor social support facilities. All the family members suffer from anxiety and depression along with the patient. Therefore the health crisis in the family disturbs the mindset of a youth to a great extent.

Stress caused by academic pressure or poor performance

Stress in daily life caused by high parental expectation for better academic performance is a big challenge for some youth especially in a developing country like India where unemployment rate is very high. Indian social system is such that a youth should become economically independent immediately after completion of education so that they can give support to the family economically as there is no social support in terms of economic support. Youth with poor academic performance experiences humiliation within and outside the family as academic performance is one of the core parameters of social status of an individual. Youth with poor academic performance also struggle a lot to get a job.

Mental health challenge

Like physical health, mental health challenges are a normal phenomenon. Therefore, when one suffers from any mental health challenges, family members should consult mental health professionals immediately for medication to help that person to lead a quality and meaningful life. However, in an Indian society social stigma discourses parents to seek mental health support services for their child and child remains unattended. This issue requires attention of policy makers to sensitize the larger society about the social stigma attached to mental health challenges.

Adversities caused by natural disaster

Natural calamities such as flood and cyclone cause tremendous problems for people of all sections of the society. Children and women are the worst victims of natural disasters. According to Aneelraj et al. (2016),

> Himalayan tsunami of Uttarakhand, India in 2013 was associated with considerable psychosocial adversities among the resident children and adolescents. Two hundred (66.7%, 200/300) children/adolescents reported one or the other psychosocial adversities attributable to the disaster. Psychological distress was present in 54/300 (18%) of the

individuals. Loss of shelter and loss of playing space were the social issues having a statistically significant association with psychological distress signals such as feelings of anxiety, helplessness, insecurity, grief, and uncertainty.

Causes behind adversities

The causes behind different types of adversities of youth are different. Nature and extent of adversities also varies from individual to individual across different social situations. The factors which are responsible for adversities include familial, social, economic, and psychological.

Familial factors

Family environment, educational background of the family members, occupation, economic status, family values, family social network are some of the crucial factors related to youth adversity in life. In every society, a large number of children and youths become victims of family violence. It does not affect them mentally; it affects their studies and personality. Children and youths of disturbed family environments feel inferior and prefer to withdraw from social interaction.

Social factors

Social factors include social policy, equal opportunity for education, quality and job-oriented education, community services, and social perception about rights of the children and youths as well as social support facilities. Inequality and/or unequal distribution of resources cause deprivation from education because of social disadvantaged conditions, non-availability of educational facilities in remote areas are some of the major challenges for children and youths of backward communities. There are various social policies related to education, health, and income-generating activities. Non-implementation of all the policies and/or lack of awareness cause hurdles for background children and youths to get the benefits of the same policies.

Economic factors

Job opportunity, industrial growth, and overall economic condition of the country are directly related to the welfare of youth. Lack of industries and job opportunities lead to high unemployment for youth. Access to quality education and enhancement of communication skills of the children and youths are prerequisite to get good placement. Both the issues need the attention of administrators of educational institutions. Poor communication skills of a large number of children and youths are a challenge to get a good job.

Psychological factors

Congenial family environment is a prerequisite for good mental health of youth and if youth remain mentally unhappy because of disturbed family environment or other factors like stress, experience of abuse, and neglect they will not be able to contribute for social development. Therefore, psychological factors are very important and it needs the attention of policy makers to make mental health support facilities in different institutions like hospitals, community health centres and in educational institutions.

Consequences of adversities

Impact of any adversity is different on different youth and it depends upon the coping capacity of youth. Some youth can cope with any stressful situation easily interpreting the situation from a positive perspective while some youth become very nervous and struggle to deal with the situation and suffer from stress. As a result, some youth cannot make the right decision during any crisis situation. During any crisis and/or adversity a youth should remain calm and discuss the issue with family members and close friends. Discussion with family members and close friends would help to find a suitable solution in the given situation.

Social support during any crisis in life is found to be immensely beneficial. However, any adversity or crisis has both positive and negative impacts. So far as positive impact is concerned, adverse situations teach a lot of lessons and one becomes very strong mentally to deal with similar situations in future. Regarding the negative impact of adversity, in addition to physical harm, one becomes psychologically disturbed and even some youth become dependent on substances and some get involved in socially undesirable activities.

Youth involvement in risk behaviour and various crimes

Involvement of youth in risk behaviour under the influence of peer group members during early age is a common phenomenon across the country since an individual during the transition phase from childhood to adolescence becomes more curious to explore and experiment. An individual becomes more matured physically and mentally during adolescence phase and as a result they remain more curious about various issues in particular about sexuality and try to experiment. Thereby some of them become vulnerable to risk-taking behaviour. In addition to sexuality, some of them also try various substances under the influence of peer group members and become dependent. However, involvement of mostly school drop-out youth in petty offence and even in heinous crime like rape followed by murder of the victim to suppress evidences has been reported by Crime in India.

Available data highlight that a good number of youths are involved in a range of risk behaviours like early unprotected sex, smoking, tobacco chewing, and alcohol consumption which finally leads to usages of illicit drugs, antisocial behaviour like eve-teasing, theft, murder, robbery, cheating, blackmailing, sexual abuse of minors, and so on.

In addition, some of them become dependent on Internet and social networking sites (SNSs), phone sex, unsafe driving, and even gambling. Blais and Weber (2006) categorized these risk behaviours under five broad categories viz., (i) health risk behaviours, (ii) social risk behaviours, (iii) recreational risk behaviour, (iv) ethical risk behaviour and (v) financial risk belabours. Some of the risk behaviours are interrelated and/or overlapping. For example, a youth dependent on substances like alcohol or drugs may be engaged in unprotected sexual behaviour.

Health risk behaviours are those behaviours that increase the risk of disease or injury because of some activity beyond a limit, i.e. with high frequency and/or intensity (Steptoe & Wardle, 2004). Social risk behaviour involves job transfer from one place to another place, placing personal views about sensitive issues in public places and/or in group situations might antagonize people with opposite views, to name a few. Another example of social risk behaviour is that one was attending a party and during the dance programme there was an argument with another person for some misunderstanding which resulted in fighting and an unhappy situation. As a result, a youth might experience threat and/or maladjustment in social situations and/or in group situations or humiliation (Blais & Weber, 2006). Recreational risk behaviour includes certain behaviour that calls risk while enjoying life in a natural environment (Ewert & Vernon, 2013). Examples of some of the recreational risk behaviours are fast driving, diving, motor racing, mountain climbing, and rock climbing.

Ethical risk behaviour may result because of various factors. For example, pressure to compromise organizational standards, misconduct of employees in an organization, not reporting of observed misconduct of an employee to the higher authority and retaliation against reporter's, i.e. not taking appropriate disciplinary measures for misconduct allowing it to continue similar misconduct by other employees in an organization

Financial risk behaviours are those behaviours that cause a threat to financial security or big financial loss of the individual and/or family. Gambling, betting, investing more money in the share market without having any experience or analysing the share market properly are some of the common examples of financial risk behaviours.

Involvement of youth in criminal activities

Involvement of youth in criminal activities has become a serious concern for the law enforcement agencies and policy makers, as it is not only a loss of potential human resources, it causes serious concern for the safety of common people. Youth of lower social strata, with poor educational background and skills, unemployed for longer time get involved in various criminal activities mostly under the peer group influence.

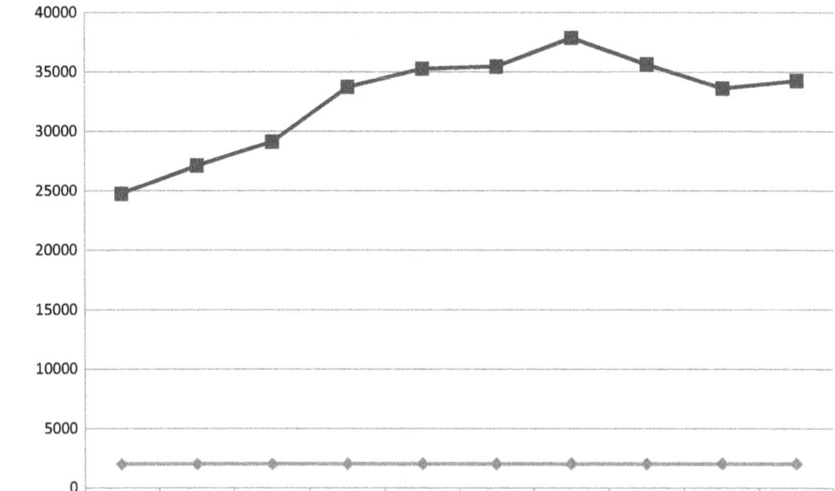

	1	2	3	4	5	6	7	8	9	10
Cases	22,740	25,125	27,125	31,725	33,256	33,433	35,849	33,606	31,591	32,235
Year	2010	2011	2012	2013	2014	2015	2016	2017	2018	2019

Figure 6.1 Trends in cases reported crimes committed by juveniles (NCRB, 2010, NCRB, 2011, NCRB, 2012, NCRB, 2013, NCRB, 2013, NCRB, 2016, NCRB, 2018).

Let us have a look at the year-wise trend of criminal activities in which children and youths were involved. According to the National Crime Records Bureau, Ministry of Home Affairs, Government of India, an increasing trend of involvement of children and youths in criminal activities has been observed from 2010 to 2019 except little decline in 2017 (Figure 6.1).

There is an increasing trend of crimes committed by juveniles during 2010 to 2016 (Figure 6.1). However, Chart 6.1 indicates the declining trend of crimes in 2017 and 2018 and again it is gone up in 2019. Most of the juveniles belonged to the 16–18 years age group. As compared to male juveniles, a significantly less number of female juveniles were involved in criminal activities (28,694 Vs. 173) as per National Crime Records Bureau Report, 2018.

As far as family background is concerned, an overwhelming number of the juveniles were living with parents, followed by guardians and the rest were living on the street.

Regarding the educational background of the juveniles, it has been observed that the majority of them studied above primary level to matriculation (17,024) while 10,666 studied up to primary level (Figure 6.2).

Figure 6.3 demonstrates types of offences committed by juveniles during 2018 under Indian Penal Code (IPC). Offences against human body are the highest type of crime (11,935) committed by juveniles, followed by offences against property (11,901), miscellaneous crimes (3,871), offences against public tranqulity (1,181), and relating to documents (136).

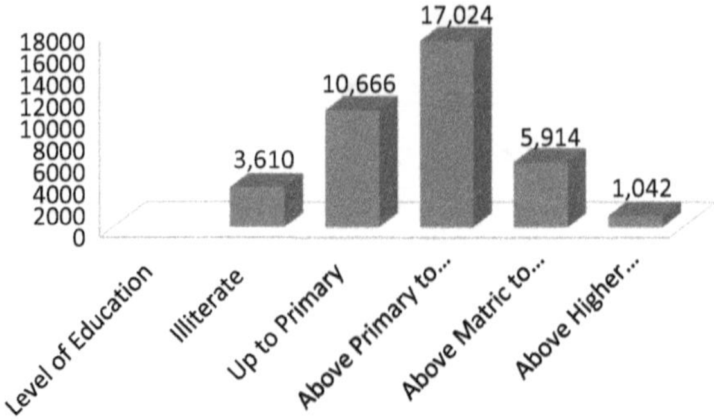

Figure 6.2 Educational background of youth involved in criminal activities.

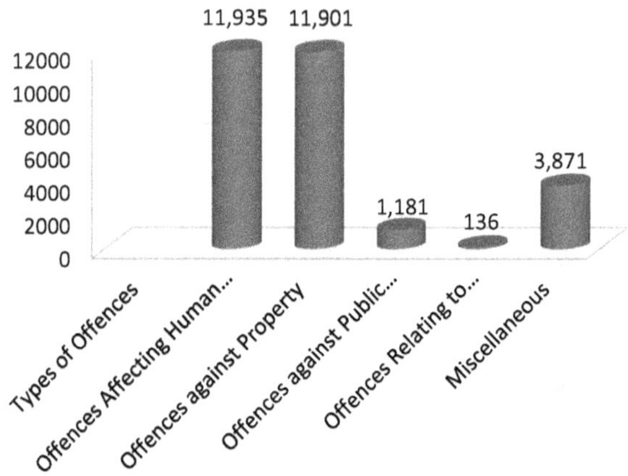

Figure 6.3 Types of offences committed by juveniles in 2018.

So far as crimes under Special and Local Laws (SLL) is concerned, juveniles were mostly involved in children related (1176), Liquor and Narcotic Drugs (691), arms and explosives related (203), other regulatory acts (333), and other miscellaneous crimes like intellectual property, foreign and passport related, finance and economic related and environment and pollution (111).

Number of juvenile crimes varies from state to state. For example, the highest number of juvenile crimes were reported in Maharashtra (5,880), followed by Madhya Pradesh (5,232), Delhi/UT (2,727), Tamil Nadu (2,304), Rajasthan (2,068), and so on.

Rajalakshmi (2016) reported that 41% younger generation aged between 18 and 30 years, irrespective of socio-economic disparities, engage in crimes such as murder, rape, burglary, and kidnapping. Children from lower social strata who experienced adversities in childhood such as abuse, broken family, and parental conflicts were more vulnerable to antisocial behaviour. Ahuja (1996) found that more than half of the young offenders were from lower and middle economic class social groups.

Prevalence of dependence of youth on substances

So far as prevalence of various types of risk behaviour among youth, especially on substance dependence is concerned, evidence demonstrates that it varies from place to place mostly because of local availability of different types of substances. For example, Avasthi et al. (2019) conducted an epidemiological study to assess the prevalence of substance dependence among people aged between 11 and 60 years from all the 22 districts of Punjab following two different methods that are Rapid Assessment Survey (RAS) and Punjab Drug Use Monitoring Survey (P-DUMS) to get a better picture. A group of 6600 was recruited in the case of RAS, while in the case of P-DUMS 7421 inpatients under medication were covered from 19 districts of Punjab. Both the surveys provide a similar picture that is 83% to 88% of people were dependent on opioid, followed by dependence on heroin (inhaled/injected) (RAS: 46% vs. P-DUMS: 52%). About one-third of the RAS sample was also dependent on opioid. The problem lies in access to treatment facilities in remote areas of Punjab and misuse of doctor's prescription.

In another recent study, covering school children of grades 7–12, in Uttar Pradesh, it was found that 14.3% of students were using continuously or often alcohol or tobacco and it was more among boys as compared to girls (Narain, Sardana, & Gupta, 2020). About one-third of the students developed the habit of taking alcohol or tobacco before 11 years of age. School students from government schools were more dependent on substances like alcohol or tobacco than that of students from private schools. Family history of taking alcohol or tobacco was found to be one of the risk factors for students' substance dependence. For one-third of students, making friends with alcohol or tobacco dependence students was found to be the purpose of taking alcohol or tobacco.

Street children are vulnerable to substance since nobody is there to guide and look after their welfare. Peer group members and drug peddlers can easily allure the street children and make them dependent on substances. A number of studies disclosed that first the drug peddlers provide free drugs to the street children and once street children become dependent they use them for drug peddling and in turn they give street children free drugs for maintenance of dependence habit (Embleton, Mwangi, Vreeman, Ayuku, & Braitstein, 2013). One Delhi-based study covering 766 street children following the Respondent Driven Sampling Methodology, it was found that street children were mostly dependent on tobacco (31.1 %), alcohol (13.5 %), and inhalants (11.3 %) during the last one year (Dhawan et al., 2020).

Saddichha and Khess (2010) carried out a study in Ranchi to ascertain the prevalence of tobacco use among young adult males following confirmation of cotinine levels. A group of 500 students were covered from five universities in Ranchi and they were selected following a systematic randomized process. Findings disclosed that the prevalence of tobacco uses mostly cigarettes, followed by khaini and gutkha among students was

55.6%. Findings also disclosed that most of the students wish to quit smoking and other substances.

Tripathy, Mohanty, Palo, and Jena (2013) reported that usages of cannabis and chewing tobacco are common among educated emerging adults (Tripathy et al., 2013) in India. Another study carried out in 2006 observed that about 41% of the students were using tobacco in Chennai and the prevalence of usages of tobacco was higher among boys as compared to their counterparts (Madan, Poorni, & Ramachandran, 2006). The prevalence of smoking among college students in India varies from 6.9 to 22.5% in case of males and 0–2.3% in cases of females (Chadda & Sengupta, 2002).

A large number of Indian youth (65.3%) are involved in non-smoking forms of tobacco like pans and gutkha as disclosed by a study in Bhopal (Bathma, Likhar, Agarwal, Mishra, & Shukla, 2015). Consumption of alcohol by college students in India varied from 60.5% to 22% across states (Tumge, 2009). For example, 60.5% of college students in Arunachal Pradesh are dependent on alcohol while about 22% of youths in Kerala reported frequent consumption of alcohol.

The incidence of substance dependence increases when youth grow up to 18–25 years of age (Ambekar et al., 2016; Gurpreet, Garg, Manjit, Rajiv, & Aseem, 2016; Jupinderjit, 2015). One study reported that the dependence of youth on substance is prevalent in every rural bely of Punjab (Mohan, Sundaram, & Sharma, 1986).

Sexual behaviour of youth

During teen age after attaining the puberty phase every child becomes more curious about sexuality and they explore more information from the literature. Internet facilities made their task easier to learn more about sexuality. Some of the children and youths become more obsessed about it and wish to experiment. Evidence indicates that a good number of grown-up children and youths across the society go for premarital sex and some even without any protection. For example, one Indian study reported that about 72% of sexually active youth had sex with new partner with protection (Reporter, 2011) while another study disclosed that 13.7% of male youth in Jamnagar, Gujarat had one or more pre-marital sex (Dave, Makwana, Yadav, & Yadav, 2013) and it was more among youth who are economically independent (Yadav, Barati, & Singh, 2015). A cross-sectional study conducted by Mohanan, Swain, Sanah, Sharma, and Ghosh (2014) in 2011 covering 376 adolescents aged between 15 and 19 years in different schools and colleges in Udupi, Karnataka, India using the Youth Risk Behaviour Survey questionnaire revealed that 5.7%, 7.2%, and 5.5% adolescents were taking alcohol, using tobacco and engaged in sexual activity.

In a study, Ghule and Donta (2011) observed that youths aged between 15 and 24 do not lack adequate scientific information on various reproductive health issues only; they have a lot of misconceptions about the same. Findings also disclosed that male members have more liberal attitudes towards premarital sex compared to their counterparts and 29.8% of males had experience of pre-marital sex against 4.9% females.

Injury or death caused by fast driving

Accidents caused by fast driving violating the traffic rules by youth are another serious concern for parents and local administration. The incidence of bike or car accidents in India is increasing especially in the cities with large populations. Youth feel very tempted to drive fast especially when they are with their friends to prove their masculinity.

As per National Crime Records Bureau (2014), 32.6% of persons injured and died due to road accidents are aged between 18 and 30 years. There is an increasing trend of accidental deaths among emerging adults in India (Ruikar, 2013; Thomas & Deb, 2016) and it is mostly because of over speeding (47.9%) and careless driving and/or overtaking (41.5%) (NCRB, 2014, 2015). Mohanty and Gupta (2015) reported that road accidents in urban areas are closely associated with over speed, age, and gender, while in rural areas speed alone is associated with it in India.

Dependence on mobile, social networking sites, and internet

Mobile has become indispensable in our daily life. It helps us connect to our friends, gather information, pay phone and electric bills and transfer funds in addition to various other usages like email facility, calculator, searching information, on-line purchase, using it as scanner and so on. As it makes our daily life much easier, there are examples of misuse of mobile phones and waste of valuable time in addition to creating social distance among the family members. As a large number of youths are enjoying the benefits of mobile and SNSs and interest, some are becoming dependent on it to the extent that it is adversely affecting their studies and misleading them. Spreading false information and creating confusion is another worst misuse of this platform. Findings of some of the latest studies in respect of misuse of mobile, SNSs, and Internet have been presented in the following section.

Mobile dependence has become another challenge for children and youths. In this regard, Jamir, Duggal, Nehra, Singh, and Grover (2019) did a study covering 885 school students in north India aged between 13 and 18 years and found that 30.3% of students met the criteria of mobile dependence syndrome and they also reported that their academic performance has deteriorated. The study also reported that boys were more addicted to mobile phones, especially those having a personal smartphone with additional gadgets and those who were depressed psychologically.

Sahu, Gandhi, and Sharma (2019) did a secondary study to examine the nature and extent of mobile phone addiction among children and adolescents and to ascertain the possible causes for the same. Findings revealed that 6.3% of children and adolescents were dependent on mobile which was more among boys. However, another study disclosed that the prevalence of problematic mobile phone use was 16%. The findings also disclosed that

> excessive or overuse of mobile phone was associated with feeling insecurity; staying up late at night; impaired parent–child relationship; impaired school relationships; psychological problems such as behavioural addiction like compulsive buying and pathological gambling, low mood, tension and anxiety, leisure boredom, and behavioural problems, among which most pronounced association was observed for hyperactivity followed by conduct problems and emotional symptoms.

The findings of the study need urgent attention of parents and teachers to sensitize the children and adolescents to use mobile for essential services only.

Another study in Saudi Arabia in 2018 highlights that 73.4% of medical students used mobile phones 5 hours a day. Of them, about two-thirds reported suffering from sleep disturbances. Female medical students having smartphones were more dependent on mobile phones (Ibrahim et al., 2018). For academic achievement, it is necessary for medical students to use mobile phones judiciously.

Seabrook, Kern, and Rickard (2016) did secondary research to examine the association of mental health challenges like depression and anxiety in the context of usages of SNSs. Findings disclosed that

> positive interactions, social support, and social connectedness on SNSs were consistently related to lower levels of depression and anxiety, whereas negative interaction and social comparisons on SNSs were related to higher levels of depression and anxiety. SNS use is related to less loneliness and greater self-esteem and life satisfaction.

However the findings were mixed in the context of impact of use of SNS with reference to frequency of SNS usages and networks of friend circle.

SNSs have become very popular over a short span of time as billions of people use it for various purposes. In order to ascertain the predictive factors of addictive SNS use beyond Facebook use, a study was conducted by Pontes, Taylor, and Stavropoulos (2018) covering a group of 511 English-speaking people mostly aged between 20 and 35 years. The study highlights that

> about 4.9% ($n = 25$) of all participants could be classified as having a high SNS addiction risk profile. Moreover, the results further indicated that fear of missing out (FoMo), maladaptive cognitions, and psychiatric distress significantly predicted SNS addiction and accounted for about 61% of the total variance in SNS addiction, with FoMo providing the strongest predictive contribution over and above the effects of sociodemographic variables and patterns of SNS use.

Tang and Koh (2017) conducted a study to ascertain the prevalence of addiction to social networking sites/platforms (SNS) and its comorbidity with other behavioural addiction and affective disorder among college students in Singapore. A total of 1110 college students in Singapore participated in the study voluntarily. The study disclosed that the

> prevalence rates of SNS, food and shopping addiction were 29.5%, 4.7% and 9.3% respectively for the total sample. SNS addiction was found to co-occur with food addiction (3%), shopping addiction (5%), and both food and shopping addiction (1%). The comorbidity rates of SNS addiction and affective disorder were 21% for depression, 27.7% for anxiety, and 26.1% for mania. Compared with the total sample, students with SNS addiction reported higher comorbidity rates with other behavioral addiction and affective disorder. In general, females as compared to males reported higher comorbidity rates of SNS addiction and affective disorder.

Suicide among children and youths is increasing every year in India as reported by Crime in India. In 2019, about 28 students committed suicide every day in India (i.e. 10,335 in 2019) mostly because of academic failure (NCRB, 2020). In the US, the incident rate of suicide among children is increasing. For example, Arielle et al. (2016) did a study to examine the characteristics and precipitating circumstances of suicide in elementary school-aged children relative to early adolescent decedents and identify potential within-group racial differences. Findings disclosed that

> mostly black male children in the US committed suicide by hanging/strangulation/suffocation, and died at home. Children who died by suicide more often experienced relationship problems with family members/friends (60.3% vs. 46.0%) and less often experienced boyfriend/girlfriend problems (0% vs. 16.0%) or left a suicide note (7.7% vs. 30.2%). Among suicide decedents with known mental health problems (*n* = 210), childhood decedents more often experienced attention-deficit disorder with or without hyperactivity (59.3% vs. 29.0%) and less often experienced depression/dysthymia (33.3% vs. 65.6%) compared with early adolescent decedents.

Factors responsible for youth involvement in risk behaviour and crime

There are various factors responsible for involvement of youth in risk behaviour and criminal activities. The surrounding social environment and personality characteristics of a youth have significant contributions on the formation and continuation of risk behaviours. In some communities, family approval of certain social behaviour, parental unconscious approval, and presence of risky behaviour among family members had a significant impact on youngsters' risk behaviour. However, youth mostly get involved in risk behaviour because of curiosity about various issues especially about sexuality and addiction and in most of the cases peer group influence plays a very important role. Other factors which contribute significantly behind risk behaviour include family discordant relationships, school or college drop-out, poverty, break-up of relationship, sudden financial crisis in the family, chronic health problem of any of the family members which requires immediate money for treatment, disturbed family environment and/or family permissive behaviour, local availability of drugs and alcohols. Some girl children get involved in risky behaviour because of compulsion. Broadly, the factors which play an important role in diverting youth in risk-taking behaviour are discussed in the following section. Fear of losing peers, fear of losing social acceptance if not engaged in these behaviours, easy accessibility to substances are some of the factors that encourage youth to be involved in risk behaviour.

Psychological factors

During the development phase children, adolescents and youth become more curious about various issues and they attempt to have first-hand experience. For example, when they see an elderly person smoking a cigarette or consuming alcohol, they wish to get the taste of the same substances and taste it once or twice. Some even continue to show their masculinity and present them as heroes before the peer group members. Similarly, sexuality is another issue that creates temptation among adolescents and youth to make friendships with the opposite gender. Attempting to make friends and/or to interact with the opposite gender is a normal phenomenon that helps them to feel psychologically happy. In order to fulfil mental desires, some read adult magazines, and some view adult Internet sites which stimulate some of them to experiment with sexuality. In most of the cases, adolescents and youth when they experience sexuality a good number of them do not take the preventive measure to safeguard them from sexually transmitted diseases and some adolescent girls conceive a child.

Social and cultural factors

In some cultures consumption of alcohol is a cultural practice. Therefore, a child during the development phase follows the same practice. Every child from the same cultural background does not become dependent on alcohol while some become regular consumers of alcohol. Local availability of substances and its price also play a significant role for consumption of alcohol or other substances. In some cultures, premarital sexual behaviours are permissible while in some cultures it is considered to be socially unacceptable. In India, premarital sexual relationship is not permissible behaviour although a good number of adolescents and youth are involved in similar behaviour.

Family-related factors

Family culture and values are very important in upbringing a child with good values and outlook. If parents lead an honest and decent life, it greatly influences a child in developing a positive outlook about life and it is reflected in their behaviour, while they interact with people of larger society. In a study Álvarez-García, García, Barreiro-Collazo, Dobarro, and Antúnez (2016) made an attempt to examine the importance of parenting styles and its dimensions in predicting antisocial behaviour of adolescents. The study revealed that "the six dimensions of parenting styles namely promotion of autonomy, affection and communication, behavioural control, self-disclosure, humor, and psychological control were significant predictors of antisocial behaviour".

Another Indian study carried out in Maharashtra by authors made an attempt to find out the role of family in the formation of problem behaviour among adolescents (Jogdand & Naik, 2014). The study found that "parents or cake takers alcohol use and problem behaviour of children were significantly associated with children and youth risk behaviour. Children from nuclear families and loss of parents were also significantly associated with problem behaviour". Baharudin, Krauss, Yacoob, and Pei (2011) examined the relationship between family processes such as family value, family competency and parenting and anti-social behaviour among urban adolescents with single mothers. The study revealed that "the family background variables did not show any significant relationship with antisocial behaviours. However, two of the family process variables like parenting styles and family competency significantly predicted antisocial behaviour of adolescents".

Financial factors

Crisis in life might arise in anybody's life. One has to be emotionally strong and stable to deal with the crisis. When an adolescent or youth experiences a financial crisis because of the sudden death of a main earning member of the family or chronic health problems of any family member and there is a support facility, this situation causes a lot of mental pressure on adolescent and youth. As a result, this sort of crisis situation pushes an adolescent or youth in risk-taking behaviour to arrange money immediately to deal with the situation. The following case study is a clear example of consequences of financial crisis.

Theories of risk behaviour and crime

Theories of risk behaviour

Over the time there has been the emergence of several theoretical frameworks that varied from each other on the importance they laid on the biological, social, and other influences. For its effectiveness in accommodating the various realms of individual, society, and their interactions, the psychosocial theories gain larger acceptance in explaining risk behaviours. Arrnet, a key proponent of the theory identified risk behaviour in adults as key to the identification and expression of one's personal freedom. In accordance with this perspective, the Problem Behaviour Theory by Jessor and Jessor (1977) explains dysfunction and maladaptive behaviour in a psychosocial framework.

(i) Problem behaviour theory

Problem behaviour, whether minimal or extreme, is perceived as a source of concern by the conventional society due to the disturbance found in the social system. Jessor (1977) brings a field theory perspective into the picture by attempting to explain problem behaviour as a function of person–environment interaction. The theory proposed three major systems viz., (a) the perceived-environment system, (b) the personality system, and (c) the behavioural system in explaining problem behaviour. It is the balance between the instigation and control variables that decides the degree of proneness of problem behaviour. In this way, psychosocial variables are used to explain unconventionality and departure from regulatory norms.

(ii) The Perceived-environment system

The system comprises two types of variables based on its proximity to problem behaviour, which are as follows: proximal and distal variables. As the name suggests, proximal variables such as peers exhibit more links to the behaviour than the distal variables such as poor parental control. Variables such as low parental disapproval-high peer approval or low compatibility between peer and parental expectation highlight the influence of perceived environment on problem behaviour.

(iii) The personality system

The personality system comprises relatively stable variables such as ones' values, beliefs, expectations, etc., towards self and society. Socio-cognitive variables such as higher values on independence and low value on self-esteem, that showcases one's social learning and life experiences predicted high proneness to problem behaviour.

(iv) The behaviour system

Problem behaviour and conventional behaviour are the two components of this system. While conventional behaviour consists of those that are socially approved and expected (For example, attending school, obeying parents), problem behaviour consists of the inappropriate behaviours such as smoking, alcohol use, and unprotected sexual activities. Low involvement in conventional behaviours and high involvement in problem behaviours indicate the vulnerability to problem behaviour. The system also works on the basis of age-graded norms as some behaviour may not be acceptable at a certain age and the same behaviour may become acceptable at later stages of life.

Theories of criminal behaviour

Various theories in behavioural science have explained criminal behaviours.

Biological roots to criminal behaviours talk about the interplay between heredity and biology for crime causation. For instance, Lombroso (1876) used physical characteristics such as the shape of head, body hair, ear lobes to distinguish "born criminals" and offenders from others. Modern biological theories also utilized the functions related to biochemistry (diet and hormones) and neurophysiology (brain dysfunction) to explain risky behaviours.

Psychological perspectives on criminality take contributions from various theories such as psychodynamic, behavioural, and cognitive theories in explaining risk behaviour. Freudian explanations on delinquency discussed the inherent antisocial human nature and inadequate ego development leading to delinquent impulses. Erik Erikson's identity crisis that emerges during the Identity vs Role Confusion stage is also used to theories of out-of-control behaviours.

The behavioural explanation of crime stems from the idea that crime is also a learnt behaviour due to ineffective conditioning, harsh and inconsistent punishment during childhood. Albert Bandura, through his social learning theory has also discussed the learning of aggressive skills and pro-violence values through observational learning and modelling. Cognitive theories, such as Kohlberg's theory of moral reasoning focuses on people's cognitive structure and content in learning risk behaviours.

In sum, the theories of risk and criminal behaviour are closely connected with local environment, family dysfunction, dependence of parents on substances, school drop-out, peer influence, poverty, unemployment, poor locus of control of youth, impulsive behaviour and situational factors like sudden death of main earning members of a family, provocation, local availability of substances and so on.

Consequences of youth involvement in risk behaviour and crime

There are various consequences of the risk behaviour of youth. Broadly consequences may be classified under the following categories.

Legal consequences

If any youth is involved in any risk behaviour that causes harm to another individual it will come under the purview of legal intervention that is and might be arrested by the police for or involvement of a particular behaviour that is unlawful. For example, if any youth is becoming dependent on drugs and taking more amounts of drugs as prescribed in the narcotic drugs and control substances act police might suggest that youth. If a youth is found to be inboard in drug peddling that issue will also come under the purview of the law enforcement agency and then you will be detained by the police for false ceiling drugs and subsequently will undergo legal procedure and will be penalized. Another example of risk behaviour is driving Bike very fast beyond the speed limit as prescribed by the transport department or not using the helmet while riding a motorcycle. In both cases, the transport department will penalize youth. There are several other risk behaviours that are prohibited by the respective authority e or law enforcement agencies like ok not taking alcohol while going to academic institution and not getting involved in peer bullying Preacher prohibited in educational institutions. Sometime some your get involved in criminal activities like stealing, dacoity, smuggling and other offences which heart other individual which calls for legal intervention a summit is found to be engaged in some of the above activities feature and low full which are harmful which hurt others an individual night be arrested by the police as per the law and will be prosecuted for panel measures. When a youth is found to be in conflict with law it is going to affect the social image of the same youth as well as eternal the image of the family in the society. Legal intervention will also cause problems if a new Earth is employed in some organizations. And even a youth might be under suspension or terminated from the job for his or her involvement in risk behaviour and criminal behaviour.

Health consequences

Evidence clearly highlights that risk behaviour has various forms of physical consequences and this consequence depends upon the nature of risk behaviour one is involved in to stop for example if somebody becomes dependent on taking intravenous drugs it will not only make an individual dependent on the particular substance it will cause other serious health consequences. Another example of health consequences is driving a car first. One might meet an accident and suffer from serious physical injuries and or death. Physical injuries caused by accidents are a global problem and in order to prevent car accidents on the highways there are various public health measures that have been adopted in the developed countries. For example in Australia beside the highway after a certain distance, that is a place where one can stop the car, refresh themselves and have a cup of tea or coffee free of cost so that one does not suffer from fatigue from driving long distances and become vulnerable to an accident. This public health measure helps to prevent a large number of accidents on the highways in developed countries. Similar strategies could be adopted in developing countries like India to prevent car accidents on the highways. Driving a motorbike fast at a young age is a big excitement among youth. Parents without giving much thought about the consequences of presenting an expensive motorbike to their young child make a child vulnerable to accidents. There is a common tendency among youth because of youthfulness to prove their masculinity there they feel tempted to drive a motorbike very fast in a group. Parents should sensitize youth about the issue. I am closely monitoring their behaviour while riding a motorbike.

Previous findings highlight that physical consequences of risk behaviour are many and they include non-fatal injuries, violence, and involvement in income-generating crimes, unintended pregnancies, and sexually transmitted diseases (Hingson, Heeren, Zakocs, Kopstein, & Wechsler, 2002; Perkins, 2002). Meeting accidents while driving car or bike in a drunken state is quite common among youth resulting in accidental death, fatal injuries, multiple disabilities, brain or spinal injuries, or even paralysis (Ansari, Akhdar, Mandoorah, & Moutaery, 2000; Kohli, Aathi, & Sethi, 2013). Finally, it affects the entire life of the youth and even some become dependent on others.

Social consequences

Like health consequences, social consequences are equally serious for youth who get involved in risky Android criminal activities under the influence of we are group members. If the risk behaviour of youth is disclosed within the family and in the neighbouring community the youth might experience social discrimination, social boycott, and/or social isolation. The consequence does not stop here also if it is their social relationship of siblings and or agar members of the family and finally the family gradually gets alienated in the community. As a result at times of crisis, the same person and his family may not get social support. Living in a community or society in an isolated manner is not only a big humiliation, but it also causes mental pressure which might lead to suffering from frustration depression and it will affect the daily life activities of an individual.

Psychological consequences

Psychological consequences are equally harmful for an individual and for the family when risk behaviour of youth is exposed to others. It might affect the individual emotionally and youth might suffer from inferiority complex and depression. Family members also feel psychologically embarrassed for the problematic behaviour of their child. In a number of cases, it has been observed that the youth who are involved in risk and/or criminal behaviour develop suicidal ideation.

Evidence indicates that risk behaviour has long-run negative impacts. Some risk behaviours cause cognitive impairments and even some become vulnerable to various other mental health challenges like depression, anxiety, suicidal thoughts, suicidal attempts and committing suicides, personality and conduct problems (Maguire, Pastore, & Flanagan, 1992; Paradis, Koenen, Fitzmaurice, & Buka, 2016; Pickard & Fazel, 2013), apathy, withdrawal, isolation from peers and families. Research also highlights that risk behaviour impairs psychosexual and emotional development among young adults (Alimen & Alimen, 2012; Volkow, Baler, Compton, & Weiss, 2014). One study by Tapert, Caldwell, and Burke (2004) reported that heavy drinking in young adulthood is associated with poor visuo-spatial skills and attention.

Academic and career-related consequences

Academic achievement required discipline and systematic study in a planned manner without any external disturbances. If one becomes dependent on drugs or alcohol and or high-risk behaviour like premarital sexual relationship one cannot concentrate and focus in his or her studies. As a result, academic progress will be affected and one will not be able to perform better and proceed for better career growth and development. A good number of youths during this development phase undermine the need to become serious in studies and take studies very likely. This group of people under the influence of peer group members or provocative situations get involved in various risk behaviours easily without realizing the consequences. Once one deviates from the mainstream of career preparation it is very difficult to come back in the mainstream of academics and pursue education satisfactorily. Therefore youth should be very careful during the development phase so that they remain focused in studies continuously and perform better.

In particular, risk behaviour of some youth causes maladaptive behaviour in the classrooms and to score poorly. A good number of youths involved in risk behaviour fail to attend regular classes and get involved in income-generating activities such as adultery, violent crimes, and so on resulting in poor academic performance. A previous study revealed that a good number of youths involved in risk behaviour are unable to concentrate in studies (Ibrahim, Mahmud, Abubakar, Harazimi, & Abdulkadir, 2016). Some drugs like Marijuan affect the short-term memory and learning. Alcohol abuse is the most common form of substance abuse among youth and it causes hang-over, nausea, vomiting, and blackouts (Jackson, Sokolovsky, Gunn, & White, 2020). In the long run, a youth with poor academic performance struggles a lot in getting a job and leads a poor quality of life.

Prevention of youth involvement in risk behaviour and crime

There is a popular saying, i.e. prevention is better than cure. So early childhood safety and healthy development of children is very important to ensure norm-bound behaviour among youth and motivate them for their proper career growth and development. However, the following are some of the pertinent issues requiring attention of all parents and guardians for keeping the children in the right direction:

- Ensuring healthy family environment and good parent–child relationship so they remain emotionally connected to parents, siblings, and family
- Listening to children/youth voices and deciding their future career accordingly.
- Providing basic care, guidance, and support facilities for education and encouraging them for small achievement.

- Monitoring youth social networks (both physical and virtual) and engagement in Internet and regular activities.
- Providing youth value education and guiding in positive activities.In the following section, each of the above issues is discussed at length with some practical examples.

Role of the family

Early childhood quality upbringing with proper values is very important for every child to follow family tradition, family culture, and other good practices in later life and become socially acceptable. In addition, the lifestyle of parents, their occupation, sources of earning, and social network greatly influences the outlook and lifestyle of the younger generation. If parents do not lead decent and honest lives, it will have an adverse impact on the lifestyle and social interaction pattern of the next generation. Therefore, parents should be very careful and should be an example before their children as a role model in terms of positive outlook, dissent occupation, good interpersonal relationship, and their nature. What behaviour and lifestyle of the parents a child observes that becomes a norm to their child and consciously or unconsciously they accept the same lifestyle in real life. However, there are some exceptional cases where children have the opportunity to interact with larger society while attending the higher learning institutions and/or working with others and in the process they develop broader perspectives about various issues in life and they largely follow the same code of conduct and imitate in their life. As a result, those children and youths do not engage in any risk behaviour. In this regard, there is a role of psychological component called locus of control. The children whose locus of control is very high they take a decision about any issue based on their own judgement and rational thought instead of following others blindly. On the other hand, the children with poor locus of control fail to apply their judgement and interpret any situation from the wrong perspective. The second category of children and youths become vulnerable to different risk behaviour as well as involve them in criminal activities under different circumstances. Therefore, a healthy family environment and good interpersonal relationship within the family and with people of larger society is very crucial to remain within the main tract of the society. In addition to basic human values, the role of elderly people in the family plays an important role in shaping the character of the younger ones. In a family where bondage is very high a child will remain emotionally connected with family members particularly with parents and siblings and in turn a child during the development phase will not be involved in any risk behaviour.

Listening to children and youth voices

It is very important for parents to give a feel to the children that their views are important about various family-related issues and invite their suggestions. And even in deciding the future career parents should discuss the issue with their child. In general, there is a wrong notion among a large number of parents that children are immature and not capable of giving valuable inputs in any decision-making process including their career. Evidence clearly demonstrates that most adolescents and youth are capable of thinking rationally and judiciously to provide valuable inputs in the decision-making process related to various issues. That is why there is a growing trend across the society to involve and engage youth in various decision-making processes. If youth are empowered and guided properly they can contribute significantly to indifferent community development initiatives and they can also play a major role in implementing various community development activities.

As far as future careers are concerned parents should discuss the issue with their child and try to understand their interest, their attitude and accordingly they should be guided in the right direction. If necessary, parents should consult a professional educational psychologist for career guidance. In a number of cases, it has been observed that parents hardly discuss career-related issues with their child and impose their ideas of future education resulting in demotivation among children and poor academic performance. Therefore every parent should give importance to the views and opinions of their child and in turn it will make a child happy and motivate them to remain committed to their future goal which is decided by them. Parents might have a lot of new ideas since they have seen life and they can share their ideas about the future career of their child with a note that children are free to make appropriate decisions reviewing the pros and cons of various options.

Basic minimal facilities

During early childhood, every child requires basic minimal facilities like adequate nutrition, medical care, congenial home environment, love and affection of parents, safety, and education which are prerequisite for healthy mental physical and career growth of a child. Unfortunately, a large number of children are deprived from some of those basic minimum facilities and some even experience neglect and abuse in different forms. A child who did not receive the basic minimal facilities invariably will remain backward in terms of education, good health, and positive mental health. During childhood children also require proper guidance and values from the elderly people. Continuous encouragement from parents and teachers for better academic performance and/or any good work or positive gesture further boost the morale of the children. It is very important to become a good human being then becoming a rich person compromising with human values and ethics. There are a lot of examples where we see that children from difficult circumstances and facing a lot of hardship are able to perform extremely well in academics and/or their creative talent. They are special cases and they are the source of motivation for other children. Similarly in our society, there are various support facilities to help disadvantaged children to come forward. Parents should seek guidance from educated people to help their child in their career by supporting them in indifferent manners.

Children and youths, irrespective of socio-economic and cultural background, should be under close observation of parents so that they are not misguided and/or not involved in any socially undesirable activities. During the transition from childhood to adolescence, children become curious about various issues and try to explore and experiment which is a normal phenomenon. While exploring various issues especially about various substances and sexuality some of them feel psychologically tempted to experiment under the influence of peer group members. Some experiment once or twice and control their pulses while some fail to control their impulses and become dependent which leads them to various high-risk behaviour and face serious health, social, psychological, and financial consequences. In the twenty-first century when the virtual world has created a lot of opportunities for entertainment and for connecting people easily through different SNSs, youth are also taking advantage of the same facilities and enjoying the benefits to gather more knowledge and make friendship with unknown people and/or connect with old friends. Though virtual world connected youth with the people of large society and with a large number of people across geographical boundaries and provided a lot of options to have more knowledge and for entertainment, it has also been observed that a large number of youths waste a good amount of valuable time engaging them in those activities leading to compromising with study, sleep, and mental disturbances. Undoubtedly, the virtual world enriched the knowledge of the youth and gave them adoption of spending time but it has disconnected them from the close family members and friends. As a result, emotional bondage of a child with siblings and parents has reduced substantially and created psychological distance although they are in close physical proximity. This is a danger for the younger generation to suffer from psychological distress in different adverse situations. Therefore, monitoring the behaviour of a child and youth by the parents is essential so that they do not spend much time in the virtual world.

Children and youths are very innocent and soft. They need to value education in terms of social manners, responsible behaviour, supporting others at times of crisis, taking initiative in family affairs and community development activities, respecting others, being kind to others, studying sincerely, and not getting involved in any socially undesirable activities. Children and youths also need proper orientation on resilience and they should be given some responsibility of the family from time to time so that they become disciplined, independent and develop a positive outlook about family and social life and take part in any group activities and work with others maintaining cordial relationships. Cordial relationships with all family members as well as with different social agents make an individual socially well accepted and they remain more likely to get any support at times of crisis. At the end family values make a child responsible citizen and they can make a difference in different spheres of social life.

Intervention and merging youth in mainstream of the society

The children and youths who are involved in high-risk behaviour and/or criminal activities need to be brought under the purview of intervention programmes for behaviour modification so that they could be merged in mainstream society. During the intervention programme, an effort should be made to assess their skills and look into their educational background so that skill-based training could be arranged for them keeping their interest, aptitude, and job market into account. Empowering children and youths with vocational skills will vary from individual to individual. Simultaneously every child and youth should be counselled to address their psychological distress, if any and give them confidence that there is scope to change their future in a positive direction and in this regard they have to be proactive and cooperate with the personnel of the intervention programme and/or with the psychologists and other professionals. In addition to individual counselling, group counselling should also be arranged which will help them to have better realization of life in terms of positive thinking to make a difference in life.

Intervention through educational institutions, in case of school-going children and/or youth attending higher learning institutions, is the best option to motivate youth in studies and impart values among them and give them a feel that their responsible role is very important for their personal happy life, family happiness and national prosperity and development.

Poor functioning of educational institutions and poor quality teaching is demotivating for the children and youths and as a result a large number of children and youths become dropouts. This issue needs the attention of school inspectors and administrators of educational institutions.

Engaging children and youths in social welfare activities and inculcating ideas of sharing and belongingness and supporting others at times of crisis are found to be very beneficial to impart values among youth.

Every educational institution should organize periodic special lectures for youth to motivate them in studies and engage them in extra-curricular and creative activities on a regular basis. Parents should also be invited in motivational lectures in school especially when parents come to the institute to collect the report card. The issues which could be addressed in motivational lectures include importance of good interpersonal relationships, need to become a good human being, role of parents in child upbringing, child rights and protection, violence and its impact, quality teaching, and/or importance of participatory method of teaching and so on. Feedback of the parents and students about methods of teaching needs to be introduced in every educational institution and based on the feedback proactive measures to be taken to improve the school academic ambiance and overall quality of teaching.

Engaging some parents in different school bodies to listen to their view and opinions for healthy child and youth development is another option to bring positive change in the school.

In the case of children and youths who are out of educational institutions, community-based intervention strategies should be adopted with the help of local non-government organizations to bring them under the intervention programme for giving them hope for the future. Parents should also be engaged in such intervention activities. Parents' involvement will facilitate developing bondage between parent–child relationships and changing the mindset of the children and youths faster.

Legislative measures for youth involvement in risk behaviour and anti-social activities

As per the National Youth Policy of the Government of India an individual aged between 15 and 29 years is regarded as youth. All the legislative measures which are applications for adults are applicable for youth aged between 19 and 29 years. Youth who are below 19 years of age come under the Juvenile Justice (Care and Protection of Children) Act 2020. This JJ Act 2020 deals with two categories of children viz., children in need of care and protection and children in conflict with law. The JJ Act 2020 allows for juveniles in conflict with Law in the age group of 16–18, involved in Heinous Offences, to be tried as adults.

Conclusion and recommendations

Happy family environment and proper guidance from the parents with basic minimal care and support facilities create an environment for healthy growth and development of a child in terms of physical, mental, and social health. Children from such families become dynamic, well-adjusted, and possess a positive outlook about career and life. If the family environment is not congenial and parents lead an indiscipline life and/or the family suffer from a serious financial crisis that might adversely affect the overall mental and physical growth of a child. Academic careers may also get affected. Nevertheless, adversities in life are normal phenomena and any child and youth may experience adversities at any point of life, irrespective of their social, economic, and cultural background. Children from well-to-do families are able to cope with the adversities better as compared to their counterparts because of strong social support from the extended family members. However, the children from middle-class and lower-middle-class families with poor social networks struggle a lot to overcome the crisis. Whatever might be the situation a child or youth shall remain emotionally strong and stable to deal with the situation and should not take quick decisions in order to overcome the crisis. They should also consult extended family members, if available, and/or trustworthy people of the locality for suggestion and guidance. In addition, they should talk to the teachers for their advice and support.

Engagement in risk and/or criminal behaviour has various negative consequences. So a child or youth should be very careful during any crisis so that nobody can misguide them in the wrong direction taking advantage of their helpless condition. If any child experiences abuse and violence in any form they should share the same with the parents and inform the law enforcement personnel for justice. Remaining silent about any abuse or violence means indulging the perpetrator to take advantage again and again and victimize many more innocent children and youths in helpless conditions. There are various legislative measures for prevention of violence and abuse of children and youths. Children and youths should be sensitized about the same which will in turn give them confidence and encourage them to report incidents of abuse and neglect to the concerned authorities.

It is the responsibility of the biological parents and significant others to protect the children and youths from all adversities and support them so that they can come out of this crisis situation and engage them in studies sincerely. Every educational institution as well as law enforcement authorities should organize sensitization programmes for children and youths on child rights and encourage them to report any abuse. Through institution and community-based efforts should be made to create a congenial and safe social environment for healthy growth of children and youths for optimum utilization of their potentials and in turn, it would contribute to overall social prosperity.

References

Ahuja, R. (1996). *Youth and crime* (pp. 51–53). New Delhi: Rawat Publications.

Alimen, R. A., & Alimen, M. C. D. (2012). Incidence of substance use among selected adolescents in the City of Iloilo. *Liceo Journal of Higher Education Research*, 8(1), 1–1.

Álvarez-García, D., García, T., Barreiro-Collazo, A., Dobarro, A., & Antúnez, Á. (2016). Parenting style dimensions as predictors of adolescent antisocial behavior. *Frontiers in Psychology*, 7, 1383.

Amani, J. (2017). Prevalence of, and factors associated with, unemployment among graduates: evidence from Tanzania. *Africa Education Review*, *14*(3–4), 230–244.

Ambekar, A., Rao, R., Agrawal, A., Mishra, A., Kumar, R., & Kumar, M. (2016). *Punjab opioid dependence survey: brief report*. New Delhi: SPYM and NDDTC, AIIMS.

Aneelraj, D., Kumar, C. N., Somanathan, R., Chandran, D., Joshi, S., Paramita, P., … & Math, S. B. (2016). Uttarakhand disaster 2013: a report on psychosocial adversities experienced by children and adolescents. *The Indian Journal of Pediatrics*, *83*(4), 316–321.

Ansari, S., Akhdar, F., Mandoorah, M., & Moutaery, K. (2000). Causes and effects of road traffic accidents in Saudi Arabia. *Public Health*, *114*(1), 37–39.

Avasthi, A., Basu, D., Subodh, B. N., Gupta, P. K., Goyal, B. L., Sidhu, B. S., … & Ghosh, A. (2019). Epidemiology of dependence on illicit substances, with a special focus on opioid dependence, in the state of Punjab, India: results from two different yet complementary survey methods. *Asian Journal of Psychiatry*, *39*, 70–79.

Baharudin, R., Krauss, S. E., Yacoob, S. N., & Pei, T. J. (2011). Family processes as predictors of antisocial behaviors among adolescents from urban, single-mother Malay families in Malaysia. *Journal of Comparative Family Studies*, *42*(4), 509–522.

Bathma, V., Likhar, S., Agarwal, S., Mishra, M., & Shukla, U. (2015). Tobacco Use Among Adolescents: a Burning Issue in Bhopal city. *National Journal of Community Medicine*, 6(1), 103–107.

Blais, A.-R., & Weber, E. U. (2006). A domain-specific risk-taking (DOSPERT) scale for adult populations. *Judgment and Decision Making*, 1(1), 33–47.

Chadda, R., & Sengupta, S. (2002). Tobacco use by Indian adolescents. *Tobacco Induced Diseases*, 1(2), 111.

Connell, R. (1994). Poverty and education. *Harvard Educational Review*, *64*(2), 125–150.

Corriveau, D. (2001). *Trail mix: stories of youth overcoming adversity paperback – import*, Corvo Comm.

Dave, V. R., Makwana, N. R., Yadav, B. S., & Yadav, S. (2013). A study on high-risk premarital sexual behavior of college going male students in Jamnagar city of Gujarat, India. *International Journal of High Risk Behaviors & Addiction*, 2(3), 112–116.

Deb, S., Ray, M., Bhattacharyya, B., & Sun, J. (2016). Violence against the adolescents of Kolkata: a study in relation to the socio-economic background and mental health. *Asian Journal of Psychiatry*, *19*, 4–13.

Deb, S., & Walsh, K. (2012). Impact of physical, psychological, and sexual violence on social adjustment of school children in India. *School Psychology International*, *33*(4), 391–415.

Deb, S. et al., (2020). *Childhood to adolescence: issues and concerns*, India: PEARSON.

Dhawan, A., Mishra, A. K., Ambekar, A., Chatterjee, B., Agrawal, A., & Bhargava, R. (2020). Estimating the size of substance using street children in Delhi using respondent-driven sampling (rds). *Asian Journal of Psychiatry*, *48*, 101890.

Embleton, L., Mwangi, A., Vreeman, R., Ayuku, D., & Braitstein, P. (2013). The epidemiology of substance use among street children in resource-constrained settings: a systematic review and meta-analysis. *Addiction*, *108*(10), 1722–1733.

Ghule, M., & Donta, B. (2011). Correlates of sexual behaviour of rural college youth in Maharashtra, India. *Eastern Journal of Medicine*, *16*(2), 122.

Gurpreet, S., Garg, P. D., Manjit, S., Rajiv, A., & Aseem, G. (2016). Emerging trends and prevalence of drug abuse: a study conducted at Swami Vivekananda Drug DeAddiction and Dual Diagnosis: Open Access Treatment Centre. *Dual Diagnosis*: Open Access, 1(8). doi:10.4172/2472-5048.100008

Hingson, R. W., Heeren, T., Zakocs, R. C., Kopstein, A., & Wechsler, H. (2002). Magnitude of alcohol-related mortality and morbidity among US college students ages 18–24. *Journal of Studies on Alcohol*, *63*(2), 136–144.

Ibrahim, N. K., Baharoon, B. S., Banjar, W. F., Jar, A. A., Ashor, R. M., Aman, A. A., & Al-Ahmadi, J. R. (2018). Mobile phone addiction and its relationship to sleep quality and academic achievement of medical students at King Abdulaziz University, Jeddah, Saudi Arabia. *Journal of Research in Health Sciences*, *18*(3), e00420.

Ibrahim, H. A., Mahmud, S., Abubakar, A., Harazimi, A. C., & Abdulkadir, S. (2016). Effect of drug abuse among youth and its impact on learning. *Journal of Pharmacy and Biological Sciences*, 11(1), 14–17.

Jackson, K. M., Sokolovsky, A. W., Gunn, R. L., & White, H. R. (2020). Consequences of alcohol and marijuana use among college students: prevalence rates and attributions to substance-specific versus simultaneous use. *Psychology of Addictive Behaviors*.

Jamir, L., Duggal, M., Nehra, R., Singh, P., & Grover, S. (2019). Epidemiology of technology addiction among school students in rural India. *Asian Journal of Psychiatry*, *40*, 30–38.

Jessor, R. (1991). Risk behavior in adolescence: a psychosocial framework for understanding and action. *Journal of Adolescent Health*, 12(8), 597–605.

Jessor, R., & Jessor, S. L. (1977). *Problem behavior and psychosocial development: a longitudinal study of youth*. New York: Academic Press.

Jogdand, S. S., & Naik, J. D. (2014). Study of family factors in association with behavior problems amongst children of 6–18 years age group. *International Journal of Applied and Basic Medical Research*, *4*(2), 86.

Jupinderjit, S. (2015). *How use turned to abuse in Punjab*. The Tribune. www.tribuneindia.com/news/bathinda/how-use-turned-to-abuse-inpunjab/31353.html

Kaburise, P. (2016). Improving soft skills and communication in response to youth unemployment. *International Journal of African Renaissance Studies-Multi-, Inter-and Transdisciplinarity*, *11*(2), 87–101.

Kobulsky, J. M., Dubowitz, H., & Xu, Y. (2020). The global challenge of the neglect of children. *Child Abuse & Neglect*, *110*, 104296.

Kohli, G., Aathi, M. K., & Sethi, M. (2013). Road accidents among adolescents. *Journal of Asia Pacific Studies*, *3*(2).

Kumar, M. T., Kar, N., & Kumar, S. (2019). Prevalence of child abuse in Kerala, India: an ICAST-CH based survey. *Child Abuse & Neglect*, *89*, 87–98.

Lombroso, C. (1876–1896/7). *L'uomo delinquente*. Milan: Hoepli.

Madan, K. P., Poorni, S., & Ramachandran, S. (2006). Tobacco use among school children in Chennai city, India. *Indian Journal of Cancer*, 43(3), 127–131.

Maguire, K., Pastore, A. L., & Flanagan, T. J. (1992). *Sourcebook of criminal justice statistics*. New York: The Hindelang Criminal Justice Research Center.

Michael, T. G. (2014). *Youth and adversity: psychology and influences of child and adolescent resilience and coping*, Nova Science Publishers.

Mohan, D., Sundaram, K. R., & Sharma, H. K. (1986). A study of drug abuse in rural areas of Punjab (India). *Drug and Alcohol Dependence*, 17(1), 57–66. doi:10.1016/0376-8716(86)90036-0

Mohanan, P., Swain, S., Sanah, N., Sharma, V., & Ghosh, D. (2014). A study on the prevalence of alcohol consumption, tobacco use and sexual behaviour among adolescents in urban areas of the Udupi District, Karnataka, India. *Sultan Qaboos University Medical Journal*, *14*(1), e104.

Mohanty, M., & Gupta, A. (2015). Factors affecting road crash modeling. *Journal of Transport Literature*, 9(2), 15–19.

Narain, R., Sardana, S., & Gupta, S. (2020). Prevalence and risk factors associated with substance use in children: a questionnaire-based survey in two cities of Uttar Pradesh, India. *Indian Journal of Psychiatry*, *62*(5), 517.

NCRB. (2010). *Crime in India 2013*. New Delhi: Ministry of Home Affairs, Government of India.

NCRB. (2011). *Crime in India 2013*. New Delhi: Ministry of Home Affairs, Government of India.

NCRB. (2012). *Crime in India 2013*. New Delhi: Ministry of Home Affairs, Government of India.

NCRB. (2013). *Crime in India 2013*. New Delhi: Ministry of Home Affairs, Government of India.

NCRB. (2014). *Accidental deaths and Suicides in India 2013*. New Delhi: National Crime Records Bureau, Ministry of Home affairs, Government of India.

NCRB. (2015). *Accidental deaths and Suicides in India 2014*. New Delhi: National Crime Records Bureau, Ministry of Home affairs, Government of India.

NCRB. (2016). *Crime in India 2013*. New Delhi: Ministry of Home Affairs, Government of India.

Paradis, A. D., Koenen, K. C., Fitzmaurice, G. M., & Buka, S. L. (2016). Impact of persistent and adolescent-limited antisocial behaviour on adult health outcomes. *Journal of Epidemiology and Community Health*, 70(10), 1004–1010.

Perkins, H. W. (2002). Social norms and the prevention of alcohol misuse in collegiate contexts. *Journal of Studies on Alcohol, Supplement*, (14), 164–172.

Pickard, H., & Fazel, S. (2013). Substance abuse as a risk factor for violence in mental illness: some implications for forensic psychiatric practice and clinical ethics. *Current Opinion in Psychiatry*, 26(4), 349.

Pontes, H. M., Taylor, M., & Stavropoulos, V. (2018). Beyond "Facebook addiction": the role of cognitive-related factors and psychiatric distress in social networking site addiction. *Cyberpsychology, Behavior, and Social Networking*, *21*(4), 240–247.

Rajalakshmi, S. (2016). Crime trends among youth. *International Journal of Research in Arts and Science*, 2(2), 7–10.

Reporter. (2011, Sun Oct 02). *Indians rank top in unprotected sex: survey*. The Indian Express Retrieved from http://archive.indianexpress.com/story-print/854636/

Saddichha, S., & Khess, C. R. J. (2010). Prevalence of tobacco use among young adult males in India: a community-based epidemiological study. *The American Journal of Drug and Alcohol Abuse*, *36*(1), 73–77.

Sahu, M., Gandhi, S., & Sharma, M. K. (2019). Mobile phone addiction among children and adolescents: a systematic review. *Journal of Addictions Nursing*, *30*(4), 261–268.

Seabrook, E. M., Kern, M. L., & Rickard, N. S. (2016). Social networking sites, depression, and anxiety: a systematic review. *JMIR Mental Health*, *3*(4), e5842.

Sheftall, A. H., Asti, L., Horowitz, L. M., Felts, A., Fontanella, C. A., Campo, J. V., & Bridge, J. A. (2016). Suicide in elementary school-aged children and early adolescents. *Pediatrics*, *138*(4).

Tang, C. S. K., & Koh, Y. Y. W. (2017). Online social networking addiction among college students in Singapore: comorbidity with behavioral addiction and affective disorder. *Asian Journal of Psychiatry*, *25*, 175–178.

Tapert, S. E., Caldwell, L., & Burke, C. (2004). Alcohol and the adolescent brain: human studies. *Alcohol Research & Health*, 28(4), 205–213.

Tilak, J. B. (2002). Education and poverty. *Journal of Human Development*, *3*(2), 191–207.

Tripathy, R., Mohanty, S., Palo, S. K., & Jena, D. (2013). Socioeconomic, demographic study on substance abuse among students of professional college in a southern town, Berhampur of Odisha state (India). *Journal of Forensic and Legal Medicine*, 20(8), 1057–1062.

Tumge, L. (2009). Prevalence and patterns of alcohol use among college students: comparing scenarios in Arunachal Pradesh and Kerala. (Msters Dissertation), SCTIMST.

Volkow, N. D., Baler, R. D., Compton, W. M., & Weiss, S. R. (2014). Adverse health effects of marijuana use. *New England Journal of Medicine*, 370(23), 2219–2227.

Yadav, J., Barati, K., & Singh, K. J. (2015). Pattern of substance abuse, sexual behavior and its determinants among unmarried youth in India. *Global Journal of Human Social Science*, 15(8), 14–24.

7 Virtual world and its impact on youth development

> The internet is...reflecting and amplifying the best and worst of human nature. It is a tool that will always be used for good and for ill...
>
> Our job is to mitigate the harms and expand the opportunities digital technology makes possible. By protecting children from the worst digital technology has to offer, and expanding their access to the best, we can tip the balance for the better.
>
> Anthony Lake, UNICEF Executive Director (UNICEF, 2017)

The twenty-first century has been an era of digitalization, with life as was known earlier transformed beyond recognition with the advent of the World Wide Web. Digital technology has revolutionized modern industries beyond recognition, adding precision and speed in operations, knowledge management, and connectivity. At the same time, technology has transformed human lives through improved healthcare, access to remote resources, and greater visibility of thoughts and ideas. The resulting changes have both positive and negative implications for the stakeholders, one of them being the youth. According to the State of the World's Children Report 2017, the youth, or those aged between 15 and 24 years, is the most connected group in the world, accounting for one in every three persons using the internet (UNICEF, 2017). The Internet has been one of the largest engagements of the waking time of the youth (Rideout, Foehr, & Roberts, 2013. According to a 2015 study, youth spend between 2.5 and 3.5 hours in a day on the internet (Žumárová, 2015), much of which duration is spent on social media platforms (Naeemi, Tamam, Hassan, & Bolong, 2014). Approximately 95% of the youths surveyed in the United States of America owned a smartphone and 45% reported using it almost constantly (Anderson & Jiang, 2018).

When it comes to new technology, the youths have a distinct advantage in adoption. While adults who are already trained in alternative methods of working face negative transfer of training as well as innovation resistance (e.g. van Esch & Black, 2019), children and young people are relatively more open to innovations in practices. Further, the growing cognitive abilities of young people make them better suited to keep up with the demands of a

DOI: 10.4324/9781003170587-7

technology that is transforming at a rapid pace. Researchers have regarded the youths as frequent early adopters of innovations in digital platforms and new media tools (Khane, Middaugh, & Allen, 2015). In many homes, the youths are the harbingers of digital technology, acting as the guide and expert for the rest of the family. The virtual world also eliminates the barriers of physical space and wealth, making knowledge and resources accessible to youths from less-privileged backgrounds. However, at the same time, the virtual world opens the access of the youth to a space way beyond the safe boundaries of their home, leaving them vulnerable to the risk of overexposure, exploitation, and harassment.

At 451 million, India has the second-largest population of active internet users globally, of which more than 66% are aged between 12 and 29 years. The 2019 report by IAMAI states that 66 million active internet users in India are aged between 5 and 11 years. Further, this number is slated to grow, as only approximately 36% of Indians presently have access to the internet (Mandavia, 2019). The digital policies that India and the rest of the world adopt when it comes to the youth and virtual access will go a long way in determining the efficacy of these interactions in the long run.

Being digital natives

With the ubiquitous presence of the digital media, the limelight turns to the Digital Natives. Digital Natives are youths aged between 15 and 24 years, who have been using the Internet for at least the last 5 years (International Telecommunication Union, 2017). This group closely corresponds to the generational cohort of post-millennials, those born between 1990 and 2010 (sometimes called the Zoomers), causing the terms to be often used interchangeably. Unlike the previous generations, the Digital Natives have exposure to digital technology from a very early age – having been brought up in homes with at least one or more digital gadgets present and interacting with digital contrivances on almost a daily basis. This is likely to make them highly efficient with the use of technology and open towards digital innovations. Digital natives tend to be among the pioneers who adopt new digital media contrivances as soon as they arise (Kesharwani, 2020) and use them extensively. The youth is among the forerunners when it comes to the adoption of digital offerings, particularly in the developing nations of the world (United Nations, 2020b). At the same time, they are unfamiliar with many non-digital ways of negotiating the world that were available to the earlier generations. This is leading to significant changes in the ways the youth socialize, form identities, and express themselves.

Way and Redden (2017), in their review, indicate several interesting patterns prominent in the way youth negotiate the virtual world. Young people are likely to let the digital media replace the traditional means of communication, co-create online experiences with content generation activities such as blogging, and prefer instant messaging (Bamezai et al., 2011; Fogel, 2011; Williams & Merten, 2008). Several researchers showed that youth growing up as Digital Natives preferred the instant gratification of online communication over the delayed gratification of physical meetings (e.g. Green & Brock, 2008). The impact of being Digital Natives extends beyond comfort with using technology. For example, Ghobadi and Mathiassen (2020) found that millennials growing up as Digital Natives were far more creative when designing digital technology and more likely to anticipate user-relevant queries than their colleagues who were Digital Non-Natives.

Virtual world and youth development: The gates of influence

Beyond the obvious advantages of digitalization of operations, the most transformational impact of digital technology is the Internet. The World Wide Web redefined access as it is understood for generations, making resources earlier limited by physical barriers available at a click. The web also opened immense possibilities for building connections and engaging with others, making the individual's world open to influences from across the globe. All these have important implications for youth development as they open low-cost avenues for the youth to access resources critical for cognitive, social, and career development. Figure 7.1 depicts the various ways in which the virtual world influences the youth.

Access to education

While primary and secondary education is almost taken for granted in the developed nations of the world, for the developing world, the large population size makes it difficult to provide a classroom and teaching resources available to the entire youth population. Children and youth located in

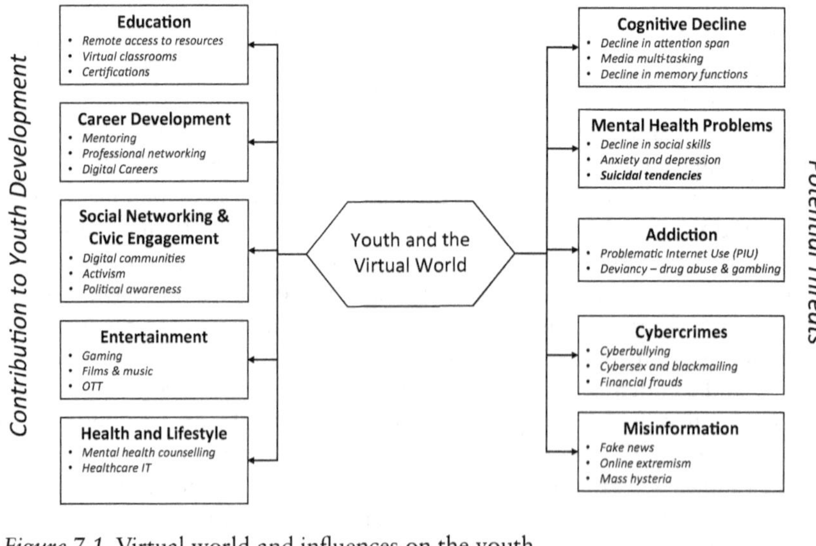

Figure 7.1 Virtual world and influences on the youth.

remote areas of India often must make do with suboptimal teaching and crowded classrooms with inadequate laboratory or library facilities. Children also must walk for miles to reach schools and colleges, which leads to early dropouts from the education system. The problem is particularly true for adolescent girls, for whom safety and housework tend to be primary reasons for premature ending of formal education (Kotwal, Kotwal, & Rani, 2007). At the other end, youth located in areas fraught with violence, civil unrest, economic deprivation, or natural disasters, also face a threat to their education, as being physically present in the classroom is often out of the question (e.g. Silwal, 2016).

Virtual education initially gained popularity as a means for extended education for adults, to provide them access to live or recorded sessions beyond work hours. Massive Online Open Courses (MOOCs) organized by the premier universities of the world have grown popular since the early 2000s among the youth, who accessed these resources as a supplement to their regular education, or to complete education while working. The last two decades have also seen a 900% growth in the online education industry, with firms such as Edx, Coursera, and Udemy providing ready access to different forms of academic and professional knowledge to people (Pappas, 2019). Virtual tools have also been a part of formal education systems, as teachers are increasingly using social media platforms such as Twitter and Facebook, emails, and instant messaging apps as pedagogical tools to facilitate communication with students and to stay connected beyond the class hours (Manca, 2020). Use of virtual media in the classroom has been found to facilitate teacher–student communication, learning, and student engagement (e.g. Dragseth, 2020).

Online education has been regarded as one of the most important benefits of the virtual world when it comes to youth development – empowering the youth to access remote resources, get educated from the best in the world, and learn at a comfortable pace. Further, skill is not limited to academic knowledge alone. The Indian youths are increasingly using the Internet to acquire various professional skills such as video editing, website design, or cooking, and other skills such as painting or music. According to the 2020 IGPP Report (IGPP, 2020), over 70% of youths use the Internet for studies and learning new skills along with accessing social media and playing games.

The COVID-19 pandemic that effectively stalled the world for several months following a viral outbreak from Wuhan, China, in December 2019 led to one of the biggest crises in education systems across the globe and in India. Nationwide lockdowns and social distancing norms made physical classrooms impossible, depriving millions of Indian youths of formal education. The pandemic saw, as a result, large-scale adoption of virtual education. The COVID-19 pandemic and the closure of normal life have led to the spread of online teaching and learning in mainstream formal education across schools and colleges in India, and even have normalized online administration and evaluation for competitive examinations. The internet also provided opportunities for education to the youths who are differently abled or placed in remote locations (United Nations, 2020b)

Career development

A positive impact of the virtual world that is closely tied to education is the development of career skills. The World Youth Report (United Nations, 2020a) lists positive implications of emerging technologies such as digital connectivity and the social media for social entrepreneurship among the youth – as access to ICT has been connected to innovation and entrepreneurial success. According to this report, "young people that have internet access may have opportunities to extend their social networks, strengthen their knowledge base, and identify financing opportunities to support venture creation and development" (pp. 73).

The role of the virtual world in career development comes from three aspects. First, the virtual world offers the youth opportunities for skilling and developing professional skills. With the advent of the COVID-19 pandemic, Technology and Vocational Education (TVET) across many nations were delivered on the online mode, to continue training for youth who could not access physical classrooms and workshops (UNESCO-UNEVOC, 2020). Similarly, access to online professional certifications and training allows youths from remote locations or with multiple engagements to prepare themselves professionally, in parallel with their academic endeavours. Second, the virtual world offers opportunities for professional networking and connecting with potential employers. Virtual networking sites such as LinkedIn allow youth to showcase their professional qualifications, seek internship or volunteering roles, join professional communities, and learn more about the latest developments and the real-life nuances of their selected trades, beyond the scope of the academic syllabus. Virtual sites also afford the youth visibility to potential employers and recruiters, facilitating a quick absorption in the workforce in the desired roles (Leader-Chivee, Hamilton, & Cowan, 2008). With 76 million accounts, India has the second-largest user base of LinkedIn in the world. Further, approximately 80% of the users of LinkedIn are youths aged between 18 and 34 years (Iqbal, 2021).

Another critical area where the digital world is aiding career development for the youth is availability of digitally enabled career options. The internet has opened several vocations that were non-existent even a couple of decades ago, such as website designers, animators and digital art designers, digital content writers, tele-counsellors, online after-sales service providers, and influencers, to name a few. Most of these digitally driven vocations have low or minimal entry and age barriers, remote working possibilities, and flexible hours, affording the entry of skilled youth who are pursuing academic or vocational degrees. Youths form one of the biggest cohorts of content generators on YouTube, Instagram, and TikTok, where they are earning significant revenue from advertisements on their channels and handles (Yarosh, Bonsignore, McRoberts, & Peyton, 2016). India's YouTube and online video market is presently valued at 700 million USD, with youths forming the prime viewers and content generators (Poonam, 2019). Youth-driven channels from India on social media sites range across a variety of areas such as product review, cooking and baking, DIY art, tutorials in software and daily life skills, travel, and political and social issues – providing the Indian youth a way to pursue the parallel objectives of pursuing their interest, showcasing their talent, and earning a living (Burgess & Green, 2018).

Social networking and the voice of the youth

While online education and skilling is a direct pathway for youth development, by far the most pervasive influence of the virtual world on the youth is through social media. Social networking is connecting with friends, families, acquaintances, and strangers on the online media on various platforms that permit content generation by the user and interacting with them on a regular basis. Social networking is the single greatest reported reason for the youth to access the internet. Radhakrishnan, Sriram, and Manivannan (2020) reported that 75% of the rural youths surveyed in India use connectivity primarily to access social media sites such as Facebook, Twitter, and Instagram.

The importance of social networking for the Indian youth stems from the need for the youth to form an identity, connect with like-minded peers, find a voice, and seek validation for their actions, beliefs, and persona. In traditional settings, the need for socialization and validation was satisfied through real-life interactions with friends, families, and other like-minded peers. However, social media widens the boundaries of one's social circle exponentially, beyond local and even national boundaries. Secondly, social media affords low-cost engagement, where one can initiate social interactions on the spot without having to spend the resources of building and maintaining functional relationships with the same people in real life.

Yang and Lee (2020) proposed that interaction on social media involved three kinds of interaction. In *directed interaction*, individuals interact with specific others, with a pre-decided purpose – for instance, sharing college notes or seeking information about classroom activities with peers. In *information broadcast*, the user puts up a status or shares a content with no specific audience in mind, expecting interaction to flow with those who express interest in engagement. Finally, in *content consumption*, the individual goes to social media primarily to passively read the content of others. Burke and Kraut (2016) reported that social media interaction with strong ties facilitates psychological well-being but only when people engage in direct interaction rather than information broadcast or content consumption. According to a Pew Research Report on Social Media Technology (Anderson & Jiang, 2018), the youth surveyed reported being connected with family and friends, meeting people with similar interests, and finding news and information, among the main advantages of the internet.

The social validation effects of virtual communities have been explored by several researchers. Cuzzocrea and Collins (2020) proposed the concept of *wiki transition* to explain how the online media was used by the youth to make a transition to adulthood – characterized by co-learning, pro bono creation of knowledge, dynamism, experience sharing, and informed risk-taking. The social networking platforms thus afford many youths in India a safe space to learn about social issues and politics, voice their opinions, find like-minded peers, and find validation for their thoughts and opinions. Landau, Eisikovits, and Rafaeli (2019) reported that online followers and supporters for one's voice build self-confidence in the youth. Further, they help combat feelings of any offline exclusion the youth face in their immediate surroundings, because of broken homes, poor parenting, or isolation in schools and colleges. Gray (2009) also states that the internet affords the youth an opportunity for sexual identity formation and healthy sexual self-expression (Ringrose & Barajas, 2011). According to McAfee's Tweens, Teens & Technology Report 2014 on Indian youths, 66% respondents said they felt more accepted on social media than in real life, and 64% reported reinventing or even faking their image online to gather "likes" and "comments" (IndiaStats, 2014).

Youth is a time for exploration and forming one's identity. At the same time, the affinity of the youth towards novelty makes them open to ideas that call for transformations in the existing order of things and what is understood to be entrenched injustices. Social media offers substantial opportunities to self-advertise, show risqué group affinities (through posts, endorsements, and hashtags), and essentially maintain an alternate or enhanced persona at a low investment of resources, without having the effect spill over into one's real life. Social media has been found to provide youth with information that helps them to form their identity (Elias & Lemish, 2009).

One of the major advantages of online social media is to make the voice of the youth heard in contexts that matter. The youths form close to 16% of the population of the world (UNICEF, 2017), and are the stakeholders of most of the public policy interventions, including the Sustainable Development Goals 2030. However, early youth is deprived of voting rights and the representation of the youth among the public policy influencers tends to be negligible across the world. All these often make the internet the only avenue where the youth can speak about public policy issues of importance, voice and record their opinions without being silenced, and present their unique perspectives into things that matter. Spöri, Oross, and Susánszky (2020) reported that the youth have a much higher rate of online participation in political activities as compared to people from other age cohorts. Kligler-Vilenchik and Literat (2018) proposed that social media enables the youth to develop a sense of agency towards politics, and challenge political institutions (Huntington, 2013). More than 50% of Indian millennials and post-millennials surveyed in 2020 said that they have participated in social media political campaigns, while 20–40% reported engaging in other online political activities, such as campaigning for a political party or signing a petition (Pathania, 2020). Youth are also increasingly found to use the internet to create their own definitions of citizenship (Bennett, Wells, & Rank, 2009).

Penney (2020) states that social media empowers the youth to share their political voice, particularly using political memes and humour. He lists several advantages of the youth having a political voice online – such as connection with peers with similar views, growth of communal spirit, formation of political identity, and being a part of influential political discussions. Further, engaging in political discourses online allows the youth an opportunity for civic engagement that otherwise is uncommon for young people. Way and Redden (2014) report that political activities online are strongly correlated with the participation of youth from the marginal sections of the society into politics and civic responsibilities However, other researchers have shown that this aspect engagement in online political activities is common among youth already interested in politics and not those with little prior interest in political matters (Keating & Melis, 2017).

Entertainment and healthcare

The internet has been one of the chief sources for the entertainment of the Indian youth in recent times. Along with social networking, entertainment features such as online single-player or multiplayer games, music and films, and entertainment videos pull the biggest youth traffic to the internet across the world. While entertainment is mostly not considered among the targeted outcomes of digital empowerment of children and youth, it invariably remains one of the fastest-realized outcomes from the internet when it comes to the younger generations. The online gaming industry is one of the biggest revenues generating industries in the world, with the youth as their chief consumers. Games such as Pokémon Go, Pub-G, or Clash of Clans involve millions of young people worldwide and consume a significant percentage of their virtual hours. At 930 million USD, India is considered among the world leaders in the online gaming market, with more than 7.3 billion installations of mobile games in India in 2020 (Navani, 2021). The popularity of the online gaming industry can be assessed from the fact that sports that simulate real sports (e.g. FIFA) will be played along with the Summer Olympics in 2024 (IOC, 2018; Morgan, 2019), as a "part of the IOC's current political and strategic aim to make the Olympic programme more 'youth-friendly'" (Tjønndal & Skauge, 2021).

While the entertainment aspect of the internet tends to be downplayed when it comes to youth development, several researchers have drawn attention to the many positive outcomes of accessing the virtual world for entertainment. For instance, websites devoted to gaming activities are also rich avenues of social networking, where gamers join transnational networks of gaming activities, and gain familiarity with global audiences with similar interests (Kuss, Louws, & Wiers, 2012). Video games have also been seen as a spurring source of creativity in design among the youth (Prensky, 2001a) – familiarizing them with digital platforms and motivating them to develop dexterity with digital technology. Again, virtual gaming has been found to promote positive youth development through happy experiences (Beniwal, 2020) – something particularly significant for youths from disadvantaged backgrounds or locations of civil unrest, who do not have access to playing fields or other resources needed for physical playing activities. The positive impact of virtual gaming had been prominent during the COVID-19 pandemic. Balhara, Kattula, Singh, Chukkali, and Bhargava (2020) reported an increase in virtual gaming among the Indian youth during the pandemic, to combat the monotony of physical restrictions (Bora, 2020). Ettekal and Agans (2020) reported that use of skill-building and parallel play on virtual platforms has been one of the major sources of entertainment for the youth during the pandemic that contributed positively to their cognitive and social development.

The popularity of smartphones among the youth and the growing digital literacy has also made practitioners utilize the digital medium as a route to channelize health and wellness interventions to the youth. Chan and Ngai (2019) reported that social media is useful for providing social services to youth by overcoming geographical and time boundaries. Such services include suicide prevention helplines, assistance for reporting child abuse and domestic violence, and anti-bullying and anti-ragging helplines, specifically targeted at the children and the youth. Several digital mental health interventions came up in India during the COVID-19 pandemic, with the youth as one of the main stakeholders. The Government of India also launched the programme *Manodarpan*, under which a website and helplines were launched to provide mental health assistance during the pandemic (PIB, 2020b).

Buttazzoni, Brar, and Minaker (2021) confirmed the evidence of smartphone-based mental health interventions for the youth, and their effectiveness in combating depression and anxiety. Such interventions make use of text messages and digital apps to diagnose and treat mental disorders. Mental health apps are popular among the youths as they are easily accessible to them and allow relative anonymity, beyond peer pressure and parental control. Virtual trainer systems (VTS), as a part of healthcare IT, has been found to be useful in motivating participants, including young people, for engaging in exercise routines and healthy habits (Kwok, Leung, Hui, & Wong, 2021). The internet is also one of the chief sources of information for the youth to answer their health-related questions, particularly those relevant to their sexual health, getting them an access to timely assistance they are often too embarrassed to ask for otherwise. This is particularly relevant for youth growing up in conservative societies, where social taboos often prevent dissemination of critical information to the youth relevant to their health and well-being (e.g. Nik Farid et al., 2018; Purdy, 2011).

Approximately 72% of Indian youths surveyed reported visiting online resources for health seeking and medical solutions, with the trend being more common among affluent and literate sections of the society (Parija, Tiwari, Sharma, & Saha, 2020).

The dark face of the virtual world: Potential threats to the youth online

The internet has been called by many a double-edged sword (e.g. Keene, 2011). This euphemism is particularly true in the context of youth development. Access to the virtual world also exposes the youth to multiple threats to their identity, safety, and sanity. Firstly, the online behaviour of children and youth is relatively removed from the parental scanner and control. Most parents of youths in India are new to digital technology, making them ill-equipped to understand and monitor their ward's online behaviour. Secondly, despite many interventions in this regard, digital regulations in India are still in a nascent stage, leaving the internet relatively free of national laws and restrictions on content targeted at young people. Finally, the close coexistence beneficial digital resources and the Dark Web of pornography, criminal activities, and exploitation often make the boundaries blur. Again, the online world leaves the user with little control over the audience of content. This lack of control leaves the user in considerable risk of their content being manipulated or exploited by predators (Adorjan & Ricciardelli, 2018). Singer and Singer (2012) drew attention to the inability of children to understand and protect themselves from the harmful effects of digital media, making the exposure particularly risky, and leading to loss of childhood innocence. Even barring external threats, prolonged exposure to the internet leads to considerable changes in the way generations negotiate social realities, compromising their effectiveness as responsible adults and global citizens.

Cognitive impact of the internet on the youth

Firth et al. (2019) draw on the concept of neuroplasticity to elucidate the impact of prolonged engagement with digital media on the human brain. For instance, six weeks of engagement with online role-playing games has demonstrated shrinkage in the orbitofrontal cortex in youths, the brain area associated with decision making and impulse control (Zhou et al., 2019). Frequent use of smartphones with connectivity also encourages compulsive checking behaviour – frequent and repetitive scanning of one's own devices for new information (Prensky, 2001b; Skinner, 1984). Other outcomes of frequent exposure to the internet are "media multitasking", or simultaneously interacting with multiple media (Ophir, Nass, & Wagner, 2009), poor performance on tasks requiring sustained attention (Uncapher & Wagner, 2018), and being easily distractible to irrelevant environmental stimuli (Ophir et al., 2009; Purcell et al., 2012), with switches happening as frequently as every 19 seconds (Yeykelis, Cummings, & Reeves, 2014). Other researchers have associated sustained use of digital media with poor overall cognitive performance (Peng, Chen, Zhao, & Zhou, 2018), lack of creativity (Altmann, Trafton, & Hambrick, 2014; Baird et al., 2012), decreased verbal intelligence in children (Takeuchi et al., 2018), and sleep interference (Van Der Schuur, Baumgartner, Sumter, & Valkenburg, 2015). Younger children appear to be more vulnerable to these negative changes than older individuals (Baumgartner, van der Schuur, Lemmens, & te Poel, 2018). Prolonged use of the internet is giving rise to what is called the transactive memory, where individuals remember the source of information rather than the information itself (Sparrow, Liu, & Wegner, 2011), causing damage to cognitive functions such as long-term storage and retrieval (Liu et al., 2018). Internet use has also been related to an inflated perception of self-knowledge (Hamilton & Yao, 2018), where people equate the information obtained on their device as their own.

The virtual world and mental health

There has been considerable research focusing on the negative impact of the Internet on the mental health of children and youth. The virtual world allows one to engage socially at one's discretion without having to face the demands and stress of real-time face-to-face interactions and sustained relationships. This often makes the internet attractive for youth who are shy or socially awkward or those who have less-than-satisfying relationships at home and among their peers. Engelberg and Sjöberg (2004) reported that youth who use the internet frequently tend to lack emotional and social skills and tend to be lonely in real lives. Such youths tend to connect with strangers online to compensate for their lack of company (Yang & Brown, 2015). While virtual interaction often compensates the need for social support in an immediately reinforcing way, in many cases, it interferes with the subsequent building of social skills and social adjustment in the individual. Sustained long-term internet browsing and social networking leads to loss of touch with reality, dependency on virtual reinforcement, and depletion of social skills (Leung, 2004).

Virtual reality offers novel means for self-identification and encourages identity pluralism. While this is beneficial for self-exploration, self-assertion, and forming cultural and social identities, researchers report negative outcomes such as formation of deviant identities in youth due to exposure to the virtual environment. For example, Pak Manesh and Razeghi (2020) reported a decline in a sense of national identity as well as religious and family identity with prolonged internet use, which have negative implications for the social adjustment of the youth. In other words, identification with deviant global trends may cause the youth to go against national laws and cultural heritage of the land, leading to destructive outcomes.

Prolonged use of the internet has also been associated with several mental health issues. According to Anderson and Jiang (2018), youths reported lack of connection with real individuals and unrealistic views of other's lives are the main challenges of being on social networking sites. Social media has a heavy positivity bias, with people tending to showcase primarily their achievements and the happy events of their lives. This in turn often leaves the observers with an unrealistic perception of one's own life trajectory when compared to that of others. Susceptibility of the online content to manipulation leads to false social comparison, increasing feelings of negative body image and negative self-concept (Royal Society for Public Health, 2017; Twenge, Joiner, Rogers, & Martin, 2018). Sustained and long-duration engagement with the virtual world is correlated with anxiety, depression, and suicidal ideations (Jelenchick, Eickhoff, & Moreno, 2013).

In their study with LGBTQ youth, McConnell et al. (2018) pointed out that online spaces require the youth to project socially desirable images, which may be a challenge particularly for those with closet or semi-closeted identities. Other studies have shown youths reporting feelings of isolation and social rejection (Common Sense, 2018), due to failure in projecting a desirable image on social media platforms. Landau et al. (2019) reported that the youth deal with online rejection in a variety of ways. These range from self-isolation mechanisms such as interacting less in the online world, quitting social media, or in more extreme cases, deviant behaviour such as drug addiction, self-destructive behaviour such as suicide, and aggression against others.

Internet addiction

Shaw and Black (2008) define internet addiction as "excessive or poorly controlled preoccupations, urges or behaviors regarding computer use and internet access that lead to impairment or distress". Some studies have shown the level of internet addiction among youth in Southeast Asia to be as high as 47% (Balhara, Mahapatra, Sharma, & Bhargava, 2018). According to the 2020 IGPP Report on the patterns of internet use among the Indian youth, 39% of the youth surveyed are active on the net for more than five hours in a day (IGPP, 2020). Internet gaming disorder has already been considered for inclusion as a pathological condition (American Psychiatric Association, 2013).

Although not identified as a full-fledged mental disorder, researchers have captured the problem of internet addiction in Problematic Internet Use (PIU) – characterized by longer-than-intended internet use, resulting distress, and hampering occupational and social productivity (Shapira et al., 2003; Spada, 2014). Demetrovics, Szeredi, and Rózsa (2008) stated that PIU is characterized by obsession with online activities even when offline, neglect of daily activities owing to prolonged engagement with online content, and difficulty to control the urge to stay connected and manage time online while Prievara, Piko, and Luszczynska (2019) reported that Problematic Internet usage correlated highly with feelings of loneliness, shyness, and lack of social support among the youth (also, Esen, Aktas, & Tuncer,

2013). In a study on Indian youths, stress, anxiety, and depression were found to be predictors of internet addiction (Gupta, Khan, Rajoura, & Srivastava, 2018). Similar findings were reported by Jain et al. (2020) in a study on Indian university students. Boys were found to be more likely to develop PIU than girls (Chen, Chen, & Gau, 2015; Choo, Sim, Liau, Gentile, & Khoo, 2015).

Internet addiction has been correlated with use of illegal drugs among the Indian youth (Arya, Singh, & Malhotra, 2018). In a recent study conducted on engineering freshmen in India, Iyer and DoraiswamyIyer (2020) reported evidence of substance abuse in students who are addicted to the internet. Similar findings have been reported by other researchers as well (e.g. Bener, Al-Mahdi, & Bhugra, 2016; Pengpid & Peltzer, 2019). Jiang et al. (2019) reported that youths with internet addiction show a higher propensity to use e-cigarettes, owing to access to the sale of these items in online shopping portals. Lopez-Fernandez (2021) found that COVID-19 pandemic has led to dependence on digital technology, putting the youth at the risk of online addiction, including obsession with cybersex, gaming, social media, smartphones, internet shopping, and gambling.

Cybercrimes against young people

The relatively unregulated nature of the virtual world and the anonymity afforded by digital presence makes the internet a fertile ground for cybercrimes. The youth are highly vulnerable to such malicious intentions due to their exploratory nature and their relative lack of awareness about potential threats. Adorjan and Ricciardelli (2018) reported two interesting patterns of behaviour when it comes to privacy and youth. While the youth express privacy concerns regularly, they also engage in oversharing online, neglecting privacy measures. Hargittai and Marwick (2016) call this phenomenon the privacy paradox – that arises from multiple sources. The 2020 IGPP report indicates a lack of awareness among the Indian youth when it comes to safe behaviour on the internet, with over 60% of youth surveyed sharing personal information on the net (IGPP, 2020). The need to be seen for the youth is much higher than their privacy concerns (Tufekci, 2008), leading to frequent risk behaviours and security breaches. Again, some youths have the belief that they have little to hide, leading to carelessness and exposure (Boyd, 2014). Finally, James (2014) reported that pre-teens are often unaware of various privacy management strategies, which contributes to their vulnerability in the digital world.

The 2018 Pew Research Center report identified cyberbullying as the topmost causes of harassment faced by the youth online (Anderson & Jiang, 2018). Cyberbullying is negative communication using the digital media targeted at harming or being aggressive against one person (Pham & Adesman, 2015). Cyberbullying may be perpetuated by strangers by a known peer group of the youth, where the former ridicule, abuse and threaten a person for being different from others or for holding an opinion contrary to the view of the majority. Cyberbullying is becoming a common phenomenon in India. According to the India Internet Report 2019, cyberbullying against teenagers increased by 36% between 2017 and 2018 (MyGov.in, 2020). In a study on Indian students by Jain, Gupta, Satam, and Panda (2020), almost 80% of respondents aged between 17 and 19 reported being cyberbullied during the lockdown. Cyberbullying can often take indirect forms like the viral internet phenomenon of "Blue Whale" – where anonymous communication blackmailing the youth with potentially disastrous consequences forced many cases of self-harm and suicide worldwide. Cases of youth falling victim to the Blue Whale challenge have been reported in India as well (Narayan, Das, Das, & Bhandari, 2019). Abreu and Kenny (2018), in their study on LGBTQ youths, found multiple negative effects of cyberbullying such as suicidal ideation, depression, low self-esteem, aggression, poor body image, and poor academic performance.

The internet is also a fertile ground for crimes of a sexual nature. Researchers have also identified the youth as particularly vulnerable to sexual predators online. The power asymmetry with older adults makes the youth easily manipulable, leaving even very young children exposed to the dangers of sexting and cybersex (Adorjan & Ricciardelli, 2018; Lenhart, 2009). It is also not uncommon to come across cases where personal photos and videos shared by the youth online have been morphed to create pornographic content. The latest addition to this is the threat of Deep Fake videos – hyper-realistic fake video content that could be potentially damaging to one's reputation (Westerlund, 2019). Such content is then used to blackmail the victim for further compromises, leading to a downward spiral. Financial frauds are also common in the virtual world, and the youth form a particularly vulnerable target, owing to their lack of awareness and gullibility. Financial frauds range from hacking of bank accounts to fraudulent transactions on online shopping portals and other e-commerce sites (Button, Nicholls, Kerr, & Owen, 2014). The FIS Pace 2021 Report revealed that in India, youth aged between 18 and 29 fall victims to cyber frauds far more frequently than Indians from the senior generations, with one in every five aged between 18 and 24 falling victim to phishing attacks (Asokan, 2021). Long time spent on exploring the internet makes young people susceptible to malware, hacking, and other potential cybercrimes.

Misinformation

Extended presence on the internet and dependence on it for information about the world makes the youth open to a flood of misinformation. Internet content being relatively unregulated often presents distorted realities or agenda-driven communication, leading to problematic outcomes for the listener or reader. Rosenberg, Syed, and Rezaie (2020) stated that the deluge of misinformation and consequent hysteria characteristic of social networking sites such as Twitter during the COVID-19 pandemic severely affect the mental health of the users, a significant number of which belong to the youth population.

The internet is also the hotbed of hate crimes and extremist opinions, and the youth is often an easy target, owing to their gullibility and desire to break the mould. In his address to the United Nations in June 2021, India's Foreign Secretary, Dr. Harsh Vardhan Shingla flagged the growing concern of the internet being used by antagonistic nations to spread hatred, violence, and false propaganda among the youth in India (PTI, 2021). The internet is a breeding ground for political violence and hate crimes due to the relative anonymity and lack of government control over online content (Hale, 2012). Social media sites that offer relative anonymity such as Reddit or YouTube are highly likely to witness violent or hate messages. The internet has been used for recruitment for terrorist groups such as ISIS, which chiefly target the youth. India, too, is combating the menace, with repeated cases of ISIS recruitment videos and video games surfacing on the Deep Web and social media sites such as Twitter, Telegram, and WhatsApp in India (e.g. Nalapat, 2017; Shukla & Das, 2020). Tynes (2006) stated that online extremist groups used tutorials and school lessons, video games, and music to lure youth to extremist materials.

According to Costello, Barrett-Fox, Bernatzky, Hawdon, and Mendes (2020), youth expressing political discontent online are singled out by like-minded extremist groups, leading to gradual indoctrination in violent beliefs. Such materials have been found to lead to gradual radicalization (Smith, 2009), emotional damage (Ybarra et al., 2008), and violence (Foxman & Wolf, 2013). Costello et al. (2020) reported that hours spent online and being politically active on social media increased the likelihood of encountering hate and extremist messages, as did dissatisfaction with the existing governments of a country. Online recruitment into terrorism activities has led to numerous instances of violence perpetrated by the youth across the world – including violent demonstrations, arson, destruction of public property, organized smear campaigns against public figures, ethnic or religious groups, and governments, and seditious activities (Bloom, 2017). Penney (2020) listed the risk of the political activity of the youth online as both trivialization of important issues and extremism. On the other hand, Marwick and Lewis (2017) connected youth political activism on the net with problematic behaviour such as trolling, cyberbullying, racism, misogyny, hyperpolarization, and spread of conspiracy theories.

The question of digital divide: Are all post-millennials Digital Natives?

As early as 2008, Palfrey and Gasser (2008) observed that there exist strong discrepancies among the post-millennials when it comes to access to the Internet. According to a report on the access to digital education during the COVID-19 pandemic by the United Nations Children's Fund and International Telecommunication Union (UNICEF, 2020), 1.3 billion children aged between 3 and 17 years presently do not have access to the internet – forming 66% of all school-age young people.

Thousands of youths in the developing nations do not have access to connectivity or digital literacy, exposing them to what is called the "digital divide" (Sambuli & Magnoli, 2019). Based on their review of existing literature, Scheerder, van Deursen, and van Dijk (2017) proposed that digital divide can happen at three levels. The first level of digital divide happens when there is a lack of access, i.e. there is a discrepancy in the access youths have to digital contrivances, connectivity, and online resources. The second level of digital divide occurs when people have access to the Internet but lack the skills to use the internet – for instance, knowledge of English, or basic computer skills. Finally, the third level of the divide can happen in terms of the lack of outcome from the use of the internet. For instance, some youths may use the internet for long-term value such as education and vocation, while the use of others may be limited to short-term benefits such as entertainment and social networking.

Despite the complex nature of digital divide, it is interesting to note that most forms of digital divides tend to arise from common markers of privileges such as gender, ethnicity, geography, or wealth (Blank & Groselj, 2014; Van Deursen, Helsper, Eynon, & van Dijk, 2017). Geographical location, for instance, is strongly correlated to access to the internet. According to a 2017 survey (International Telecommunication Union, 2017), Africa, Asia, and the Pacific zone houses 90% of the youth without connectivity. The geographical trend is mostly explained by discrepancies in national income in the regions of the world. Only 6% of the youth in low-income countries have access to the internet as opposed to 87% in the high-income countries (UNICEF, 2020). Further, this difference is prominent even among affluent households across countries – internet access is available to 97% of the richest households in developed nations but to only 16% of the richest households in developing nations (UNICEF, 2020). Further, within a country, income level of the household is a strong determinant of internet access available to the youth – as the youth from affluent homes are as much as 50% more likely to have internet access than the youth from non-affluent homes. Researchers have also found a strong link between social class and online activity (North, Snyder, & Bulfin, 2008). Gender also plays a role in likelihood of internet access. A report by IAMAI in 2019 shows that in India, the number of women with access to the internet is only half of that of men (Mandavia, 2019).

The digital divide among the youth population in India has strong implications for education and empowerment for large sections of the younger generations – often a lot more than how the digital divide affects the previous generations. This is because lack of connectivity could be a major hindrance to skill building in an increasingly digitized educational environment. Poor access to IT also challenges the career development prospects of the youth in an IT-driven country. Thus, the need for inclusivity in virtual access and use becomes particularly relevant in the context of the youth, as it is increasingly becoming difficult and often impossible to live otherwise.

Digital empowerment of the Indian youth: Public policy measures in India

Home to one of the largest youth populations in the world, India has also been known for its digital presence in the IT/ITES industry, among the biggest job generators in the country, and projected to yield 10% of India's GDP by 2025 (McKinsey Global Institute, 2019). India has one of the cheapest high-speed internet connectivity in the world (Roy, 2019), thanks to a highly competitive market led by private and public sector telecom players. The flagship Digital India initiative by the Government of India was launched in 2016 to encourage digital adoption in all aspects of governance and social welfare. The Digital India programme was bolstered by the BharatNet or the National Optic Fibre Network (NOFN) that attempts to connect the remote locations of the subcontinent using broadband internet (BBNL, 2021). Digital India also provided a significant boost to digital governance, through the digitalization of important government activities such as voter registration, land records maintenance, payment of taxes or vehicle registration, as well as digitalization of disbursement for funds through social welfare schemes such as the Public Distribution System of India, the largest in the world. The National Digital Communication Policy 2018 too emphasized on the need for providing universal access to connectivity, accompanied by digital literacy to exploit the access gainfully (NDCP, 2018).

To promote digital literacy in the rural areas, in 2017, the Government of India launched the Pradhan Mantri Gramin Digital Saksharta Abhiyan (PMGDISHA) – an initiative aimed at making at least one person in every rural household digitally literate (Darade, 2017). As of 2021, the PMGDISHA has 0.37 million digital literacy centres across rural India, providing digital education to citizens, and empowering them to apply their digital skills for vocational ends. In 2020, the Government of India has allocated close to INR 40 billion to the Digital India programme, targeting the coverage through optic fibre network, cyber security, promotion of IT/ITES, and training of human resources in digital skills (PTI, 2020a).

Empowerment of the nation can happen through the empowerment of the youth (Kesavan & Vignesh, 2020). To this end, the youth is one of the chief targeted beneficiaries of the various schemes under Digital India. In addition, there have been several initiatives specifically focused on the digital empowerment of the Indian youth. In 2020, the Ministry of Tribal Affairs launched the GOAL (Go Online As Leaders) programme for digital skilling of the tribal youth in India (PIB, 2020a). Also in 2020, the Ministry of Electronics and Information Technology, Government of India, in collaboration with Intel India, has launched the National Program for Government Schools: Responsible AI for Youth. Under this, youth in government schools of India will be introduced to the latest developments in information technology and artificial intelligence, to make them digitally prepared (NeGD, 2021).

To ensure digitalization of educational practices and higher education institutions, in 2009, the Government of India launched the National Knowledge Network (NKN) (iNOC, 2012). The NKN is focused on creating digital clusters connecting educational institutions of the country, enabling knowledge sharing and collaborative research through digital means, and setting up virtual classrooms and online teaching and learning infrastructure. The National Educational Policy (NEP) of 2020 has provided significant impetus to the digital access and empowerment of the youth. The NEP has focused on the digitalization of formal education in India, through close collaboration with educational technology firms and launch of e-courses in regional languages, making education universally accessible to all corners of the country (The Times of India, 2020). In addition, the NEP also emphasizes digital skill acquisition as a part of vocational education and inclusion of digital innovations of the industries into educational curricula, preparing the youth for the occupations of the future. Digital skilling has also been a major component of the Skill India initiative, driven by institutions such as the National Skill Development Corporation.

While India has adopted several positive steps in the direction of the digital empowerment of the youth, a lot remains to be addressed. The availability of affordable high-speed internet and low-cost digital devices such as smartphones has made the growth rate of internet users in India thrice as much as the world average (McKinsey Global Institute, 2019) and rural India contributing to 75% of the new internet users (NASSCOM, 2016). Nevertheless, the 2017–2018 National Sample Survey report revealed that only 42% of urban households and 15% of rural households in India had access to the internet (Sudevan, 2020). While the figures are expected to be improved in 2020, the COVID-19 pandemic revealed a major digital divide among the 320 million students in formal schooling systems in India, particularly when it came to access of online classes in rural India and among the disadvantaged sections of the society. A survey conducted in June 2020 revealed that only approximately 43.9% of students had access to smartphones, 0.8% had access to computers or laptops, and 12% did not have access to even basic phones (PTI, 2020b). Teachers too were challenged in terms of digital teaching skills (United Nations, 2020b), further affecting the learning outcomes. The Government tried to bridge the gap through the launch of e-learning guidelines and portal and use of the national television channel and YouTube for educational purposes (MHRD, 2020a; MHRD, 2020b). The new normal of the pandemic-ridden world necessitates that the issue of digital access, training, and empowerment is considered with utmost importance to ensure that a vast majority of the new generations of India is not left behind when it comes to the transforming world.

Youth and the virtual world: Recommendations for digital policy interventions

The virtual world with its myriad possibilities is the reality of the twenty-first century. What remains a choice is how to place oneself in the reality – as a conscious actor with agency or as a victim of the system. When it comes to the youth in India, association with the internet and digital contrivances is imperative – given the extent to which academics, occupations, and daily living is getting digitized by the day. Further, the early years are essential in picking up critical life skills such as language, locomotion, and social interactions. It is only a matter of time before digital skills get added in this repertoire of essential life skills in India, making an early exposure to digital technology and the virtual world mandatory in nature for the digital natives.

Davis (2001) described the healthy use of the internet as one characterized by a purpose and spanning over a rational duration. The importance of digital technology and its pervasiveness in human lives also alerts one to the criticality of harnessing the digital disruption in a socially constructive way. Digital empowerment being the currency of the coming decades, at one end it is important to provide access to digital technology to all youths and closing the digital divide to the extent possible. At the other end, it is critical to protect the youths from the harmful influences of the virtual world and set up guards against exploitation and systematic damage. Figure 7.2 depicts the interventions to channelize digital empowerment:

The digital divide arises out of three causal roots - access, skills, and outcomes, and therefore, to close the gap, it is essential that each aspect receive adequate In other words, for digital empowerment to happen, it is essential that stakeholders not only get an access to the technology, but

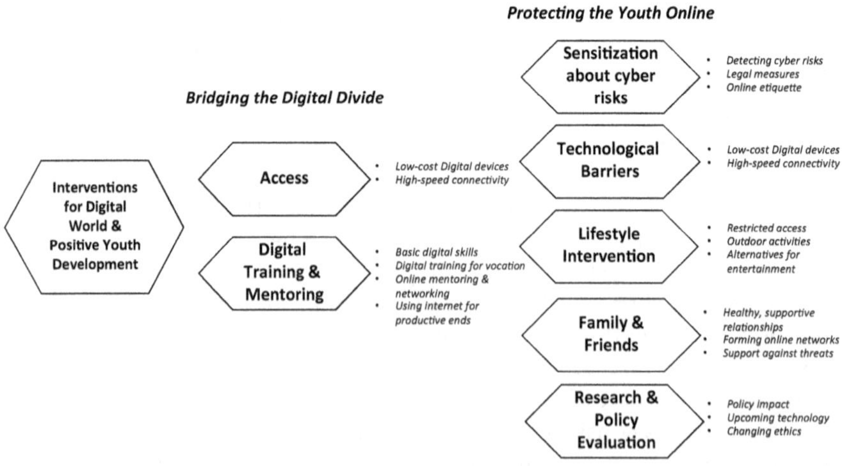

Figure 7.2 Interventions for digital empowerment and positive youth development.

also have adequate training to use it efficiently, and then receive support to exploit the technology for sustainable and profitable ends (Majumdar, Basu, & Jain, 2021).

Institutionalization of access

A significant portion of the youth population in India does not have access to the internet, high-speed connectivity that makes prolonged engagement rewarding, or even digital gadgets that would serve as the interface. Therefore, before any other intervention may happen, it is important to provide the youth across the globe access to high-speed internet on a regular basis. The UN recommends increased broadband coverage, greater digital literacy, cheaper connectivity costs, and greater access to mobile devices as useful for closing on the digital divide (UNDESA, 2018). There have been several public policy interventions as well as private initiatives to this end. While high-speed internet is readily available in most developed nations, developing nations are attempting to address this challenge through technological innovations and social welfare measures. In India, BharatNet or optic fibre network and wireless and broadband internet provided by private and public sector telecom players ensure the availability of the internet across the nation. In addition, India makes available the unlicensed spectrum of 2.4 GHz and 5.8 GHz free of cost for utilization by small players and NGOs to provide last-mile connectivity (Ponappa, 2011). Similar projects aiming at last-mile connectivity using alternate technology have been the Project Loon by Google, and the more recent satellite-based Starlink by Tesla, which is planned to enter the Indian market soon (FE Online, 2021).

Access to connectivity needs to be accompanied by access to digital devices such as computers, tablets, or smartphones. This may be achieved through proliferation of public access points as well as access to low-cost personal devices. For instance, during the COVID-19 pandemic, Indian states such as Haryana and Karnataka provided free tablets to youths in government schools and colleges, respectively, so that they could carry on with online classes (The New Indian Express, 2020; Zee Media Bureau, 2020b).

An interesting correlation of digital access among the youth is enrolment in formal education at the secondary level and beyond, (International Telecommunication Union, 2013). In India, schools are often the only places where underprivileged students have access to the internet, more so for girls (International Telecommunication Union, 2014). Hence, absorption of students in the formal education system will ensure digital access and empowerment as well. For this, there needs to be adequate infrastructure in schools and colleges in India for digital access - including IT infrastructure such as computers, laptops, and smartphones (UNESCO-UNEVOC, 2020). Access to the internet through internet cafes and portals in public places in the country is also helpful in closing the digital divide by making the internet readily available to the public (Liff & Steward, 2001).

Digital skilling for beneficial ends

To close the second and third level of digital divide in India, it is essential that the youth is trained in using the internet and accessing it for beneficial purposes. Deprived of digital training, the attention of the user is mostly captured by content consumption and information broadcast, a low-stake, low engagement form of digital interaction. Thus, even when provided with a digital device and high-speed internet, the Indian youth spends the bulk of the time on the internet scrolling through memes, watching videos or pornography, posting photos, or playing online games. Digital training empowers the youth to go beyond the easy access of social media sites for entertainment, to use the internet for education and certification, banking, e-commerce (purchase and sale of products), professional networking, and civic engagement. To this end, education of the youth must begin at an early age before Problematic Internet Usage behaviour sets in. The 2020 UNESCO-UNEVOC Virtual Conference Report (UNESCO-UNEVOC, 2020) stated that the COVID-19 pandemic had further reinstated the importance of building digital skills among the youth. It also popularized blended modes of education, giving a much-needed push for the digitalization of educational practices.

Educational institutions in India are likely to play an important role in the digital skilling of youth. Digital education is slowly becoming a part of the school and vocational education curricula. However, for greater effectiveness, it is also important to connect digital skills with immediate application. For instance, schools and colleges in India may encourage students to use online data for completing school projects, set up professional profiles online, complete online courses and certifications in parallel with their regular courses. Application of the knowledge in supervised settings is likely to ensure that the information gain is internalized, and healthy digital habits are set.

In addition to digital training and skilling, the emphasis is also on hand holding the Indian youth in their digital presence, to sustain their interest, and to provide them early fruits for their efforts. The UN report on Youth Entrepreneurship (2020) recommends online mentoring programmes for social entrepreneurs, to make guidance affordable and accessible to the youth, and promote "intergenerational alliance" between the youths and adults. It also recommended making use of social media to project youth role models in the field of entrepreneurship to inspire and educate other young people. Similar youth networks for professional and educational ends may be set up in India, where the youth may connect to stalwarts in the field and like-minded peers and get connected to opportunities and resources.

Along with digital training of the youth, many researchers also emphasize on the training of the trainers who would be imparting the knowledge and skills. Ettekal and Agans (2020) recommended training of adults who engage in online training and engagement of the youth, to ensure positive youth development. The trainers need to be provided periodic updates on the latest developments in the field, such as artificial intelligence and machine learning, and how they are transforming digital applications. They also need to stay updated about new career options in the digital world such as graphic designers, digital marketers, online content creators, online reputation managers, and social media influencers, so that they can adequately guide the youth in their career choices. Finally, trainers need to have a clear understanding of the latest developments in cybersecurity, risk behaviour, and digital regulations, so that the youth may be ensured a clear understanding in these matters. A useful model is that of the peer educator, where youth are trained to be digital educators for their cohorts (Literat, Kligler-Vilenchik, Brough, & Blum-Ross, 2018). It is likely that a peer educator would close the generational gap when it comes to discussing search behaviour on the internet and would be able to communicate and motivate in a manner that resonates with the youth. Ramsey et al. (2016) recommend peer-driven educational interventions for better outreach among the youth to prevent cyberbullying, particularly among marginalized youth such as the LGBTQ.

Interventions for protecting the youth in the virtual world

Closing the digital divide is the topmost priority to prevent the systematic victimization of the underprivileged for the future generations. What is also important is to protect the vulnerable youth once they enter the virtual world so that they do not end up as pawns in the system.

Cernikova, Dedkova, and Smahel (2018) opined that youths are co-constructors of the online world through their active engagement with other recipients. While discretion is desirable, interactions with strangers are unavoidable when it comes to online interactions. Therefore, instead of having a "risky-by-default" perception, it is important to educate the Indian youth about potential risks and to empower them to choose and terminate conversations whenever needed. Internet safety programmes targeted at the Indian youth thus should not entirely forbid online interactions with strangers but instead make the youth aware of danger signals that require cognisance and action. To this end, the following interventions are recommended.

Sensitization about risks and preventive measures

Sensitization about online risks and cyber security is one of the most emphasized interventions for protection of virtual denizens, youth included. Researchers recommend making cyber security a part of school curricula, so that the youth is made aware of the best practices by the time they enter the virtual world. Sensitization training should focus on the common threats such as financial frauds, malware, hacking, and morphing of videos and images, as well as relatively less talked about issues such as cyber bullying, and illegal use of personal data for marketing and product placement.

Cyber security trainings, focusing on the importance of regularly changing passwords on various online accounts, not sharing critical personal details of self and others online, detecting suspicious links and insecure web pages, or detecting fake profiles and chat box, are useful in making the youth aware of the means to protect themselves in the virtual world. It is also important to develop in the youth awareness of the cyber laws of India and cyber laws applicable across international boundaries, such as the GDPR, and the process of filing complaints relating to online crimes, so that they can easily access these services whenever necessary.

One relatively less-discussed issue of critical importance for the youth is the impact of controversial opinions voiced on social media on future career and life prospects. There have been several instances when the old tweets and social media posts of celebrities and even private citizens have gone viral in India, showing politically incorrect words or opinions. In 2021, one Indian student elected as the first woman president of the Oxford University Student Union was forced to resign and leave the university due to cyberbullying on her past tweets of a controversial nature (PTI, 2021). It has now become a common practice for employers to scan the social media profiles and digital presence of an applicant, to see if the person holds a contrarian/politically incorrect view or engages in online practices that may be potentially damaging for the firm's reputation going ahead. Cyber-vetting of profiles by recruiters (Jeske & Holland, 2019), necessitates that the youth is cognizant of the impact of their Internet presence not only on their current reputation but also on the future roles they foresee for themselves. While this should not discourage civic engagements and activism, the youth need to be trained in selecting appropriate forums for raising their voice about social issues, being constructive, legally sound, and respectful in their arguments, be ethical and culturally sensitive about the quality of their content and make extensive use of privacy settings so that their content only reaches the intended audience to the extent possible.

The pervasive nature of cyberbullying and its damaging consequences have shifted the focus on means to address the same. While social media activism has been instrumental in drawing attention to social wrongs and providing rapid redressal, there have been umpteen instances of the social media setting up kangaroo courts to implicate and harass a person on suspicion, without any due legal process. In 2020, an Indian school student committed suicide after being named in a #MeToo post on Instagram (Zee Media Bureau, 2020a). At the other end, there have been cases of videos of sexual crimes going viral on social media, forcing the victim to self-harm and suicide (e.g. Chitre, 2019). Researchers recommend making cyberbullying and online safety behaviour a part of the school curriculum for the youth (Bauman & Baldasare, 2015).

Doane, Kelley, and Pearson (2016) demonstrated that technology-based interventions, such as videos sensitizing the youth about cyberbullying, contribute to both awareness and empathy among the youth regarding the issues in question. Flanagan (2014) also recommends training to the youth so that they do not become passive witnesses but make actual interventions when they witness cyberbullying. Other recommended interventions include making and creating anonymous portals in Indian schools and colleges where students may flag critical issues, along with measures against those caught engaged in cyberbullying (Blumenfeld & Cooper, 2010). Further, Abreu and Kenny (2018) recommend collaborative efforts among teachers, parents, lawmakers, and executives to decrease cyber victimization.

Technological measures for preventing cybercrimes

With advancement in digital technology, there is also a constant upgrade in the technology adopted by cybercriminals. This makes even the best of vigilance efforts fail. Further, despite the best training, the efficacy of the interventions in bringing about a sustained change in the online behaviour of the youth is often beyond the control of interventionists. Therefore, researchers and technological experts are increasingly recommending barriers set up by default in the system so that the youth stays protected from criminal intentions online. India was ranked 10th in the world in the Global Cybersecurity Index 2020, attesting a tremendous improvement from its rank of 47 in 2018 (Varma, 2021), owing to emphasis on building robust cyber systems, legal checks, and promoting cyber education.

In the forward for the conference on Youth and the Internet: Fighting radicalization and extremism, the United Nations Educational, Scientific and Cultural Organization (UNESCO, 2015) recommends that internet addiction and crimes against the youth need to be countered both by monitoring and censoring content online. Such censoring may happen using child-lock or parental control; that makes problematic content inaccessible to the youth. The Government of India, in 2020, exercised a ban on the online video sharing platform TikTok, owing to the proliferation of hate messages on the platform (Singal, 2021). Similar restrictions have been exercised for the addictive online multiplayer game Pub-G and for child pornography (Business Today, 2020).

Technology is being used in a major way to protect the youth from online threats. The Counter Extremism Project works to single out extremist content on social media using technology and counter it with rational factual content (Counter Extremism Project, 2021). Similarly, machine learning has been used to identify and block online content of an offensive nature (Costello et al., 2020). Castillo-Sánchez et al. (2020) recommend use of machine learning and semantic analysis to detect content signalling suicidal ideations or signs of distress online.

Lifestyle interventions to curb addiction

Research has shown a significant link between problematic internet behaviour and lifestyle issues – making certain youths highly likely to show symptoms of internet addiction. Ying Ying et al. (2021) recommended early detection of internet addiction through screening, as well as monitoring of lifestyle correlates such as sedentary lifestyles, unhealthy eating, and drug addiction. Further, they recommended cultivation of healthy living habits such as an active lifestyle, early awareness building to combat internet addiction among the youth, restricted access to personal IT-enabled devices at a young age, and role modelling of ideal internet usage behaviour by parents and caregivers.

The UNESCO (UNESCO, 2015) too recommends suitably engaging the youth in alternative activities offline. Opportunities for outdoor games, team activities, and cultural pursuits could help the Indian youth in occupying their time and not looking at the virtual means as an alternative.

Youth who used the internet for communication purposes were far less at risk for PIU than who used the internet for content consumption or gaming purposes (Thorsteinsson & Davey, 2014). It is therefore recommended that the youths are trained to use social media to connect with family, friends, and professional ties, and exchange information, rather than simple passive content consumption or information broadcasting.

The role of strong ties: Family, school, and friends

Internet addiction often originates from compensating for felt inadequacies in offline relationships and interactions. Youths who are lonely, shunned, or socially awkward in their personal lives often take to the internet for unhealthy durations, finding the social approval and reinforcement that is absent otherwise. It has been widely recommended that healthy relationships with strong ties (Granovetter, 1973) – social relations close and influential to the person – would go a long way in curbing problematic internet behaviour. Yang and Lee (2020) reported that being connected on social media with parents and college friends led to better adjustment in college whereas being connected with strangers led to poor adjustment. Again, Landau et al. (2019), in a study on Israeli adolescents, identified different coping mechanisms adopted by youth who have faced hate and rejection online. These included seeking help from therapists, online community supervisors, or others in responsible positions, seeking support from siblings, parents, and even friends in online communities.

Family plays a critical role in developing the online behaviour of children. Parents and caregivers act as role models for online behaviour, and children and youth are likely to demonstrate similar patterns of online engagements as they grow up to see (Hefner, Knop, Schmitt, & Vorderer, 2019). Therefore, it is important for the Indian parents to role model healthy online behaviour in front of young people, such as restricted internet use, no browsing during family hours, and maintenance of a suitable online persona (Kumar, 2018).

Childhood being a period requiring adult supervision and regulation, the importance of supervision of the youth's online behaviour cannot be emphasized more (Buckingham, 2013). In a study done in Malaysia, it was found that only approximately 51% of parents were aware of parental control and only 12% used it on computers used by their children (MCMC, 2018). Researchers such as Livingstone and Bulger (2014) recommend sophisticated parental regulations to protect children from the harmful impact of the internet. Schools and colleges in India may take up the initiative in training parents of youths on censoring and monitoring technology, and teaching them the best practices of having restricted access to personal devices, and placing devices in non-private locations of the household. Parents and teachers should have free and open discussion with children and youth about advantages and disadvantages of internet and social networking sites so that unnecessary usages of the internet could be avoided to save valuable time for children and youth. Parents should also be watchful of their children and youth involvement in mobile and internet and discourage them not to spend an unhealthy amount of time in the virtual world.

Several scholars reported a relationship between Problematic Internet Use and lower parental control, broken home, and lower parental education (Chen et al., 2015; Yu & Shek, 2013). Thus, parents need to be encouraged to foster a positive home environment where children feel loved, understood, and adequate. Li, Dang, Zhang, Zhang, and Guo (2014) demonstrated the role of parental support in combating unhealthy addiction to the internet.

Healthy relationships with teachers have been emphasized to play a role in controlling internet addiction. With the growing digitalization of education in Indian schools and colleges, it is important that teachers play an active role in shaping the online behaviour of the youth and demonstrate the healthy use of the internet for educational and vocational purposes. Students who perceived their teachers to be giving them autonomy and decision-making powers in the classroom were less likely to suffer from Problematic Internet Use (Yu et al., 2015). This highlights the importance of the training of teachers in making the youth aware of healthy behaviour internet on the internet and at the same time make them feel empowered and appreciated. There should be restrictions in the college and universities for mobile usages.

The role of healthy peer relationships has also been emphasized in online behaviour and outcomes (Selfhout, Branje, Delsing, ter Bogt, & Meeus, 2009). As in the case of other strong ties, peers influence the youth's online behaviour through role-modelling, help develop the online persona. and provide support in cases of cyberbullying. Prievara et al. (2019) recommend training in social and interpersonal communication for the youth to curb internet addiction, involving both parents and peers. They also recommend training and guidance to the youth to build meaningful connections on social media with strong ties, replacing connection with strangers.

Continued research and policy evaluation

Despite the vast amount of literature on the online world and youth experiences, it needs to be recognized that the digital media is one of the fastest evolving fields in the world. State-of-the-earth interventions such as the

Internet of Things (IoT), use of humanoids such as Alexa and Siri in daily life, and increased blurring of the boundaries between human communication and advanced artificial intelligence, are going to change the virtual interactions of the younger generations in an unforeseen way. For instance, researchers have reported that prolonged exposure to service offered by AI-assisted technology is transforming an individual's expectations from human interactions that are more error-prone, require more effort, and require more cognitive and emotional investments (e.g. Bankins & Formosa, 2020). Upcoming technology enabling deviceless access to the internet (DeMers, 2016) and chip-based learning (University of Münster, 2019), are also going to revolutionize the cognitive and social impact of the virtual world as it is understood today.

The rapid changes in the technological front are also bringing about major changes on the legal and regulatory front when it comes to online behaviour. The General Data Protection Regulations (GDPR) of the European World, restricting access to personal data of consumers by businesses (GDPR, 2016), is one such example that has considerably impacted the operations of the internet. Similar updates in regulatory norms need to come up from time to time in national laws and policies as well, addressing prevention and punishment of new variants of cybercrimes, setting up standards of ethical practices in artificial intelligence, and establishing accountability in case of cybercrimes committed by digibots. Firth et al. (2019) recommend extensive research on the impact of the internet on human cognition, so that the negative effects may be mitigated, and the benefits multiplied. Cernikova et al. (2018) recommend more research on the positive aspects of youth's experience in the virtual world, so that effective interventions may be planned to multiply such positive experiences.

Along with research on regulatory norms and technology updates, it is important to assess the impact of digital policies adopted by various countries, to see if they meet the goals set and if they continue to be relevant in a rapidly changing context. Data-driven assessment of cyber policies and regulations is likely to assist policymakers, thinkers, and educationists to plan interventions to create positive experiences for the youth in the virtual world.

Conclusion and recommendations

India in the twenty-first century is witnessing the onset of a digital era that promises to be transformational in its impact, in a way probably no other technology before it has been. The youth is the prime stakeholder in this transforming society, slated to reap the benefits of the digitized world, as well as to bear its curses. What makes the task doubly challenging is that the future is in flux, making it difficult to predict what the future of digital technology will look like. Hence, the Indian youth need to be prepared to make the most of the digital experience – understanding and utilizing its numerous advantages and at the same time staying protected from the threats that the virtual world brings into one's personal space. The results of the efforts made in these directions, through digital policies and regulations, research, interventions, and practices are going to define the future of the nation and the dynamics of humanity for the coming decades.

References

Abreu, R. L., & Kenny, M. C. (2018). Cyberbullying and LGBTQ youth: a systematic literature review and recommendations for prevention and intervention. *Journal of Child & Adolescent Trauma*, *11*(1), 81–97. doi:10.1007/s40653-017-0175-7

Adorjan, M. C., & Ricciardelli, R. (2018). *Cyber-risk and youth: digital citizenship, privacy and surveillance*. London: Routledge. doi:10.4324/9781315158686

Altmann, E. M., Trafton, J. G., & Hambrick, D. Z. (2014). Momentary interruptions can derail the train of thought. *Journal of Experimental Psychology: General*, *143*(1), 215. doi:10.1037/a0030986

American Psychiatric Association (2013). *Diagnostic and statistical manual of mental disorders* (5th ed.). Washington, DC: American Psychiatric Association.

Anderson, M., & Jiang, J. (2018, May 31). *Teens, social media, and technology 2018*. Pew Research Center Internet and Technology. Retrieved July 1, 2021 from https://www.pewresearch.org/Internet/2018/05/31/teens-social-media-technology-2018/

Arya, V., Singh, H., & Malhotra, A. K. (2018). Prevalence of Internet addiction and its association with socio-demographic factors among MBBS students as medical college, Jhansi, Uttar Pradesh. *International Journal of Community Medicine and. Public Health*, *5*, 1980–1983. doi:10.25215/0803.052

Asokan, M. (2021, June 17). Youth most vulnerable to UPI scams, phishing attack: Report. *The Times of India*. Retrieved July 1, 2021 from https://timesofindia.indiatimes.com/business/india-business/youth-most-vulnerable-to-upi-scams-phishing-attack-report/articleshow/83585361.cms

Baird, B., Smallwood, J., Mrazek, M. D., Kam, J. W., Franklin, M. S., & Schooler, J. W. (2012). Inspired by distraction: mind wandering facilitates creative incubation. *Psychological Science*, *23*(10), 1117–1122. doi:10.1177/0956797612446024

Balhara, Y. P. S., Kattula, D., Singh, S., Chukkali, S., & Bhargava, R. (2020). Impact of lockdown following COVID-19 on the gaming behavior of college students. *Indian Journal of Public Health*, *64*(6), 172–176.

Balhara, Y. P. S., Mahapatra, A., Sharma, P., & Bhargava, R. (2018). Problematic Internet use among students in South-East Asia: current state of evidence. *Indian Journal of Public Health*, *62*(3), 197–210.

Bamezai, G., Kesharvani, P., Yumnam, B., Goswami, S., Pradhan, A., Roy, A., & Ambade, B. N. (2011). Impact of Internet on changing patterns of newspaper access and news-reading habits in India. *Media Asia*, *38*(2), 110–121.

Bankins, S., & Formosa, P. (2020). When AI meets PC: exploring the implications of workplace social robots and a human-robot psychological contract. *European Journal of Work and Organizational Psychology*, *29*(2), 215–229. doi:10.1080/1359432X.2019.1620328

Bauman, S., & Baldasare, A. (2015). Cyber aggression among college students: demographic differences, predictors of distress, and the role of the university. *Journal of College Student Development*, *56*, 317–330. doi:10.1353/csd.2015.0039

Baumgartner, S. E., van der Schuur, W. A., Lemmens, J. S., & te Poel, F. (2018). The relationship between media multitasking and attention problems in adolescents:

results of two longitudinal studies. *Human Communication Research*, *44*(1), 3–30. doi:10.1093/hcre.12111

BBNL (2021). *GPs to which OFC Connected & Equipment Installed.* Retrieved July 1, 2021 from www.bbnl.nic.in

Bener, A., Al-Mahdi, H. S., & Bhugra, D. (2016). Lifestyle factors and Internet addiction among school children. *International Journal of Community & Family Medicine*, *1*(118), 2. doi:10.15344/2456-3498/2016/118

Beniwal, A. (2020). Digital Gaming: a new way of programming happiness and creativity in youth. In S. Kono, A. Beniwal, P. Baweja, & K. Spracklen (Eds.) *Positive sociology of leisure. Leisure studies in a global era* (pp. 259–277). Palgrave Macmillan, Cham. doi:10.1007/978-3-030-41812-0_15

Bennett, W. L., Wells, C., & Rank, A. (2009). Young citizens and civic learning: two paradigms of citizenship in the digital age. *Citizenship Studies*, *13*(2), 105–120. doi:10.1080/13621020902731116

Blank, G., & Groselj, D. (2014). Dimensions of Internet use: amount, variety, and types. *Information, Communication & Society*, *17*(4), 417–435. doi:10.1080/1369118X.2014.889189

Bloom, M. (2017). Constructing expertise: terrorist recruitment and "talent spotting" in the PIRA, Al Qaeda, and ISIS. *Studies in Conflict & Terrorism*, *40*(7), 603–623. doi:10.1080/1057610X.2016.1237219

Blumenfeld, W. J., & Cooper, R. M. (2010). LGBT and allied youth responses to cyberbullying: policy implications. *The International Journal of Critical Pedagogy*, 3, 114–133.

Bora, G. (2020). For Indian gaming startups, Covid-19 lockdown is a boon for business. *The Economic Times*, April 13. Retrieved June 24, 2020, from: https://economictimes.indiatimes.com/small-biz/startups/newsbuzz/for-indian-gaming-startups-covid-19-lockdown-is-a-boon-for-business/articleshow/75115595.

Boyd, D. (2014). *It's complicated: the social lives of networked teens.* New Haven: Yale University Press.

Buckingham, D. (2013). *After the death of childhood.* Cambridge: John Wiley & Sons.

Burgess, J., & Green, J. (2018). *YouTube: online video and participatory culture.* Cambridge: John Wiley & Sons.

Burke, M., & Kraut, R. E. (2016). The relationship between Facebook use and well-being depends on communication type and tie strength. *Journal of Computer-Mediated Communication*, 21, 265–281. doi:10.1111/jcc4.12162

Buttazzoni, A., Brar, K., & Minaker, L. (2021). Smartphone-based interventions and internalizing disorders in youth: systematic review and meta-analysis. *Journal of Medical Internet Research*, 23(1), e16490. doi:10.2196/16490

Button, M., Nicholls, C. M., Kerr, J., & Owen, R. (2014). Online frauds: learning from victims why they fall for these scams. *Australian & New Zealand Journal of Criminology*, 47(3), 391–408. doi:10.1177/0004865814521224

Castillo-Sánchez, G., Marques, G., Dorronzoro, E., Rivera-Romero, O., Franco-Martín, M., & De la Torre-Díez, I. (2020). Suicide risk assessment using machine learning and social networks: a scoping review. *Journal of Medical Systems*, 44(12), 1–15. doi:10.1007/s10916-020-01669-5

Cernikova, M., Dedkova, L., & Smahel, D. (2018). Youth interaction with online strangers: experiences and reactions to unknown people on the Internet. *Information, Communication & Society*, *21*(1), 94–110. doi:10.1080/1369118X.2016.1261169

Chan, C., & Ngai, S. S. Y. (2019). Utilizing social media for social work: insights from clients in online youth services. *Journal of Social Work Practice*, *33*(2), 157–172. doi:10.1080/02650533.2018.1504286

Chen, Y. L., Chen, S. H., & Gau, S. F. S. (2015). ADHD and autistic traits, family function, parenting style, and social adjustment for Internet addiction among children and adolescents in Taiwan: a longitudinal study. *Research in Developmental Disabilities*, 39, 20–31. doi:10.1016/j.ridd.2014.12.025

Chitre, M. (2019, October 6). UP: Rape victim commits suicide, writes names of the accused on hand. *RepublicWorld.com*. Retrieved July 1, 2021 from https://www.republicworld.com/india-news/general-news/muzaffarnagar-gang-rape-victim-commits-suicide-writes-names-on-hand.html

Choo, H., Sim, T., Liau, A. K. F., Gentile, D. A., & Khoo, A. (2015). Parental influences on pathological symptoms of videogaming among children and adolescents: a prospective study. *Journal of Child and Family Studies*, *24*, 1429–1441. doi:10.1007/s10826-014-9949-9

Common Sense (2018). Social media, social life: teens reveal their experiences, 2018. *Common Sense Media*. Retrieved July 1, 2021 from https://www.commonsensemedia.org/research/social-media-social-life-2018

Costello, M., Barrett-Fox, R., Bernatzky, C., Hawdon, J., & Mendes, K. (2020). Predictors of viewing online extremism among America's youth. *Youth & Society*, *52*(5), 710–727. doi:10.1177/0044118X18768115

Counter Extremism Project (2021). Mission Statement. *Counterextremism.com*. Retrieved July 1, 2021 from https://www.counterextremism.com/mission-statement

Cuzzocrea, V., & Collins, R. (2020). Youth transitions as 'wiki-transitions' in youth policies platforms. *European Societies*, 22(4), 411–432. doi:10.1080/14616696.2019.1690158

Darade, P. (2017, October 7) Narendra Modi to launch Pradhan Mantri Gramin Digital Saksharta Abhiyan; Here's everything you need to know. *India.com*. Retrieved July 1, 2021 from https://www.india.com/news/india/narendra-modi-to-launch-pradhan-mantri-gramin-digital-saksharta-abhiyan-heres-everything-you-need-to-know-2519187/

Davis, R. A. (2001). A cognitive-behavioral model of pathological Internet use. *Computers in Human Behavior*, *17*(2), 187–195. doi:10.1016/S0747-5632(00)00041-8

DeMers, J. (2016, April 8). 7 Predictions for how the Internet will change over the next 15 years. *Forbes*. Retrieved March 24, 2021 from https://www.forbes.com/sites/jaysondemers/2016/04/18/7-predictions-for-how-the-Internet-will-change-over-the-next-15-years/?sh=241f49fa22e0

Demetrovics, Z., Szeredi, B., & Rózsa, S. (2008). The three-factor model of Internet addiction: the development of the problematic Internet use questionnaire. *Behavior Research Methods*, *40*(2), 563–574. doi:10.3758/BRM.40.2.563

Doane, A. N., Kelley, M. L., & Pearson, M. R. (2016). Reducing cyberbullying: a theory of reasoned action- based video prevention program for college students. *Aggressive Behavior*, *42*, 136–146. doi:10.1002/ab.21610

Dragseth, M. R. (2020). Building student engagement through social media. *Journal of Political Science Education*, *16*(2), 243–256. doi:10.1002/ab.21610

Elias, N., & Lemish, D. (2009). Spinning the web of identity: the roles of the Internet in immigrant adolescents' search of identity, *New Media & Society*, 11, 533–551. doi:10.1177/1461444809102959

Engelberg, E., & Sjöberg, L. (2004). Internet use, social skills, and adjustment. *Cyberpsychology & Behavior*, 7(1), 41–47. doi:10.1089/109493104322820101

Esen, B. K., Aktas, E., & Tuncer, I. (2013). An analysis of university students' Internet use in relation to loneliness and social self-efficacy. *Procedia – Social and Behavioral Sciences*, *84*(9), 1504–1508. doi:10.1016/j.sbspro.2013.06.780

Ettekal, A. V., & Agans, J. P. (2020). Positive youth development through leisure: confronting the COVID-19 pandemic. *Journal of Youth Development*, *15*(2), 1–20. doi:10.5195/jyd.2020.962

FE Online (2021, March 5). Elon Musk's Starlink satellite broadband service is coming to India: how to pre-order, price, availability and other details. *The Financial Express*. Retrieved July 1, 2021 from https://www.financialexpress.com/industry/technology/elon-musks-starlink-satellite-based-broadband-service-is-coming-to-india-how-to-pre-order-price-availability-and-other-details/2204606/

Firth, J., Torous, J., Stubbs, B., Firth, J. A., Steiner, G. Z., Smith, L., ... & Sarris, J. (2019). The "online brain": how the Internet may be changing our cognition. *World Psychiatry*, *18*(2), 119–129. doi:10.1002/wps.20617

Flanagan, A.Y. (2014). Cyberbullying and harassment. *NetCE*. Retrieved July 1, 2021 from https://www.netcegroups.com/1127/Course_66421.pdf.

Fogel, J. (2011). Instant messaging communication: self-disclosure, intimacy, and disinhibition. *Journal of Communications Research*, 2(1), 13–19.

Foxman, A. H., & Wolf, C. (2013). *Viral hate: containing its spread on the Internet*. New York: St. Martin's Press.

GDPR (2016). Regulation (EU) 2016/679 of the European Parliament and of the Council of 27 April 2016 on the protection of natural persons with regard to the processing of personal data and on the free movement of such data, and repealing Directive 95/46/EC (General Data Protection Regulation). *Official Journal of the European Union*, L119/1–88. Retrieved July 1, 2021 from https://eur-lex.europa.eu/legal-content/EN/TXT/PDF/?uri=CELEX:32016R0679

Ghobadi, S., & Mathiassen, L. (2020). A Generational perspective on the software workforce: precocious users of social networking in software development. *Journal of Management Information Systems*, *37*(1), 96–128. doi:10.1080/07421222.2019.1705508

Granovetter, M. S. (1973). The strength of weak ties. *American Journal of Sociology*, 78(6), 1360–1380.

Gray, M.L. (2009). Negotiating identities/queering desires: coming out online and the remediation of the coming-out story. *Journal of Computer-Mediated Communication*. *14*(4), 1162–1189. doi:10.1111/j.1083-6101.2009.01485.x

Green, M. C., & Brock, T. C. (2008). Antecedents and civic consequences of choosing real versus ersatz social activities. *Media Psychology*, *11*(4), 566–592. doi:10.1080/15213260802491994

Gupta, A., Khan, A. M., Rajoura, O. P., & Srivastava, S. (2018). Internet addiction and its mental health correlates among undergraduate college students of a university in North India. *Journal of Family Medicine and Primary Care*, 7(4), 721.

Hale, W.C. (2012). Extremism on the World Wide Web: a research review. *Criminal Justice Studies*, *25*(4), 343–356. doi:10.1080/1478601X.2012.704723

Hamilton, K. A., & Yao, M. Z. (2018). Blurring boundaries: effects of device features on metacognitive evaluations. *Computers in Human Behavior*, 89, 213–220. doi:10.1016/j.chb.2018.07.044

Hargittai, E., & Marwick, A. (2016). "What can I really do?" Explaining the privacy paradox with online apathy. *International Journal of Communication*, *10*, 21.

Hefner, D., Knop, K., Schmitt, S., & Vorderer, P. (2019). Rules? Role model? Relationship? The impact of parents on their children's problematic mobile phone involvement. *Media Psychology*, *22*(1), 82–108. doi:10.1080/15213269.2018.1433544

Huntington, H. E. (2013). *Subversive memes: internet memes as a form of visual rhetoric*. AoIR Selected Papers of Internet Research, 3. Retrieved from https://spir.aoir.org/ojs/index.php/spir/article/view/8886

IGPP (2020). *Patterns of Internet usage among youths in India*. Institute for Governance, Polices & Politics & Social Media Matters & Youth Online Learning Organisation, New Delhi. Retrieved July 1, 2021 from https://www.socialmediamatters.in/patterns-of-Internet-usage-among-youths-in-india#

IndiaStats (2014). *Internet & Social Media Usage among youth in India: Mcafee Report*. Retrieved July 1, 2021 from https://indiafacts.in/Internet-social-media-usage-among-youth-india-mcafee-report/

iNOC (2012). *National Knowledge Network Overview*. Retrieved July 1, 2021 from http://workshop.nkn.in/2012/Document/slides/NKN%20Overview.pdf

International Telecommunication Union (2013). *Measuring the Information Society Report 2013*. Retrieved July 1, 2021 from https://www.itu.int/en/ITU-D/Statistics/Documents/publications/mis2013/MIS2013_without_Annex_4.pdf

International Telecommunication Union (2014). *Measuring the Information Society Report 2014*. Retrieved July 1, 2021 from https://www.itu.int/en/ITU-D/Statistics/Documents/publications/mis2014/MIS2014_without_Annex_4.pdf

International Telecommunication Union (2017). *Measuring the Information Society Report Volume 1*. Retrieved July 1, 2021 from https://www.itu.int/en/ITU-D/Statistics/Documents/publications/misr2017/MISR2017_Volume1.pdf

IOC (2018). *Olympic Movement, eSports and Gaming Communities Meet at the eSports Forum*. Retrieved July 1, 2021 from https://www.olympic.org/news/olympic-movement-esports-and-gaming-communities-meet-at-the-esports-forum

Iqbal, M. (2021, May 21). LinkedIn Usage and Revenue Statistics (2021). *Business of Apps*. Retrieved July 5, 2021 from https://www.businessofapps.com/data/linkedin-statistics/

Iyer, G., & DoraiswamyIyer, R. (2020). Internet addiction in freshmen engineering students in India. *Journal of Management and Public Policy*, 12(1), 45–58.

Jain, O., Gupta, M., Satam, S., & Panda, S. (2020). Has the COVID-19 pandemic affected the susceptibility to cyberbullying in India?. *Computers in Human Behavior Reports*, 2, 100029.

Jain, A., Sharma, R., Gaur, K. L., Yadav, N., Sharma, P., Sharma, N., … & Yadav, K. S. (2020). Study of Internet addiction and its association with depression and insomnia in university students. *Journal of Family Medicine and Primary Care*, 9(3), 1700.

James, C. (2014). *Disconnected: youth, new media, and the ethics gap*. Massachusetts: MIT Press.

Jelenchick, L. A., Eickhoff, J. C., & Moreno, M. A. (2013). Facebook depression? social networking site use and depression in older adolescents. *Journal of Adolescent Health*, *52*(1), 128–130. doi:10.1016/j.jadohealth.2012.05.008

Jeske, D., & Holland, P. (2019). Employer and employee vetting: reputation management challenges in the Information Age. In P. Holland (Ed) *Contemporary HRM issues in the 21st century* (pp. 149–157). Bingley: Emerald Publishing Limited.

Jiang, N., Cleland, C.M., Wang, M.P., Kwong, A., Lai, V., & Lam, T.H. (2019). Perceptions and use of e-cigarettes among young adults in Hong Kong. *BMC Public Health*, 19, 1123. doi:10.1186/s12889-019-7464-z

Keating, A., & Melis, G. (2017). Social media and youth political engagement: preaching to the converted or providing a new voice for youth? *The British Journal of Politics and International Relations*, *19*(4), 877–894. doi:10.1177/1369148117718461

Keene, S. D. (2011). Terrorism and the Internet: a double-edged sword. *Journal of Money Laundering Control*, 14(4), 359–370. doi:10.1108/13685201111173839

Kesavan, C.R. & Vignesh, K.K.R. (2020, September 8). Empower the Youth First. *The Hindu*. Retrieved July 1, 2021 https://www.thehindu.com/opinion/op-ed/empower-the-youth-first/article32546714.ece

Kesharwani, A. (2020). Do (how) digital natives adopt a new technology differently than digital immigrants? A longitudinal study. *Information & Management*, *57*(2), 103170. doi:10.1016/j.im.2019.103170

Khane, J., Middaugh, E., & Allen, D. (2015). Youth, media, and the rise of participatory politics. In D. Allen & J. S. Light (Eds.) *From voice to influence: understanding citizenship in a digital age* (pp. 35–56). Chicago, IL: University of Chicago Press.

Kligler-Vilenchik, N., & Literat, I. (2018). Distributed creativity as political expression: youth responses to the 2016 US presidential election in online affinity networks. *Journal of Communication*, *68*(1), 75–97. doi:10.1093/joc/jqx005

Kotwal, N., Kotwal, N., & Rani, S. (2007). Causes of school dropouts among rural girls in Kathua District. *Journal of Human Ecology*, *22*(1), 57–59. doi:10.1080/09709274.2007.11906000

Kumar, R. (2018). Cyberbullies, bullying, and the young in India. In R. West, & C. S. Beck (Eds). *The Routledge handbook of communication and bullying*. New York: Routledge.

Kuss, D. J., Louws, J., & Wiers, R. W. (2012). Online gaming addiction? Motives predict addictive play behavior in massively multiplayer online role-playing games. *Cyberpsychology, Behavior, and Social Networking*, *15*(9), 480–485. doi:10.1089/cyber.2012.0034

Kwok, R. C. W., Leung, A. C. M., Hui, S. S. C., & Wong, C. C. K. (2021). Virtual trainer system: a tool to increase exercise participation and work productivity. *Internet Research*, *31*(3), 892–910. doi:10.1108/INTR-04-2020-0236

Landau, A., Eisikovits, Z., & Rafaeli, S. (2019, January). *Coping Strategies for Youth Suffering from Online Interpersonal Rejection*. In *Proceedings of the 52nd Hawaii International Conference on System Sciences*. Retrieved July 1, 2021 from http://128.171.57.22/bitstream/10125/59656/0216.pdf

Leader-Chivee, L., Hamilton, B. A., & Cowan, E. (2008). Networking the way to success: online social networks for workplace and competitive advantage. *People and Strategy*, 31(4), 40–46.

Lenhart, A. (2009). *Teens and sexting: how and why minor teens are sending sexually suggestive nude or nearly nude images via text messaging (Vol. 15)*. Washington, DC: Pew Internet & American Life Project. Retrieved July 1, 2021 from https://www.pewresearch.org/Internet/2009/12/15/teens-and-sexting/

Leung, L. (2004). Net-generation attributes and seductive properties of the Internet as predictors of online activities and Internet addiction. *CyberPsychology & Behavior*, 7(3), 333–348. doi:10.1089/1094931041291303

Li, C., Dang, J., Zhang, X., Zhang, Q., & Guo, J. (2014). Internet addiction among Chinese adolescents: the effect of parental behavior and self-control. *Computers in Human Behavior*, *41*, 1–7. doi:10.1016/j.chb.2014.09.001

Liff, S. & Steward, F. (2001). Community E-gateways: locating networks and learning for social inclusion. *Information, Communication & Society*, *4*(3), 317–340. 10.1080/713768550

Literat, I., Kligler-Vilenchik, N., Brough, M., & Blum-Ross, A. (2018). Analyzing youth digital participation: aims, actors, contexts and intensities. *The Information Society*, *34*(4), 261–273. doi:10.1080/01972243.2018.1463333

Liu, X., Lin, X., Zheng, M., Hu, Y., Wang, Y., Wang, L., Du, X., & Dong, G. (2018). Internet search alters intra-and inter-regional synchronization in the temporal gyrus. *Frontiers in Psychology*, *9*, 260. doi:10.3389/fpsyg.2018.00260

Livingstone, S., & Bulger, M. (2014). *A global research agenda for children's rights in the digital age*. UNICEF Office of Research. Retrieved July 1, 2021 from http://eprints.lse.ac.uk/54276/1/livingstone_global_agenda_childrens_digital_2014_author.pdf

Lopez-Fernandez, O. (2021). Emerging health and education issues related to Internet technologies and addictive problems. *International Journal of Environmental Research and Public Health*, *18*(1), 321. doi:10.3390/ijerph18010321

Majumdar, B., Basu, S., & Jain, S (2021). Digital empowerment and Indian handlooms: case-based policy recommendations. *Economic and Political Weekly*, 56 (8).

Manca, S. (2020). Snapping, pinning, liking or texting: investigating social media in higher education beyond Facebook. *The Internet and Higher Education*, *44*, 100707. doi:10.1016/j.iheduc.2019.100707

Mandavia, (2019, September 26). India has second highest number of Internet users after China: report. *ET Prime*. Retrieved July 1, 2021 from https://economictimes.indiatimes.com/tech/Internet/india-has-second-highest-number-of-Internet-users-after-china-report/articleshow/71311705.cms

Marwick, A., & Lewis, R. (2017). Media manipulation and disinformation online. *Data & Society Research Institute*. Retrieved July 1, 2021 from http://www.chinhnghia.com/DataAndSociety_MediaManipulationAndDisinformationOnline.pdf

McConnell, E., Néray, B., Hogan, B., Korpak, A., Clifford, A., & Birkett, M. (2018). "Everybody puts their whole life on Facebook": identity Management and the online social networks of LGBTQ youth. *International Journal of Environmental Research and Public Health*, *15*(6), 1078. doi:10.3390/ijerph15061078

McKinsey Global Institute (2019). *Digital India: technology to transform a connected nation*. Retrieved July 1, 2021 from https://www.mckinsey.com/~/media/McKinsey/Business%20Functions/McKinsey%20Digital/Our%20Insights/Digital%20India%20Technology%20to%20transform%20a%20connected%20nation/MGI-Digital-India-Report-April-2019.ashx

MCMC (2018). *Internet users survey 2018*. Malaysian Communications and Multimedia Commission. Retrieved July 1, 2021 from https://www.mcmc.gov.my/skmmgovmy/media/General/pdf/Internet-Users-Survey-2018.pdf

MHRD (2020a). *PRAGYATA: guidelines for digital education*. Ministry of Human Resource Development, Government of India. Retrieved July 1, 2021 from https://www.education.gov.in/sites/upload_files/mhrd/files/pragyata-guidelines_0.pdf

MHRD (2020b). *India report digital education: remote learning initiatives across India*. Ministry of Human Resource Development, Government of India. Retrieved from https://www.education.gov.in/sites/upload_files/mhrd/files/India_Report_Digital_Education_0.pdf

Morgan, L. (2019). *Liam Morgan: esports is coming to the Olympics after all as Paris 2024 reveal ideas to improve fan engagement*. Retrieved July 1, 2021 from https://www.insidethegames.biz/articles/1075990/liam-morgan-esports-is-coming-to-the-olympicsafter-all-as-paris-2024-reveal-ideas-to-improve-fan-engagement

MyGov.in (2020, November 30). *Cyberbullying – a changing trend of modern crime.* Retrieved July 1, 2021 from https://blog.mygov.in/cyberbullying-a-changing-trend-of-modern-crime/

Naeemi, S., Tamam, E., Hassan, S. H., & Bolong, J. (2014). Facebook usage and its association with psychological well-being among Malaysian adolescents. *Procedia – Social and Behavioral Sciences*, 155, 87–91. doi:10.1016/j.sbspro.2014.10.261

Nalapat, M. (2017, October 15). India at centre of ISIS recruitment drive. *The Sunday Guardian.* Retrieved July 1, 2021 from https://www.sundayguardianlive.com/news/11275-india-centre-isis-recruitment-drive

Narayan, R., Das, B., Das, S., & Bhandari, S. (2019). The depressed boy who accepted Blue Whale Challenge. *Indian Journal of Psychiatry*, 61(1), 105–106.

NASSCOM (2016). *The Future of Internet in India.* Retrieved July 1, 2021 from https://www.nasscom.in/system/files/securepdf/The_Future_of_the_Internet_in_India_19082016.pdf

Navani, R. (2021, February 24). *Why India's gaming industry is on the rise.* World Economic Forum. Retrieved July 1, 2021 from https://www.weforum.org/agenda/2021/02/why-india-s-gaming-industry-is-on-the-rise/

NDCP (2018). *National Digital Communications Policy 2018.* Retrieved July 1, 2021 from https://dot.gov.in/sites/default/files/EnglishPolicy-NDCP.pdf

NeGD (2021). *Responsible AI for Youth: a national programme for government schools.* Retrieved July 1, 2021 from https://responsibleaiforyouth.negd.in/home

Nik Farid, N. D., Mohd Arshad, M. F. B., Yakub, N. A., Ahmad Zaki, R., Muhamad, H., Abdul Aziz, N., & Dahlui, M. (2018). Improving Malaysian adolescent sexual and reproductive health: an Internet-based health promotion programme as a potential intervention. *Health Education Journal*, *77*(7), 837–848. doi:10.1177/0017896918778071

North, S., Snyder, I., & Bulfin, S. (2008). Digital tastes: social class and young people's technology use. *Information, Communication & Society*, *11*(7), 895–911. doi:10.1080/13691180802109006

Ophir, E., Nass, C., & Wagner, A. D. (2009). Cognitive control in media multitaskers. *Proceedings of the National Academy of Sciences*, *106*(37), 15583–15587. doi:10.1073/pnas.0903620106

Pak Manesh, Z., & Razeghi, N. (2020). Internet and national identity among the youth in Sari. *Sociological Studies of Youth*, *11*(39), 103–118.

Palfrey, J., & Gasser, U. (2008). Opening universities in a digital era. *New England Journal of Higher Education*, *23*(1), 22–24.

Pappas, C. (2019, September 24). *Top 20 eLearning statistics for 2019 you need to know. E-Learning Industry.* Retrieved July 1, 2021 from https://elearningindustry.com/top-elearning-statistics-2019

Parija, P. P., Tiwari, P., Sharma, P., & Saha, S. K. (2020). Determinants of online health information-seeking behavior: a cross-sectional survey among residents of an urban settlement in Delhi. *Journal of Education and Health Promotion*, 9.

Pathania, R. (2020). Young India politically conscious, more likely to take part in online and offline protest. *LiveMint.* Retrieved July 1, 2021 from https://www.livemint.com/news/india/young-india-politically-conscious-more-likely-to-take-part-in-online-and-offline-protests-11592566694673.html

Peng, M., Chen, X., Zhao, Q., & Zhou, Z. (2018). Attentional scope is reduced by Internet use: a behavior and ERP study. *PLOS ONE*, 13(6), e0198543. doi:10.1371/journal.pone.0198543

Pengpid, S., & Peltzer, K. (2019). High carbonated soft drink consumption is associated with externalizing but not internalizing behaviours among university students in five ASEAN states. *Psychology Research and Behavior Management*, *12*, 585–592. doi:10.2147/PRBM.S209611

Penney, J. (2020). 'It's so hard not to be funny in this situation': memes and humor in US youth online political expression. *Television & New Media*, *21*(8), 791–806. doi:10.1177/1527476419886068

Pham, T., & Adesman, A. (2015). Teen victimization: prevalence and consequences of traditional and cyberbullying. *Current Opinion in Pediatrics*, *27*(6), 748–756. doi:10.1097/MOP.0000000000000290

PIB (2020a, May 15). *Shri Arjun Munda launches 'Goal' programme of M/o Tribal Affairs for Digital Skilling of Tribal Youth across India in partnership with Facebook*. Press Information Bureau Press Releases. Retrieved July 1, 2021 from https://pib.gov.in/PressReleseDetail.aspx?PRID=1624021

PIB (2020b, July 21). *Union HRD Minister launches MANODARPAN initiative of Ministry of HRD to provide psychosocial support to students for their Mental Health and Well-being*. Press Information Bureau Press Releases. Retrieved July 1, 2021 from https://www.education.gov.in/sites/upload_files/mhrd/files/Manodarpan-merged_0.pdf

Ponappa, S. (2011). Open spectrum for development India case study. *Association for Progressive Communications*. Retrieved July 1, 2021 from https://www.apc.org/en/spectrum/pubs/research/open-spectrum-development-india-case-study

Poonam, S. (2019, March 14). How India conquered YouTube. *FT Magazine*. Retrieved July 5 2021 from https://www.ft.com/content/c0b08a8e-4527-11e9-b168-96a37d002cd3

Prensky, M. (2001a). *Digital game-based learning*. New York: McGraw-Hill Publication.

Prensky, M. (2001b). Digital natives, digital immigrants part 2: do they really think differently? *On the Horizon*, *9*(6), 1–6. doi:10.1108/10748120110424843

Prievara, D. K., Piko, B. F., & Luszczynska, A. (2019). Problematic Internet use, social needs, and social support among youth. *International Journal of Mental Health and Addiction*, *17*(4), 1008–1019. doi:10.1007/s11469-018-9973-x

PTI (2020a, February 3). With 23% boost, Digital India Program gets Rs 3,958 crore. *ET Government.com*. Retrieved July 1, 2021 from https://government.economictimes.indiatimes.com/news/digital-india/with-23-boost-digital-india-program-gets-rs-3958-crore/73889733

PTI (2020b, June 13). About 56% of children have no access to smartphones for e-learning: study. *The Times of India*. Retrieved July 1, 2021 from https://timesofindia.indiatimes.com/home/education/about-56-of-children-have-no-access-to-smartphones-for-e-learning-study/articleshow/76355541.cms

PTI (2021, February 18). Rashmi Samant resigns as Oxford University Student Union President-elect. *BusinessStandard.com*. Retrieved July 1, 2021 from https://www.business-standard.com/article/pti-stories/rashmi-samant-resigns-as-oxford-student-union-president-elect-amidst-row-over-her-past-remarks-121021800551_1.html

Purcell, K., Rainie, L., Heaps, A., Buchanan, J., Friedrich, L., Jacklin, A., & Zickuhr, K. (2012). How teens do research in the digital world. *Pew research center's Internet and american life project*. Retrieved July 1, 2021 from https://eric.ed.gov/?id=ED537513

Purdy, C. H. (2011). Using the Internet and social media to promote condom use in Turkey. *Reproductive Health Matters, 19*(37), 157–165. doi:10.1016/S0968-8080(11)37549-0

Radhakrishnan, P., Sriram, N., & Manivannan, N. (2020). Usage of social networking tools by rural youth in transfer of technology-an overview. *Asian Journal of Agricultural Extension, Economics & Sociology*, 44–57. doi:10.9734/ajaees/2020/v38i230309

Ramsey, J. L., DiLalla, L. F., & McCrary, M. K. (2016). Cyber victimization and depressive symptoms in sexual minority college students. *Journal of School Violence*, 15, 483–502.

Rideout, V. J., Foehr, U. G., & Roberts, D. F. (2013). *Generation M^2. Media in the lives of 8-to 18-year-olds.* The Henry J. Kaiser Family Foundation. Retrieved July 1, 2021 from https://eric.ed.gov/?id=ED527859

Ringrose, J., & Barajas, K. E. (2011). Gendered risks and opportunities? Exploring teen girls' digitized sexual identities in postfeminist media contexts. *International Journal of Media & Cultural Politics*, 7(2), 121–138. doi:10.1386/macp.7.2.121_1

Rosenberg, H., Syed, S., & Rezaie, S. (2020). The Twitter pandemic: the critical role of Twitter in the dissemination of medical information and misinformation during the COVID-19 pandemic. *Canadian Journal of Emergency Medicine*, 22(4), 418–421. doi:10.1017/cem.2020.361

Roy, P.K. (2019, March 18). Mobile data: why India has the world's cheapest. *BBC*. Retrieved July 1, 2021 from https://www.bbc.com/news/world-asia-india-47537201

Royal Society for Public Health (2017). *#StatusOfMind: social media and young people's mental health and wellbeing*. Royal Society for Public Health: Vision, Voice, and Practice. Retrieved July 1, 2021 from https://apo.org.au/sites/default/files/resource-files/2017-05/apo-nid92461.pdf

Sambuli, N. & Magnoli, S. (2019, April 29). What is digital equality? An interview with Nanjira Sambuli. *World Economic Forum*. Retrieved July 1, 2021 from https://www.weforum.org/agenda/2019/04/digital-equality-interview-nanjira-sambuli/

Scheerder, A., van Deursen, A., & van Dijk, J. (2017). Determinants of Internet skills, uses and outcomes. A systematic review of the second-and third-level digital divide. *Telematics and Informatics, 34*(8), 1607–1624. doi:10.1016/j.tele.2017.07.007

Selfhout, M. H., Branje, S. J., Delsing, M., ter Bogt, T. F., & Meeus, W. H. (2009). Different types of Internet use, depression, and social anxiety: the role of perceived friendship quality. *Journal of Adolescence, 32*(4), 819–833. doi:10.1016/j.adolescence.2008.10.011

Shapira, N. A., Lessing, M. C., Goldsmith, T. D., Szabo, S. T., Lazoritz, M., Gold, M. S., & Stein, D. J. (2003). Problematic Internet use: proposed classification and diagnostic criteria. *Depression and Anxiety*, 17(4), 207–216.

Shaw, M., & Black, D. W. (2008). Internet addiction. *CNS drugs*, 22(5), 353–365.

Shukla, M., & Das, S. (2020, July 9). ISIS trying to recruit terrorists online, raises concern for Indian security agencies. *Zeenews.com*. Retrieved July 1, 2021 from https://zeenews.india.com/india/isis-trying-to-recruit-terrorists-online-raises-concern-for-indian-security-agencies-2294700.html

Silwal, S. (2016). Resilience amidst conflict? The effect of civil war exposure on secondary education. *International Journal of Development and Conflict*, 6(2), 97–120.

Singal, N. (2021, January 25). India bans TikTok permanently; App evaluates notice. *BusinessToday.in* Retrieved from https://www.businesstoday.in/technology/news/india-bans-tiktok-permanently-app-evaluates-notice/story/429086.html#

Singer, D. G., & Singer, J. L. (Eds.). (2012). *Handbook of children and the media.* London: Sage.

Skinner, B. F. (1984). Contingencies and rules. *Behavioral and Brain Sciences*, 7(4), 607–613.

Smith, A. (2009). *Radicalization: a guide for the perplexed.* Ottawa, ON: Royal Canadian Mounted Police.

Spada, M. M. (2014). An overview of problematic Internet use. *Addictive Behaviors*, 39(1), 3–6. doi:10.1016/j.addbeh.2013.09.007

Sparrow, B., Liu, J., & Wegner, D. M. (2011). Google effects on memory: cognitive consequences of having information at our fingertips. *Science*, *333*(6043), 776–778. doi:10.1126/science.1207745

Spöri, T., Oross, D., & Susánszky, P. (2020). Active youth? Trends of political participation in East Central Europe. *Intersections: East European Journal of Society and Politics*, 6(4). doi:10.17356/ieejsp.v6i4.792

Sudevan, P. (2020, May 11). Why e-learning isn't a sustainable solution to the COVID-19 education crisis in India. *The Hindu.* Retrieved July 1, 2021 from https://www.thehindu.com/sci-tech/technology/why-elearning-is-not-a-sustainable-solution-to-the-covid19-education-crisis-in-india/article31560007.ece

Takeuchi, H., Taki, Y., Asano, K., Asano, M., Sassa, Y., Yokota, S., … & Kawashima, R. (2018). Impact of frequency of Internet use on development of brain structures and verbal intelligence: longitudinal analyses. *Human Brain Mapping*, *39*(11), 4471–4479. doi:10.1002/hbm.24286

The New Indian Express (2020, December 26). 1.55 lakh govt college students to get free tablets. *NewIndianExpress.com.* Retrieved July 1, 2021 from https://www.newindianexpress.com/states/karnataka/2020/dec/26/155-lakh-govt-college-students-to-get-free-tablets-2241300.html

The Times of India (2020, July 30). New education policy to help in digital transformation strategy: IAMAI. *The Times of India.* Retrieved July 1, 2021 from https://timesofindia.indiatimes.com/business/india-business/new-education-policy-to-help-in-digital-transformation-strategy-iamai/articleshow/77258800.cms

Thorsteinsson, E. B., & Davey, L. (2014). Adolescents' compulsive Internet use and depression: a longitudinal study. *Open Journal of Depression*, *3*, 13–17. doi:10.4236/ojd.2014.31005

Tjønndal, A., & Skauge, M. (2021). Youth sport 2.0? The development of eSports in Norway from 2016 to 2019, *Qualitative Research in Sport, Exercise, and Health*, *13*(1), 166–183. doi:10.1080/2159676X.2020.1836509

Business Today (2020, December 30). Not just in India, PUBG Mobile was banned in these countries in 2020. *BusinessToday.in.* Retrieved July 1, 2021 from https://www.businesstoday.in/latest/trends/not-just-in-india-pubg-mobile-was-banned-in-these-countries-in-2020/story/426454.html

Tufekci, Z. (2008). Can you see me now? Audience and disclosure regulation in online social network sites. *Bulletin of Science, Technology & Society*, *28*(1), 20–36. Retrieved July 1, 2021 from https://journals.sagepub.com/doi/pdf/10.1177/0270467607311484?

Twenge, J. M., Joiner, T. E., Rogers, M. L., & Martin, G. N. (2018). Increases in depressive symptoms, suicide-related outcomes, and suicide rates among US adolescents after 2010 and links to increased new media screen time. *Clinical Psychological Science*, 6(1), 3–17. doi:10.1177/2167702617723376

Tynes, B. (2006). Children, adolescents, and the culture of hate online. In N. Dowd, D. Singer & R. F. Wilson (Eds.). *Handbook of children, culture, and violence.* Sage.

Uncapher, M. R., & Wagner, A. D. (2018). Minds and brains of media multitaskers: current findings and future directions. *Proceedings of the National Academy of Sciences, 115*(40), 9889–9896. doi:10.1073/pnas.1611612115

UNDESA (2018). *World Youth Report: youth and the 2030 agenda for sustainable development.* United Nations Department of Economic and Social Affairs. Retrieved July 1, 2021 from https://www.un.org/development/desa/youth/wp-content/uploads/sites/21/2018/12/WorldYouthReport-2030Agenda.pdf

UNESCO (2015, June). *Youth and the Internet: fighting radicalization and extremism.* United Nations Educational, Scientific and Cultural Organization. Retrieved July 1, 2021 from http://en.unesco.org/youth-and-Internet-fighting-radicalization-and-extremism/about-conference

UNESCO-UNEVOC (2020). *Virtual conference on skills for a resilient youth: virtual conference report. UNESCO-UNEVOC TVeT Forum, 6–14 July 2020. Skills development, commonwealth of learning.* Retrieved July 1, 2021 from https://unevoc.unesco.org/home/Virtual+conference+on+skills+for+a+resilient+youth#

UNICEF (2017). *The State of the World's Children 2017: Children in a Digital World.* UNICEF. Retrieved July 1, 2021 from https://files.eric.ed.gov/fulltext/ED590013.pdf

UNICEF. (2020). *How many children and young people have Internet access at home?: estimating digital connectivity during the COVID-19 pandemic.* UNICEF. Retrieved July 1, 2021 from http://202.1.196.69/jspui/bitstream/123456789/8093/1/How%20many%20children%20and%20young%20people%20have%20Internet%20access%20at%20home%3F%20%3A%20estimating%20digital%20connectivity%20during%20the%20COVID-19%20pandemic.pdf

United Nations (2020a, July). *The World Youth Report: Youth Social Entrepreneurship and the 2030 Agenda.* Retrieved July 1, 2021 from https://www.un.org/development/desa/youth/wp-content/uploads/sites/21/2020/07/2020-World-Youth-Report-FULL-FINAL.pdf

United Nations (2020b, August). *Policy Brief: education during COVID-19 and beyond.* Retrieved July 1, 2021 from https://www.un.org/development/desa/dspd/wp-content/uploads/sites/22/2020/08/sg_policy_brief_covid-19_and_education_august_2020.pdf

University of Münster. (2019, May 8). Step towards light-based, brain-like computing chip. *ScienceDaily*. Retrieved March 24, 2021 from www.sciencedaily.com/releases/2019/05/190508134459.htm

Van Der Schuur, W. A., Baumgartner, S. E., Sumter, S. R., & Valkenburg, P. M. (2015). The consequences of media multitasking for youth: a review. *Computers in Human Behavior*, 53, 204–215. doi:10.1073/pnas.1611612115

Van Deursen, A. J., Helsper, E., Eynon, R., & Van Dijk, J. A. (2017). The compoundness and sequentiality of digital inequality. *International Journal of Communication*, *11*, 452–473.

Van Esch, P., & Black, J. S. (2019). Factors that influence new generation candidates to engage with and complete digital, AI-enabled recruiting. *Business Horizons*, 62(6), 729–739. doi:10.1016/j.bushor.2019.07.004

Varma, A. (2021, June 30). *India enters top 10 in global cybersecurity index 2020 rankings; jumps 37 places*. Republic World. Retrieved July 1, 2021 from https://www.republicworld.com/india-news/general-news/india-enters-top-10-in-global-cybersecurity-index-2020-rankings-jumps-37-places.html

Way, A.K., & Redden, S. M. (2014). Expression patterns and pathways among civically engaged youth, *International Journal of Communication*, 8, 210–233.

Way, A. K., & Redden, S. M. (2017). The study of youth online: a critical review and agenda. *Review of Communication*, *17*(2), 119–136. doi:10.1080/15358593.2017.1293838

Westerlund, M. (2019). The emergence of deepfake technology: a review. *Technology Innovation Management Review*, 9(11), 40–53. doi:10.22215/timreview/1282

Williams, A. L., & Merten, M. J. (2008). A review of online social networking profiles by adolescents: implications for future research and intervention. *Adolescence-San Diego*, 43(170), 253–274.

Yang, C.C., & Brown, B. B. (2015). Factors involved in associations between Facebook use and college adjustment: social competence, perceived usefulness, and use patterns. *Computers in Human Behavior*, *46*, 245–253. doi:10.1016/j.chb.2015.01.015

Yang, C. C., & Lee, Y. (2020). Interactants and activities on Facebook, Instagram, and Twitter: associations between social media use and social adjustment to college. *Applied Developmental Science*, *24*(1), 62–78. doi:10.1080/10888691.2018.1440233

Yarosh, S., Bonsignore, E., McRoberts, S., & Peyton, T. (2016, February). *YouthTube: youth video authorship on YouTube and Vine*. In *Proceedings of the 19th ACM Conference on Computer-Supported Cooperative Work & Social Computing* (pp. 1423–1437). doi:10.1145/2818048.2819961

Ybarra, M., Diener-West, M., Markow, D., Leaf, P., Hamburger, M., & Boxer, P. (2008). Linkages between Internet and other media violence with seriously violent behavior by youth. *Pediatrics*, 122, 929–937. doi:10.1542/peds.2007-3377

Yeykelis, L., Cummings, J. J., & Reeves, B. (2014). Multitasking on a single device: arousal and the frequency, anticipation, and prediction of switching between media content on a computer. *Journal of Communication*, *64*(1), 167–192. doi:10.1111/jcom.12070

Ying Ying, C., Awaluddin, S. M., Kuang Kuay, L., Siew Man, C., Baharudin, A., Miaw Yn, L., ... & Ibrahim, N. (2021). Association of Internet addiction with adolescents' lifestyle: a national school-based survey. *International Journal of Environmental Research and Public Health*, *18*(1), 168. doi:10.3390/ijerph18010168

Yu, C., Li, X., & Zhang, W. (2015). Predicting adolescent problematic online game use from teacher autonomy support, basic psychological needs satisfaction, and school engagement: A 2-year longitudinal study. *Cyberpsychology, Behavior, and Social Networking*, *18*(4), 228–233.

Yu, L., & Shek, D. T. (2013). Internet addiction in Hong Kong adolescents: a three-year longitudinal study. *Journal of Pediatric & Adolescent Gynecology*, *26*(3 Suppl), S10–S17. doi:10.1016/j.jpag.2013.03.010

Zee Media Bureau (2020a, May 9). Gurugram school boy commits suicide after girl levels allegations on him on Instagram. *ZeeNews.com*. Retrieved July 1, 2021 from https://zeenews.india.com/india/gurugram-school-boy-commits-suicide-after-girl-levels-allegations-on-him-on-instagram-2282162.html

Zee Media Bureau (2020b, December 1). COVID-19: his state gives free tablets to class 8 to 12 students of government schools. *ZeeNews.com*. Retrieved July 1, 2021 from https://zeenews.india.com/india/covid-19-this-state-to-give-free-tablets-to-class-8-to-12-students-of-government-schools-2327761.html

Zhou, F., Montag, C., Sariyska, R., Lachmann, B., Reuter, M., Weber, B., ... & Becker, B. (2019). Orbitofrontal gray matter deficits as markers of Internet gaming disorder: converging evidence from a cross-sectional and prospective longitudinal design. *Addiction Biology*, 24(1), 100–109. doi:10.1111/adb.12570

Žumárová, M. (2015). Computers and children's leisure time. *Procedia – Social and Behavioral Sciences*, 176, 779–786. doi:10.1016/j.sbspro.2015.01.540

8 Mental fitness and other psychological capitals of youth in India

Introduction

Development of a country is dependent on the development of its youth in more than one way. To assess a country's prospects, one important criterion would be the number of its youth population. This is precisely why any country who has a huge youth capital is also called a young country and is looked up to as a place with a huge scope of progress. However, the quantity of the youth alone will not translate into nation building. It is only through the appropriate nourishment and training can a country build on their quality so as to attain a prosperous youth development. In other words, children, adolescents, and youth have to be made a country's priority with all respect. This prioritization should manifest in all sectors of development including education, health, family welfare, employment, economics, law and order, and community building.

Training to be given to the youth should not be limited only in relation to employment. All-round training is the need of the hour for the youth in India. This may sound Utopian considering the huge population of India. Nevertheless, through systematic and evaluative planning, holistic training can be provided to all our youth. Holistic training should include age-appropriate skills and cognitive-behavioural patterns that match with the decorum of the socio-cultural framework of our nation. The former part of the aforementioned training is attempted to be provided through our education system to a certain extent. More appreciable changes have been introduced of late through the new education policy 2020; encouragement of multidisciplinary approach by blurring the boundaries between various disciplines, priority given to the mother tongue, and attempt to make education available in line with the age of the students are some of the accommodations. Nonetheless, the definition of training should not get limited to educational training alone. A comprehensive training should be capable of providing psychological training to the youth of the country as well and it should commence from a very young age.

The relevance of psychological training to be given to the youth is substantiated by the alarming acceleration of mental health concerns among youth. Notably, a good majority of these mental health concerns are either

DOI: 10.4324/9781003170587-8

stemming out of or are initiated by environmental factors. In other words, those factors which can be managed and controlled effectively are paving the way for mental disturbance among our youth. Hence, the management of mental disturbances among youth lies in the management of environmental factors causing them. Incidentally, this may sound easy only in words but not in action. It will take the wholehearted participation of each and every community member to work out this intervention to fruition.

First and foremost, the definition of mental health itself has to be altered in the common understanding of the society. This is considered as the very starting point of this long-term intervention towards Youth Development. More often than not, mental health is understood only in terms of absence of mental illness and the community fails to understand the importance of ensuring presence of mental fitness in the community members, particularly the youth. This will, to a great extent, take care of concern such as stigma related to seeking mental health support, discrimination of mentally ill people, and poor social support provided to people with mental health need. If equal consideration is given to addressing the presence of mental illness and the absence of mental fitness, then, there will be a significant drop in the prevalence rate of several mental health challenges our youth face today.

Care must be taken to install various aspects of mental fitness such as positive subjective well-being, rich psychological capital such as hope, self-efficacy, resilience, optimism, healthy interpersonal relationships, other positive psychological elements such as perseverance, grit, happiness, satisfaction, quality of life and so on, in our children, adolescents, and youth population. It is equally important to ensure age-appropriate training in mental fitness is provided by appropriate social agents such as parents/guardians, teachers, and community leaders. Therefore, as an initial step the social agents need to be sensitized about mental fitness, its various components, their importance, and how adequate training can be supplied effectively at the right time to our youth. Psycho-education for these social agents can be provided by making use of community setup such as village panchayats, community centres, housing societies, or even family gatherings. Once the adults in the country are fine-tuned to this understanding, training can be provided to our youth towards this direction at a rapid speed.

Youth who are thus trained and have a strong psychological capital will be capable of handling all the environmental stressors in their day-to-day life. Stressors can be found in any areas of open exchanges, such as schools/colleges, workspace, family space, or in the community. These stressors may take the shape of peer pressure, academic burden, abuse and neglect, poor work-life balance, marriage, racial discrimination, disasters, childbearing, financial insecurity, bullying, or unemployment. They can further be manifested as anxiety, low performance in studies or work, depression, impulsivity, Internet addiction, substance misuse, antisocial personality disorders, eating disorders, high sexual risk behaviour, suicidal tendencies, or violence. By controlling the environmental stresses through an educated and planned approach, the prevalence rate of all of the mental disturbances and more can be addressed effectively. Even though long and tedious, and demand for huge involvement, community participation for youth Development is the ultimate strategy towards nation building. The community can also train their youth the ideas of inclusivity, coherence, social and cultural values, and community building; these attitudes among the youth would ensure safeguarding of societal functioning.

This chapter addresses mental health from both the dichotomies: Mental illness and mental fitness. The chapter begins its exploration into the trajectory of development of today's youth by focusing specifically on the journey to maturation beginning from home to school and college life, work life, and married life. Later, various prevalent mental disturbances in our youth today are explored, particularly specific condition such as stress, anxiety, depression, suicide, Internet addiction, substance abuse, and high-risk sexual behaviour. The chapter proceeds to understand the concept of mental fitness by learning the ideas of subjective well-being and psychological capital. This is done through investigating their various components and determinants and their role in ensuring mental fitness among the youth. A session is exclusively dedicated to discuss how youth development can be attained the promotion of mental fitness through a proposed conceptual model. The chapter concludes with few effective implications.

Mental Health

Over the years mental health has been understood only in terms of malfunctioning and illnesses the trouble the health of an individual. Majority of the efforts to understand mental health of any age group, community, or time frame have shown the interest in exploring the illness aspect of it. In this chapter, we are interested to understand mental health in both the direction: Mental fitness and mental illness (Figure 8.1).

Mental illness

Youth is understood to be a critical phase of development because it sets the foundation for an adulthood life devoid of health problems. But, as per the WHO report nearly 2.6 million young adults between 10 and 24 years suffer from illness behaviours. This huge disease burden is arising out

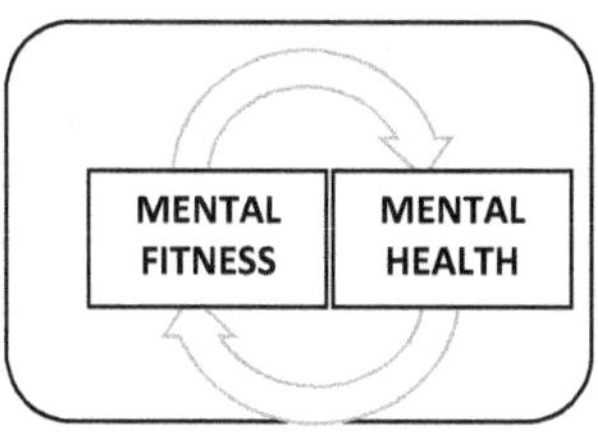

Figure 8.1 Mental health and fitness.

of certain behaviour initiated by youth such as tobacco use, violence, and high-risk sexual activities etc. (WHO, 2011). This problem's behaviours are coming from the influence of Peer groups and media coupled with their natural impulsivity and vulnerability endemic of their age (Stang & Story, 2005). These behaviour patterns can hinder appropriate development during this critical growth period and will continue to manifest as chronic health conditions later in their adult life (Adolescent Health Services, 2021). Adolescence and young adulthood are considered to be the healthiest time in one's life span. Unfortunately, of late, the prevalence of several social risky behaviours is reported at its peak during these years. Added with their vulnerability are the influence of several environmental and social factors such as unfavourable family environment, peer pressure, identity crisis, economic hardship, influence of media, unemployment, and many more that available literature indicates that the proneness to several health in impeding conditions are increasing among this age group (Sunitha & Gururaj, 2014). Substance abuse, HIV infection, road traffic accidents, violence, Internet addiction, suicidal tendencies, and stress are a few among several such conditions that are unfortunately being reported among Indian youth.

The prevalence of mental disorders among children, adolescents, and young adults in India is far beyond imagination. Shastri (2009) reported that childhood mental disorders are as prevalent as 50 million in India at any given time. World Health Organization estimated that in India, children and adolescents between the age of 0–19 are the largest proportion of people who committed suicide in 2012. Let us look into a few Indian-based studies that substantiate this statement. The National Mental Health Survey 2016 estimated 7.3% prevalence of mental disorders among adolescents age 13–17 years: "Depressive disorders, agoraphobia, intellectual disability, autism spectrum disorders, psychotic disorders and anxiety work reported" (Ministry of Health and Family Welfare, 2016). The estimated child and adolescent mental disorder (CAMH) in Lucknow are 12.1%; specific prevalent illnesses identified work nocturnal enuresis (4.16%), Pica (2.38%), conduct disorders (1.78%), and developmental disorder (1.26%) (Srinath et al., 2005). Prevalence of CAMH disorders in Haryana and West Bengal there estimated to be 20.7% and 33.3% respectively (Malhotra & Patra, 2014). Alcohol and tobacco consumption were found to be highly prevalent in Himachal Pradesh (Ministry of Health and Family Welfare, 2016).

As we know, the aetiology of mental disorders can be biological or psychosocial in nature. In other words, these illnesses can be innate or acquired. Since there is only a little that we can do about illnesses that are innate, let us discuss further on the increasingly acquired mental illnesses that our country faces today.

Stress

Stress is an inevitable phenomenon for everyday life. But it is also a phenomenon that can be well managed using the resources available. As it doesn't have a manifestation of its own, it may be explained in terms of sadness, worries, and tensions exhibited by the young adult. Understanding the causes would make management better and if those are psychosocial in nature, available resources can be effectively utilized to track all the conditions. According to Lazarus and Folkman (1984)

> Stress is a mental or physical phenomenon formed through one's cognitive appraisal of the stimulation and is a result of one's interaction with the environment.

Stress can take up different roles. It can be a stimulus, a response, or a transaction. Therefore, identifying the source of stress is important. Cherian and Charian (1998) provided a list of probable main sources of stress for students:

> studies, work, career and future, sensitivity and confidence, family, economic problems and lack of facilities, mild neurosis, sex and marriage, self-schedule and independence. social problems, health and physical matters, self and self– image.

Presently in India, the pressure exerted by academic institutions is becoming unbearable. Students are loaded with several assignments, examinations and many other evaluative processes that they have to constantly undergo. Added to this is the huge pressure put on by the teachers and parents in the name of expectations which force them to work relentlessly. The constant racing to meet with the deadlines and still be excellent at the job burns them down. With academics comes the pressure to be an all-rounder, and be actively participating in several extra-curricular activities with ease. Sometimes, students are not able to choose their career path based on their interest and are forced to take up courses depending upon the job market. This rigorous studying pattern, lack of interest, and huge expectations builds stress in students. Lack of support is one of the most important reasons for stress among students. Parents and teachers are more or less inaccessible to the personal concerns of students as a result of which they feel lost and directionless (Jain & Singhai, 2017). McKean, Misra, West, and Tony (2000) identify stress as a single reason for the development of anxiety and depression. However, one should not find all kinds of stress unhealthy, rather, mild stressors are important for effective functioning that provides a drive to meet the daily challenges for the young adults.

Anxiety

Talking in clinical terms, anxiety disorders among adolescents and young adults are understood to have an early onset. The earliest version of anxiety disorder that can be found in any individual would be the separation anxiety in early childhood. This may be manifested in the form of disinterest or refusal to leave the parent and go to school/play/any other social function. During early childhood, an advanced version of anxiety disorder could take place that manifests as avoidance of certain specific objects or situations which is labelled as specific phobia. This might aggregate into social anxiety or social phobia during late childhood or early adolescence where an adolescent is so worried about the negative evaluation that can happen in any social setting which will lead them to avoid that particular situation due to highly intense anxiety. The specific situations can, at a later stage, become the generalized anxiety disorder that is very prominently found among adolescence and young adults. Now, the anxiety of being evaluated and of the negative outcomes may spread from a specific situation or an event to several activities. Sometimes, this anxiety can go out of control and affect different aspects of one's life which includes school/college or workspace. This can further aggravate panic disorder where physical symptoms such as palpitation, shortness of breath, or even nausea can be triggered by such society-provoking situations. Agoraphobia is another extreme version of anxiety disorder that is commonly seen in late adolescence and early adulthood. People may attempt to avoid and escape from situations where negative outcomes are anticipated and thus causing significant impairment in multiple areas of one life (Olofsdotter, 2017).

A major contribution to the aetiology of anxiety is genetics and biological dispositions. But equally important is the contribution of psychosocial risk factors in the proneness to anxiety. Parental influence is found to be contributing to the development as well as the maintenance of anxiety disorders in both children and adolescents. Parental psychopathology (Wei & Kendall, 2014), parental anxious behaviour that may be modelled and accommodated by children (Thompson-Hollands, Kerns, Pincus, & Comer, 2014), parental rejection and control (Waite, Whittington, & Creswell, 2014) are given prominent roles in understanding anxiety. A Calcutta based study has validated this understanding, where adolescence perceived that they did not get quality time with their fathers (32.1%) and mothers (21.3%); they also share the discomfort in disclosing their personal issues with their fathers (60%) and mothers (40%) (Deb, Chatterjee, & Walsh, 2010). Apart from the parent child relationships, adolescence is also marked by the development of peer relationships. Most adolescents and young adults do feel difficulty in developing close relationships with the peer group which can also lead to chronic stress. Even when they are able to form such relationships, the quality and functioning of the same would decide the genesis of stress and anxiety. La Greca and Harrison (2005) identified that problematic relationships increase the risk of anxiety development. Young adults, at this time, feel vulnerable to the demands of unhealthy relationships and tend to experience stress and anxiety within those relationships. In fact, it is the internalization of these symptoms that results in development of anxiety and depression (Rose & Rudolph, 2006).

Depression

Depressive disorder is a commonly found condition among the youth population that often goes unrecognized. There has been a notable increase in the prevalence of depression soon after puberty and by the end of adolescence. It is understood as a very significant risk factor for suicide and the leading cause for death in this age group (Costello, Erkanli, & Angold, 2006). It is found to cause serious social and educational malfunctioning (Fletcher, 2008) and is often found as a comorbid condition with substance abuse (Keenan-Miller, Hammen, & Brennan, 2007). There have been mixed reviews about the influence of gender in proneness to depression. However, several studies have found girls to be more vulnerable to depression soon after puberty (Thapar, Collishaw, Pine, & Thapar, 2012). These estimates and prevalence would be far below the actual rate, as depression tends to go unnoticed because the presence of irritability, mood fluctuations, and state of confusion are so common in adolescence and early adulthood. Unless there are any indications of physical symptoms such as decline in school performance or behavioural problems displayed by students, depression goes unnoticed and can accelerate something beyond control. This early-onset of depression has a strong linkage with recurrence in later life, and if gone unnoticed, management would be challenging (Birmaher et al., 2014).

Both genetic and psychosocial risk factors contribute to the development of depression among young adults. But let us restrict our discussion to psychosocial risk factors alone, which is a much-researched area. Exposure to acute stress and chronic adversity such as child abuse and neglect or even bullying by peers, or poverty can increase the likelihood of developing depression in adolescence (Pine, Cohen, Johnson, & Brook, 2002). Those who have high genetic risk tend to be more susceptible to the effect of psychosocial stressors (Hariri, Mattay, Tessitore, et al., 2002). Children who got exposed to traumatic events such as natural calamities, war, orphanhood have higher susceptibility (Patel, Fisher, Hetrick, & McGorry, 2007). Academic stress, sudden hormonal change associated with puberty, stressful home environment, moving away from home for higher studies and loneliness, peer bullying, abusive romantic relationships, poverty, cultural and racial factors are causes of depression among adolescents. Work pressure, unemployment, workplace discrimination, burnout, unbearable responsibilities and expectations from family, breakage in relationship, early pregnancy, marriage when not ready are reason specific to the youth population. As can be understood, the probability increases as multiple stressors act in unison.

Suicide

Suicide rate among adolescents and young adults is increasing at an alarming rate and has become a fear-inducing social problem. It is true that suicide is underreported in India, but its highest rates are among youth under

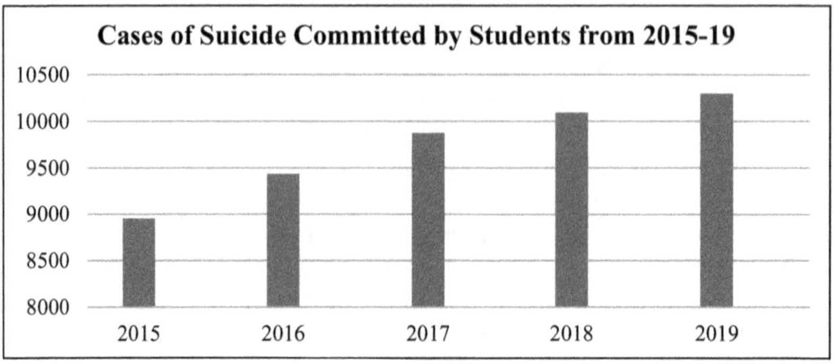

Figure 8.2 Depicting cases of suicide by students from 2015–19.

Source: NCRB Report on Suicides in India 2019.

the age of 30 (Samuel & Sher, 2013). The most common environmental predisposing factors to suicide among adolescence are reported to be anomalous life conditions such as childhood trauma, negative life events, academic failure, negative consequences of disciplinary action, and family problems (Mukherjee, 2011) (Figure 8.2).

Pillai, Andrew, and Patel (2009) observed that suicide behaviour is associated with "female gender, not attending school or college, independent decision making, premarital sex, physical abuse at home, lifetime experience of sexual abuse, and probable common mental disorder". The high rates of suicides among youth stress on the importance of providing psychoeducation to the youth as well as their family, encouraging family and social support, and promoting social Integration (Samuel & Sher, 2013).

Internet Addiction

An alarming number of young adults seem to be vulnerable to addiction in the digital world which is deteriorating their academic and job performance. However, since the time of COVID-19 pandemic, the educational and occupational sector has completely shifted to online mode of communication. This has forced the youth to spend more time online in the name of their studies or work. Therefore, it is not really possible to officially diagnose the condition as Internet addiction, but the health consequences such as loss of sleep and irritability continue to aggravate (Wallace, 2014). Compulsive Internet usage is no joke. Traffic news from across the world has caught our attention about the darker sides of online platforms, violent and addictive game, exposure to pornography, dark verb, and black markets, all of which have frightening capacity to alter youth development (Figure 8.3).

As depicted in the model, Internet addiction among youth can be initiated by three broad aspects namely physical, psychological, social-cognitive. Physical aspects may be influenced by conditions such as poor dietary behaviour, sleep hygiene, or lack of physical activity found among

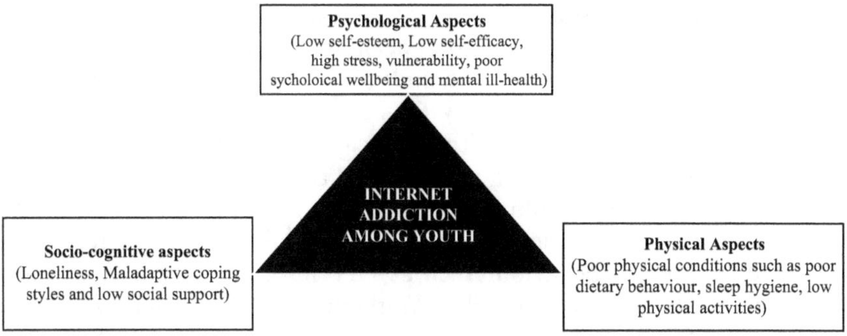

Figure 8.3 Showing the various aspects of Internet addiction among youth.

Source: Model adapted from Deb et al. (2020) Childhood to Adolescence: Issues and Concerns. Pearson India foundation Services Pvt. Ltd.

youth today. Psychological aspects can be related to mental illnesses such as depression or anxiety, or personal aspects like low self-esteem, loneliness, poor self-efficacy, poor well-being, high-stress vulnerability. While, socio-cognitive aspects would include maladaptive coping styles, unhealthy learning practices, and low social support.

Substance Abuse

Substance misuse is a concern worldwide and early initiation of it would result in poor prognosis and lifelong repercussions. Prevalence of adolescence and youth involved in substance abuse is increasing tremendously in India. A West-Bengal-based study conducted among high school students found that 12.5% have abused any one of the substances; the rate is found to be higher among urban students as compared to the rural counterpart. Interestingly, even though 73% longed to quit substance abuse, 57% of them couldn't do it even after trying to stop (Tsering, Pal, & Dasgupta, 2010). The study found out that easy access and availability to the substances as well as the immediate relief it provides to tension and stress faced by the students are the reason for the continuation of substance abuse among them.

Several awareness programmes have been implemented and executed among the teachers, parents as well as students to discuss epidemiology, aetiology prognosis, and management of substance abuse. Despite the amount of awareness provided adolescents and young adults continue to indulge in the misuse of substances. The situation highlights the need for more effective implementation and community participation in the management of abuse among youth.

High-risk sexual behaviours

Impulsivity and lack of control are two key characteristics of adolescence. A manifestation of this would be engagement and risky sexual activity too early in life that are associated with severe negative outcomes. Sharma and Vishwakarma (2020) attempted to understand this phenomenon using the national family health survey. The findings of the study found that risky sexual behaviour has increased by 64–70% among adolescent boys and 18–27% among young adults within a decade. There has been an increase in the live-in relationships both in urban and rural India.

Several physiological, cultural, and social factors are there besides the sexual awakening in adolescence and young adults. Concerns related to such reckless sexual behaviour such as HIV infection, teenage/unwanted pregnancies, adolescent motherhood/fatherhood are of high risk. Easy availability of information, in this scenario, has both positive and negative effects. However, it all depends on how the individual makes use of this information.

Trajectory of maturation

Youth are transitioning from their adolescence to adulthood and are in need to have a stable and well-developed self, with strong decision making and conflict management skills. This is so because the trajectory from childhood to adulthood will require them to handle multiple issues, conflicts, and dilemmas. They will need to manage people, issues, and relationships in multiple contexts including their homes, schools/colleges, workspaces, and in the case of at least few, married life. The number and nature of experiences they encounter during this travel would determine the nature of their mental health.

In most of the cases, a child would have lived through multiple challenges and disruptive events by the time they reach adulthood. Childhood trauma, family violence, peer bullying, poor academic performance, interpersonal violence, addiction, unemployment, and teenage pregnancy could be a few of many such instances that today's youth may encounter. Along with these negative experiences and trauma there may be additional and unexpected problems coming their way that can hamper their psychological well-being and result in poor development. Unexpected problems could be pronounced during adolescence, a period that is known for its vulnerability. All these points, unanimously, highlight the importance of providing a positive and nurturing environment for the continued development of young adults. For the ease of understanding, let us divide this trajectory of growth into 5 stages as depicted below. We, in the section, intend to explore various challenges that might come the way of an individual in their journey to maturation (Figure 8.4).

A. Home environment

Family plays a significant role in an adult's behaviour and functioning in society. In fact, it is the most basic and utmost important entity that shapes an individual's identity and their world view. It can affect a person's behaviour and functioning in both positive and negative ways. Many family

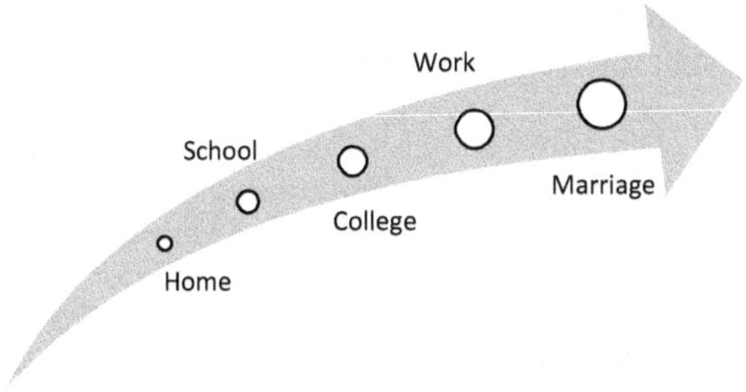

Figure 8.4 Showing the trajectory of maturation of youth.

factors such as genetic loading, attachment patterns, parenting style, family structure, healthy and unhealthy familial relationships, and unfortunate and traumatic events, if any, can all influence the way an individual grows up. Some of these factors such as malnutrition, poverty, physical ill health, or any genetic disorders are permanent and can only be managed. However, there are amenable risk factors, such as child abuse and neglect, family violence, sibling rivalry, and family conflict, that needs immediate intervention to ensure positive child development. Depending upon the nature, parent–child relationship can be a protective factor or a risk factor. It is the attachment pattern that lays the foundation to trust, feeling of security, and belongingness in a child. The impact of insecure attachment style between the child and the parent can have lasting impressions on all the relationships the child may develop as an adult.

Fear-inducing and life-threatening experiences such as family breakdown, divorce, parental separation, addition of a new step-parent, domestic violence, abuse, family violence, and neglect can affect the growing physical and psychological integrity of a child. In most of such situations, children become the ultimate victim as being helpless units in the family. Their feeling of vulnerability accentuates and they begin to internalize that the world is an unfair place to live and that they only have little control over situations. Such children will continue to develop our tendency to escape from such situations which will subsequently lead to long-term problems. Addiction, behavioural problems, poor conflict management skills, and reckless behaviour are all manifestations of these at a later time.

Abuse and neglect have become a significant social problem. This could be the result of an intentional or unintentional action of omission or commission by a parent or any caregiver that can have an adverse impact on the child or adolescent (Gilbert et al., 2009) and can take the form of physical, emotional, and sexual abuse. The 1999 WHO Consultation on Child Abuse Prevention drafted a broader definition, which is:

> Child abuse or maltreatment constitutes all forms of physical and/or emotional ill-treatment, sexual abuse, neglect or negligent treatment or commercial or other exploitation, resulting in actual or potential harm

> to the child's health, survival, development or dignity in the context of a relationship of responsibility, trust or power.

Consequence of child abuse and neglect affect all domains of development in an individual. Problematic peer relationships in adolescents and troubled interpersonal relationship in adulthood (Meadows, Tunstill, George, Dhudwar, & Kurtz, 2011), learning disability and poor academic achievement (Gilbert et al., 2009), mental ill health including post-traumatic stress, attention deficit hyperactivity disorder, oppositional defiant and contact disorder, substance abuse, mood disorders and adjustment disorders (Kearney, Wechsler, Kaur, & Lemos-Miller, 2010), increased risk of suicidal ideation and attempted suicide in adolescence and adulthood (Miller, Esposito-Smythers, Weismoore, & Renshaw, 2013), alcohol and drug abuse problem in both adolescence and adulthood (Perkins & Jones, 2004), behavioural problems, aggression, violence, and involvement in criminal activities (Trickett, Negriff, Ji, & Peckins, 2011), teenage pregnancy (Gilbert et al., 2009) and certain physical ill health are all reported to be long term effects of abuse and neglect faced from families.

A. School life

Contrary to the common colourful description given to adolescence, growing up into adulthood is a tough period of negotiation for many. Often found confused between mixed messages and demands from their environment including parents, teachers, and peer group, adolescence should be understood as a time that requires support (Gupta, 2003). The transition can evidently be seen when a child who was previously dependent on their family now seeks independence and enjoys the company of their peer group more. Changing bodily appearance, identity crisis, sexual development, peer pressure, and academic anxiety can all add up to cause stress and uneasiness in them. Most of them display symptoms of maladjustment and anxiety which may or may not worsen on the basis of the support system that they have. Societal expectations and cultural variations can also contribute to the internal conflict and its resolution by adolescents.

Puberty is more than just physical development. Although it is a normal process that everyone goes through, the experience of puberty can vary widely from adolescent to adolescent. It is so because one's own body is identified as a representation of oneself and is upheld as a symbol of competence. They spend more time than usual to make their appearance in line with what they perceive it should be and are often found to be anxious and unsatisfied by their physical appearance. Culture plays a significant role in establishing an adolescent as a full-fledged adult of a community after puberty. In some cultures, with puberty comes new prescribed norms and regulations for the boy and the girls to follow henceforth. This can be particularly stressful for adolescents who had early physical maturation as compared to their counterparts. This is more commonly seen among adolescent girls and is found stressed and vulnerable (Kim et al., 2003). They seem to be carried away by the unreal images put out by the media that play a deciding role in setting up expectations on the ideal physical appearance of adolescents. Adolescents who are struggling to understand their sexual orientation get trapped into reality vs. expectation conflict.

Impulsivity is another characteristic of adolescence that can lead to risky behaviours such as rash driving, substance abuse, early sexual activity, and teenage pregnancy. Risk of contracting human immunodeficiency virus (HIV-AIDS) and other sexually transmitted diseases are also heightened during this time. Impulsivity can take its origin in infant temperament; when not addressed, can be manifested in childhood as disruptive behaviour and later to ADHD and conduct disorders (Krueger et al., 2002). `Drug and alcohol addiction, Internet addiction in the form of uncontrollable and compulsive indulgence in video game and pornography are also widely prevalent among young adults (Sharma & Sousa, 2016). High academic pressure and inability to meet the expectation of teachers and parents are issues of great importance. Peer pressure, ragging, and bullying can take different maladaptive forms in the students. Bullying in school; be it direct or cyber-bullying, is increasing out of proportion to which many adolescents are vulnerable. Poor academic performance, low self-esteem, depression, anxiety and suicidal thoughts, violent outbreaks, and aggression are after-effects of being subjected to bullying (Oliveira, de Menezes, Irffi, & Oliveira, 2018). Discriminatory Peer bullying on the basis of race, gender and ethnicity e is increasing at an alarming rate among adolescents.

B. College life

Many of the issues discussed as part of school life may continue to interfere with the healthy functioning of a young adult's college life. Concerns related to academic attainment and performance can be at the centre, as competition and requirement for employment become the need of the hour. These students face difficulty in adjusting to situations such as moving away from home, hostel life, money management, bullying and ragging, culture shock and a hectic learning schedule. Due to the difference in the teaching–learning mechanism in school and college, some students may find it difficult to adopt new learning skills. Added to this would be the struggle to meet the expectation of parents in terms of their academic performance. Students working under such stress may be uneasy and anxious, further curtailing their performance. The burden of educational loan requires a mention here, particularly in the Indian context, as most of the college students who have taken a professional course will be under the pressure of obtaining a job soon after graduation. As the unemployment rate in the country increases students as well as their family will be in the fear of being pushed into debt.

Conflict relationships with parents, particularly in need of autonomy and negotiating power, are also commonly observed among young adults. A lot of these have to be resolved naturally and would be the outcome of early parent–child relationships and family environment. Development of intimate relationships is endemic to youth life, and so are relationship issues. Young adults may get involved in romantic relationship issues arising out of their huge emotional investment. When young adults are unable to resolve these issues, it can take a toll on their mental health and academic performance. When in a smooth romantic relationship, they tend to indulge in unsafe sexual activities and exploration with their partners leading to unwanted pregnancy and sexually transmitted diseases.

Mental health needs of college-going students are increasing more than ever. Depression, anxiety, adjustment disorders, eating disorders, and stress are highly reported. This is a topic that is extensively discussed elsewhere in this chapter. However, the need to intervene to ensure mental fitness of young adults is getting reinstated time and again.

C. Work space

For those youth who have succeeded in getting a job and are in a workspace would require good mental health to adapt to the needs of the environment. Work can be hectic and can lead to burn out. Young adults may constantly be required to upgrade their knowledge and skills to meet with the ever-growing demand at their workspace. Competition among peers may be high at all the points and the employer may demand for higher productivity. Young adults may find it difficult to balance work and life, and may lose touch with their interests and hobbies.

Employment would also bring additional household responsibilities to these individuals as they have become breadwinners of the family. Sometimes when their earning does not meet all the required needs, they may be put under further stress. Physical and mental health of working young adults are found to be compromised not just in terms of occupational hazards but also in line with their quality of life. Discrimination on the basis of culture, gender and socio-economic background as well as phenomenon such as glass ceiling can also make work space unfavourable for growth.

D. Married life

Unlike all the other stages that we discussed so far, marriage becomes part of an individual youth's life by choice. In most cultures in India, women tend to be married around the age of 25. The general trend is such that the young college-going girls or young women newly into work are expected to get married before their thirties. This has a potential to confuse these women into choosing one over the other. Those who decide to continue studying or working while married are forced to be multi-taskers and are expected to continually rattle between family and career. This leaves them tired and unhealthy. Child bearing and motherhood may also take its way during this time. However, one should not fail to see that many men are also preparing to get married before their thirties and do willingly take up these responsibilities. The issue lies where marriage becomes a forced choice for many, leading to many unprepared and unsupported couples struggling to work out the marriage.

Mental fitness

Mental fitness as a concept was developed by Dr. Luthans et al. (2007) after identifying the dire need for a concept to explain positive mental health.

> Positive mental health has been left on the doorstep of the public and professional community as a neglected and starving stepchild…it would be useful to have some new term to replace positive mental health… that retains the good will and enthusiastic participation of members of the mental health profession and their medical, health and welfare colleagues, and yet effectively elicits the involvement of members of the social sciences.
>
> (pp. 303–304)

Despite being referred to on several platforms repeatedly, only very little is the concept exercised every day. Let us get familiarized with the topic by exploring two key concepts of positive psychology, namely, subjective well-being and psychological capital.

Subjective well-being

Mental fitness has two dimensions: (a) it is the absence of mental illness, disability, or malfunctioning; and (b) it is the presence of positive thinking towards life which is the subjective well-being of an individual. Subjective well-being is the perception of an individual about his or her life on the basis of factors such as life experiences, interpersonal relationships, and accomplishments. It also marks the level to which an individual is able to identify their fullest potential and become a flourishing being. Therefore, subjective well-being is an individual's perception of their functioning in life: their social and psychological functioning. Social functioning has to do interpersonal relationships and societal functions and is manifested in terms of one's social acceptance, integration, and partaking in social responsibilities. Psychological well-being is about self-acceptance, autonomy, purposefulness, and personal growth of an individual (Keyes, 2006). Therefore, if the intention is to assess the mental fitness of youth, one needs to not only check their mental health status but also tap on their psychological capital through factors such as resilience, perseverance, grit, flourishing, self-determination.

Innumerable studies have assessed the important outcomes of subjective well-being in adulthood including better mental health (Bolier et al., 2013), disease progression and recovery (Howell, Kern, & Lyubomirsky, 2007), cardiovascular function (Steptoe & Kivimäki, 2013), health behaviour (Sin, Moskowitz, & Whooley, 2015), and vocational success (Diener, Pressman, Hunter, & Delgadillo-Chase, 2017). Taking cognizance of these findings, a few comparable results have been found that demonstrates the positive association of subjective will-being with important outcomes among adolescents such as positive health behaviour (Kalak, Lemola, Brand, Holsboer-Trachsler, & Grob, 2014), mental health (Chervonsky & Hunt, 2019) and academic achievement (Steinmayr, Wirthwein, Modler, & Barry, 2019). However, the general tendency that continues is to only access the physical and mental health components of adolescence and youth to determine their overall health (González-Carrasco, Casas, Malo, Viñas, & Dinisman, 2017). Since this is the time of optimal physical health for any individual, most assessments only tap on to certain common mental health conditions among youth such as addiction and risky behaviour. But in order to understand their subjective well-being, it is inevitable to get into the strength of the psychological capital of young adults. Therefore, the psychological capital has to be identified as indicators of mental health among youth, and ways to improve upon these variables have to be included when assessing the overall health and well-being of youth. In spite of being an important topic of exploration in identifying health and well-being, there are hardly any longitudinal studies that investigate the development and correlates of subjective well-being among adolescents and young adults.

Determinants of subjective well-being

Empirical studies investigating the correlates of subjective well-being in youth are scarce. However, from the available studies that have been dedicated to examining these correlates let us discuss the influence of some of these variables. There are a multitude of variables that can influence youth Development, such as, gender, family and school/college environment, socio-economic background, and social support.

Broadly speaking, quality of the environment of growth is found to be a significant determinant of subjective well-being among youth. Particularly, family, school, and other layers of environment are important for positive youth development. Two specific variables can be particularly derived from the environment of growth: (a) academic achievement and (b) social support.

Academic achievement: There are only little studies that connect academic achievement directly to subjective well-being. However, good academic performance has been identified as a protective factor against mental illness (Herman, Lambert, Reinke, & Ialongo, 2008). Substantiating this understanding, Bücker, Nuraydin, Simonsmeier, Schneider, and Luhmann (2018) in a meta-analysis has found a correlation of 0.16 between the aforementioned variables. Another related variable namely life satisfaction is found to have higher correlation value (r = 0.20) with academic achievement, while that with the affective component of well-being being 0.16. Likewise, academic achievement was found to be correlated with the cognitive component of well-being of youth aged between 16–18 (Steinmayr et al., 2019). Even though General Intelligence is found to be highly correlated with academic achievement (Kuncel Hezlett & Ones, 2004), only a very little attention has been given to this variable as a determinant of subjective well-being. This could be because of a heterogeneous range of correlation values (–0.06 to 0.44) between subjective well-being and general intelligence found across studies (Sirin, 2005).

Social support: Social Support and subjective well-being variable that has been widely studied (Siedlecki, Salthouse, Oishi, & Jeswani, 2014). In fact, perceived social support plays a significant role in the cognitive and affective well-being of an individual (Chu, Saucier, & Hafner, 2010). Family support including the parent child relation and certain specific parental behaviour is found to have high impact on subjective well-being (Thomas, Liu, & Umberson, 2017). Adolescents and young adults spend most of their time in their educational institution, peer support is also found to be crucial in determining subjective well-being.

Personality: There are several studies which investigated the association between personality and subjective well-being. Out of all factors, extraversion and neuroticism have been found to be substantially related to the cognitive and affective aspects of well-being (Anglim & Grant, 2014). In a study conducted by Suldo, Minch, and Hearon (2015) among adolescents aged between 13 and 19 years, a high negative correlation ($r = -0.65$) was found between neuroticism and life satisfaction, while a positive correlation ($r = 0.30$) was found between extraversion and life satisfaction.

Demographic variables: Mixed reviews have been obtained about the influence of demographic variables such as gender and economic status. Gender is a frequently investigated variable in relation to subjective well-being which has received mixed results (Sirin, 2005). Salmela-Aro and Tuominen-Soini (2010) found that young women had lower life satisfaction than men and their age of 17; however, the study does not provide any more direction to this understanding. Socioeconomic status is also a variable that provides divergent results about its correlation with subjective well-being (Durlak, 2015).

Hence, these studies imply that personal characteristics such as personality, academic achievement, and social support tend to be more relevant in terms of subjective well-being as compared to demographic variables the chess Gender and economic status.

Psychological Capital (PsyCap)

Psychological capital is understood as "an individual's positive mental state of development" (Luthans et al., 2007), that contains "measurable, developable, and effectively controllable applications related to the potential and psychological capacity of human resources with the salt in better performances" (Keles, 2011). PsyCap as per Luthans, Youssef, and Avolio (2007) is:

"An individual's positive psychological state of development characterized by:

(1) Having confidence (self-efficacy) to take on and put in the necessary effort to succeed at challenging tasks;

(2) Making positive attribution (optimism) about succeeding now and in the future;
(3) Persevering toward goals and, when necessary, redirecting paths to goals (hope) to succeed; and
(4) When beset by problems and adversity, sustaining and bouncing back and even beyond (resilience) to attain success. (p. 3)"

Even though the concept of psychological capital was introduced into the context of organizational behaviour, it could be effectively utilized to discuss positive youth development. Just like how social capital is imperative for the success of any enterprise, psychological capital is a necessary and sufficient wealth for any individual, particularly the youth, to attain their optimal functioning. It has four fundamental characteristics namely, hope, self- efficacy, resilience, and optimism. According to Page & Donohue (2015), a positive and rich psychological capital enhances an individual's personal capacity and helps them to identify their full potential and perform at their highest level. Interestingly, PsyCap is also understood as a predictor of subjective well-being as well. To fully understand Psychological capital, let us first explore its components (Figure 8.5).

1. Hope

It is true that people are largely driven by certain expectations and goals to be attained in their lives. However, it is the "internalized determination and willpower to invest their energy" (Luthans & Youssef, 2004) in order to attain their goals that lead to success, and this drive is hope. In other words, it is a wakeup call for motivation to act. Snyder (2000) in his concept building study describes hope in terms of three fundamental dimensions: (a) an agency (the will to reach the goal) (b) pathways (the systematic plan made) and (c) goals (the target that drives the individual). Several empirical studies have found positive and recommended relationships of hope with life satisfaction (Luthans & Youssef, 2004), job performance (Synder, Irwing, &

Figure 8.5 Four components of psychological capital.

Anderson, 1991), and coping skills even during extremely stressful events. (Cavus & Goken, 2015).

2. Self-efficacy

Self-efficacy is an inner thought or agent that will guide people to perform effectively in all the different tasks and roles in their everyday life (Caprara & Cervone, 2003). "An individual's conviction of confidence about his/her abilities to mobilize the motivation, cognitive resources and courses of action needed to successfully execute a specific task within a given context" is self-efficacy (Stajkovic & Luthans, 1998). It has to be noted that self-efficacy is not entirely related to competencies or particular capabilities of an individual, rather, it is related to the belief an individual has about oneself (Özkalp, 2009). Outcome expectancy and efficacy expectancy are the two key elements of this trait. People with high self-efficacy are found to be confident and are eager to improve their motivation and challenge themselves by taking up difficult tasks and fighting against all the obstacles faced until their goals are accomplished. In fact, this is one of the fundamental traits that we should be able to inculcate in our youth today.

3. Resilience

Resilience is a very crucial characteristic the youth in our country should have presently. It is so because it is a capacity that allows people to look at every overwhelming situation from a positive lens. While multifaceted life situations arise, people need to get into a complex process that includes endurance, tolerance, flexibility, and willingness to adapt (Özkalp, 2009). Resiliency also provides people with the needed coping skills at the most pressing hours of uncertainty and obstacles. Hence it is defined as the "capacity to bounce back from adversity and grow stronger from overcoming negative events" (Luthans, 2002). Frederickson, Tugade, Waugh& Larkin (2003) has proposed the four components that support resilient characteristics: (1) ability to make pragmatic plans and work it out, (2) optimistic view about one's own strengths and abilities, (3) good problem solving and communication skills, and (4) strong impulse control. According to Masten (2001), resiliency in itself has three major components that equip people to succeed in mischances: (1) assets that increase resiliency at a personal level, (2) risk factors that can reduce the level of resiliency, and (3) influence processes. Young adults who are resilient are capable of addressing any challenging situations that come their way.

4. Optimism

Optimism is a word that is casually used in everyday life and it is considered as an area of active research in positive psychology. An individual is called to be an optimist when they have a generalized positive expectation for a better future (Keles, 2011). Several studies prove that optimism in an individual positively influences their physical and mental health. Seligman (1998) defines an optimist to have internal, stable, and global attribution relating to positive events and external, unstable, and specific reasons for negative events. Luthans (2002) established its links with positive emotions, motivation, and ability to work in a realistic manner have been established by numerous studies.

PsyCap and academic domain: Of late, Education Psychology has investigated the role of psychological capital in the education domain as well. School and college-going students face several challenges such as high academic expectation, pressure, hectic and cumbersome class homework, obtaining the degree, job preparations, highly competitive job market, unemployment and low security (Rioli, Savicki, & Richards, 2012). As Luthans, Luthans, and Avey (2014) rightly pointed out that developing psychological resources of students is the heightened need of the hour to foster their inner strength and thereby promoting better adaptability, learning, and overcoming hurdles to academic success. Positive emotions in students can go a long way by both fostering them motivation so as to adapt to new learning strategies catering to their abilities as well as the need. A similar study conducted among college students indicated that psychological capital among them has a very significant and positive relationship with student engagement and learning empowerment (You, 2016). A Bhutan-based study has provided an indirect link between psychological capital and high quality of learning, reduced dropout rates, psychosocial development, and promotion of lifelong learning among students at college level (Jafri, 2017).

PsyCap and work domain: Being a concept that is widely used in Industrial Psychology, many studies have explored the relationship between psychological capital and organizational effectiveness (Avey, Luthans, & Youssef, 2010). Since work life is another significant area of consideration among youth, the status of psychological capital needs further exploration. Innumerable studies have significantly associated psychological capital with high performance (Avey et al., 2010), organizational commitment (Luthans & Avolio, 2007) protection from work stress, and high work turnover (Avey, Luthans & Jensen, 2009). It also has a favourable impact on employee attitude, behaviour, and performance (Luthans & Mhatre, 2011). Undoubtedly, psychological capital provides the youth with a positive state of mind that equips them to remain at their best shape while in during their stressful job demands.

PsyCap and well-being: Subjective well-being, as discussed earlier, is multidimensional that regulates the well-being of young adults. Psychological capital and subjective well-being are two constructs that are closely related. When subjective well-being equips the young adults with the needed resources and coping styles to mitigate the negative and extremely stressful environment, there develops positive psychological capital (Rask, Astedt-Kurki, & Laippala, 2002). PsyCap and the components of subjective well-being are also connected. Hope, a component of psychological capital, has been proved, time and again, to have a significant relation with both subjective as well as psychological well-being (Davidson, Wingate, Rasmussen, & Slish, 2009). Likewise, recent studies have obtained the benefits of optimism on both physical and psychological well-being of young adults. Scheier, Carver, and Bridges (2001) observed that optimism reduces stress by inducing positive emotions and reduces the influence of daily stressful events that trouble one's mental health. A study among Chinese University students found that optimistic people are more satisfied in life and have high subjective well-being. This finding was found to be relevant to both eastern and western cultures. Diener et al. (2003) has found self-efficacy and resiliency as significant predictors of subjective well-being. A longitudinal study conducted among young adults of Australia indicated that subjective well-being intervene with mental health, particularly depression and anxiety, by increasing positive affect and decreasing negative affect (Burns, Anstey, & Windsor, 2010); it is found to widen the thoughts and actions of people and so their coping skills (Fredrickson, 2001).

PsyCap and health: There have been several indirect links between psychological capital and health. Research in organizational behaviour points out how individuals' with positive psychological capital survive stress and burnout with better health and high performance (Lupsa & Virga, 2020). This could be because the positive psychological capital that they have acts as a shield and protects them from stress and maintains their health (Mäkikangas, Kinnunen, & Feldt, 2004). In other words, these positive personal resources have become very strong protective factors against illness. This promotes well-being and behaviours among young adults (Krasikova, Lester, & Harms, 2015). In a recent research conducted among Australian school students, psychological capital was found to be a stronger predictor of decreased levels of depression and anxiety when all the four components of PsyCap were in combination (Finch, Farrell, & Waters, 2020).

Research shows that psychological capital can be developed in individuals through training (Luthans, Avey, Avolio, & Peterson, 2010). Therefore, intervention strategies for the youth could be developed to accentuate their psychological capital and thereby empower them with the needed resources for positive functioning in all the arenas of day-to-day life.

Youth development through mental fitness

In light of our discussion so far, the most evident factor is that mental health and well-being of our young adults are facing challenges that are innumerable. Undoubtedly, mental health is of paramount importance when it comes to positive youth development. Considering the fact that prevalence of mental illness is increasing on a day-to-day basis, our youth are in dire need of mental health support. Two factors may hinder accessibility to mental health support systems to those in need: (a) the social stigma associated with seeking mental health support and (b) scarcity of mental health professionals available across the country. These are stemming out of socio-political issues that may not be easily addressed. Several advocacy and awareness creation programmes are widely done to avoid the stigma related to seeking mental health, but, in effect, its impact is minuscule. Solution to the non-availability of mental health professionals is also not pragmatic, since it requires political, social, and educational domains at a national level to intervene. This is when the need for a pragmatic, effective, and holistic intervention strategy gains its prominence.

The key to successful life is in the ability to adapt, cope and endure with the various experiences that come one's way. These experiences are varied and unpredictable in nature. In other words, there is no direct way in which anybody can be prepared to face these challenges and obstacles. No parent or education institution can spoon-feed their children/students the formula to succeed in life. But what can possibly be done by these social agents is to provide a congenial and conducive environment for the development of needed life skills. The proposed conceptual model is attempting to come up with a pragmatic solution that will ensure positive youth development. Promotion of mental fitness seems to be the most inevitable and effective key to successful life. This is a long-term process that will require the participation of multiple social bodies including families, education institutions, workspaces, and community in general (Figure 8.6).

This conceptual model resonates with Bronfenbrenner's ecological systems theory, which views child development as a complex system of relationships influenced by multiple layers of environment beginning from one's own home to broad socio-cultural and legal environments (Ettekal & Mahoney, 2017). Therefore, promotion of psychological capital should be

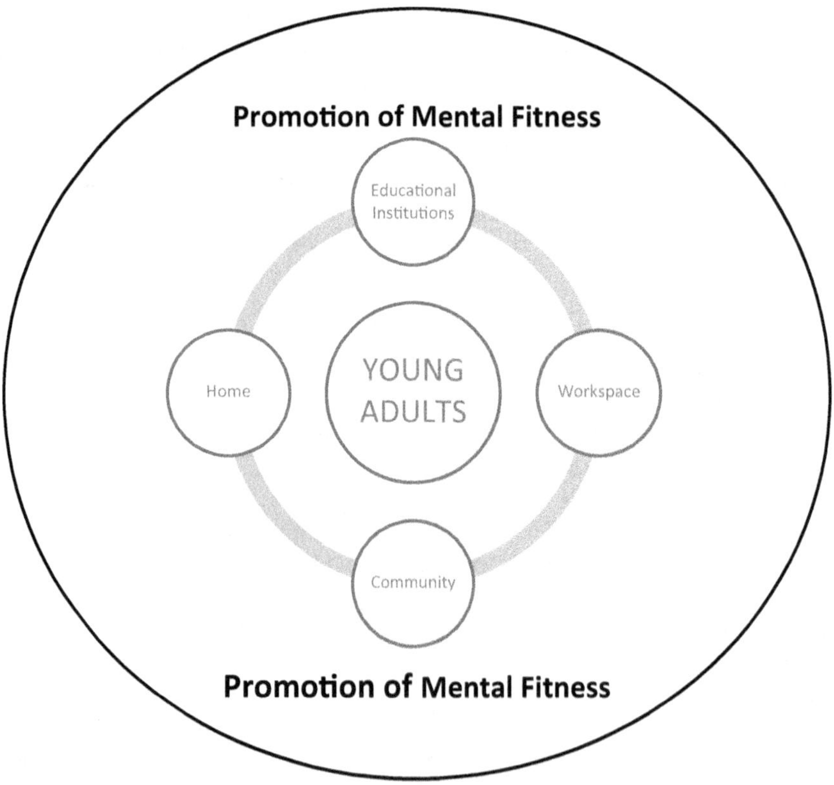

Figure 8.6 Conceptual model proposing promotion of mental fitness for positive youth development.

visible and encouraged in all these layers of environment the young adult is part of. Precisely, the promotion of mental fitness should begin quite early in one's life and have to be continually nurtured until adulthood. One should not forget that these skills are not learnt by the child in isolation, rather through their interaction with their environment.

Home, school/college, and workspace are the closest social systems an individual lives. These are the immediate environments where an individual explores, engages, and learns through transactions. Hence, promotion of mental fitness should begin from these immediate social systems. Home, being the primary and long-standing influential agent, should encourage development of psychological capital, i.e. hope, self-efficacy, resilience, and optimism in an individual from childhood. According to the socio-cognitive perspective of learning, observation plays a determinant role in learning of any new behaviour. When influencers from these immediate environments such as parents and teachers exercise psychological capital in their daily transactions, children and adolescents model this behaviour and acquire them to their contexts. This learning can be further reinforced through the deliberate involvement of teachers and parents by giving children/ adolescents activities/events where psychological capital has to be exercised. When important social agents take active participation in ensuring the promotion of psychological capital among children/adolescents, it is quite likely that they imbibe these skills. As young adults who are either studying or working will, by now, be able to adapt the primary learning of psychological capital to their matured world. In fact, youths whose mental fitness are promoted from their childhood will be in a better state of mind in dealing with the world of adults.

When the quantity and quality of interactions between social agents grow, the manifestation of psychological capital becomes stronger and richer in individuals. For instance, when an adolescent grows up in an environment where both home and school appreciate that encourages the development of psychological capital, the adolescent gets the best support needed to practice those skills in day-to-day life. Similarly, a young adult who grew up in an optimistic environment is more likely to view every hurdle in his or her job from a positive framework. And when he or she gets back to a home that further promotes psychological capital, then issues related to burn out and work-life balance can be positively attained.

The contribution of the community in the promotion of mental fitness is huge. It is a system or a group of systems in which youth do not directly participate. Nevertheless, the influence this system can have on the thoughts, behaviours, and belief systems of young adults is noteworthy. Community agencies have a huge power in determining what type of messages have to be sent to children/adolescents and how they have to be conveyed. This is why the process is told to be lengthy, as each individual community member has to be tuned in this direction. Thus, over a period of time, the community needs to realize the need to inculcate such values in our youth, align its blueprint, and volunteer to promote mental fitness for positive youth Development.

The new education policy 2020 and mental fitness

The new education policy has several direct and indirect impacts on the mental health of students. The policy has been receiving appreciation from several corners of experts and it is found to be considerate to mental health concerns among students. Some of the highlights of NEP, 2020 in favour of mental health are discussed here.

Holistic learning experience: The policy has serious consideration in providing holistic education to the students. Lifting of 10th standard board examination, introduction of more practical-based hands-on-training, encouragement of multi-disciplinary approaches towards higher learning, and so on are found to reduce the stress among children about competitive exams such as NEET and IIT-JEE which may be outside their interest area. Children through their practical exposure will now be in a situation to judge their interest and skills in pursuing their career path quite early in life. In addition to taking away the stress, this will build interest and confidence in our students to make appropriate and suitable career choices for themselves. The new pedagogical structure which eliminates rigid streams in higher secondary education and multiple exit points would bring clarity and structure to learning.

Digital learning: By incorporating digital learning, the students of our country will be tuned in the direction where development is progressing. Learning will become interesting and children can adopt learning styles suitable to their preferred modalities. With this empowerment comes reduction in stress, and confidence for competing in international spear.

Sports integration: The high positive correlation between regular physical activity and mental health has been proved time and again, including stress reduction and enhanced productivity. Along with it, we equip our student population to prepare themselves to work in teams, to create a winning attitude, and to be goal directed.

Focus on pre-primary courses: Psychological and social skills such as empathy, communication, assertive skills, logical and critical thinking, and so on have to be developed from a very early age. Since NEP 2020 aims to train children along these directions from an early age their mental health will be taken care of to a great extent.

Vocational training: Even with people who are mentally disturbed, vocational training would help them to develop skills and attitudes in line with their interest to obtain employment. Vocational training is found to be positively correlated with mental fitness.

The Ministry of Youth Affairs and Sports (GOI) and Mental Fitness

The Ministry of Youth Affairs And Sports, Government of India has several programmes under its guidance that directly or indirectly but towards mental fitness through attaining positive Youth Development, some of which are mentioned here as follows:

- **Nehru Yuva Kendra Sangatham:** The world's largest community organization exclusively for youth which works towards developing volunteerism and self-help India's youth between the age group of 13–35 years.
- **National Service Scheme:** A centrally sponsored scheme that aims at personality development of India's youth through community participation and services.
- **National Service Volunteer Scheme:** It provides opportunities for student volunteers in nation building by involving them in various activities for a specific purpose. This will develop in them commitment, empowerment, and teamwork.
- **Scheme of Promotion of National Integration:** Through several youth programmes youth are analysed to build nation integration and community harmony.
- **Rajiv Gandhi National Institute of Youth Development:** An educational institution exclusively dedicated to training documentation research and extension activities for youth affairs in the country.
- **Rashstria Sadbhavana Yojana:** An attempt for leadership development among youth by Linking various youth clubs and development centres across the country.

Please see for elaborate discussion on each of these programmes in Chapter 10.

Conclusion and recommendations

As a concept, mental health needs to be perceived as an attempt to address all the obstacles to attain mental fitness. Considering today's scenario, society's perception about mental health and well-being will need to undergo transformational change. The process is time-consuming and demands the participation of all members of the society. Primarily, this change should begin among responsible social agents such as parents and teachers. Mental fitness of our children should be upheld from the youngest age possible. Concepts such as well-being and quality of life have to be taken up seriously because resilience, girt, optimism, hope, and such related concepts will be optimally required for their day-to-day life. Therefore, if positive youth development is our target, then, the path toward it is through the promotion of mental fitness of youth.

Based on the discussion, a few recommendations to promote mental fitness are made:

- Training school and college teachers in incorporating and encouraging development of mental fitness among the students. This could be in the form of classroom activities or interactions where such concepts are shared and discussed. They may be trained to exhibit warm and encouraging approach towards students that they may like to model and accommodate

- School/college management should be instructed to hold seminars and workshops on mental fitness and its varied components. Service of a trained and qualified counsellor must be mandated.
- Every educational institution should have a mental health centre that is open not just to students who are facing psychological difficulties, but also for wellness coaching.
- Youth wing should be established which contains peer leaders and members. The wing can be utilized to reach out to every adolescent/youth with information, activities, or any initiatives. This would encourage more students to participate in community activities.
- Members of Nehru Yuva Kendra and NCC should be utilized to reach the youth in the respective localities for training, community building, and nation building.

References

Adolescent Health Services: Missing Opportunities. Available from: http://books.nap.edu/openbook.php?record_id=12063&page=1, accessed on March 25, 2021.

Anglim, J. & Grant, S. L. (2014). Incremental criterion prediction of personality facets over factors: obtaining unbiased estimates and confidence intervals. *J. Res. Pers.*, 53, 148–157.

Avey, J. B., Luthans, F., & Youssef, C. M. (2010). The additive value of positive psychological capital in predicting work attitudes and behaviors. *J. Manage.* 36, 430–452.

Birmaher, B., Williamson, D. E., Dahl, R. E., et al. (2014). Clinical presentation and course of depression in youth: does onset in childhood differ from onset in adolescence? *J. Am. Acad. Child. Adolesc. Psychiatry* 43, 63–70.

Bolier, L., Haverman, M., Westerhof, G. J., Riper, H., Smit, F., & Bohlmeijer, E. (2013). Positive psychology interventions: a meta-analysis of randomized controlled studies. *BMC Public Health*, 13, 119.

Bücker, S., Nuraydin, S., Simonsmeier, B. A., Schneider, M., & Luhmann, M. (2018). Subjective well-being and academic achievement: a meta-analysis. *J. Res. Pers.* 74, 83–94.

Burns, R. A., Anstey, K. J., & Windsor, T. D. (2010). Subjective well-being mediates the effects of resilience and mastery on depression and anxiety in a large community sample of young and middle-aged adults. *The Austr. New Zealand J. Psychiatry*. 45(3), 240–248.

Caprara, G. V., & Cervone, D. (2003). *A Conception of personality for a psychology of human strengths: personality as an agentic, self-regulating system. A psychology of human strengths: fundamental questions and future directions for a positive psychology*. (Edt: L. G. Aspinwall & U. M. Staudinger). American Psychological Association, Washington, 61–74.

Cherian, V., & Charian, L. (1998). University student's adjustment problems. *Psychol. Rep.*, 82, 1135–1138.

Chervonsky, E. & Hunt, C. (2019). Emotion regulation, mental health, and social wellbeing in a young adolescent sample: a concurrent and longitudinal investigation. *Emotion*. 19, 270–282.

Chu, P. S. Saucier, D. A., & Hafner, E. (2010). Meta-analysis of the relationships between social support and well-being in children and adolescents. *J. Soc. Clin. Psychol.* 29, 624–645.

Costello, E. J., Erkanli, A., & Angold A. (2006). Is there an epidemic of child or adolescent depression? *J. Child. Psychol. Psychiatry*. 47, 1263–1271

Davidson, C., Wingate, L. R., Rasmussen, K., & Slish, L. (2009). Hope as a predictor of interpersonal suicide risk. *Suicide and Life-Threatening Behavior*. 39(5), 499–507.

Deb, S., Chatterjee, P., & Walsh, K. (2010). Anxiety among high school students in India: comparisons across gender, school type, social strata and perceptions of quality time with parents. *Austr. J. Educ. Develop. Psychol. 10*, 18–31.

Deb, S. et al., (2020). *Childhood to adolescence: issues and concerns*, India, Pearson Education.

Diener, E., Oishi, S., & Lucas, R. E. (2003). Personality, culture, and subjective well-being: Emotional and cognitive evaluations of life. *Annual review of psychology*, *54*(1), 403–425.

Diener, E. Pressman, S. D. Hunter, J., & Delgadillo-Chase, D. (2017). If, why, and when subjective well-being influences health, and future needed research. *Appl. Psychol. Health Well-Being*, 9, 133–167.

Durlak, J. A. (2015). *Handbook of social and emotional learning: research and practice*; Guilford Publications: New York, NY.

Ettekal, A., & Mahoney, J. L. (2017). Ecological systems theory. *The SAGE Encyclopedia of Out-of-School Learning*, April. doi:10.4135/9781483385198.n94

Finch, J., Farrell, L. J., & Waters, A. M. (2020). Searching for the HERO in youth: does psychological capital (PsyCap) predict mental health symptoms and subjective wellbeing in Australian school-aged children and adolescents? *Child. Psychiatry Human Develop. 51*(6), 1025–1036. doi:10.1007/s10578-020-01023-3

Fletcher, J. M. (2008). Adolescent depression and educational attainment: results using sibling fixed effects. *Health Econ.* 17, 1215–1235.

Frederickson, B. L., Tugade, M. M., Waugh, C. E., & Larkin, G. R. (2003). What good are positive emotions in crises? A prospective study of resilience and emotions following the terrorist attacks on the United States on September 11th, 2001. *Journal of personality and social psychology*, *84*(2), 365–376.

Fredrickson, B. L. (2001). The role of positive emotions in positive psychology: the broaden-and-build theory of positive emotions. *Am. Psychol.* 56, 218–226.

Gilbert, R., Spatz Widom, C., Browne, K., Fergusson, D., Webb, E., & Janson, J. (2009). Burden and consequences of child maltreatment in high-income countries. *The Lancet*, *373*, 68–81.

González-Carrasco, M., Casas, F., Malo, S., Viñas, F., & Dinisman, T. (2017). Changes with age in subjective well-being through the adolescent years: differences by gender. *J. Happiness Stud.*, *18*, 63–88.

Gupta, S. G. (2003, October). Teen depression. *Femina girl*, 26–27.

Hariri, A. R., Mattay, V. S., Tessitore, A, et al. (2002). Serotonin transporter genetic variation and the response of the human amygdala. *Science*. 297, 400–403.

Herman, K. C., Lambert, S. F., Reinke, W. M., & Ialongo, N. S. (2008). Low academic competence in first grade as a risk factor for depressive cognitions and symptoms in middle school. *J. Couns. Psychol.* 55, 400–410.

Howell, R. T., Kern, M. L., & Lyubomirsky, S. (2007). Health benefits: meta-analytically determining the impact of well-being on objective health outcomes. *Health Psychol. Rev.* 83–136.

Jafri, H. (2017). Understanding influence of psychological capital on student's engagement and academic motivation. *Pacific Business Rev. Int. 10*(6), 16–23. www.pbr.co.in

Jain, G., & Singhai, M. (2017). Academic stress amongst students: a review of literature. *Prestige E-Journal Manage. Res. 4*(2), 58–67. http://pimrindore.ac.in/vol4-issue2-vol5-issue1/5.

Kalak, N., Lemola, S., Brand, S., Holsboer-Trachsler, E., & Grob, A. (2014). Sleep duration and subjective psychological well-being in adolescence: a longitudinal study in Switzerland and Norway. *Neuropsych. Disease Treatment. 10*, 1199.

Kearney, C. A., Wechsler, A., Kaur, H., & Lemos-Miller, A. (2010). Posttraumatic stress disorder in maltreated youth: a review of contemporary research and thought. *Clin. Child Family Psychol. Rev. 13*, 46–76.

Keenan-Miller, D., Hammen, C. L., & Brennan, P. A. (2007). Health outcomes related to early adolescent depression. *J. Adolesc. Health.* 41, 256–262.

Keles, N. H. (2011). Positive psychological capital: components and their effects on definition, organization and management sciences. *BJESBS*, 3, 343–350.

Keyes, C. L. M. (2006). Mental health in adolescence is America's youth flourishing. *Am. Psychol. Assoc. 76*(3), 395–402.

Krasikova, D. V., Lester, P. B., & Harms, P. D. (2015). Effects of psychological capital on mental health and substance abuse. *J. Leadership Organiz. Stud.* 22, 280–291. doi:10.1177/1548051815585853

Krueger, R. F., Hicks, B. M., Patrick, C. J., Carlson, S. R., Lacono, W. G., & McGue, M. (2002). Etiologic connections among substance dependence, antisocial behavior and personality: modeling the externalizing spectrum. *J. Abnormal Psychol.* 177, 411–424.

Kuncel, N. R., Hezlett, S. A., & Ones, D. S. (2004). Academic performance, career potential, creativity, and job performance: Can one construct predict them all?. *Journal of personality and social psychology*, *86*(1), 148.

La Greca, A. M., & Harrison, H. M. (2005). Adolescent peer relations, friendships, and romantic relationships: do they predict social anxiety and depression? *J. Clin. Child Adoles. Psychol.* 34, 49–61.

Lazarus, R.S., & Folkman, S. (1984). *Stress, appraisal and coping*. New York: Springer.

Lupsa, D., & Virga, D. (2020). Psychological capital, health, and performance: the mediating role of burnout. *Psihologia Resurselor Umane*, *18*(1), 7–22. doi:10.24837/PRU.V18I1.458

Luthans, F. (2002). The need for and meaning of positive organizational behavior. *J. Organ. Behav.*, 23, 695–706.

Luthans, F., Avey, J. B., Avolio, B. J., & Peterson, S. J. (2010). The development and resulting performance impact of positive psychological capital. *Human Resource Develop. Quart.* 21(1), 41–67.

Luthans, F., Avolio, B. J., Avolio, J. B., & Norman, S. M. (2007). Positive psychological capital: measurement and relationship with performance and satisfaction. *Pers Psychol.*, 60, 541–572.

Luthans, B. C., Luthans, K. W., & Avey, J. B. (2014). Building the leaders of tomorrow: the development of academic psychological capital. *J. Leadership Organ. Stud.* 21(2), 191–199.

Luthans, F., & Youssef, C. M. (2004). Human, social, and now positive psychological capital management: investing in people for competitive advantage. Organizational management: investing in people for competitive advantage. *Dynamics*, 33(2),143–160.

Luthans, F., Youssef, C. M., & Avolio, B. J. (2007). *Psychological capital*. New York, NY: Oxford University Press.

Mäkikangas, A., Kinnunen, U., & Feldt, T. (2004). Self-esteem, dispositional optimism, and health: evidence from cross-lagged data on employees. *J. Res. Personality*, *38*(6), 556–575.

Malhotra, S., & Patra, B. N. (2014). Prevalence of child and adolescent psychiatric disorders in India: a systematic review and meta-analysis. *Child Adolesc Psychiatry Ment Health* 8, 22.

Masten, A. S. (2001). Ordinary magic: resilience processes in development. *Am. Psychol.* 56, 227–238.

McKean, M., Misra, R., West, S., & Tony, R. (2000). College students' academic stress and its relation to their anxiety, time management, and leisure satisfaction. *Am. J. Health Stud.* 16, 41–51

Meadows, P., Tunstill, J., George, A., Dhudwar, A., & Kurtz, Z. (2011). *The costs and consequences of child maltreatment: literature review for the NSPCC*. London: NSPCC.

Miller, A. B., Esposito-Smythers, C., Weismoore, J. T., & Renshaw, K. D. (2013). The relation between child maltreatment and adolescent suicidal behavior: a systematic review and critical examination of the literature. *Clin. Child Family Psychol. Rev.* *16*(2), 146–172.

Ministry of Health and Family Welfare, Government of India. (2016). *National Mental Health Survey of India*; [Last accessed on 2021 March 21]. Available from: http://www.indianmhs.nimhans.ac.in/Docs/Summary.pdf.

Mukherjee, P. (2011). *Functional disconnection and social cognition in schizophrenia*.

Oliveira, F. R., de Menezes, T. A., Irffi, G., & Oliveira, G. R. (2018). Bullying effect on student's performance. *EconomiA*, *19*(1), 57–73.

Olofsdotter, A. (2017). *Anxiety among Adolescents. Measurement, clinical characteristics, and influences of parenting and genetics. digital comprehensive summaries of Uppsala dissertations from the faculty of medicine 1356* (Vol. 108). http://urn.kb.se/resolve?urn=urn:nbn:se:uu:diva-323578

Özkalp, E. (2009). *A new dimension in organizational behavior: a positive (positive) approach and organizational behavior: a positive (positive) approach and organizational behavior issues*. In: *Proceedings of 17th National Management and Organization Congress*. 491–498. Turkish.

Page, L. F., & Donohue, R. (2015). *Positive psychological capital: A preliminary exploration of the construct*.

Patel, V., Fisher, A. J., Hetrick, S., & McGorry, P. (2007). Mental health of young people: a global public-health challenge. *Lancet*, 369, 1302–1313.

Perkins, D., & Jones, K. (2004). Risk behaviors and resiliency within physically abused adolescents. *Child Abuse & Neglect*, *28*, 547–563.

Pine, D. S., Cohen, P., Johnson, J. G., & Brook, J. S. (2002). Adolescent life events as predictors of adult depression. *J. Affect. Disord.*, 68, 49–57.

Rask, K., Astedt-Kurki, P., & Laippala, P. (2002). Adolescent subjective wellbeing and realized values. *J. Adv. Nurs.* 38(3), 254–263.

Rose, A. J., & Rudolph, K. D. (2006). A review of sex differences in peer relationship processes: potential trade-offs for the emotional and behavioral development of girls and boys. *Psychol. Bull.* 132, 98–131.

Salmela-Aro, K., & Tuominen-Soini, H. (2010). Adolescents' life satisfaction during the transition to post-comprehensive education: antecedents and consequences. *J. Happiness Stud.* 11, 683–701.

Samuel, D., & Sher, L. (2013). Suicidal behavior in Indian adolescents. *Int. J. Adolescent Med. Health 25*(3), 207–212. doi:10.1515/ijamh-2013-0054

Scheier, M. F., Carver, C. S., & Bridges, M. W. (2001). Optimism, pessimism, and psychological well-being. In: E. C. Chang (Ed.), *Optimism and pessimism: implications for theory, research, and practice* (pp. 189–216). Washington, DC: American Psychological Association.

Seligman, M. E. P. (1998). *Learned optimism.* New York: Pocket Books.

Sharma, P., & Sousa, A. De. (2016). Internet addiction in adolescents – an overview. *Ind. J. Mental Health (IJMH)*, *3*(4), 394. doi:10.30877/ijmh.3.4.2016.394-404

Sharma, S. K., & Vishwakarma, D. (2020). Transitions in adolescent boys and young Men's high-risk sexual behaviour in India. *BMC Public Health 20*, 1089. doi:10.1186/s12889-020-09191-6

Shastri P. C. (2009). Promotion and prevention in child mental health. *Ind. J. Psych.* 51, 88–95.

Siedlecki, K. L. Salthouse, T. A., Oishi, S., & Jeswani, S. (2014). The relationship between social support and subjective well-being across age. *Soc. Indic. Res.* 117, 561–576.

Sin, N. L., Moskowitz, J. T., & Whooley, M. A. (2015). Positive affect and health behaviors across 5 years in patients with coronary heart disease: the heart and soul study. *Psychosom. Med.*, 77, 1058–1066.

Sirin, S. R. (2005). Socioeconomic status and academic achievement: a meta-analytic review of research. *Rev. Educ. Res.* 75, 417–453.

Snyder, C. R. (2000). The past and possible futures of hope. *Journal of social and clinical psychology*, *19*(1), 11–28.

Srinath, S., Girimaji, S. C., Gururaj, G., Seshadri, S., Subbakrishna, D. K., Bhola, P., et al. (2005). Epidemiological study of child & adolescent psychiatric disorders in urban & rural areas of Bangalore, India. *Ind. J. Med. Res.* 122, 67–79.

Stajkovic, A. D., & Luthans, F. (1998). Social cognitive theory and self-efficacy: going beyond traditional motivational and behavioral approaches. *Organ. Dyn.*, 26, 62–74.

Stang, J., & Story, M. (2005). Adolescent growth and development. In: *Guidelines for adolescent nutrition services.* Minneapolis, MN Center for Leadership, Education and Training in Maternal and Child Nutrition, Division of Epidemiology and Community Health, School of Public Health, University of Minnesota; 2005. Available from: http://www.epi.umn.edu/let/pubs/img/adol_ch1.pdf, accessed on March 20, 2021.

Steinmayr, R., Wirthwein, L., Modler, L., & Barry, M. M. (2019). Development of subjective well-being in adolescence. *Int. J. Environ. Res. Public Health*, *16*(19). doi:10.3390/ijerph16193690

Steptoe, A. & Kivimäki, M. (2013). Stress and cardiovascular disease: an update on current knowledge. *Annu. Rev. Public Health*, 34, 337–354.

Suldo, S. M., Minch, D. R., & Hearon, B. V. (2015). Adolescent life satisfaction and personality characteristics: investigating relationships using a five factor model. *J. Happiness Stud.*, 16, 965–983

Sunitha, S., & Gururaj, G. (2014). Health behaviours & problems among young people in india: cause for concern & call for action. *Ind. J. Med. Res.*, *140*(AUG 2014), 185–208.

Thapar, A., Collishaw, S., Pine, D. S., & Thapar, A. K. (2012). Depression in adolescence. *Lancet*, *369*(9820), 1056–1067.

Thomas, P. A., Liu, H., & Umberson, D. (2017). Family relationships and well-being. *Innovation in Aging*, *1*(3), igx025.

Thompson-Hollands, J., Kerns, C. E., Pincus, D. B., & Comer, J. S. (2014). Parental accommodation of child anxiety and related symptoms: range, impact, and correlates. *J. Anxiety Disorders*, 28(8), 765–773.

Trickett, P. K., Negriff, S., Ji, J., & Peckins, M. (2011). Child maltreatment and adolescent development. *J. Res. Adoles.*, *21*(1), 3–20.

Tsering, D., Pal, R., & Dasgupta, A. (2010). Substance use among adolescent high school students in India: a survey of knowledge, attitude, and opinion. *J. Pharm. Bioallied Sci.* 2(2), 137–140. doi:10.4103/0975-7406.67005

Waite, P., Whittington, L., & Creswell, C. (2014). Parent–child interactions and adolescent anxiety: a systematic review. *Psychopathol. Rev.* 1(1), 51–76.

Wallace, P. (2014). Internet addiction disorder and youth: there are growing concerns about compulsive online activity and that this could impede students' performance and social lives. *EMBO Reports*, *15*(1), 12–16. doi:10.1002/embr.201338222

Wei, C., & Kendall, P. C. (2014). Parental involvement: contribution to childhood anxiety and its treatment. *Clin. Child Family Psychol. Rev.* 17(4), 319–339.

World Health Organization (2011). Young people: health risks and solutions. *Fact sheet no.* 345. Available from: http://www.who.int/mediacentre/factsheets/fs345/en/index.html, accessed on March 25, 2021.

You, J. W. (2016). The relationship among college students' psychological capital, learning empowerment, and engagement. *Learning and Individual Differences*, *49*, 17–24. doi:10.1016/j.lindif.2016.05.001

9 Youth Participation in Crisis Management, Social Development and Policy Formulation

Introduction

Youth Development is a concept that sounds simple but has been challenging to define for many theorists. There are two broad ways in which the various definitions of youth development can be categorized. If one looks into the initial days of defining the concept, those had more to do with discussing the defects and problems that youth of the time was dealing with. Later, a few definitions emerged about youth development from a holistic perspective and concepts of growth as well as concepts of deficits. Sandles (2006) define this significant concept as follows:

> A process which prepares young people to meet the challenges of adolescence and adulthood through a coordinated, progressive series of activities and experiences which help them to become socially, morally, emotionally, physically and cognitively competent. Positive youth development addresses the broader developmental needs of youth, in contrast to deficit-based models which focus solely on youth problems.

If one were to break down the aforementioned definition, there are three important points that are worth discussing. First, it talks about the challenges that are faced for which they need to be prepared. The nature and type of these challenges have been adapting from time to time. Challenges related to physical development and awakening of sexuality are endemic to any development process, and one should not nullify youth's issues as part of the natural development process. Along with this, as time progressed, there were several associated problems that the youth had to face. Most of the time, these issues have come to the notice only when the youth or an observable number of youths has visible manifestations that deteriorate their life conditions. Until such indications were visible, all the social agencies including parents were aware of them. It is only after the Genesis and advancement of such issues that the user approaches social scientists to learn about them. Until then, adolescence and young adults are kept outside the scene without any contributory value given to them. The point that is to be highlighted here is a lack of involvement of youth in issues concerning them.

DOI: 10.4324/9781003170587-9

Secondly, the definition highlights the importance of youth gaining competence in all domains of their life. An individual with social competence would be able to deal with any situation or interpersonal issues with confidence. Moral competence helps an individual to make the right decisions at the right time without getting carried away by certain undue/undeserving advantages that may come their way. Emotional competence is the one that provides an individual the psychological fitness and frame of mind to behave in any range of situations. Physical competence has to do with health and physical fitness as well as mental fitness. Cognitive competence has to do with one's knowledge base and how higher order cognitive status decision-making and problem-solving are handled. Out of the five domains of competencies a young adult should be able to develop, our society and our education system are primarily interested only in developing the cognitive competence of our youth. This is a very narrow way of thinking, where all the other domains of competencies that are required for an individual to live a life of success and quality are completely ignored. None of the stakeholders of youth, including parents, kinship, teachers, or community does not invest in training for youth to develop competencies in all these significant areas. This leaves the youth unprepared to face the challenges that come their way. The point is to be highlighted here is the lack of sufficient training provided for the youth for their appropriate development.

The definition also talks about the need to have experience for the youth to develop these competencies. Another word for this experience could be the opportunity to participate in serious societal functions. Considering the culture in India, most of the significant decisions to be taken until one's adulthood are taken by the guardians or other authority figures on behalf of the youth. Young adults are then forced to implement the decisions taken for them, without their consultation by their guardians. In no arena of life, young adults are given the opportunity and experience to participate in any significant decisions or positions. In other words, the set of experiences that is required for the youth to develop various competencies for their life is completely cut off from them. Young adults who grow up in such a situation with a gross lack of opportunity would be flustered in their adulthood and be struggling to manage the challenges of everyday life. The lack of opportunity to participate is the point to be noted in this context.

Youth participation is not a new topic of discussion in relation to nation building. There have been several documents produced by several renowned agencies both nationally and internationally that talk about the advantages of youth participation in social development. This is a topic that has been overlooked by all the policy makers, governments, and the stakeholders. The present chapter attempts to understand the contribution of youth participation in Youth Development. Throughout the chapter, we discuss the various nuances of youth participation including its meaning, characteristics, merits and demerits as well as obstacles to youth participation in India. The highlight of the chapter lies in the process of re-envisioning the role of youth in various domains in India, such as Politics, education, health and social care sector, art, and policy making. Various ways in which youth can participate at an operational level are also discussed. A session is exclusively set aside to briefly describe the existing policies and programmes for youth in India.

Youth participation

Children and youth contribute to nearly 50% of the developing world population (World Bank, 2010). Therefore, it must be seen as an opportunity to develop the largest, youngest, and most prepared workforce for a country's development (UNFPA, 2007). For this truth has to be recognized collectively as an asset who can make remarkable contributions at local, national, and international levels (DIDD, 2010). Instead of perceiving them as risk and threat, they can be involved in meaningful activities where their creative problem-solving and reasoning skills could be utilized for building social cohesion (UNFPA, 2005). Their participation has to be beyond mere working for the young people instead working with and by young people.

Participation as a prominent concept within development that has been defined in numerous ways. According to World Bank (1994), participation is

> a process through which stakeholders influence and share control over development initiatives and the decisions and resources which affect them.

The UK Department for International Development (Britain & Baldry (2003) links participation to an individual's perception of one's on right and comments as that participation is

> enabling people to realise their rights to participate in, and access information relating to, the decision-making processes which affect their lives.

It is true that there has been an increasing interest in youth participation across various agencies worldwide. But, youth participation is restricted to just gathering of information through surveys or listening to very few of their representatives to draw conclusions. The DFID (2007) has figuratively viewed and represented the current trend of global youth participation in the form of an Iceberg, as depicted in the following Figure 9.1.

At the moment, youth participation is mostly restricted to having formal dialogue, followed by gathering of views of a small group of youth only. Their potentials are not properly tapped and utilized and a lot is remaining untouched and unexplored. The UK DFID urges to widen youth participation to several less visible areas such as governance, youth-adult partnership (Y-AP), capacity building, outreach programmes, community engagement, and so on. Through these and many more engagements, the youth will be provided with an enabling environment where they actively participate in the process of democracy, economy, and law.

Figure 9.1 Youth participation represented as an Iceberg by the UK Department for International Development.

Source: Department for International Development. (2010). Youth Participation in Development: A guide for Development Agencies and Policy Makers.

Obstacles to youth participation

EARPO (2006) identified key obstacles to youth participation in the "Child and Youth Participation Guide" for UNICEF. Inadequate education and training are the foremost in the list. The present education system is predominantly interested in providing subject-specific knowledge, i.e. most of the time, a degree holder would have been trained in preparing oneself to become a professional in that specific area of study. They are not trained in analytical thinking or decision-making and this lack of training is reflected in the output of youth participation. Even in cases where chances for such analytical work are provided, those were not followed by systematic and adequate training. Therefore, the lack of active learning and engagement is acting as an obstacle to youth participation. Followed by this is the concern related to weak systemic infrastructure in our country. Young people face trouble in accessing institutional structures within our governments. This lack of transparency in their transmission affects their involvement in the decision-making process. Even the ones who have tried to break over the barriers of this complicated structure were not able to overcome the limitation it can have on their implementation. Inequality and exclusion are a barrier as always, the case. Social discrimination acts as a double negative. A youth who belongs to a minority group finds it extremely difficult to participate. Another pragmatic hindrance is the financial cost involved. As students or youth with little or no money, meeting the financial requirements to involve them in society events restrict themselves from doing so.

Key stake-holders of the youth

Because youth participation is a process that will take a long time to finally attain its full form, effective management of relationships that are directly or indirectly crucial to the youth is important. By relationship we mean, the power dynamics that may undergo in giving the youth opportunity for decision-making. If there has to be a change in the pattern of how youth are often exerted with decisions taken by older adults and other institutions, the key stakeholders of youth have to be oriented to allow the youth to take decisions on vital matters that will alter their lives. Figure 9.2 represents the key stakeholders of youth who enjoy enormous power in deciding the nuances of youth participation.

Productive youth participation should begin to get encouraged within one's family and kinship. This is the most comfortable zone for youth to indulge in the decision-making process, as they are surrounded by their own family members who will not take undue advantage of them. This is the in-house corrective system that can help youth streamline their thought processes that would leave them to make a decision. Youth can exercise these skills without feeling vulnerable and feeling being taken advantage of. Over time, when several such exercises take place in the comfort of their homes and under the guidance of their parents, youth will be able to accumulate their experiences and learn how to make effective decisions. If parents can

Figure 9.2 Stakeholder of youth in India.

encourage their children to be part of the decisions that they take for their own children, then they may feel involved in the decision-making process and would be motivated to adhere to it. This will be an opportunity for them to learn the various reasons behind it, the information being collected for it, and finally the pattern of the decision being taken. This would be one way in which parents can make sure that children and youth would not get into destructive behaviours and troublesome activities. In times of confusion and vulnerability, they will be in a better shape to choose the wisest path.

Educational institutions should act as the platform of formal training for youth in terms of their civic participation. As would be extensively discussed at a later portion in the chapter, a multidisciplinary training has become the need of the hour, to model our youth to be effective youth participants of a country. In order to actually make a difference, youth has to be trained in critical thinking, reasoning, health and wellness, basic science, and social science subjects for pragmatic use. This training to develop their skills and attitudes in the direction of positive Youth Development can be done by the educational system, starting from two institutions of higher learning.

Workplace would be one of the first independent contexts our youth may become part of, which requires them to behave effectively without any guidance. Being in a dog-eat-dog- world; youth in work need to function both strategically and smartly. For the youth who are able to exercise the training they have received from their homes and educational institutions, would be able to display a remarkable performance at their workspace. They will be noted for their outstanding temperament that will work in favour of them in the career as well. Other significant stakeholders such as community, religious organizations, and governments should be motivated to take in the views of today's young adults. They need to take proactive measures and deliberate initiations to include youth not only as beneficiaries but as leaders and collaborators in policy making. All these stakeholders should have one motive in common, which is to empower the young adults to develop their personal skills and capabilities, by effective collaborations.

Despite being a topic of whose enormous advantage on the social development of a country is highlighted a time in again, governments and their citizens across the world fail to bring this to action. Here we are going to re-envision the role of youth in India in the succeeding session.

Re-envisioning the role of youth in India

On the basis of the discussion so far, the scope and relevance of youth participation in India is made clear. It is also evident that our country has been reluctant in exploring and leveraging the precious human resource of a country in almost all the spheres of its development. Having understood the enormous contribution youth can bring in, not just an issue related to their population but on aspects on a very general ground, let us try to imagine the various ways in which this can be brought to a reality. In the following section, we imagine India and its advantages.

Youth in politics

For its creative and dynamic nature, youth is undoubtedly a population who can be a catalyst of important changes in the political system of any country. Throughout history, their participation in power-sharing dynamics and political–economic development of the country has proved their effectiveness as leaders for change. Despite the case, the proportion of youth parliamentarians in their twenties is only 1.65% and that for those in their thirties is 11 is 87% (UNDP, 2012). Despite being a cohort that constitutes a fifth of the world's total population, their representation in politics is feeble; and that leads the average age of a parliamentarian to be 53 years globally (UNDP, 2012). Youth are politically active in Universities and their educational institutions, but this does not get converted to political activism into an organized and formal engagement by playing a prominent political role.

India's case is no different. Approximately 65% of the population are people below the age of 35 and this is why we call ourselves a young country. Hence, it would not be surprising that all political parties target these youth populations, who are so vibrant, enthusiastic and seem to be easy to convince, to be part of their election campaign propaganda, rallies, and other demonstrations to display their party power. However, the reality is that, when it comes to you actually giving the power in the hands of these party workers who are youth, not many parties in our country have shown a green flag. Hence only 6% of our political leaders in the current Lok Sabha are below 35 years and can fit into being called as "young leaders".

Political engagement of youth is not encouraged by providing them ample opportunities in the actual political field. For most active youth members of political parties, their engagement does not translate into a reliable income source as they need not get an elected position through their parties. Limited number of political seats is definitely one of the practical reasons for them not getting the opportunities. In the present Indian scenario, for an active youth who is a strong party ally is required to invest many years in politics to get their scope visible to contest as a candidate representing their political party. It wouldn't be an exaggeration if one comments that "our country is growing young with older leaders" (Kumar, 2019). The problem here is circular in nature: young people who have shown political engagement find their opinions unnoticed, they lose their interest as well as their aspirations in the institutionalized political processes. As they feel increasingly excluded lose interest in the process and stop to try voicing the needs of the youth despite being aware of social equity and Justice. However, the role of the Ministry of Youth Affairs and Sports, Government of India cannot be ruled out. The Youth Club Leaders of NYKS are provided with avenues to engage in community service which enables them to enter into local governance institutions and later paves way to join the mainstream politics. Further, the National Service Scheme (NSS) and National Cadet Corps (NCC) also provide similar opportunities to gain leadership skills and people skills which can be of advantage to the aspiring youth to enter into politics. The Ministry also annually organizes the National Youth Parliament at district, state, and national levels coinciding with the National Youth Festival. During District and State Youth Parliaments, the participants will deliberate on a key theme and will be judged by a Jury. The finals National Youth Parliament competitions this year (2021) was held in the Central Hall of the Parliament on wherein 84 winners from various States and Union Territories got an opportunity to speak before the Lok Sabha Speaker; Deputy Chairman of Rajya Sabha along with Minister (IC), Ministry of Youth Affairs and Sports, important dignitaries and a national jury comprising of eminent personalities judging the deliberations. The first three winners got a rare opportunity to speak before the Hon'ble Prime Minister of India who also interacted with the other participating youth during the occasion. This endeavour kindles the inquisitiveness among the youth to assume politics as their career.

At the very structure of it itself, there are few concerns that act as a practical obstacle to engaging youth in politics. Age restriction can pose challenges of varying degrees in different countries. Age restriction to cast a vote, to run for office, or even to be involved in election campaigning has been understood to be coming in the way. Another important hurdle is the huge financial requirement that may not be possible to be met by a youth candidate. Most of the time, when the party is not financially stable, the candidate would be told to pull in as much money as possible to be visible while the campaigning is ongoing. This would be of particular interest for young candidates as they may have poor/no income as well as the contacts required to arrange for the same. Sometimes the demographic characteristic of a particular area will be such, where only older people have been contesting an election for all the years and youth leaders tend to be looked down on and their capabilities are underestimated. Breaking this bias would be highly challenging as it has to do with the deeply-rooted attitude of that area. Of course, gender bias does exist in this scenario as well, where women and other gender minorities have to surpass double discrimination to explore their political involvement. Several countries have come up with reservation strategies to ensure equal representation; but in most of the places, only little has been brought to practice. Political sphere continues to be male-dominated across the world. Marginalization and social exclusion are related topics of discussion that come in the way to pursue politics at a serious level. Particularly in countries like India, sometimes the political parties and their inner-party politics itself hinders youth participation due to their age-old bias that may favour party workers from certain groups/ages/gender/socioeconomic status and the like.

Lack of knowledge about political processes and its importance is also widespread among today's youth. To a certain extent, this has been manifested in the form of poor voting rate among our youth population. There seems to be a lack of clarity and understanding of the democratic practices of their country among the youth, even among the educated ones. Sometimes, it can be a case of like/dislike, while, sometimes it can arise out of ignorance. Either the case, a youth who is unaware and disinterested in a country's political processes is not indicative of its development.

When youth is underrepresented in the political system, their voice is only little heard. Inclusive political participation is definitely crucial in the identification as well as management of the specific needs of young adults. In fact, this is the only way to tackle the authoritarian practices that have been dominating any system. However, obstacles to youth participation in politics are many and need to be tactfully handled.

Youth as educators and researchers

The role youth play in terms of their contribution to society development is remarkable. But they are a group that is, for various reasons, being kept aside from engaging in research and policy development. Earlier, youth in research were limited to mere data collection points only, but of late, youth engagement calls to bring them into the entire research process as full-time researchers (Kirshner, O'Donoghue, & McLaughlin, 2005), in a variety of roles that would "reflect their interest level, availability, commitment and skills" (Checkoway & Richards-Schuster, 2003). This brings in several reciprocal advantages such as "skill building, empowerment and social engagement of the youth, along with increase in feasibility of youth- friendliness and ecological validity of research" (Powers & Tiffany, 2006). They can be contributors in the traditional academic research, community-based research or youth-led research designs. There is a heightened need to motivate youngsters to get into research, and consultancy so that their needs are highlighted whenever required.

Unfortunately, statistics from across the world shows that the number of youths to pursue higher education and who express interest in getting into research is reducing. This is, to a great extent, is due to the increased promotion of autonomy and self-reliance among youngsters. During the teenage ages itself, they are engaged in one job or the other that provide them with needed pocket money. This trend has both positive and negative sides to it. When adolescence and young adults become financially independent, their motivation to get back to studies drop down significantly. Most of them would prefer to go for part-time studies or undertake certificate programme that would fetch them easy jobs. This could be a reason by youth is not attracted to academics and related career opportunities such as teaching and research. Emergence of professional courses could also be one of the reasons. This is so much in relation to the job market and its demands. Over the past few decades, youth has been extensively getting into technical jobs that would require them to be undergoing professional courses. Since such courses would give them a better probability of job, a better payment and less time in studies, youth tend to be attracted to pursuing search programme.

Time becomes a huge investment for youth to get into teaching and research. The path to becoming a teacher as well as a researcher is long which requires the youth to remain interested, perseverant, and consistent. For instance, you are required to continue pursuing degree programmes one after the other to finally be qualified as a teacher. Considering the case in India, youth will have to join for an undergraduate programme after the completion of their schooling. Soon after this 3–4 years programme, they need to get into a post-graduation programme to attain a master's degree. Ideally, both these degrees have to be in the same subject or with the same discipline. In order to become a school teacher in India, this candidate has to pursue another undergraduate degree in education (Bachelor of Education) lasting for a year. Despite securing all these degrees, the youth would still be required to prove their capability by passing a certain eligibility test. In sum, to become a school teacher in India, youth has to spend a minimum of 6–8 years. This story is no different for a youth who is interested in becoming a college teacher. In this case, they have to have their Ph.D. to be done in the same subject in which you would like to teach, in addition to qualifying a national eligibility test. Therefore, a youth has to invest 8–12 years in their pursuit of becoming a teacher at an institution of higher learning. In fact, in India this is one of the very few ways to get into research as well. The general trend that is observed is that teachers who get into colleges and universities set up their own labs and research centres to pursue their interest in research. Independent research Agencies accept, but its longevity and effectiveness would rely on the funding it gets.

This extensive investment in education in terms of both time and money is definitely pulling down the factor of our youth from pursuing a career in teaching. As can be imagined, a youth who aspires to become a teacher or a researcher will be required to remain patient for many years until they reach their goal. This also means that until then they will have to rely on their parents or other financial sources for many years when their counterparts who pursue professional courses start earning. Another detrimental factor is the lack of opportunity in the teaching profession in India. The number of permanent teaching posts in India are also few. Most of the time and particularly in the recent past, all these sanctioned posts are made to be run with the help of guest lecturers. By this it means that a youth who gets into teaching in a temporary post will continue to remain in the same job for years without any job security or salary for the work they do. Moreover, teachers who work in private schools and other educational institutions do not get well paid in India. In other words, there is no guarantee that despite investing a lot of time and effort to meet the eligibility criteria, a youth who has become a teacher or a researcher in India may not be able to attain the same. For all these reasons and many more, candidates who applied for the very few permanent posts that may come up, are forced to bribe the institution or any allied agencies with huge amounts of money in order to secure a job. Most of the time, youth who would not have huge savings, may not be considered for such positions despite being eligible. Discrimination based on reservations, caste, gender, and culture also prevents eligible candidates from getting into teaching positions in India.

Contribution of young researchers to positive Youth Development could be many. Having a youth researcher in any investigation will easily open several research issues that may otherwise go unnoticed. They are at a better place in terms of latest skills and are updated about various methods of data collection, analysis, and information dissemination. Many youth are involved in research activities related to Youth Development that can have a greater impact on the participants and the audiences. This also brings in the feeling of active engagement in the youth on topics that are affecting their own as well as their peers' lives. About all these, these young researchers actively learn about the various methods of investigations and its impact from their early adulthood and thereby growing up to researchers of significant experiences in their own fields of interests. In this way, youth becomes the force of change rather than just being a recipient of the product that is developed for them by people who do not have first-hand information about the issues and concerns of youth (International Planned Parenthood Federation, 2008). Therefore, in order to ensure youth participation, an organization needs to value their contribution, acknowledge and recognize it both in terms of acceptance and remuneration. They need to be continuously trained by competent adults with a welcoming attitude towards youth. Their works need to be recognized, credited, and should be offered due respect. Their roles should be defined with clarity and their genuine needs should be taken into consideration. Attracting youth to teaching and research is possible only by making these professions rewarding and recognized.

Youth-Adult partnerships (Y-APs) is an enterprising programme that was initially conceptualized to be implemented in organizational decision-making and programming. These are collaborative programmes where youth and adults engage in active discussions and sharing of opinion that would lead to several important decision-making (Zeldin, Camino, & Mook, 2005). Y-APs are found to be successful in several social-economic contexts such as civic engagement (Carlson, 2006), community programmes (Jones & Perkins, 2006), education (Mitra, 2009) research (Kirshner et al., 2005), and health care system (Ramey & Rose-Krasnor, 2015).

The McCain Model of Youth Engagement was developed by the McCain Centre based on systematic literature reviews. The model provides strategic methods to ensure youth engagement through different environment opportunities for youth. The key attributes of the model include flexibility, mentorship, authenticity, and reciprocal learning (Wong, Zimmerman, & Parker, 2010).

As can be seen from the figure, Y-APs show various levels of youth participation. The progression of engagement would range from very little to excellent. At a non-participatory level, youth are involved only to a very

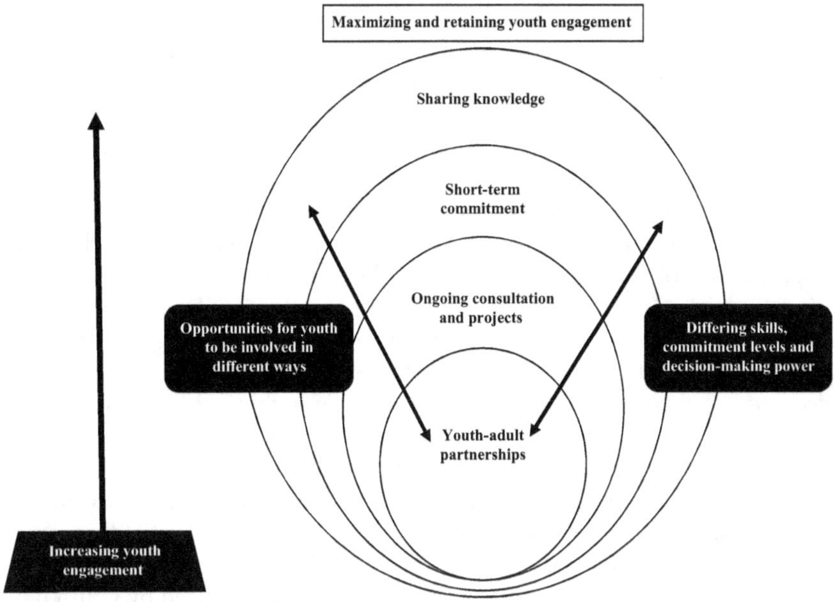

Figure 9.3 The model of youth engagement developed by Herzog, Heffernan, Chaim & Henderson (2014).

Source: Adapted from Hampton's Model of Civic Youth Engagement by Carlson (2006).

small degree and may only participate in sharing of knowledge. From there youth may be entrusted with short-term commitment which demands more engagement and resources. The graduation continues where youth may be involved in ongoing consultations and projects which will require different skills and commitment levels as well as opportunities to work in various ways. This includes the opportunity to plan and execute one's own creative ideas with complete liberty. Finally, the youth participation becomes more authentic and they may be given control over very important decisions at the highest level along with the adults (Heffernan et al., 2017). Skill development is the highlight of Y-APs. Evidence of positive youth development arising out of improved social trust (Heffernan et al., 2017), school achievement (Zeldin, Christens, & Powers, 2013), lifelong community citizenship, and positive health outcomes (Suleiman, Soleimanpour, & London, 2006) were reported.

Youth in health and social care sector

It is motivating that the health and social sector have become the biggest employer of youth people over the last few decades. In fact, more than any other age groups, it is youth who have leveraged these employment opportunities to a noticeable degree (WHO, 2016). The International Labour Organisation (2017b) has estimated the rise in youth employment rates in the United Kingdom, Canada, Mexico, Columbia, Bangladesh, and Philippines from 2005 to 2015 to be 38%, 30.5%, 38%, 90%, 200%, and 100%. ILO (2017) in another related survey predicted that the health and social care sector has the potential of creating 40–120 million employment opportunities by 2030, further indicating the probabilities of positive youth development.

Social care jobs are poorly paid even though they are demanding; hence job opportunities in this sector would be sought by people when there is a huge cost in job availability and when they exhaust all the other possibilities (Scottish Care, 2015). This is because search jobs do not provide job security and also do come with a poor or slow career progression. If the focus is to attract more youth into jobs in the sectors, then a lot has to be done to enhance the image of these jobs as something above that of a job taken when there are no other alternatives available. A 2015 Scottish-based qualitative study conducted among youth and employers in the social care sector has identified their perception about employment in the social care sector. The study reported about resource scarcity in the field as youth would be required to undergo specialized skill and aptitude training to be kept up to deal with vulnerable populations. Concerns raised by youth have more to do with the nature of the job. "Opportunities to move up the pay scale are limited and training is infrequent and basic. In addition, working conditions are often poor" (Gardiner & Hussein, 2015).

A practical difficulty the study found was the mismatch between the job requirement and the skills processed by the youth. For instance, personality match could be one characteristic that would determine the quality of one's service in the social care sector. The skills and expertise required for a sector of this nature would more be dependent on experience rather than formal qualifications. Therefore, it may not always be possible to match the youth with certain values and attributes that could be required to effectively function in the sector. Even though some of them may be able to secure a job in the sector, they may find it difficult to continue in the same and provide effective services. Another significant concern is the insecure nature of the job. "Insecure contracts, in particular zero-hours contracts, are prevalent among care workers, particularly in domiciliary care" (Gardiner & Hussein, 2015), thereby leaving the young adults with the burden of inconsistent income.

Global Health Workforce Network (2019) reported two significant factors that may motivate youth to enter in the sector. Gender stereotyping, discrimination, and associated violence are widely experienced by youth and early career professionals during their training as well as work period (International Labour Organisation, 2017a). There have been a few studies that also mentioned about discrimination based on age and ethnicity that prevent students and new graduates to get into the profession. Issues related to work-life balance and burnout are also widely reported. Lack of mentorship and occupational segregation have acted against the overall quality of work life in the youth population.

The benefits of youth involved in the social care sector are bilateral. Youth being the healthiest time, is the best human resource to take care of people who are unhealthy and vulnerable. In pursuit of doing so, young people will gain several social skills and philanthropic attitudes that will nurture their growth as an individual. But, since youth are not attracted to the service care sector, changes have to be incorporated from a policy level that will impact the labour market and make these professions attractive and respectful. These policies could also be capable of inculcating the skills required for the jobs among young people to match the huge demand. By this way provision of care for needed as well as concerns of employability among youth are both taken care of.

Youth as artists and liberal thinkers

Like never before, choosing an educational path that would align with the demand of a career in the future has become increasingly difficult due to the transformation that is happening in the employment sector. It appears that a youth requires more than just a specific education to excel in the career but rather needs an education that will empower them to design that future in this rapidly changing employment sector (Hollis, 2021). This is exactly where the relevance of liberal art education comes into play, which typically provides abroad exposure to different subject disciplines that will prepare an individual to deal with the complexities and diversity in today's society. The Association of American Colleges and Universities (2014) found that 93% of the Liberal Arts students displayed better ability in critical thinking, communication, and problem-solving in comparison to their undergraduate major counterparts. Approximately 80% of the employers also acknowledged the importance of Liberal Arts and Sciences among aspiring youth to succeed in their careers. This is more so because of the genesis of several jobs that don't require a very specific college degree, instead constantly evolving and adapting to handle the unexpected shifts in the job market. The change in this trend is visible even in the tech-dominated sector that requires ability to come up with creative solutions. Moreover, people change jobs more than before, each of them with varied job descriptions and expectations even when they may be within the same domain of work. The Liberal Arts seems to be a one-stop solution to these changing demands that presses the youth to be versatile and knowledgeable in several domains.

As Cuseo (2016) explains Liberal Arts and Sciences cover six broad disciplines: (1) Humanities: subjects that discuss human experiences in general such as literature and language, and theology and philosophy; (2) Fine Arts: Subjects that helps to explore art of human experiences like Visual Musical and Performing arts; (3) Mathematics: Basic algebra, statistics and calculus required for pragmatic calculations, reasoning and analysis; (4) Natural Sciences: to trains in systematically observing the physical world and gather inferences through subject such as Biology, Chemistry, Physics, Geology and Astronomy; (5) Social and Behavioral Sciences: that learns

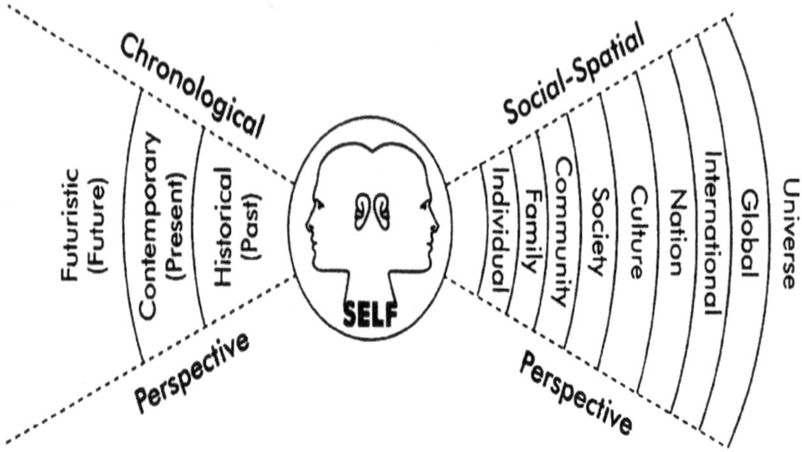

Figure 9.4 Liberal arts broadening the perspective of youth.

Source: Cuseo (2016). Liberal Arts & General Education What it Means to be a Well-Educated Person in the 21st Century. In *Thriving in College & Beyond: Research-Based Strategies for Academic Success and Personal Development* (4th ed., pp. 1–35). Kendall Hunt.

human individual and group behaviour true subjects like History, Political Science, Psychology, Anthropology Economics, and Sociology; (6) Physical health and wellbeing: that promotes optimal health and functioning through physical education, sexuality and nutrition. Along with providing a huge knowledge base, liberal Arts would also help an individual to think in a variety of ways by studying them and later by applying these to various instances that comes across. Youth will be tuned to think "chronologically, symbolically, scientifically and aesthetically" Cuseo (2016).

As the term stands for, liberal Arts will liberate a youth from the restrictions of narrow thought processes that exist in today's society. They will be able to broaden their perspective in a comprehensive way and will be able to see the world through a panoramic perspective (Braskamp, 2008). This process of liberation is effectively described in the Figure 9.4.

Youth is the centre of the model that fans out to two sides namely (a) chronological and (b) social- spatial. On either side, the perspective fans out progressively from an arrow perspective to a broader and wider perspective.

The chronological perspective: the range of chronological perspective begins from the past and extends up to the future. The youth will be able to perceive their world from historical, contemporary and futuristic perspectives. This means that they will be in a position to imply from their past learning, comprehend the current situation and predict various possibilities. Liberal arts will help youth to see beyond the here and now and broadens their perspective to appreciate the experiences in the past and welcome the future that is waiting for them.

The social-spatial perspective: The effect that begins from the individual will move to the perspective of family and help the youth understand the multi directional influence family can have on one's intellectual development, physical health and even economic security (Pascarella & Terenzini, 2005). As a move further to the perspective of community, which includes that school/college and work environment, you understand that the relationship between individual and community is reciprocal in nature. As Cronon (1998) said

> In the act of making us free, it [liberal arts education] also binds to the communities that gave us our freedom in the first place; it makes us responsible to those communities. It is about exercising our freedom in such a way as to make a difference in the world and make a difference for more than just ourselves

By this, the youth will be encouraged to participate in community services and civic affairs. Self-interest and volunteerism could be nurtured in them, stemming out of the feelings of humanitarianism and compassion for the welfare of one's' community (Pascarella & Terenzini, 2005). As the youth get the perspective of society table be able to think beyond their own communities. Unequal society ratifications on the basis of caste, creed, gender or economic resources (Feagin & Feagin, 2012) will become their areas of concern. They begin to understand how much stratification are based out of inequality and power play. This will help to nurture empathy and fellow feeling for the less privileged members of one society. It is a national perspective that engages the youth with the right meaning of citizenship and civic responsibility. Sensitive youth will be able to understand unfavourable and biased representation that worked out in our political system. They will be motivated to voice their opinion and participate in the governance through voting processes. Liberal art would also help the youth in developing interesting cross-cultural transactions and go beyond the boundaries of one own nation. They will be able to take sensible viewpoints about various inter-border disputes existing between various countries. The Global perspective is the one which teach them the interface between the human and non-human life on earth. Here is the idea of global citizen that motivates them to have environmental responsibility and sustainable development as they focus. The broadest of all perspective is that of universe which is required for developing reflective thoughts about the mysterious existence of universe which may direct the youth to something that can be called as "spiritual experience". In nutshell, liberal art takes multiple perspective, and it is integration of all this perspective that make it a meaningful whole (King, Brown, Lindsay, & Vanhencke, 2007).

An interesting and relevant write up by Cardenas (2021), a Political Pcience Professor at Trinity College, discusses multiple ways in which liberal art graduates become best prepared candidates for over 25 characteristic needs of today's society. Today's society requires critical and curious thinkers who have the capacity and patience to slowly become the masters of their work by thinking creatively and also by working in challenging situations. Their communication skills have to be clear and should have the vigour to build their community responsibly. They should be passionate as well as empathetic, who care about societal justice and equality. They should be self-aware and globally minded who are able to take various chronological perspectives. They should be resilient and open-minded who care about others and are capable of thinking ethically. They should be able to express their emotions freely and find personal meaning in literature and art, while being driven by the latest technology. Overall, they should be able to be adaptive thinkers who are capable of re-imagining the world by finding balance amidst ambiguities. This is so true because in the study conducted by Association of American Colleges and Universities (2014), 55% of employers wanted their employees to have a combination of both field- specific knowledge as well as a broad range of skills.

As Santa J Ono, the vice chancellor city of British Columbia, opinionated the discipline of Liberal Arts is often under-promoted and poorly funded. He found that there has been a decline in the study of and encouragement for taking up Liberal Arts over the past one decade (CBC Radio, 2020). Countering the argument about poor employability prospects of Liberal Arts by saying that most of the successful people had at least one liberal art studies in the past. He also highlighted the importance of having some Liberal Arts studies along with the professional courses for students to take up. This once again highlights the point that "In a future with unscripted difficult-to-predict problems, how one learns is more important than what one learns" (Godwin & Pickus, 2017).

Therefore, youth in our country should be encouraged to take up liberal art for their studies as well as their profession. They should be encouraged to be free thinkers and be motivated to express their thought processes through their art forms. This will also enhance their civic responsibility and better them as an individual. Parallel this will enhance the aesthetic sense of the nation altogether.

The narrow perspective of restricting oneself to only one particular subject has to be stopped and a multidisciplinary approach should be adopted in all education institutions in the country. Appreciably, the New Education Policy 2020 aims at doing the same. Artists have to be given more platforms to display the work. Politicians and policy makers have to make use of these expressions as a way to understand the challenges and issues faced by the society. If youth is motivated to undertake art, then this will enhance the vitality of a nation altogether.

Youth as policy makers

Youth wellbeing, youth policy and youth development are three significant concepts that are mutually inclusive of each other. Effective balancing of these three elements requires a coordinated and wholehearted effort from all stakeholders. The Global Youth Well-being Index (2014) is an appropriate reference point to understand the effort needed to be taken along these lines. This index that comprised six main domains namely health, citizenship, education, economic opportunity, safety and security, and ICT, was measured across 30 countries of which India ranked 26. This is an indicator of how much we need to work on our youth policy to improve the youth wellbeing and thereby use development across various sectors. Hence as depicted in the figure, these three are a continuous process that has no end, and which requires constant effort from all the stakeholders (Figure 9.5).

Youth policy in India needs to work on several general and specific topics that are related to youth that will help them not only to become adults but also to remain young as they can be (Williamson, 2009). However, what happens most of the time is that the voice of the youth that highlights their concern goes unnoticed by the policy makers at higher levels (United Nations, 2004). Understanding youth issues is the ultimate basis of proper policy formulation and implementation at all levels (Ashing, 2010). Therefore, the five preconditions of policy formulation process as suggested by UNESCO (2005) games in men's significance in this context. They are:

(a) Adequate resource allocation
(b) Strong stakeholders' partnership
(c) Active youth participation at all stages
(d) Action plans
(e) Mainstreaming of youth policies.

The Department for International Development (2007) conducted a youth mapping study in 2007 that led to increasing awareness about the need to address youth issues with their cooperation. The study proceeded to

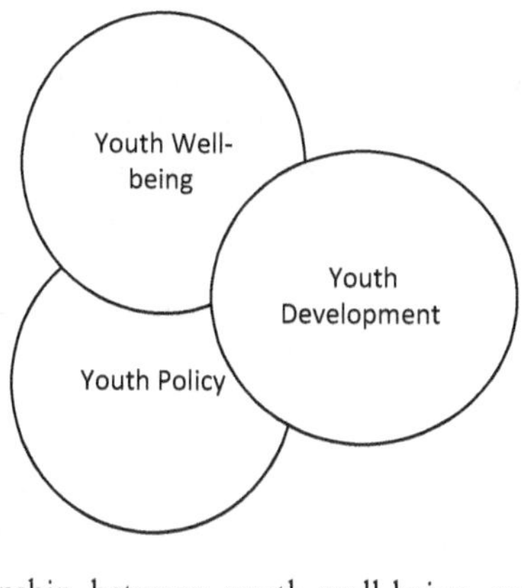

Figure 9.5 Interrelationship between youth well-being, youth policy and youth development.

Source: Motcham, C. R. (2014). Forming Youth Policy for Performing Youth Development. In J. H. Razario & M. C. Antonysamy (Eds.), *Emerging Trends in Youth Development* (Issue February).

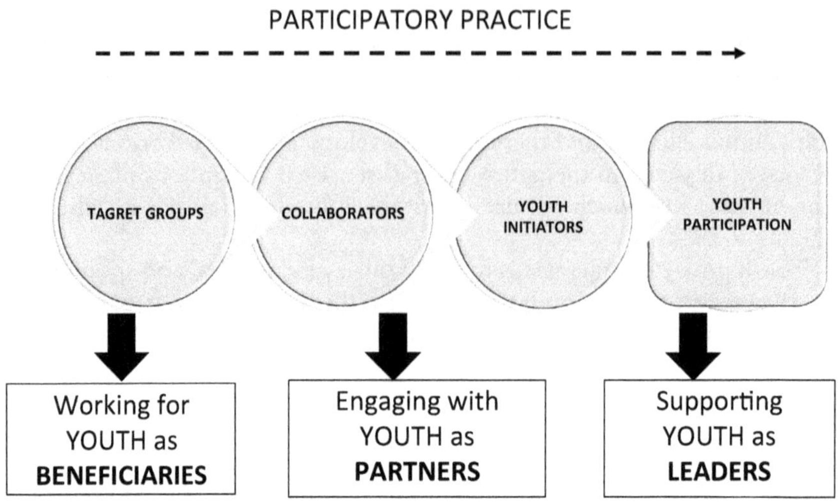

Figure 9.6 The three-lens approach to youth participation.

Source: Department for International Development. (2010). Youth Participation in Development: A guide for Development Agencies and Policy Makers.

conceptualize a three-lens approach to youth participation which was adapted from the 2007 world bank development report as depicted in the following Figure 9.6.

The approach in set conversion is used as partners and leaders in their own developmental models. Youth agency, their capacity to act, their ability to change their own life and the skills and capabilities are considered. In this way youth will become the beneficiaries, partners and leaders of their own development.

(a) When working with youth as beneficiaries they will be considered as a target group of whose issues are learnt through documentation.
(b) When engaging with youth as partners they will be fully consulted to develop collaborative interventions that would require mutual cooperation and responsibility.
(c) When youth become leaders, several youth-initiated and directed interventions will be appreciated, and they will be given in decision-making power within the process.

The application of this dynamic approach would depend on the context at which the work is done as well as the issue that is being addressed. Even though the combination of all three lenses works at its best, sometimes one may be more appropriate and prominent over the others. The situation has improved in India as there are more avenues created by the Ministry of Youth Affairs and Sports for the youth to voice out their concerns. In a recent exercise to revise India's National Youth Policy, the draft policy document was circulated among various key stakeholders including the youth belonging to different categories. A separate forum to obtain their reactions on the draft national youth policy document and seek their suggestions was created wherein, youth leaders, and youth from various walks of life were engaged in discussions with the policy makers and provided valuable inputs for revision of the draft policy document.

Youth volunteerism

Youth population is in its highest proportion in the history of the world today. Their contributions to nation building, national emergencies, innovations, and reforms are distinctive and contemporary. Towards this, youth volunteerism has been identified as a significant contributor and an increasingly popular mechanism towards sustainable development. The United Nations general assembly (2001) defined youth volunteerism as

> an activity undertaken out of free will, for the general public good, and where monetary reward is not the principal motivating factor.

The benefits of youth volunteering are obtained for all stakeholders. The economy, various service organizations, community and the youth volunteers receive its benefit either directly or indirectly. Huge literature supports the positive effect of youth engagement and volunteering in their overall development Guzman (2007) explain the various lifelong impact of volunteerism on our youth today: Healthy lifestyle, better psychological and intellectual development, increased interest in learning and applying new social skills, improved physical and mental health including higher self-esteem, confidence and responsibility, and overall greater life satisfaction are visible among the youth that may be visible in their adulthood. Further studies have proved that volunteerism can reduce at risk behaviours like addiction and academic disinterest among the youth (Torres, 2003). Studies prove that voluntourism can enhance social, cognitive, and psychological development (Kuperminc, Holditch, & Allen, 2001), identity development and political awareness (Youniss, McLellan, & Mazer, 2001) development of feeling of autonomy and belongingness (McKinney, 2002).

Several factors can influence volunteering behaviour among youth. Participation motivation is a key factor that was identified in China through a case study of the 2009 world games, where the youth do not want to miss an event that can provide them irrelevant learning and knowledge (Liao, Chang & Tsai, 2012). It was suggested that provision of a Remarkable and unforgettable experience with which the youth can identify can increase the probability of volunteering. In a study conducted among University students of the United States have identified employability, acquisition of skills and personal values as the top motivators to volunteer (Holdsworth, 2010). Altruism, and personal improvement were identified as a chief motivator in Turkey (Boz, 2007), while respect and recognition earned out of volunteering activity were identified to be the main motivating factors among the youth in Africa (Wijeyesekera, 2011). Konidari (2010) identified barriers to volunteering through a survey conducted among the youth who have not volunteered and found that busy academic schedules, lack of volunteering opportunities and inability to find a suitable role that matches with their career goals were causing major hindrance. Nevertheless, the Ministry of Youth Affairs and Sports, Government of India has been endeavouring to engage youth in nation building activities through volunteerism. The Nehru Yuva Kendra Sangathan (NYKS) is one platform where the rural youth can choose to volunteer and partake in the community development process through the youth clubs at village levels and also can assume leadership roles of the youth clubs that cater to the developmental needs of rural youth. The National Service Scheme (NSS) promotes personality development and nation building through volunteerism among the students in higher secondary and colleges/universities wherein, the volunteers engage in regular and special campaigns in adopted villages and render various volunteering services for community development. The National Cadet Corps (NCC), functioning under the Union Ministry of Defence, forms the youth section of India's Armed Forces which is open to the students at the high school and in colleges across the country on voluntary basis which builds in youth the ideals of community and social service than the military related training and youth management. The Bharat Scouts and Guides (BSG) recognized by the Government of India promotes the Scouts and Guides Movement, Builds character, confidence, idealism and spirit of patriotism and Service among young boys and Girls. The Bharat Scouts and Guides contributes to the education of young people through a value system based on the Scout Promise and Law to help build a better world where people are self-fulfilled as individuals and play a constructive role in society. Bharat Scouts and Guides were selected as honorary "Peace Messengers" for their significant and concrete contributions to the International Year of Peace in 1986. While these are various organized forms of volunteering avenues available among other volunteering forms for the youth of India, there are several non-formal ways of engaging in volunteering activities for social action.

The volunteer process model

Snyder and Omoto (2008) proposed the volunteer process model which has three sequential stages and activities at multiple levels of analysis. The model talks about volunteerism as a Process of various stages that interact with each other. As the model progresses it expands to Cater to the need of a wider audience. As depicted in the table, there are four levels at which volunteerism can take place which are (a) individual, (b) interpersonal, (c) organizational, and (d) societal/cultural. Each of these levels has three stages that interact with each other which are the antecedents, the experiences and the consequences (Table 9.1).

Table 9.1 Volunteer Process Model

Levels of Analysis	*States of the Volunteer Process*		
	Antecedents	*Experiences*	*Consequences*
Individual	Personality, motivation, life circumstances	Satisfaction, stigma, organizational integration	Knowledge and attitude change, health
Interpersonal/ Social Group	Group memberships, norms	Helping relationship, collective esteem	Composition of social network, relationship development
Agency/ Organization	Recruitment strategies, training	Organizational culture, volunteer placement	Volunteer retention, work evaluation
Societal/ Cultural Context	Ideology, service programmes and institutions	Service provision, programme development	Social capital, economic savings

Source: Snyder, M., & Omoto, A. M. (2008). Volunteerism: Social issues perspectives and social policy implications. *Social Issues and Policy Review*, 2(1), 1–36.

The antecedents would be factors such as personality, life circumstances, recruitment strategies and ideology. The experiences that can influence the process could be stigma, organizational culture or programme development. The consequences that would arise out of this would be e knowledge and attitude, relationship development or even economic savings. The model identifies volunteerism as a bridge between the various levels of analysis, which ranges from individual level to a societal level. This model has been developed based on extensive literature review and empirical evidence.

Volunteerism for employability

A commonly identified practical advantage of volunteerism is skill development required for the job market. It can enhance two key factors that are related to positive employment outcomes: namely social capital and human capital (Wollbaeck & Selle, 2002). Some of the evident benefits of volunteering in terms of employment are the opportunity for unemployed people to explore, maintain and develop their skills, widen their contacts, enhance their resume, and find out their job preparedness, all of these while making their dedicated contribution and involvement in work. Several researchers have identified civil engagement as an expression of that community's ability to bounce back from their social or economic recession (NCoC, 2012). Despite the lack of quantitative evidence several governments, non-profit sectors, or media have promoted volunteerism as a powerful technique for youngsters who are seeking a job (Institute for Employment Studies, 2011).

Even though there have been several anecdotal evidences that identify volunteerism as a strategy for employment, there is much empirical evidence supporting this. A United States based study identified volunteerism as a pathway to attaining employment; 27% probability increase in employment attainment was found to be associated with volunteering even among people from rural areas who have limited exposure in terms of education (Spera, Ghertner, Nerino, & DiTommaso, 2013). Antoni (2009) conducted a study among volunteers in Italy to find that only 24 % of them have attributed successful employment finding to their volunteering experience; participation in informal activities are also reported to have a positive effect on job finding. Similar findings have been found by a longitudinal survey where women reported that volunteering has brought them into a prestigious position related to their formal employment status (Statham & Rhoton, 1986).

Of the few studies that have attempted to understand the conversion rate of volunteerism to employment, most of them highlighted the key characteristics of volunteerism such as teamwork, work experience, conflict resolution and decision-making to enhance the chances of finding a job. Hirst (2001) estimated an average of six months or more of volunteerism to be needed for maximum output. Based on extensive literature review Spera et al. (2013) has attempted to identify the association between volunteering and employment through the enhancement of social and human capital as is depicted in the following Figure 9.7.

Volunteering enhances the probability of employment attainment by facilitating the individual's social capital and human capital. Volunteering provides access to various areas outside immediate reach both in terms of the quantity and quality of resources available. This also involves the social network that is not naturally given to an individual but has to be constructed through constant involvement and go to work exhibited, which can actively increase the opportunity of finding a placement. In a similar way human capital can also be elaborated through a deliberate investment in all the available opportunities. Knowledge acquisition, application of the theories learnt, training and skill development, availability to role models and enhanced psychological wellbeing such as increased confidence and self-esteem can all add up to the human capital which is proven to be positive at the labour market. This is why several prominent studies that try to understand the link between human capital and volunteering understand that volunteer work can "race one future earning power by providing work experience and providing potentially valuable contacts" (Menchik & Weisbrod, 1987).

Impact of volunteering need not be the same for every individual. This is particularly found to be advantages for individuals who come from a deprived background, who have to struggle for resources and accessibility. In other words, for individuals with low human capital and social capital will be more benefited from volunteering as they can expose themselves to a job market that they aspire for. However, research shows that volunteerism is generally shown by people from higher socioeconomic status, who are better educated and have an extensive social network (Wilson, 2000). People from lower strata may not be in a position to provide free services

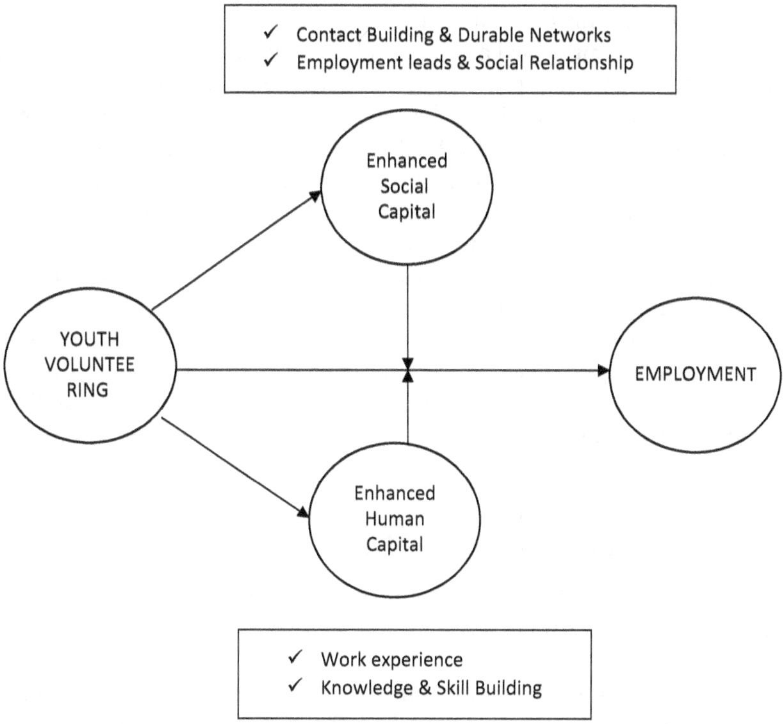

Figure 9.7 Volunteering leading to employment.

Source: Spera et al. (2013). Volunteering as a pathway to employment: Does volunteering increase odds of finding a job for the out of work? Office of Research & Evaluation, Corporation for National and Community Service.

as they make their daily living from the jobs that they do. Since people from higher socioeconomic backgrounds can afford to provide free services because of the backing that they already have, volunteerism can further reiterate their prospects in the labour market. Therefore, the paradox here is that, volunteerism can become a challenge to employment for people from lower socioeconomic status.

Parents and educators play a pivotal role in encouraging youth to experience volunteering. They need to provide the youth with needed information about the opportunities available for them in their communities, schools, local organizations, or religious sites. They can ensure that the facilities provided in the places where the youth volunteers are safe, engaging and positive by all means. They also need to help the youth overcome the various barriers in the form of Logistic issues for the youth to actually take part in such activities. Transportation, food and lodging, and finances could be some of these issues that would be preventing the Youth from engaging themselves in volunteering activities. Parents and educators can also help the children to find out volunteering activities that will suit their interest and age. This is important to ensure that the youth enjoy these activities and can utilize them for their benefit at a future time. Reward for volunteering can also be provided as an encouragement to undertake similar such activities in the future. Parents and educators need to be the role models for them by being volunteers themselves and setting them the right examples.

Supervision and mentorship: Adult involvement and acceptance are particularly important in volunteerism. Youth need to be guided in finding out the right place to render the service. Adults need to act as their mentor, friend, supervisor and guide all throughout the volunteering. Adults, who could be the parents or educator's for vendors at the organization, could help the youth identify relevant and age appropriate volunteering services they can engage in. Moreover, at the place of volunteering, the others need to take proactive steps in guiding them with needed information and knowledge along with opportunities for them to explore their skills and capabilities. It is only with the help of the adult, and their acceptance and guidance can a youth attend the volunteering activity.

Youth participation at operational level

The World Bank in 1992 has laid out four ways in which youth can be participating at an operational level.

(a) **Information sharing:** Youth can be part of carrying over any individual or collective activity at the fastest pace. Youth can be the people who are informed, knowledgeable and trained to spread any relevant information needed for societal functioning. For instance, consider the present COVID-19 scenario in a locality. A well-informed youth community will be the best suited population who can get into the workforce through knowledge dissemination and field work.

(b) **Consultation:** Youth can be consulted on any topic that is directly or indirectly linked to them. This does not restrict to mere surveying for data points, but their appearance and feedback can be taken under

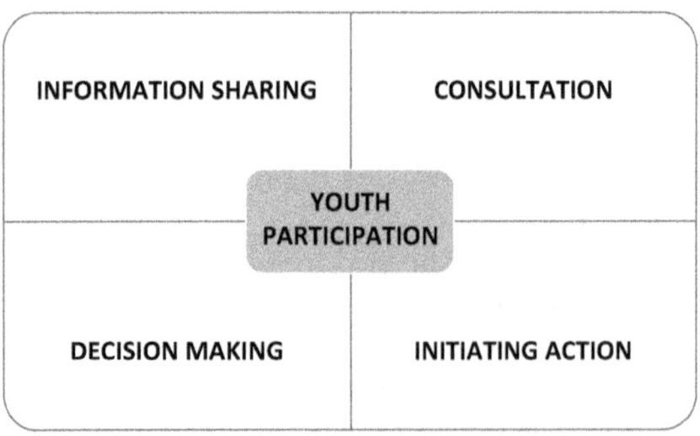

Figure 9.8 Youth participation at an operational level.

Source: Bhatnagar, B. & Williams, A.C., 1992. "Participatory Development and the World Bank.; Potential Directions for Change", World Bank - Discussion Papers 183, World Bank.

serious consideration. Youth will be the primary data-point for issues concerning their population in particular, the effectiveness of which cannot be substituted by any other mode of data collection or be fetched from other data sources.

(c) **Decision-making:** Youth have the capacity for problem-solving and decision-making which can be coordinated jointly with the others. The highlight of Youth-Adult Partnership is the same. This is particularly applicable for special issues in terms of policy development or intervention strategy formulation. Youth can be given a central role in decision-making which will ensure that the needs and requirements of their population are also represented.

(d) **Initiating action:** Youth can be given the responsibility to take any of the intervention strategies that were developed. It is only through their pro-activity and commitment that need to be leveraged for the benefit of the recommended strategy.

Ensuring youth participation will be an on-going process where they may be converted from the target of an outreach programme or a policy to the planners and implementers of the same. Co-management could be a starting point where youth are given the opportunity to work with older adults who are professional and begin to learn to lead to their own development. "Co-management is a form of youth participation that sets youth people on an equal level with older partners to work towards a common goal" (Peace Child International, n.d.). In other words, empowering youth to become the builders of their own future is the core of youth LED development.

The youth population belongs to the most suitable phase for training to effective participants of nation building. Two inputs have to be given to

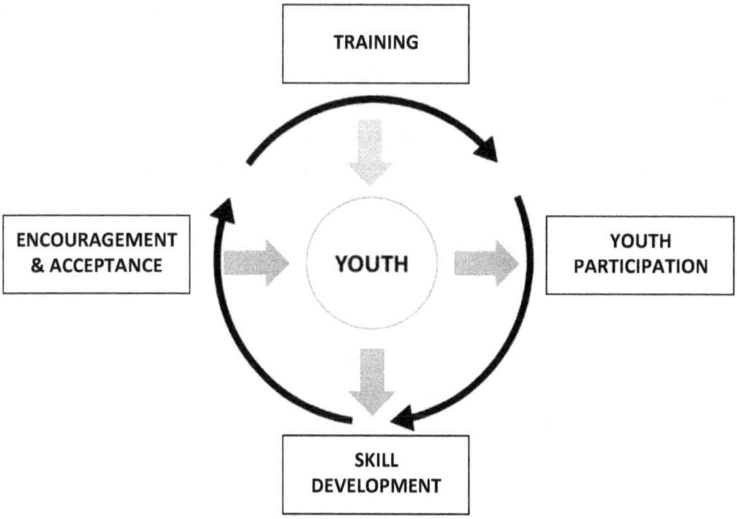

Figure 9.9 Input–output diagram of youth participation.

the youth at the appropriate time to get to effective outputs which will lay the cornerstone of youth development. First one being the training, that is required for them not just in terms of skills and competencies for employment, but also for facing the challenges of life. This training will lead to effective skill development which can be translated into effective output of youth participation. Along with training, adults and other social agents have to encourage the youth to participate and accept their contributions. This will invoke in them a sense of volunteerism that will translate into effective youth participation.

Conclusion and recommendations

Youth participation is the key to Youth Development. All the stakeholders of the youth have to take active steps in encouraging youth participation. They should begin from one's homes and education institutions, so that youth can participate in important decision-making processes. The contributions in various domains of society will have A Remarkable impact on social development altogether. Important facts that need to be understood is that youth participation should not be limited to working for youth, it should also include ways to work with youth and also to accept the work done by the youth. Along with exchange waiting for Youth Development, appreciating youth participation will also help the youth build on competencies that are required for them to face the challenges of life.

Encouragement for youth participation should begin from their home and must be visible in all areas of their active participation.

- Parents have to encourage their children to actively participate in age appropriate tasks at home. As a training, children can be involved in discussions or interactions that would lead to decision-making
- Schools have to introduce various activities that would help the children and adolescents to exercise their higher order processes from an early stage. Schools should motivate children to participate in group activities and joint ventures that will teach them teamwork, cooperation, and decision-making processes.
- Parents and teachers should ensure that the psychological capital of the children have received ample attention and training.
- Teachers and parents have to be trained on the importance of youth participation and should be equipped with needed skills and practices to encourage their children/students to participate.
- Volunteerism has to be encouraged and appreciated. More openings have to be provided for the youth to engage as a bridge between education and employment.

Adults have to create an attitude of acceptance to allow our youth to participate and engage in serious decision-making processes.

References

Antoni, G. (2009). *Getting a job through voluntary associations: the role of network and human capital creation*. (Working Paper No. 14). Retrieved from EconPapers.org at http://econpapers.repec.org/paper/entwpaper/wp14.htm.

Ashing, L. (2010). *Introduction to Youth Policy - Swedish and Turkish Perspectives* [online].

Association of American Colleges and Universities. (2014). Liberal arts graduates and employment: Setting the record straight. In *Association of American Colleges and Universities*. http://www.aacu.org/leap/nchems/index.cfm

Braskamp, L. A. (2008). Developing global citizens. *J. College Charact.*, 10(1), 1–5

Britain, G., & Baldry, T. (2003). *Department for International Development: Departmental Report 2002: Government Response to the Committee's Sixth Report of Session 2001-02: First Special Report of Session 2002-03*. Stationery Office.

Cardenas, S. (2021). *Why society will need liberal arts graduates*. Issues in Higher Education.

Care, S. (2015). *In the front line: social care providers survey report on recruitment and retention*.

Carlson, C. (2006). The Hampton experience as a new model for youth civic engagement. *J. Community Pract.* 14:89–106.

CBC Radio. (2020). *Education without liberal arts is a threat to humanity, argues UBC president*. CBC Newletter. https://www.cbc.ca/radio/ideas/education-without-liberal-arts-is-a-threat-to-humanity-argues-ubc-president-1.5426112

Central Statistics Office. (2017). *Youth in India*. http://mospi.nic.in/sites/default/files/publication_reports/Youth_in_India-2017.pdf

Chaim, G., & Henderson, J. (2014). *Youth System Services Review Phase 2 Report: A review of the continuum of Ontario services addressing substance use available to youth age 12–24*. Toronto: authors

Checkoway, B., & Richards-Schuster, K. (2003). Youth participation in community evaluation research. *Am. J. Eval.*, 24:21–33.

Cronon, W. (1998). "Only Connect": the goals of a liberal education. *The American Scholar*, 67(4), 73–80.

Cuseo, J. (2016). Liberal arts & general education: What it means to be a well-educated person in the 21st century. *Thriving in College & Beyond: Research-Based Strategies for Academic Success and Personal Development*.

Department for International Development. (2010). *Youth Participation in Development: A guide for Development Agencies and Policy Makers*.

DFID/Maguire, S. (2007) 'Youth Mapping Study – DFID's Approach to Young People'.

EARPO, U. (2006). *Child and Youth Participation Resource Guide*.

Elaine, S. C., Holosko, M. J., & Lo, T. W. (Eds.). (2008). *Youth empowerment and volunteerism: principles, policies and practices*. City University of HK Press.

Feagin, J. R., & Feagin, C. B. (2012). *Racial and ethnic relations* (9th ed.). Saddle River, NJ: Prentice Hall.

Gardiner, L, & Hussein, S. (2015). *As if we cared: the costs and benefits of a living wage for social care workers*, Resolution Foundation Report.

Godwin, K. A., & Pickus, N. (2017). *Liberal Arts and Sciences Innovation in China: Six Recommendations to Shape the Future*. 8. https://www.bc.edu/

content/dam/files/research_sites/cihe/pubs/CIHEPerspective/CIHEPerspectives8_ENGLISH_13NOV2017.pdf

Goldin, N. (2014) The Global Youth Wellbeing Index [online]. available: http://www.youthindex.org/reports/globalyouthwellbeingindex.pdf

Guzman, M. (2007) *Youth volunteerism.* University of Nebraska-Lincoln Extension, Institute of Agriculture and Natural Resources.

Heffernan, O. S., Herzog, T. M., Schiralli, J. E., Hawke, L. D., Chaim, G., & Henderson, J. L. (2017). Implementation of a youth-adult partnership model in youth mental health systems research: Challenges and successes. *Health Expect.*, *20*(6), 1183–1188. doi:10.1111/hex.12554

Hollis, J. (2021). *The benefits of a liberal arts education.* Coalition for College.

Institute for Employment Studies. (May 2011). *Volunteering: supporting transitions.* Retrieved from http://www.employment-studies.co.uk/press/1108.php.

INTERNATIONAL LABOUR OFFICE-ILO. (2017). *World employment and social outlook: Trends 2017.* Geneva, Switzerland: Author.

International Labour Organisation. (2017a). *Improving employment and working conditions in health services. Report for discussion at the Tripartite Meeting on Improving Employment and Working Conditions in Health Services.* Geneva: International Labour Organization.

International Labour Organisation. (2017b). *Global employment trends for youth 2017: paths to a better working future.* Geneva: International Labour Organization.

International Planned Parenthood Federation. (2008). *Explore: ideas for youth involvement in research.*

Jones, K.R., & Perkins, D.F. (2006). Youth and adult perceptions of their relationships within community- based youth programs. *Youth Soc.*, 38:90–109.

King, P. N., Brown, M. K., Lindsay, N. K., & Vanhencke, J. R. (2007). Liberal arts student learning outcomes: an integrated approach. *About Campus*, September/October, pp. 2–9.

Kirshner, B., O'Donoghue, J., & McLaughlin, M. (2005). Youth-adult research collaborations: bringing youth voice to the research process. In: Mahoney JL, Larson RW, Eccles JS, (eds.) *Organized activities as contexts of development extracurricular activities, after-school and community programs.* Mahwah, NJ: Lawrence Erlbaum Associates, 131–156.

Kumar, S. (2019 October 15). Young country, old leaders: while politics engages large numbers of youth, it does not serve their interests. *Times of India*, 1–8.

Kuperminc, G.P., Holditch, P.T., & Allen, J.P. (2001) Volunteering and community service in adolescence. *Adoles. Med.: State of Art Rev.*, 12, 445–457.

McKinney, K.G. (2002). Engagement in community service among college students: is it affected by significant attachment relationships? *J. Adoles.*, 25, 139–154.

Menchik, P., & Weisbrod, B. (1987). Volunteer labour supply. *J. Public Econ.*, 32, 159–183.

Mitra, D.L. (2009). Collaborating with students: building youth-adult partner-ships in schools. *Am. J. Educ.* 115:407–436.

Motcham, C. Raj. (2014). *Youth policy in Ireland and India: a Comparative Study*, unpublished thesis (Ph.D.), National University of Ireland, Maynooth.

National Conference on Citizenship. (September 2012). *Civic health and unemployment II: the case builds*, Washington, D.C.

Pascarella, E.T., & Terenzini, P. T. (2005). *How college affects students: a third decade of research (volume 2).* San Francisco: Jossey-Bass.

Peace Child International. (n.d.). *Co-management: a practical guide.*

Powers, J.L., & Tiffany, J.S. (2006). Engaging youth in participatory research and evaluation. *J. Public Health Manage. Pract.*. 12: S79–S87.

Ramey, H.L., & Rose-Krasnor, L. (2015). The new mentality: youth- adult partner-ships in community mental health promotion. *Child Youth Serv Rev.* 50: 28–37.

Sahri, M., Murad, K., Alias, A., & Sirajuddin, M. D. M. (2013). Empowering youth volunteerism: the importance and global motivating factors. *J. Educ. Social Res.*, *3*(7), 502–502.

Sandles, S. (2006). '*What do you mean, "youth development"?*' [online].

Snyder, M., & Omoto, A. M. (2008). Volunteerism: social issues perspectives and social policy implications. *Social Issues and Policy Review*, 2(1), 1–36.

Spera, C., Ghertner, R., Nerino, A., & DiTommaso, A. (2013). *Volunteering as a pathway to employment: does volunteering increase odds of finding a job for the out of work?*. Office of Research & Evaluation, Corporation for National and Community Service.

Statham, A., & Rhoton, P. (1986). Mature and young women's volunteer work, 1974–1981. *Columbus: center for Human Resource Research*, The Ohio State University.

Suleiman, A.B., Soleimanpour, S., & London, J. (2006). Youth action for health through youth-led research. *J Community Pract.* 14:125–145.

Torres, G. (2003). *The future of volunteering: children under the age of 14 as volunteers.* Service Leader.

UNDP & IPU (2012). *Global Parliamentary Report.*

UNESCO (2005). Guidelines for inclusion: Ensuring Access to Education for All. París: UNESCO. *EDUCACIÓN INCLUSIVA: ABRIENDO PUERTAS AL FUTURO*, 82.

UNFPA. (2005). '*The case of investing in young people as part of a national poverty reduction strategy*'; New York: UNFPA.

UNFPA. (2007). '*Framework for action on adolescents and youth: opening doors with young people: four keys*'; New York: UNFPA.

UNFPA. (2008). *Annual report 2007.* United Nationals Population Fund. Geneva.

United Nations. (2004). World youth Report 2003 – The Global Situation of Young People, United Nations [online]. available: http://www.un.org/esa/socdev/unyin/documents/worldyouthrcpofi

Wijeyesekera, D. (2011). The State of Youth Volunteering in Africa. In *International Forum on Development Service.*

Williamson, H. (2002). *Supporting young people in Europe: principles, policy and practice: the Council of Europe international events of national youth policy l997–2001-a synthesis report*, Council of Europe.

Williamson, H. (2009). *Integrated or targeted youth support services: an essay on 'prevention'. Prevention and youth crime: Is early intervention working*, 9–20

Wilson, J. (2000). Volunteering. *Annu. Rev. Sociol.*, 26, 215–240.

Wollbaeck, D. & Selle, P. (2002). Does participation in voluntary associations contribute to social capital? The impact of intensity, scope, and type. *Nonprofit and Voluntary Sector Quarterly*, 31, 32–61.

Wong, N.T., Zimmerman, M.A., & Parker, E.A. (2010). A typology of youth participation and empowerment for child and adolescent health promotion. *Am. J. Community Psychol.* 46:100–114.

World Bank. (1994). *World development report 1994: Infrastructure for development.* The World Bank.

World Bank. (2007). '*World Development Report 2007: Development and the Next Generation*'; Washington: World Bank.

World Bank. (2010). *World development indicators 2014*. The World Bank.

World Health Organisation. (2016). *Working for health and growth: investing in the health workforce. Report of the High-Level Commission on Health Employment and Economic Growth*. Geneva: World Health Organization.

Youniss, J., McLellan, J.A., & Mazer, B. (2001). Voluntary service, peer group orientation and civic engagement. *J. Adoles. Res.*, 16, 456–468.

Zeldin, S., Camino, L., & Mook, C. (2005). The adoption of innovation in youth organizations: creating the conditions for youth-adult partnerships. *J. Community Psychol.* 33:121–135.

Zeldin, S., Christens, B.D., & Powers, J.L. (2013). The psychology and practice of youth- adult partnership: bridging generations for youth development and community change. *Am. J. Community Psychol.* 51: 385–397.

10 Skill development programmes, entrepreneurship, and international and national policies and programmes for youth

> Education, vocational training and lifelong learning are central pillars of employability, employment of workers and sustainable enterprise development
>
> —International Labour Organisation

Introduction

Pursuit of education is contingent upon various factors that are beyond the control of an individual. Particularly in a country like India, which is densely populated and intrinsically layered, education may not be an accessible option for many of its youth. This doesn't mean that the youth who are illiterate or have little access to education are incapable or lack any cognitive ability or intellectual capacity. Rather, it is the interplay of several factors that has hindered their access to education. Poverty, inaccessibility to and unavailability of educational institution, poor access to and limited exposure of parents to education, social exclusion and discrimination based on caste, locality or gender, adverse life conditions that have pushed them into job market as an unskilled labour, distance, poor education to employment ratio and so on are a few among the very many reasons that is curtailing individuals' access to education. Even though it is true that education is a pillar to employability, there are several other access points to acquiring success in their jobs. Two of the highly recommended alternatives to attain employability are skill training and entrepreneurship. This is precisely why economies across the world, both developed and developing, are investing a lot of their time, effort and money into encouraging the youth to get themselves skill trained and also enter into enterprising initiatives that are sustainable sources of income.

The relationship between education and employment is complex. Education cannot be seen as an assurance to employability. Rather, it is only one of the elements that can increase the probability of securing a job. The International Labour Organisation (2019) reports that young people (age 15–24 years) are three times more likely to be unemployed than adults (25 years and above). This is reflected in the figure given below that depicts the ratio of youth to adult unemployment rate. The highest ratio of unemployment

DOI: 10.4324/9781003170587-10

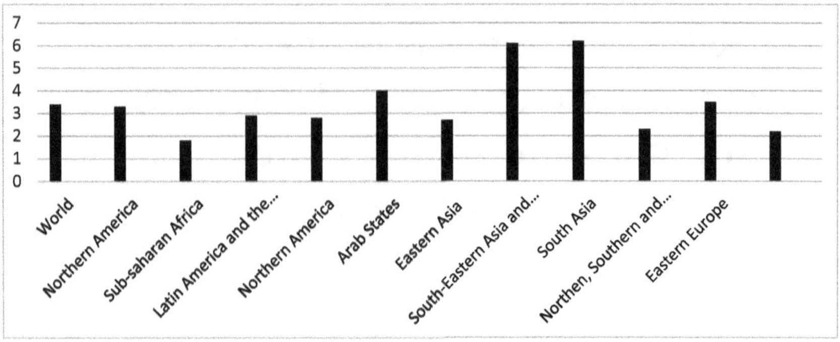

Figure 10.1 Youth-to-adult unemployment rate in 2019.

Source: ILO (2020). Global Employment Trends for Youth 2020: Technology and the future of jobs. In the International Labour Organization. https://www.ilo.org/wcmsp5/groups/public/---dgreports/---dcomm/---publ/documents/publication/wcms_737648.pdf

is at 6.4 which is estimated in the southern Asian region followed by South-east Asian at 6.2. Drawing inference from the graph given below, it is evident that educated youth from countries like India are not able to translate their qualification into a job opportunity (Figure 10.1).

This is where the long-term vision and quality of education is put under question. Are educational institutions able to futuristically ideate and train their students to meet the demand of the job market that they are aspiring to meet in due course of time? A growing body of literature says no. Despite spending nearly two decades into education, the students in countries like India are barely given any hands-on experiences, or training to translate their theoretical knowledge to practice. Therefore, when these youth enter into a global job market, where they are supposed to compete with youth from across the world, they appear to be lacking and poorly equipped in front of the employer. Once again, the relevance of skill training is highlighted even for educated and qualified youth.

Skill development is essential for youth development. This chapter attempts to explore the relevance of skill development in India by studying various international and national reports on employment and unemployment in the youth today. The chapter talks about the various employability skills and interest points from the perspective of the employer on which our youth needs to be trained from the very beginning. The chapter also identified entrepreneurship as another significant contributor to employability of our youth. The trend of entrepreneurship in the emerging economy of India is explored along with learning the various determinants of entrepreneurship in a country. The chapter learned the process of entrepreneurship and identified a proposed conceptual model that highlights the importance of the same to the national economy growth. Towards the end, an exclusive section is dedicated to exploring the various policies and programmes for youth in the country. Educational institutions and training programmes dedicated to vocational training and skill development and various International and national youth development policies and programmes are also highlighted in the chapter. The chapter also concludes with a few recommendations which will be of interest to stakeholders such as parents, teachers, employers, NGO, and various government agencies.

Skill development

Youth worldwide face serious challenges in acquiring the needed skills for the highly competitive job market. The struggle today's youth go through is very different from that of the previous generation. The global trend is such that specialization is given predominant importance and hence, youth, even after having the required educational qualification, are expected to further specialize or do advanced studies in certain targeted areas of their studies. In other words, the employee is keen to identify whether the youth in employment have the needed specialized skill that meets the job demands. With the rapid technological advancements happening in all job sectors, competition has intensified to a great extent. Today the employer requires the workers to have a high level of skills so that they can adapt to the quickly changing systems at the workplace, improve the quality of both the services as well as the product generated and engage in innovations and upgradation. Even the local firm can have an international market, and so the potential employee base has also widened. Therefore, the number of youths outnumber the employment opening tremendously, making it difficult for them to attain jobs of their aspirations. At an individual level, the relevance of skill training and development is highlighted as a key determinant for development. Similarly, at a national level too, a skilled workforce is a key determinant for attracting multinational companies and firms to invest in our country. As a developing country that is making earnest efforts to become involved in global value chains, India is in dire need to meet the global standards of efficiency. Today we need a more skilled workforce for expanding our foreign trade and boosting economic development (Okada, 2012).

Skill development is particularly important in Indian context for various reasons. Firstly, India has the world's largest population in terms of its youth strength. Additionally, according to the World Bank report (2012), nearly 86% of India's total employment is in the informal sector and continues to be segmented. Incidentally, India has been experiencing a comparative progress in its economy, but unfortunately it has not translated to employment growth. This is another reason why youth in the country end up working in informal job sectors that offers little wages and security. Moreover, Indian youth, especially the ones in rural areas, have received only limited education and training and remain unfit for the competition in the job market. Considering all these conditions and more, there have been several policies and programmes that the country has instituted by taking special interest in skill development among youth. However, the matter still requires serious consideration of the community as well as the policy makers.

The traditional and widely accepted linkages between education and labour market are a three-tiered association. Determinants of education, including those related to personal level to societal level, will decide the educational outcome. This was to decide the labour market outcome of the individual which sums up to the country's growth outcome. The close association between educational attainment and availability of employment opportunities is widely known as established (Desai et al., 2010). The ratio of education to employment transition in a country is not smooth and direct. India is facing a huge shortage in the number of skilled workers and so employers are forced to recruit people who are unskilled and have to invest time and money in training them to meet the requirement of the job (Ansari, 2018). The following table provides an overview of vocational training received by the workforce in a country which further validates this statement (Table 10.1).

As per the table, over 75% of the country's workforce has not received any training, be it formal or non-formal. The workforce in the agriculture sector has received the highest formal training yet and currently it is the workforce at the service sector that is getting the highest degree of formal training. Hence, in order to address the negligible work skills of our youth entering into the workforce every year, comprehensive and globally proven

Table 10.1 Vocational Training received for India's Workforce

Vocational Training	*Agriculture*	*Manufacturing*	*Non-manufacturing*	*Services*	*Total*
Receiving formal training	0.80	0.13	0.05	0.39	0.64
Received formal training	0.22	0.51	0.20	1.48	2.41
Non-formal hereditary	3.05	0.77	0.15	0.47	4.44
Non-formal self-learning	0.60	061	0.23	0.79	2.23
Non-formal learning on job	0.86	2.02	0.98	1.49	5.35
Non-formal others	0.07	15.0	0.04	0.18	0.44
Did not receive any training	38.2	7.56	9.45	20.5	75.8
Nr	5.81	0.85	0.55	1.48	8.69
Total	48.9	12.6	11.65	26.84	100

Source: National Sample Survey Scheme 2011–12 (68th Round).

skill development and vocational training has to be provided. The result of an assessment study conducted by Saini (2015) on the skill capacity of Indian workforce age between 15 to 59 found that only 10% of the workforce have occasionally trained of which 2% received formal training while the remaining 8% had received informal training, as compared to 96% in Korea, 75% in Germany, 80% in Japan and 68% in the United Kingdom. Some of the key challenges faced for skill development in India, according to Saini (2015) are mismatch between demand and supply, demographic and geographical problems, poor educational attainment, minimal vocational training, little participation by private sector, poor consideration for minority population, skill-gap between various sectors, infrastructural challenges, lack of trained trainers, and poor labour market information.

A recent study based on NSSO data has found a 4.7% increase in the wages of those who had formal training as compared to their counterparts without training. This was found to be highest in the primary sector where the weight increase has gone up to 36.9% while it was17.6% in the secondary sector. However, the study found that being a male and an urban dweller decreases the probability of receiving formal vocational training. The paper confidently suggests the existence of a good economic return related to formal vocational training and recommends further investment in providing vocational training for skill development (Kumar, Mandava, & Gopanapalli, 2019).

Employability Skills

The relevance of skill development for youth has been established time and again by several literatures. However, there needs to be a clarity on the core skills that are required for employability on which our youth needs to be trained. Related to this in the year 2000, international Labour Organisation adopted a resolution that define employability skill as the following

> ... the skills, knowledge and competencies that enhance a worker's ability to secure and retain a job, progress at work and cope with change, secure another job if he/she so wishes or has been laid off and enter more easily into the labour market at different periods of the life cycle. Individuals are most employable when they have broad-based education and training, basic and portable high-level skills, including teamwork, problem solving, information and communications technology (ICT) and communication and language skills. This combination of skills enables them to adapt to changes in the world of work.
>
> (ILO, 2004)

Skill gap refers to "the degree of alignment or misalignment between the skills youth develop through education and training, and the skills needed by employers" (4). Since it is difficult to predict the exact nature of economic and professional change, educational institutions find it difficult to offer skill training from a futuristic perspective.

Soft skills training

Soft skill seems to be top in the priority of an employer who looks for placement across industries (World Economic Forum, 2020). This is so because of the proactive need to effectively navigate through the various demands of the job, which is only possible with soft skills. According to the World Economic Forum Study,

> more than one third (36%) of all jobs across all industries are expected to require complex problem-solving as one of their core skills, compared to less than 1 in 20 jobs (4%) that will have a core requirement for physical abilities such as physical strength or dexterity.
>
> (Costello, 2017)

The translation of soft skills to workplace behaviour and later to business impacts are given below (Figure 10.2):

Development and quality of soft skill attained by the youth can depend upon several factors, such as, positive early and Middle childhood development experiences, home environment that is facilitated through active learning of soft skill, and a rewarding and stimulating school environment. Once acquired, soft contributes to a wide range of developmental outcomes. Evidence suggests that soft skill can result in positive social and health behaviour practice conflict prevention, improved reproductive health and even active citizenship behaviour (Gates et al., 2016). Taking cognizance from this, WHO report emphasizes on the importance of developing life skills in the young people in order to help them to deal with conflict, improve their competencies as well as in finding employment (World Health Organization, 2005). Soft skill development can be understood only as a

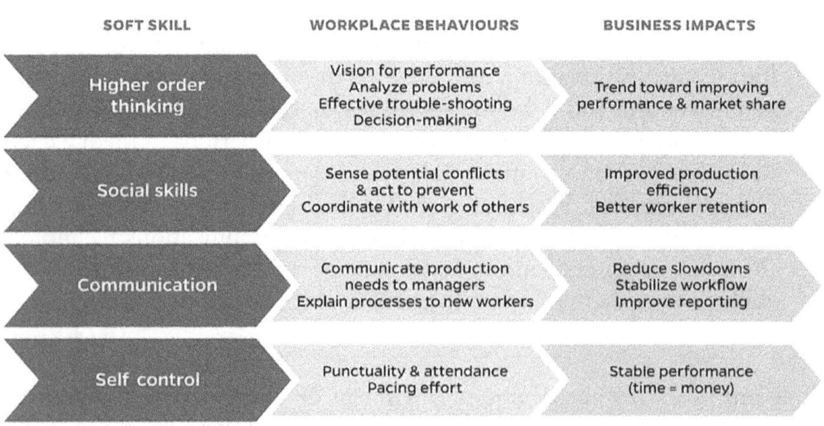

Figure 10.2 Link between Soft Skills and Business Impact in Manufacturing Sector.

Source: Youth Employment Funders Group. (2019). What Works in Soft Skills Development for Youth Employment?

dynamic and interactive process between all the stakeholders. Education institutions, household and extended community, government as well as employers' employees and organizations at search should be actively participating in implementing opportunities for soft skill development among youth. This is a process that will also contribute to awareness building and group commitment that are inevitable for generating better the search for the youth.

Entrepreneurship

Unemployment and under-employment have become a long-standing problem for many economies across the world. Due to several reasons, countries are unable to create new jobs that can assure enough earning for our youth as fast as it is required to absorb the growing youth population entering the job market. This is where entrepreneurship has become the widely promoted policy agenda in many of these countries as a means to address issues related to unemployment. Entrepreneurship is a term that is of wide usage of late and lacks a simple precise definition. In simple terms it means to be self-employed by making use of one's personality traits as well as managerial skills efficiently. Entrepreneurship is "the process of doing something new and something different for the purpose of creating wealth for the individual and adding value to society" (Kao, 1993). As per the Global Entrepreneurship Monitor (GEM), entrepreneurship is

> Any attempt at new business or new venture creation, such as self-employment, a new business organization, or the expansion of an existing business, by an individual, a team of individuals, or an established business

It is a wholehearted effort to discover and create goods and services that is capable of extracting economic values from one's environment to eventually make a new and independent source of income. Three main characteristics will remain after several iteration of the popular definitions of entrepreneurship:

(a) the ability to wear uncertainty and risk-taking behaviour,
(b) effective and Competent management skills such as planning, accounting and marketing, and
(c) ability to explore and exploit available opportunities.

(Kruger, 2004)

Apart from this there are certain entrepreneurship-based traits such as creativity, determination, and confidence that are endemic to success (Valerio, Parton, & Robb, 2014).

Given the current Global trends, democracy across the world is doing youth entrepreneurship as an important means as well as an effective alternative for income generation for the country as well as its young people 14. As technological advances, the traditional career paths are also acquiring different appearances, gaining acceptance as a way to boost the labour market as well as to overcome poverty through the active participation of the youth. Several countries view entrepreneurship as a way to convert educated and skilled youth available in the job market to an income-generating member and so have aroused new policies and programmes that support youth entrepreneurship 15. Alam (2019) has found to main approaches in which policy discourse is has viewed entrepreneurship as a solution to youth unemployment:

1. **Growth approach:** Your entrepreneurship is identified as a token to economic growth. Individuals of any age group are self-employed and this becomes an enhancer of job opportunities for the youth in the country. In this way, the country's economy will accentuate, also by generating employment for youth.
2. **Livelihood approach:** When youth initiate entrepreneurial initiatives for themselves, they become the creator of their own means of livelihood. Such youth entrepreneurs make use of their thinking and management skills to acquire productive employment for oneself as well as other youth in the country.

Both these approaches are known for its contribution to youth employment and as a result, have found an appreciable position in policies. Besides these, Chigunta (2002) has provided a number of reasons for the promotion of youth entrepreneurship.

- It can lead to job creation and income generation for the young entrepreneurs themselves as well as for other youngsters that may get employed in the process.
- Marginalized and excluded youth can be brought to the economic mainstream through their active participation and contribution to the economy through their entrepreneurial venture. Different directories still in them a sense of belongingness and meaning as well as can act as a fuel for the progress.
- Several psychological and social problems found in the youth today that arise out of joblessness such as delinquent behaviour, impulsivity, addiction, and antisocial traits can be addressed.
- The youth can be trained in developing new skills and responsibilities which will work towards facing other difficult challenges in life. Psychological capital that was discussed elsewhere in the textbook would also be indirectly inculcated in the youth.
- Local communities particularly in rural areas can gain larger visibility through the valuable goods and services that they can provide through the entrepreneurial venture taken up by the youth in the community.

- Youth can be the barriers of new economic opportunities and trends that will cater to the need for international standards and thereby uplift the glory of the country.

However, youth entrepreneurship should not be viewed as a solution to unemployment all together. Situations in which it cannot be exercised particularly in conditions where the economic atmosphere is unfavourable and labour market has very few opportunities in the developing countries remain minimal. In other words, a country should be very well aware of these terms and conditions that are conducive to entrepreneurship and promote its youth in accomplishing their aspirations by providing appropriate policies and support systems.

Entrepreneurship in the emerging economy of India

The key characteristic of an emerging economy is the fast-changing institutional framework and market. The strength of their industrial ways as well as the labour market is in their infancy as compared to the developed economies. Therefore, the factors that affect the transition from employment to self-employment could be different than that is in the case of developed countries. As per the economic survey conducted by the World Bank for 2019 to 2020, the entrepreneurial activity in India is less as compared to several other developed economies like the United Kingdom and the United States (World Bank, 2020).

However, as compared to the year 2014, nearly 80% increase can be seen in the number of new forms opened in the year 2018. As per the reports of the Ministry of Corporate Affairs most of these new forms have been created in the service sector as compared to the agriculture or manufacturing sector. Agriculture is lowest in the list while manufacturing and infrastructure maintains a more or less similar trajectory (Figure 10.3).

There are only very few studies that talk about the various factors responsible for promoting self-employment in emerging economies. The "recession-push" hypothesis has been found to have a considerable influence in the emerging economies as it talks about how necessity should drive people to opt for self-employment rather than opportunities and like the case in developed countries (Valliere & Peterson, 2009). This means that in countries like India, a structural shift would work well that would attract the youth to getting into entrepreneurship than a sudden trend or spirit for search self-initiatives. Moreover, in developing economy self-employment in the informal sector is rather a voluntary affair and since the income generated from self-employment will always be compared against other occupations, the resource availability and support in terms of policy and programmes will also have an influencing impact on the decisions taken by the youth to indulge in self-employment. The study conducted by Earle and Sakova (2000) on self-employment trends in India identified several factors to play an influential role including factors such as gender, marital status,

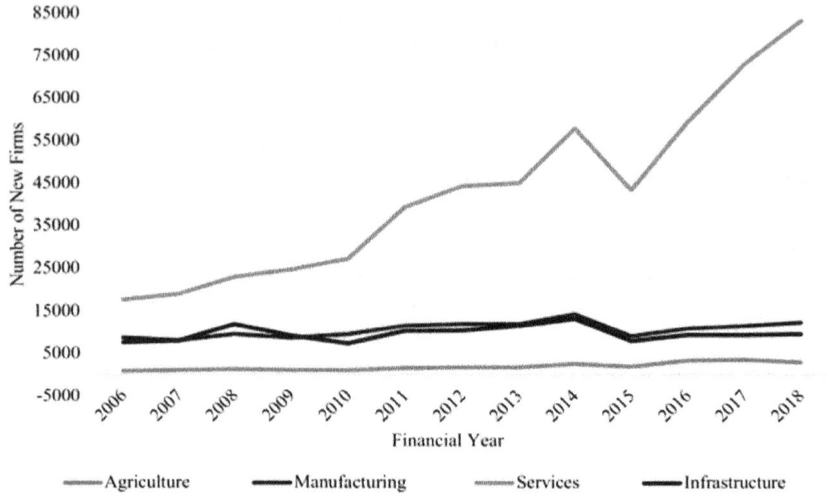

Figure 10.3 Growth of New Firms in India from 2006–2018.

Source: Economic Survey (2020). Entrepreneurship and Wealth Creation at the Grassroots. www.devdatalab.org/shrug_download/

attitudes to self-reliance, parents' education and entrepreneurial experiences, trends in the local market, and the unemployment rate in the country.

Determinants of entrepreneurship in India

It is true that there has been a surge in self-employment in India. Several studies have validated that self-employment in India is need-based more than opportunity driven, as most of the self-employed individuals report that their income is not sufficient to meet their needs (Chandrasekhar& Ghosh, 2007). Majumder (2007) and a few other researchers have identified these initiatives to be driven out of the distress and have found their roots in unemployment, economic exclusion based on religion and caste, distinct opportunity differences between rural and urban regions as well as educational differences. The economic survey, 2020 also substantiates this correlation between educational status and entrepreneurial activities undertaken by the youth. Determinants of entrepreneurship in India are as varied and intricate as the country. Within the limitations of research and literature, let us analyse three important determinants of entrepreneurship namely unemployment, education, and regional differences.

Entrepreneurship due to unemployment

As a premise to the following discussion, there are two factors that need to be understood as the push-pull factors leading to entrepreneurship because of unemployment. The recession push factor that was discussed before talks about how high unemployment pushes people to get into self-employment and rely on one's own ideas and initiatives to generate income. On the contrary, the "prosperity-pull" factor discusses the higher risk of bankruptcy that is arising out of lack of demand for the service and products provided by search initiatives that have stood out for financial stability (Parker, 2004). Interestingly, literature has studies supporting both these factors. However, several cross-sectional studies are in support of the prosperity-pull hypotheses (Cowling & Taylor, 2001), while longitudinal and time series studies support the former hypothesis (Schuetze, 2000).

In India, the tendency to encourage self-employment as a solution to unemployment and poverty has been observed for a couple of decades (Ahluwalia, 1999), and it is evident from the various economic policies that have existed in the country. But statistics show that in India the unemployment rates of the states with high incidence of poverty are low in comparison to their counterparts (Bhalotra, 2002). This could be because the people in these areas would be engaging them in hard labour work and hence cannot be categorized as unemployed, even though their income may not be sufficient to run the household. The relationship between entrepreneurship and poverty appears to be puzzling and the idea of viewing entrepreneurship as a solution to poverty may require a re-visit. Nonetheless, the substantial decrease in the regular employment that was faced by the country following economic liberalization has definitely resulted in an increase in entrepreneurship and self-employment (Monsen, Mahagaonkar, & Dienes, 2010).

Education leading to entrepreneurship

A key highlight of self-employment literature is the definite impact of education on the entrepreneurial decision an individual may take (Casson, 2003). The knowledge and skill provided by education is reflected in the economic growth of India over the past few decades particularly in the service and manufacturing sector. However, the link between education and entrepreneurship is slightly tricky.

Of course, entrepreneurial decision relies to a great extent on the necessary skills an individual has, which can be provided by education to a great extent. However, the analysis of returns expected from a salaried employee mint and entrepreneurship has a crucial role to play to decide whether to take up self-employment. In other words, higher education provides a better return from a salaried job than from entrepreneurship then, an individual may not take a high risk in initiating a new venture. Therefore, higher education may not always be considered as a requirement for entrepreneurship. Substantiating evidence is reported by a study conducted in the United States, where the return to education of self-employed American was 6% that of an employed American was up to 9% (Sluis, Praag & Vijverberg, 2003). But Parker (2004) observed that this may not be the case in emerging economies due to the compromised and perfect market system in the present occupational choices. Moreover, they may be individuals who may not consider the monetary benefit as the primary driving force for entrepreneurship (Hamilton, 2000). Although there is a link between education leading to self-employment, there are specific, personal, socio-economic, and cultural factors that play as determinants.

Entrepreneurship out of exclusion

The impact of stratification of economic groups in a society is highly relevant in a country like India with diverse communities and social groups. It is evident that entitlement and social exclusion due to the involvement of the economy in forces is a key determinant two entrepreneurship among youth. The theoretical model of joblessness and social exclusion proposed by Akerlof and Kranton (2000) depicts that members of socially excluded communities are unlikely to engage in remunerative activities including entrepreneurship. Several racial and ethnic studies across the world have similar study findings.

The influence of the caste system in India or individual choices of an individual cannot be ignored. The clear wage disparity and earning differential found in India can be readily related to the current topic of discussion (Darity & Deshpande, 2000). Out of the very few studies available, it can be understood that the involvement of people from scheduled castes and scheduled tribe communities are relatively poor (Majumder, 2007) as compared to the privileged community. As Amartya Sen (1976) opinionated:

> the initial inequalities in entitlements prevent capacity formation among the EGs, which in turn prevents them from entering the job market even when the economy is vibrant and growing.

An associated determinant is the locality of one's occupancy. Urban Vs rural location of stay additional e influence once entrepreneurial decision. Chandrasekhar and Ghosh (2007) found that self-employment is more evident in rural India and is prominently found in the non-farming sector.

The Entrepreneurial journey

The growth and development of an entrepreneurial initiative travels through many thoughts and crusts. Several theories have come out with models that depict the stages of entrepreneurship. The figure given below is taken from a 2019 – report published by UNICEF and is found to be effectively depicting the various important stages of the entrepreneurial journey. Clearly as can be seen from the figure the journey is a dynamic one (Figure 10.4).

1. **Gestation:** The very first stage in the entrepreneurial journey can be called the gestation period and the interested individual can be called as a potential entrepreneur. The innovation phase could be time-consuming

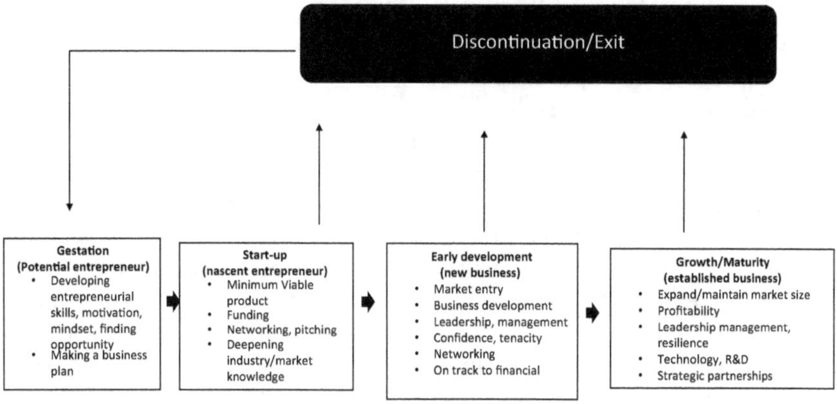

Figure 10.4 Growth and development of an entrepreneurial initiative.

Source: Alam (2019). *Youth entrepreneurship: concepts and evidence (Issue February.*

and involves the transformation of the generated idea to an actual product or service. The aspiring entrepreneur will be required to investigate the various market opportunities and feasibility of implementing conceptualized ideas. He or she should be able to calculate the ways to extract values from the available environment to develop saleable products or services. This is also the time when the potential entrepreneur should be working towards developing his or her skills and psychological characteristics required for the initiative. The individual is required to remain consistently motivated and maintain a mindset that is willing to explore all the possible opportunities and not to feel disheartened when things do not turn out as per expectation. It is also important for the potential entrepreneur to begin to make a business plan as a frame of reference in their mind about the time and resources required to materialize their ideas. Gestation stage begins from the triggering event that is the seed for the business idea all together. The potential entrepreneur should do risk assessment by making use of all of their far and wide contacts. Resource acquisition should also be extensively done during this stage.

2. **Start-up:** This is the stage of actual implementation of the idea. The new entrepreneur in his infancy can be addressed as a nascent entrepreneur at this stage. The initiative will be at its infancy stage and includes the setting up and launching of the same by making a tactful business strategy through a proper display of available resources. The entrepreneur may begin to run the business in a slow and steady manner by making use of minimum viable products. The initiative would be actively looking for funding and other agents of support. They may try to actively represent in the market through networking and pitching events and thereby trying to enhance their visibility to a larger audience. The nascent entrepreneur would begin to exhibit their entrepreneurial and

managerial skills to effectively handle their venture. This is also a time when the entrepreneur is able to acquire market knowledge through their first-hand experience and as a result is able to deepen their industrial knowledge and skills.

3. **Early development:** A venture at this stage can be considered as a new business. The entrepreneurship has entered the market and would probably be exploring the various trajectories. Depending upon its performance in the market, the entrepreneur can explain various strategies for business development. This is also a period when entrepreneurs need to explore his/her managerial skills and leadership quality to lead their staff and strategies. The number of staff may vary depending upon the performance of the business and accordingly would require the entrepreneur to explore his or her leadership skills. They need to be confident and determined; should be able to explore new options with tenacity and fortitude even when the initial acceptance and market is very feeble. Networking seems to be the backbone of the business at the stage. Through networking, pitching, and advertising the new business can try to maintain its economic health and stability.
4. **Growth/maturity:** This is the final stage of the entrepreneurship process where the initiative can be now confidently called as an established business. The entrepreneur at the stage would be engaged in expanding their market size, and increasing their profitability. They may be interested in involving other strategic partners and also incorporating the advantages of the latest technology. They may have a specific wing for research and development based on finding the business that seems to explore other related opportunities. Leadership and management skills need to be at its best as the business has established and flourished then before. The entrepreneur should continue being resilient, optimistic, motivated, and determinant to expand one's business. Planning, organizing, and effectively controlling the various goods and services provided by the business continues to be addressed with caution.

As represented in the figure, the process can lead to discontinuation or cancellation from the second stage onwards and can get back to the gestation stage to continue to travel through the same trajectory. Therefore, an entrepreneur should be very vigilant, informed, and adaptive to the needs and demands of the market and continue to strive to attain their goals. The aforementioned flowchart, which takes a cyclic format, is successful in communicating the dynamic nature of the entrepreneurial process.

The global entrepreneurship monitor (GEM) model

The Global Entrepreneurship Monitor (2002) has conceptualized a model that highlights the importance of entrepreneurship in the economic development of a country. This model which was created two decades ago still

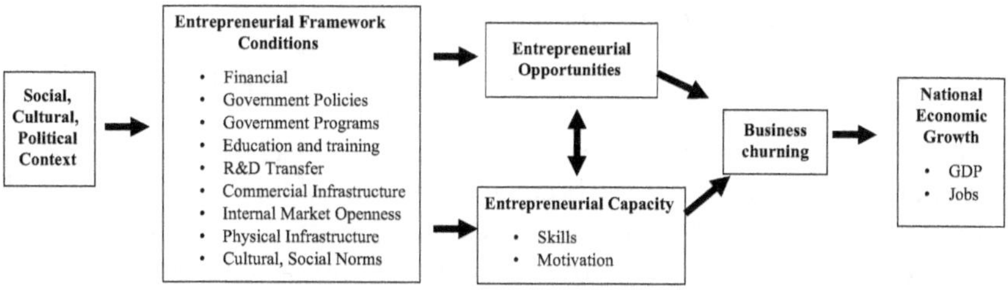

Figure 10.5 The conceptual model proposed by global entrepreneurship monitor.

Source: Manigart, Clarysse, Crijns, and Goossens (2002). *The Global Entrepreneurship Monitor: Executive Report Belgium and Flanders 2001.*

stands valid in the current Indian scenario and is worth a mention. The model is depicted in the figure given below (Figure. 10.5).

The proposed model views entrepreneurship as a way to economic growth. Towards this, two important components are identified as entrepreneurial opportunities and entrepreneurial capacity. It is highlighted that a best entrepreneurial initiative will arise when the appropriate opportunity can meet that need of skills and motivation. Therefore, care must be given for the provision of appropriate skill training as well as the ability to identify the right opportunity. The confluence of these two elements results in the creation of a new initiative that would also inevitably lead to the demolition of old and non-functioning forms that accept. Even though it may sound negative this process should be identified as a creative destruction which is depicted in the model as a business churning. This process will ensure the decline of non-functioning businesses and that's a way for newer and competitive start-ups to proceed into the market.

A few framework conditions are required for the achievement of the above-mentioned framework to work out financial support, government policies and programmes, education and training, availability of commercial infrastructure, and cultural and social norms in Alliance with the processes are all some of the necessary conditions that will facilitate the creation of appropriate opportunities and capacities. This will in turn facilitate national economic growth and can be evidently seen in the form of GDP growth and job creation. The model also emphasizes on the importance of having unappreciated and accommodative social, cultural, and political context for this construction model to get executed effectively.

Existing policies and programmes for youth in India

Having discussed various aspects of youth skill building and entrepreneurship, it is important to discuss accessing policies and programmes that are available for youth in our country. The following session discusses both International and national initiatives for youth in India.

Educational institutions and training centres

1. Rajiv Gandhi National Institute of Youth Development (RGNIYD), Ministry of Youth Affairs and Sports, Government of India

The Institution of national importance that had begun as a centre for training for youth has now expanded to become an institute of higher learning as well offers academic programmes in social science subjects that are directly linked to Youth Development. Apart from this, the institution is devoted to providing training programmes for youth vocational training and certification that are in line with contemporary job demands. The institution is also keen to cooperate with other state agencies and youth organizations that are directly involved in Youth Development. The institution also has several extension and outreach programmes across the country. RGNIYD provides a platform for many relevant online training programmes and discussions in line with youth development. Apart from the post-graduate programmes, the institution also offers PhD programmes and also engages in research in youth development.

The institution directly under the Ministry of Youth Affairs and Sports (GoI) works in close Association with National Service Scheme (NSS) and Nehru Yuva Kendra Sangatham (NYKS) in implementing several training programmes for youth across the country. This premium Institute is responsible for the preparation and presentation of "India Youth Development Index" that has been referred to as the standard assessment of Youth Development in the country. Together with all its stakeholders, RGNIYD is devoted to training the youth to become responsible professionals and citizens of the country

2. Tata Institute of Social Sciences (TISS)

This is Asia's oldest Institution of higher learning that is devoted to professional social work education. Currently, TISS is a deemed university that is widely known for its public research as well as action projects across its various campuses. The various academic programmes that this institution offers are in Social Sciences, such as developmental Studies, Public Policy, Rural Development, Applied Psychology, Education, and Management and Labour Studies to name a few.

The institution has a Centre exclusively dedicated for training education and is called the School of Vocational Education (TISS-SVE). This initiative which was set up in 2011 is committed towards providing immediate intervention through skill training and vocational programmes for the youth. Both organized and unorganized workforces across various industries can be beneficiaries of the programmes offered by the school. This initiative works towards a vision of creating an ecosystem that respects the dignity of labour. They also hope to create a sustainable and reliable source of income for the youth in the country by helping them in developing employable skills. TISS-SVE adopted the work-integrated training programme to focus on providing jobs specific skills to its participants through several programmes: diploma courses, bachelor's degree programme, and standalone certification awarded by the home University.

3. National Institute of Rural Development and Panchayati Raj (NIRD & PR) An education institution under the Union Ministry of Rural development that offers programmes in over seven brought social science disciplines such as Social Justice, local governance, public policy, rural management science and technology, and sustainable development to name a few. The institution is known to provide support services for the rural youth through their eminent research and capacity building programmes

International initiatives for youth

The thoughtful and timely initiatives for youth by the United Nations have helped many member states, particularly the developing nations to focus on their youth population. The UN has been identifying youth as one of their top priority and has been coming up with initiatives that will enhance their response to the needs of the youth, and address their developmental needs as much as possible. Some of the Agencies that work specific to youth-related concerns are given here:

1. **UN Department of Economic and Social Affairs Division (DESA)**: The World Programme of Action for Youth was set up by DESA with the aim of increasing their understanding about the global situation of the youth. This has played an important role in strengthening National Youth policies of their member states. They also provide youth the opportunity to partake in the country's official delegations to the UN.
2. **UN Centre for Human Settlements (UCHS)**: Particular emphasis is given to the livelihood aspects of the youth, specifically for the disadvantaged and underprivileged youth who stay in slums and unplanned settlement. It also provides financial support to many developing countries through the UN-Habitat Urban Youth Fund. Poverty reduction and employment generation are also included in their objectives.
3. **United Nations Development Programme (UNDP)**: Programme provides an array of initiatives: both short and long in nature. Equality, national ownership and leadership, volunteerism, knowledge sharing, and working by, with, and for young people are a few among their guiding principles. UNDP being the first to explicitly state their commitment to the youth, expect economic empowerment of the youth, their civic participation in political processes and engagement in resilience building
4. **United Nations Environment Programme (UNEP)**: Promotion of environmental awareness among youth has been taken up as a global agenda. Through regular conferences, information exchange, and capacity-building programmes, the intention is to cultivate an environmental consciousness youth population across the world.
5. **United Nations Population Fund (UNPF)**: Empowerment of youth is done first by understanding their conditions, and then by bringing together governments through advocacy for more investment in young

people. They also provide support to sustainable organizations that are led by young people with the intention of promoting human rights as a priority.

6. **Voice of the youth (VOF) by UNICEF**: Online platform for young people to share their thoughts and opinions as well as understand the issues affecting the world in terms of youth population. The topics may vary from education to violence to conflict to disaster management to human rights. This has various online subsidiaries: Cross-cultural interactions are entertained through 'Voice of Youth Connect' and information is gathered through 'Voice of Youth Citizens' and skill training is provided through 'Voice of Youth Maps'.
7. **International Labour Organisation (ILO):** Dedicated to enhancing working opportunities and conditions for young men and women across the world. ILO actively associates with various alliances at various sectors of different countries and is involved in the development of youth employment policies and programmes. It has a crucial role to play in the UN Secretary General's Youth Employment Network.
8. **Food and Agriculture Organisation of United Nations (FAO):** FAO has a new strategic objective that has considered youth as their priority. The Feeding Minds, Fighting Hunger Portal, Education for Rural People (ERP) are some of their education resources provided to children and young adults across the world. Specific needs of vulnerable youth in the rural parts of developing countries, FAO has developed the Junior Farmers Field and Life School Program (JFFLS) that is intense to work towards long-term food security.
9. **United Nations Volunteer (UNV)**: UNV has a long history of working for youth across the world. As per reports, "by 2011 23% of UN volunteers and 62% of UN online volunteers were under the age of 30" (National Youth Policy, 2017). Through youth volunteerism and partnerships, the United Nations agencies ascribe that best to work for and with youth.
10. **The World Programme of Action Youth (WPAY)**: it is an initiative that provides a framework for policy building and guidelines action plans that can be taken up by national or international agencies to work towards improving the conditions of young people. They aim to ensure constructive participation of youth by improving the quality and quantity of opportunities available for them. Hunger and poverty, drug abuse, juvenile delinquency, armed conflict are some of the priority areas identified by them.

National initiatives for youth in India

Ever since its inception, the Government of India has been keen in undertaking various policies and programmes for its youth. In the year 1985, a department exclusively dedicated to working for youth was installed, and today, we have the Ministry of Youth Affairs and Sports as an integral part of our government. Under the strong headship of this ministry, the National Youth Policies have been formulated and updated in a timely fashion. The latest being the National Youth Policy (NYP) 2014 viewed as the right and duty of the youth to participate in the country's development. The NYP 2014 was implemented with the mission to empower youth of the country to achieve their full potential, and through them enable India to find its rightful place in the community of nations with the objectives of creating a productive workforce that can make a sustainable contribution to India's economic development; develop a strong and healthy generation equipped to take on future challenges; and instil social values and promote community service to build national ownership among the youth of India. The policy document encompassed five well-defined objectives, eleven priority areas, and policy interventions in each priority area. The priority areas include the following: Education; Employment and Skill Development; Entrepreneurship; Health and healthy lifestyle; Sports; Promotion of Social values; Community engagement; Participation in politics and governance; Youth engagement; Inclusion; and Social Justice (National Youth Policy 2014). Along these lines, the National Policy for Skill Development and Entrepreneurship 2015 laid great emphasis and defined skill development of the youth as a joint responsibility of all stakeholders. The conceptualization behind NYP 2014 was in line with the vision of "Skill India" which aimed at enabling the youth in the country to attain their full potential as a lifelong process. With the growth of individuals comes the growth of the country and is found to be one of the most sustainable ideas. The draft National Youth Policy 2021 is under the final round of review process after gathering the feedback about the same from various stakeholders including youth of the country.

Programmes for youth by the central government

The central government of India has initiated several programmes for the youth in the country catering to the needs of the diversity of the population. The following session provides a brief description of some of these programmes.

1. **National Young Leaders Programmes (NYLP)**: The primary aim is to encourage the leadership skills of a youth and utilize it for nation building. Its components are as follows: Neighbourhood Youth Parliament (educating through debates and discussions at a village or community level), Youth for Development Programme (promoting dignity of labour through volunteerism), National Youth Leaders award (rewarding youth for their outstanding performance in their respective areas), National Youth Advisory Council (involving youth leaders and stakeholders in important decision-making processes) and National Youth Development Fund (mobilizing financial resources for Youth Development).

2. **Nehru Yuva Kendra Sangathan (NYKS):** With nearly 8.5 million members, NYJS is the largest youth organization in the world. It works in a diversity of activities that primarily focuses on personality building of a youth. Some of its focal activities include education, health, sanitation, rural development, disaster management, and order friendship skill development. The Tribal Youth Exchange Program, the Adolescent Health and Development Programme, the Promotion of Folk Art and Culture, and the National Integration Camps are some of their outstanding programmes.

   A recent review study of NYK in Jaipur found that the educational level and social participation of the rural youth play a crucial role in their involvement in NYK (Verma, 2012). A similar study conducted in Tumakuru in the district identified the lack of need-based and periodic guidance and training programmes that are affecting the performance level of NYK (Yadav, 2019). Of however both studies highlighted the interest and participation of youth in the country in various activities of Nehru Yuva Kendra
3. **National Service Scheme (NSS):** A programme that is inspired from the ideologies of Mahatma Gandhi which encourages voluntary community services among the youth. The NSS volunteers are given the opportunity to learn through their field experience while working with real-life issues of the citizens of a country. This includes issues related to women empowerment, disaster management, environmental conservation and the list continues.

   Being an initiative that has remained popular for so many years, several evaluation reports from across the country on NSS are available. The number of education institutions covered under the scheme has been found to be increasing with every passing year (Parmer, 2019). The study report conducted by the Tata Institute of Social Sciences commended it as one of the greatest experiments in the field of youth work in the world. The recommendations made by the reports were towards a direction of installing a strong administrative mechanism that would introduce innovative activities that can motivate people in running the scheme. Financial constraint was also highlighted as one of lacunas of the programme (Parasuraman, Khalil, Saman, & Saigita, 2010).

   The midterm evaluation report of the project to integrate NYKS and NSS highlighted the importance of both these initiatives to work together towards the betterment of their common target group, which is the youth (Sharma, 2018).
4. **Rajiv Gandhi National Institute of Youth Development (RGNIYD):** As has been discussed earlier, RGNIYD is a resource centre that offers academic programmes that cater to the diverse requirements of today's youth. It is also an active research Centre on topics of Youth Development along with offering a wide array of post-graduate courses. It also functions as a training centre and renders capacity-building programmes in Youth Development routinely. There are also several online training programmes, outreach activities, and extension initiatives taken up by

the institution. RGNIYD is offering various Training, Orientation and Capacity Building Programmes for the Youth, Youth Functionaries in the Government and Voluntary Sector to enhance the youth development services in the country besides enabling the youth themselves to become partners of youth development through organizing youth-led programmes on various themes in alignment with the National Youth Policy. To enhance the competencies of the youth of the country during the COVID-19 pandemic period in various ICT skills, RGNIYD organized series of 5-Day Short-term Skill Training Certification Programmes in collaboration with prominent technological institutions of national importance in the country such as NIT-Tiruchirappalli, NIT-Jalandhar, and industry partners such as Neoware Technology Solutions, Seagate Technology-USA, Boston Scientific-USA on cyber security; artificial intelligence & machine learning; recent advances in data science; cloud computing; Internet of things and automation; nanotechnology and its applications. Several programmes particularly for the benefit of the youth in north-eastern region are being organized through the RGNIYD's newly established Regional Centre in the North-Eastern Region and in partnership with Higher Educational Institutions across the North-Eastern States. Further, exclusive programmes for empowerment of youth of north-eastern region are being conducted besides undertaking research studies in collaboration with higher educational institutions in the north-eastern region. Imparting skill training programmes is of vital significance to the rural and less educated youth. With a view to mainstream and include the youth of the north-east, RGNIYD is organizing a series of skill training programmes for the youth of the north-eastern region in rural technologies which will enable them to build specific income generation skills and set up small entrepreneurial units. Further, RGNIYD also networks with various institutions providing micro-credit, mentoring, market linkages, etc., to the benefit of the trained youth to engage in sustainable livelihood.

5. **National Programme for Youth and Adolescence Development (NPYAD):** This scheme provides financial assistance to five major objectives focusing youth and adolescence development, which are personality development, national integration, promotion of adventures, adolescence empowerment, adolescent empowerment, and resource development.

Skill development programmes for youth

Besides these government school programmes, there are other initiatives that AIMS at skills

1. **Mahatma Gandhi National Rural Employment Guarantee Act (MGNREGA):** Provide employment opportunities to unskilled workers through the promotion of self-reliance.

Table 10.2 Key Indicators of MGNREGA

Year	*No. of Households Provided Employment (in crore)*	*Average No. of Persons Days of Work Per Household*	*Total Expenditure (in crore)*
2006–07	2.10	43	8823.35
2007–08	3.39	42	15856.88
2008–09	4.51	48	27250.10
2009–10	5.25	54	37905.23
2010–11	5.49	47	39377.27
2011–12*	4.99	43	38034.69
2012–13**	4.25	36	28073.51

Source: Ministry of Rural Development. (2019). Standing Committee on Rural Development (2018–2019).

As can be inferred from the given table from the standing committee report on the seven years of performance of MGNREGA, the programme has succeeded in providing jobs for people in rural areas where participation of women, SC/ST, and other marginalized societies has been ensured (Table 10.2).

The challenges highlighted in the report included delay in the payment, increasing number of incomplete works, and creation of fake job cards. Regular monitoring, appropriate utilization of funds, and training were the few recommendations provided (Ministry of Rural Development, 2019). Notable and encouraging reports have come from the state of Kerala, as 100% implementation of the scheme was possible at the Grama Panchayat level. Review studies have commented that the state has benefited "in better cooperation among people and reduced the social economic gap" through the Systematic establishment of MGNREGA (Kumar & Muthulakshmi, 2018).

2. **Deen Dayal Upadhyaya Grameen Kaushalya Yojna (DDU-GKY):** Improving employability through skill development that particularly focuses on youth from poor socioeconomic background. It is a part of the Skill India Campaign that has initiated several renowned programmes such as Make in India, Digital India, and Stand-up India campaigns.

   A Karnataka best evaluation report provides the performance of the programme from 2014–2015 to 2018–2019. The number of youths who were trained during 2018–2019 is a significant 10,13,430 youth (Karnataka Evaluation Authority, 2020) (Figure 10.6).

As the chart depicts, despite the inconsistency in the pattern of participants being trained under DDU-GKY, there has been a steep increase in the number of trainees at an all-India level. However, this is not the case in the national level average placement rate. And therefore, the report recommends

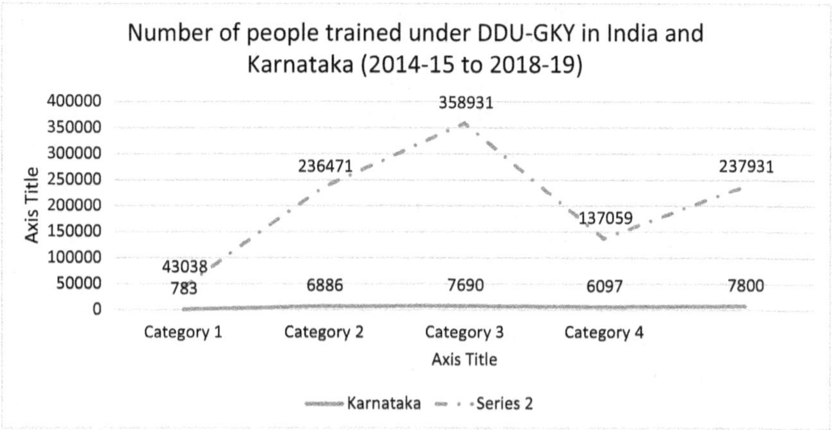

Figure 10.6 Number of people trained under DDU-GKY in India and Karnataka.

Source: Karnataka Evaluation Authority. (2020). Evaluation of Deen Dayal Upadhyaya Grameen Kaushalya Yojana in Karnataka. October.

to ensure more focus to be laid on local employment. The performance of the state of Karnataka is not encouraging.

3. **Deen Dayal Antayodaya Yojana (DDAY):** The programme that was initially known as National rural livelihood mission (NRLM), that aims at providing an institutional platform for youth from socio-economic backgrounds that offers easy access to financial services which can be converted to sustainable livelihood options. Some of the key objectives of the programme are: (1) are creation of a productive workforce, (2) strengthening and diversifying livelihoods, (3) skill training and placement support (4) rural entrepreneurship development. Mahila Kisan Sashaktikaran Pariyojana (MKSP) that empower women in agriculture and Start-up Village Entrepreneurship Programme (SVEP) that motivates and promotes start-up Enterprises for the youth are to other programmes coming under this programme.
4. **Prime Minister's Employment generation programme (PMEGP):** Credit linked subsidy programme that aims at promoting opportunity through micro-enterprises. The primary target of this programme is artisans and unemployed youth interested in the non-farming sector. The programme is interested in investing in both urban and rural areas. The Khadi and Village Industries Commission (KVIC) has been reported to have achieved more than 100% of its target under the PMEGP theme in the year 2016–2017. Press Information Bureau (2018) has further reported that in the same year, the PMEGP has achieved the set target of Rs 1,100 crore and 4 lacs new jobs were created. As per a review study, the scheme has created 41000 jobs in 2015 (Asaraf & Amulya, 2016).

5. **Enterprise and skill development:** Along with the focus on entrepreneurial skills, specific skills relating to electronics and food processing are particularly encouraged. The programme also includes Entrepreneurship Development Programmes (EDP), Entrepreneurial Skill Development Programme (ESDP), Management Development Programme (MDP), Industrial Motivation Campaign (IMC), and Vocational Education Training (VET).
6. **Pradhan Mantri Kaushal Vikas Yojana (PMKVY):** This is a skill certification scheme that trains in industry-relevant skills and aptitude that can increase the probability of youth having a better livelihood. Fees for both training and assessment are completely taken care of by the government and are implemented through the ministry of skill development and entrepreneurship. Several states are to assess the impact of PMKVY training on youth skill development by providing encouraging reports (Agrawal & Thakur, 2019). However, most of the studies recommended for improvement in the awareness programme in terms of a continuous process that promote skill upgradation and skill enhancement (Suhagin, Patnaik, & Satpathy, 2018).
7. **UDAAN Scheme:** It is a special industry initiative, particularly for the youth of Jammu and Kashmir. Its objective is to provide skill training for the unemployed youth. In Jammu and Kashmir where unemployment among youth is an alarming cause of concern, nearly 18,560 Udaan candidates received job offers after the completion of the training (NITI Aayog, 2019). Hindustan Times reported that the programme has facilitated the employment of around 3% of unemployed people in the state (Hindustan Times, 2012).

Conclusion and recommendations

Skill development and entrepreneurship are the two smart routes to employability and Youth Development. Training the children on life skills, employability skills, soft skills, and entrepreneurial skills should begin from very young and must be made part of the curriculum that is served in the country. The skill training should be done as a joint effort by all stakeholders directly linked to children. Parents should provide the opportunity to inculcate the several skills in the children from their homes. Experts and policy makers in education should proactively participate in creating a curriculum that has evident links between theory and practice. Nations should channelize a systematic and scientific approach to use development through skill training and entrepreneurship.

The following steps are recommended for effective implementation of various schemes for welfare of youth:

- Awareness should be created among parents about the importance of training the children with needed psychosocial skills within the home right from their childhood.

- Experts in education should focus on creating a curriculum that has a direct link between theory and practice. This should be age appropriate, and activity-based where the children get to explore and develop the various psychosocial skills that are required for them to succeed in the career.
- Policymakers should be able to draw a futuristic inference from the available data and rhetoric to develop a curriculum that will be able to meet the demand of the job after years when these children are in the job market.
- Community should take interest in promoting the local start-up initiatives and support the young entrepreneurs by buying their goods and services.
- The entrepreneurs should take their employees from the local community and fetch the raw materials from within the locality so that the community can prosper altogether.
- Governments should make policies and programmes that are conducive of entrepreneurship and skill development.
- Stakeholders should take proactive efforts to make a support system for the youth to explore the various career options by respecting the dignity of every job.

References

Agrawal, M., & Thakur, K. S. (2019). Impact of Pradhan Mantri Kaushal Vikas Yojana on the Productivity of Youth in Gwalior Region, India. *International Journal of Recent Technology and Engineering*, *8*(4), 801–806. doi:10.35940/ijrte.d7385.118419

Ahluwalia, M. S. (1999). India's economic reforms: an appraisal. *India in the era of economic reforms*, 26–80.

Akerlof, G. A., & Kranton, R. E. (2000). Economics and identity. *The Quarterly Journal of Economics*, *115*(3), 715–753.

Alam, A. (2019). *Youth entrepreneurship: concepts and evidence* (Issue February).

Ansari, T. (2018). Role of education and skill development to promote employment in India. *Skill India Opportunities and Challenges, December*, 208–215.

Asaraf, U., & Amulya, M. (2016). Prime Minister's employment generation programme (PMEGP): a review. *Global Journal of Commerce & Management Perspective*, *5*(3), 1–3.

Bhalotra, S. (2002). *The impact of economic liberalization on employment and wages in India*. ILO, Geneva, 121–132.

Casson, M. C. (2003). *The entrepreneur: an economic theory*, 2nd ed. Elgar, Cheltenham.

Chandrasekhar, C. P., & Ghosh, J. (2007). Recent employment trends in India and China: an unfortunate convergence? *Social Scientist*, 19–46.

Chigunta, F. (2002). *Youth entrepreneurship: meeting the key policy challenges*. Wolfson College, Oxford University, England.

Costello, B. (2017). The future of us. *The Plural of Us, January*. doi:10.23943/princeton/9780691172811.003.0009

Cowling, M., & Taylor, M. (2001). Entrepreneurial women and men: two different species?. *Small Business Economics*, *16*(3), 167–175.

Darity, W., & Deshpande, A. (2000). Tracing the divide: intergroup disparity across countries. *Eastern Economic Journal*, *26*(1), 75–85.

Desai, S. B., Dubai, A., Joshi, B. L., Sen, M., Sharif, A., & Vann Man, R. (2010). *Human development in India: challenges for a society in transition*. New Delhi: Oxford University Press.

Earle, J. S., & Sakova, Z. (2000). Business start-ups or disguised unemployment? Evidence on the character of self-employment from transition economies. *Labour Economics*, *7*(5), 575–601.

Economic Survey. (2020). Entrepreneurship and wealth creation at the grassroots. www.devdatalab.org/shrug_download/

Gates, S., Lippman, L., Shadowen, N., Burke, H., Diener, O., & Malkin, M. (2016). Key soft-skills for cross-sectoral youth outcomes. *Washington, DC: USAID's Youth Power: Implementation, Youth Power Action*.

Hamilton, B. H. (2000). Does entrepreneurship pay? An empirical analysis of the returns to self-employment. *Journal of Political Economy*, *108*(3), 604–631.

Hindustan Times. (2012). *J & K has over 6 lakh unemployed youth*. 4–7.

International Labour Office. (2020). *Global Employment Trends for Youth 2020: Technology and the future of jobs*. International labour office.

International Labour Organization. (2004). *Resolutions adopted by the International Labour Conference at its 93th Session. June 2005*, 1–21. http://www.ilo.org/wcmsp5/groups/public/---ed_norm/---relconf/documents/meetingdocument/wcms_098017.pdf

Kao, R. W. (1993). Defining entrepreneurship: past, present and?. *Creativity and Innovation Management*, 2(1), 69–70.

Karnataka Evaluation Authority. (2020). *Evaluation of Deen Dayal Upadhyaya Grameen Kaushalya Yojana in Karnataka. October*.

Kruger, Maria E., (2004). *Creativity in the entrepreneurship domain*, University of Pretoria.

Kumar, R., Mandava, S., & Gopanapalli, V. S. (2019). Vocational training in India: determinants of participation and effect on wages. *Empirical Research in Vocational Education and Training*, *11*(1). doi:10.1186/s40461-019-0078-y

Kumar, C. V., & Muthulakshmi, R. (2018). Role of panchayati raj institutions for inclusive growth under Mahatma Gandhi NREGS-a review in Kerala context. *Indian Journal of Economics and Development*, 6(10), 1–5. www.iseeadyar.org

Majumder, R. (2007). *Earning differentials across social groups: evidence from India*.

Manigart, S., Clarysse, B., Crijns, H., & Goossens, H. (2002). *The global entrepreneurship monitor: executive report Belgium and Flanders 2001*.

Ministry of Rural Development. (2019). *Standing Committee on Rural Development (2018–2019)*.

Monsen, E., Mahagaonkar, P., & Dienes, C. W. (2010). *Entrepreneurship in India: the question of occupational transition*.

NITI Aayog. (2019). Review of Udaan Scheme in Jammu & Kashmir. *In the Bureau of Research on Industry and Economic Fundamentals Private Limited*.

Okada, A. (2012). Skills development for youth in India: challenges and opportunities. *Journal of International Cooperation in Education*, *15*(2), 169–193.

Parasuraman, S., Khalil, A., Saman, A., & Saigita, C. (2010). An evaluation study of NSS in India. *Indian Journal of Social Work*, *71*(3), 417–431.

Parker, S. C. (2004). *The economics of self-employment and entrepreneurship*. Cambridge University Press.

Parmer, H. H. (2019). National Service Scheme an opportunity for youth to contribute in nation building. *NSS and Nation Building*, 7(4), 2277–7733.

Press Information Bureau. (2018). *KVIC has achieved a more than 100 percent target in the PMEGP scheme, says an independent report*. 2–3.

Saini, V. (2015). Skill development in India: Need, challenges and ways forward. *Abhinav National Monthly Refereed Journal of Research in Arts & Education*, 4(4), 1–9.

Schuetze, H. J. (2000). Taxes, economic conditions and recent trends in male self-employment: a Canada–US comparison. *Labour Economics*, 7(5), 507–544.

Sen, A. (1976). Famines as failures of exchange entitlements. *Economic and Political Weekly*, 1273–1280.

Sharma, P. (2018). *Project on strengthening NYKS and NSS: mid-term evaluation report* (Issue January).

Suhagin, S., Patnaik, B. C. M., & Satpathy, I. (2018). ICT and skill development of the workforce-a review of literature (With special reference to Pradhan Mantri Kaushal Vikash Yojana.PMKVY). *International Journal of Civil Engineering and Technology*, 9(9), 256–262.

Valerio, A., Parton, B., & Robb, A. (2014). *Entrepreneurship education and training programs around the world: dimensions for success*. The World Bank.

Valliere, D., & Peterson, R. (2009). Entrepreneurship and economic growth: evidence from emerging and developed countries. *Entrepreneurship & Regional Development*, 21(5–6), 459–480.

Van der Sluis, J., van Praag, M., & Vijverberg, W. (2003). *Entrepreneurship Selection and Performance* (No. 03-046/3). Tinbergen Institute Discussion Paper.

Van der Sluis, J., Van Praag, M., & Vijverberg, W. (2005). Entrepreneurship selection and performance: a meta-analysis of the impact of education in developing economies. *The World Bank Economic Review*, 19(2), 225–261.

Verma, H. L. (2012). Attributes affecting the extent of involvement of rural youths in different activities of Nehru Yuva kendra in Jaipur District of Rajasthan. *Hind Agri-Horticultural Society*, 7(3), 358–361.

World Bank. (2012). *South Asia development matters: more and better jobs in South Asia*. Washington, D.C.: World Bank.

World Bank. (2020). *Ease of doing business entrepreneurship data. in business formation statistics of the U.S. Census Bureau*. doi:10.7256/1812-8688.2014.6.12196

World Economic Forum. (2020). The Future of Jobs Report 2020 | World Economic Forum. *The Future of Jobs Report, October*, 1163. https://www.weforum.org/reports/the-future-of-jobs-report-2018%0Ahttp://reports.weforum.org/future-of-jobs-2016/shareable-infographics/%0Ahttp://reports.weforum.org/future-of-jobs-2016/chapter-1-the-future-of-jobs-and-skills/%0Ahttps://www.weforum.org/rep

World Health Organization. (2005). *Violence prevention: the evidence*.

Yadav, S. (2019). *Performance of Mahila Mandals of Nehru Yuva Kendr in Tumakuru District*.

Index

www.ingramcontent.com/pod-product-compliance
Lightning Source LLC
LaVergne TN
LVHW021118300926
849160LV00010B/765
* 9 7 8 0 3 6 7 7 7 2 7 5 8 *